SEVEN SHOTS

SEVEN SHOTS

AN NYPD RAID ON A TERRORIST CELL AND ITS AFTERMATH

JENNIFER C. HUNT

THE UNIVERSITY OF CHICAGO PRESS · CHICAGO AND LONDON

Jennifer C. Hunt is professor of sociology at Montclair State University.

The University of Chicago Press, Chicago 60637
The University of Chicago Press, Ltd., London
© 2010 by The University of Chicago
All rights reserved. Published 2010
Printed in the United States of America

20 19 18 17 16 15 14 13 12 11 10   1 2 3 4 5

ISBN-13: 978-0-226-36090-4   (cloth)
ISBN-10: 0-226-36090-3   (cloth)

Library of Congress Cataloging-in-Publication Data

Hunt, Jennifer C.
    Seven shots : an NYPD raid on a terrorist cell and its aftermath / Jennifer C. Hunt.
        p. cm.
    Includes bibliographical references and index.
    ISBN-13: 978-0-226-36090-4 (alk. paper)
    ISBN-10: 0-226-36090-3 (alk. paper)
1. New York (N.Y.). Police Dept.   2. Police—New York (State)—New York.   3. Police—
Special weapons and tactics units—New York (State)—New York.   4. Terrorism—New York
(State)—New York. I. Title.
    HV8148.N5H858 2010
    363.325'16097471—dc22

2010013702

Contents

Preface

STUDYING THE POLICE

I didn't begin graduate school with an interest in studying police. I wanted to do fieldwork among tropical forest Indians in the Amazon. My curiosity about police dates to when I began teaching a college course in introductory anthropology to police officers in the 1-0-3 Precinct in Queens, New York. It was a fascinating time in the New York Police Department (NYPD). The Knapp Commission investigation had ended an era of systemic corruption, but instances of abuse of force remained frequent. The most flagrant had just occurred in the 1-0-3 when Anti-Crime (plainclothes) Unit police officer Thomas Shea shot and killed an unarmed ten-year-old African American boy named Clifford Glover.

The incident took place on April 28, 1973, as Clifford was accompanying his fifty-one-year-old father to work. Shea and his partner pulled up next to the pair, whom they viewed as suspects in an incident that had happened not long before. Both officers got out of their unmarked car with weapons drawn. Assuming they were being robbed, the father and son took off. Shea opened fire, hitting Clifford Glover in the back. The father kept running until he found a patrol car and asked the police for help. After alerting Central Communications that he'd shot someone, Shea accidently left the microphone on. All of New York would soon hear the words that were preserved on tape: "Die, you little fuck!"

I taught in the back room of the first floor of the old precinct building. My students were dressed in jeans and flannel shirts, with one or two guns either clipped to their waist or strapped to their bodies in shoulder or ankle holsters. One officer wore a string of ammunition across his chest, reminding me of the poster I'd tacked on my college dorm room wall depicting the Mexican revolutionary Emiliano Zapata. A first-time instructor, I stood behind the podium reading my lectures, and finally the cops intervened. "Are you scared of us?" they asked. "Damn right I'm scared!" I replied, and relaxed after that. Still, I doubt that I taught them much. I didn't know enough about their culture to communicate in a language that could traverse the boundaries of experience.

Among the assigned readings was Napoleon Chagnon's short ethnography on the indigenous Yanomamö of South America, with their warrior ethos and paranoid worldview. *Yanomamö, the Fierce People* contained photographs of the native men with their lanky, black bodies and wads of green snot clotting their nostrils, a remnant of the hallucinogenic drugs they smoked. Males were dominant in Yanomamö culture and husbands were permitted to beat their wives. Occasionally, a village would invite a neighboring community to a "betrayal feast." While the guests lay satiated and vulnerable in their hammocks, the hosts would attack, kill the males, and steal their wives.

I tried my best to instill the concepts of cultural relativity and ethnocentrism. But what the cops learned was filtered through cultural assumptions they already shared. I came to realize this when a group of my students called me outside to listen to some transmissions on the radio. "We're in pursuit of four Yanomamö males running south on [Elm Street] heading for the subway," I heard an officer say against the backdrop of student giggling. In retrospect, I realize that something significant had occurred. They trusted me sufficiently to show me a glimpse of their backstage world.

If there is truth in the expression that opposites attract, then it certainly pertained to me. I was a young woman from an educated, middle-class, liberal Democratic family. My father was a psychiatrist who finished his training in psychoanalysis in the 1950s during the heyday of Freud in the United States. My grandfather was a well-known Cincinnati mayor who spearheaded the fight against the patronage politics of the infamous George "Boss" Cox. After H. T. Hunt, for Henry Thomas—or "Hell and Trouble," as he was better known—lost the election for a second term, he moved to Washington, D.C., took an anthropologist as his bride for his second marriage, and worked with Franklin Delano Roosevelt on the New Deal.

Although my father was not close to his never home politician parent, he shared his liberal sentiments. My father and I walked side by side through Central Park in the first big march against the Vietnam War in 1964. Years later, when I was in college, I got arrested along with three hundred others in an all-night nonviolent antiwar protest in front of the

Induction Center in Washington, D.C. A few hours before the prearranged morning bust, I noticed a young cop standing around looking tired and uncomfortable. I offered him some of my breakfast granola, which he politely declined. While we waited in sex-segregated district detention cells to be transferred to jail, we taunted the cops with protest songs from Country Joe and the Fish. "And it's one, two, three, what are we fighting for? Don't ask me, I don't give a damn. Next stop is Vietnam."

Most of my police students were working-class Irish and Italian men who leaned to the right of the Republican Party. All were Vietnam veterans and probably felt betrayed by people like me. Nevertheless, a month or two into the semester, a group of them surrounded me during a class break, wanting to know if I'd been at the wrong end of their nightsticks during the protest at Columbia University in 1968. Their guilty apologies couldn't help but endear them to me and give me a deeper sense of the moral complexities of living in a world in which the use of coercive force is the defining feature of the work and an ever-present possibility.

Shortly after the end of my teaching stint, I began working as a participant-observer in a comparative study of male and female New York City police officers. For a year, I rode on patrol in two-person cars with veteran police in Harlem; the Bronx; Midtown South, Manhattan; and Bedford-Stuyvesant, Brooklyn. I still remember one Christmas Eve when I was riding with two of my favorite cops in the 2-5 Precinct in east Harlem. My partners had just picked up a six-pack of beer when the sound of gunshots erupted a block away. When we arrived at the scene, we saw a man standing in the snow, waving a pistol in the air. The officers jumped out of the car and wrestled him to the ground. His sweat smelled stale and pungent, and I could almost taste the booze on his breath when the officers moved him past me and put him in the backseat of the patrol car. When we got to the station house, one of my police partners pulled the man outside, threw him up against the hood, and pummeled him three or four times. "This is for ruining our party!" the officer said.

I won't ever forget those New York cops. They took me under their wing and treated me almost like I was a rookie one of them. They showed me how to perceive incongruity on the street and determine who might or might not belong.[1] They gave me tactical lessons, showing me where to stand when we approached apartment doors, stopped a car, or responded to jobs like a man with a gun or a knife. One night in east Harlem, a cop and I were kneeling next to the body of a child who had been hit by a car.

The frightened driver was sitting in his vehicle a few yards away. We could hear the sirens and see the headlights as additional police units began to arrive en masse. I felt the heat of restless bodies all around me as more people joined the swelling crowd. The officer explained to me that he wasn't going to turn on his flashlight because he didn't want the people to see the blood, lest it incite their rage and have them try to turn over the driver's car.

OUTSIDE WORK AND THE ISSUE OF GENDER

For every lesson I learned about how officers viewed the street, there was another that corresponded to their perceptions of working "inside." Just about everything negative in police work—procedural rules, limits on discretion and the use of force, paperwork that had to be processed after almost every job, and orders that didn't seem to make sense—were associated with the "pencil-pushing administrators" downtown. Lieutenants and above were viewed with suspicion unless they had earned reputations as "cop's cops" and had run outside commands. In this era, the distinction between inside and outside, street cop and management, was also mediated by gender.[2] "Real" police work was linked to stereotypical masculine attributes like aggressiveness, physical and sexual prowess, and the moral dilemmas inherent in policing a corrupt and dirty world.[3]

As there was no known category of "real woman cop," the presence of female officers on patrol presented the men with a quandary that reminded me of something I'd learned about the Nuer of Africa. Having no word for deformed newborns, the Nuer transformed them into baby hippopotami, the closest living thing, and put them in the water where they belonged. In a similar vein, the police identified their women colleagues as "dykes" or "whores," two known types of females who belonged on the street, and treated them accordingly. Of course, the female officers thought that the men's view of them was as naïve as I did, although they saw it in terms of harassment and I as culturally managed fear. One woman officer, the daughter of a cop and wife of a fireman, explained, "These guys think their wives don't fool around, their mothers don't fool around, and their sisters and daughters don't fool around. What do they think, that there's one perpetrator in sneakers fooling around with all these cops?"

At the time I conducted my first stint of fieldwork, I was a participant-observer on a study sponsored by the Vera Institute of Justice and the

NYPD as part of the latter's effort to integrate women on patrol. Street cops therefore viewed my work as part of the agenda of pencil-pushing members of the top brass. I remember sitting in the roll call (muster) room asking officers questions so I could fill out the required survey. Proclaiming the survey to be "bullshit," even the friendliest officers refused to cooperate until I told them that I also had to indulge the whims of superiors by completing a pile of ridiculous paperwork. Their cooperation was superficial. They knew that I knew they were lying to me. If there had been a doubt in my mind about the value of ethnographic versus applied survey research, it disappeared then.

The flavor of patrol in my veins, addicted to the street, and seduced by the world of big-city police, I seized another opportunity to do fieldwork among police. In a *New York Times* article I learned that the Justice Department had hired an independent consulting firm to do a comparative analysis of men and the first hundred women assigned to uniformed patrol. I signed on shortly after I was interviewed in New York. My younger brother helped me pack up and move to Philadelphia to work as a consultant and participant-observer. As it turned out, the mayor and the police commissioner there were embroiled in a legal battle with the Justice Department and a policewoman plaintiff to keep women off patrol. The City of Philadelphia and the Philadelphia Police Department had contracted the firm that hired me and three other field observers. I soon found myself neck-deep in the crazy world of big-city politics, not unlike what my grandfather probably experienced two generations earlier.

CULTURAL PARANOIA

One of the scariest moments in my fieldwork took place several weeks after I arrived at the Philadelphia Academy, when I was observing a class. I was standing in the back of the auditorium, watching a training film on the police handling of demonstrations, when I saw a mirror image of myself sitting on the grass in front of the Induction Center in Washington, D.C. I was wearing my boyfriend's shirt and Levi's jeans. My hair was long and tangled, resembling what my mother would call a "rat's nest." Alarm spread like liquid fire from my abdomen to my extremities as I waited for someone to recognize me and kick me out of their world. No one did. The only other time that I felt so scared was when my "crazy" rookie partner pulled up alongside a car we were sure contained armed men.

It was during those months in Philadelphia that I developed a deeper understanding of a state of mind that I'd noticed among police in New York City: cops were culturally paranoid, suspicious, and hypervigilant.[4] Their paranoia seemed to be an adaptive response to the risks they experienced in their working environment. Some sociologists have also suggested police paranoia is one dimension of the authoritarian personality style that develops with socialization into the job.[5] Police training in tactics and the use of force underscores danger in police work and instructs recruits regarding the importance of body positioning, spatial distance from suspects, and awareness of dangerous objects in their environment. When officers leave the academy and go on patrol, they become alert to patterns of dress and behavior and incongruities in appearance that "look wrong," "don't belong," and might indicate the presence of criminal activity.[6] Most important is what suspects are doing with their hands.[7]

Officers thus begin to divide the public into affectively infused categories of people who cannot be trusted because they are civilians, not cops. Depending on the flow of interaction, some of these people may be attributed status as symbolic (or actual) assailants or suspects, assholes, know-nothings, or some rotating combination of the three.[8] Complexity, difference, and ambiguity may also generate emotions like anxiety, fear, hate, and loathing, resulting in police engaging in degrading or violent behavior to crush what is little understood and therefore frightening.[9]

I soon came to realize that paranoia was also a response to a highly politicized and segmented organizational environment in which power can shift at any time. Officers who one day are viewed in a positive light suddenly find themselves out of the loop or in the "penalty box." Life within the department sometimes seems to constitute a brutal game in which different players cement their power and neutralize political threats by tormenting those below them in rank, subverting the efforts of peers, or working to get something on them. The viciousness with which police handle their opponents is reflected in the language used in the NYPD today, where you "crush," "kill," "burn," "crucify," and "do" an officer-enemy.

POLITICAL PARANOIA

I learned a lot about corruption and violence while I was in the Philadelphia Police Department that early summer in 1976 through the fall of 1977, but the most profound lessons came from the realm of politics.

Mayor Frank Rizzo and police commissioner Joseph O'Neill were intent on using the study to prove that women couldn't handle patrol. The department's opposition to women was based on primitive myths about the female sex that had little to do with the question of physical strength and its relationship to police work as stated in the department's case against the Justice Department and the ACLU, who had filed the sexual discrimination lawsuit on behalf of a class of women officers and one individual plaintiff named Penelope Bracc.[10] The police commissioner and his associates seemed to view menstruation as a form of lunacy, resulting in "emotional instability" that rendered women incapable of functioning on the street.[11] Women of childbearing age were also viewed as being in a practically unavoidable and chronic state of pregnancy and patrol was seen as so demanding and dangerous that miscarriage or death to the fetus was inevitable. "There is also the risk of the unborn child. . . . We should propose that sterilization be a requirement for female police officers," suggested a high-ranking city official in a meeting I attended while scribbling notes until my hand hurt. I'd been in Philadelphia only a few weeks, and the top brass seemed to assume I was a secretary for the consulting firm.

The effort to dominate and control the women sometimes bordered on ludicrous. One female cop was disciplined because her bra straps showed underneath her shirt although she was wearing the required T-shirt underneath. Several women were investigated and charged with moral turpitude for sleeping with married cops. The women rookies were not allowed to train with veteran officers lest an orgy take place. Petty harassment of the women and their assignment to one-person cars in high-crime districts without sufficient training with veterans were only a few of the ways the department tried to undermine their confidence.

I soon became aware that the city and the police commissioner were trying to manipulate the study to prove that women couldn't handle the job so they could get them off the street for good. By then I'd learned that the CEO of the consulting firm that had hired me had caved to political pressure and had signed a contract that came up for renewal every three months. Eventually, three out of the five of us involved in the fieldwork banded together to try to keep the study honest and out of the department's hands. When I confided what was going on to my older brother, he advised me to get an attorney. He gave me the name of a partner from a prominent labor firm, who took the case pro bono. "I finally get to work for the good guys," he said.

"Be careful what you say on the phone and don't sleep with a cop because he might be a Rizzo plant," my lawyer warned not long after he sent a letter threatening to sue the consulting firm and the city if they tried to fire us or mess with the data. By this time, my experience in Philadelphia had begun to resemble the movie *The Conversation*, with Gene Hackman as a wire-tapping specialist. By the end of the film, Hackman is frantically destroying the walls of his house, looking for bugs. Neither he nor the audience knows if his actions are based on an accurate assessment of reality or a paranoid fantasy that he is under surveillance.

"I didn't have to go to the Amazon. The Yanomamö are alive and well in Philadelphia," I wrote in a letter to the chair of the anthropology department where I was enrolled in graduate school. An ethnographer herself, she probably guessed that I was becoming a little like Yanomamö. I was beginning to see the world like a Philadelphia cop. I realized this one day when I found myself stifling the impulse to punch out some obnoxious people who were fat-mouthing my partner, our backups, and me, who they assumed was plainclothes police. I was as amused as any female cop when I watched the reaction of male colleagues to a phenomenon they didn't anticipate: the nasty, recalcitrant, "three-hundred-pound" gorilla they'd warned the women about suddenly became docile when he saw us there. "I'm sorry for cursing like that. I don't mean you no disrespect! Ain't seen no women po-lice before!" the "gorilla" said as he put his hands behind his back, waiting to be handcuffed.

It was a relief when I finally got back to New York after more than a year in the field. I was glad to be in a place where I could walk down the street with a black friend without risking a stop and frisk. Black men didn't automatically walk to the wall, raise their hands, and spread their legs when a patrol car approached as they had in Philadelphia. Finally I could sit back, relax, and begin to deny the violence that I had discovered existed inside me. I was also a basket case, pleased with the fieldwork I'd done but traumatized by the paranoid politics of the fight we'd fought and barely won. Like many ethnographers back from the field, I felt painfully liminal to the academic world and wasn't sure where I belonged.

I sought a temporary fix by doing another three months of fieldwork among officers in Midtown South, the precinct that covered the then seamy neighborhood in and around 42nd Street and Eighth Avenue. I was standing around with my NYPD police partners who were engaged in an exchange with a civilian who was blatantly challenging one officer's authority, like a typical "asshole."[12] I felt my body tense up in anticipation of the beating I'd come to expect. The officer's face contorted, his mouth tensed, but he did not respond with physical force. I felt relieved. Even in the 1970s, cops in the NYPD had a much longer fuse than those in Philadelphia.

At the end of the summer, I was ready to take a breather from fieldwork. It took a year to decompress and stop seeing the world in terms of danger signs and incongruities, to sit in a restaurant without feeling uncomfortable when my back was to the door. Finally, I developed sufficient distance from the police to make sense of my field notes and write up the results. Nevertheless, regardless of what I wrote, researched, taught, presented, or read through the following years, something seemed to be missing from my professional life. It was shortly after the World Trade Center disaster that I realized what "that something" was: the police.

9/11: THE ROAD BACK HOME TO THE POLICE

Toward the end of September 2001, I got out of the subway at Broadway and 72nd Street and walked up the stairs, passing the photographs and descriptions of the missing that were plastered on every inch of wall. I picked up a couple things at Fairway, then headed uptown. My eyes felt as though clouds had formed on the lids and were weighing them down. When I got to the northwest corner of 79th Street, I noticed a cop standing alone on the sidewalk, staring at nothing at all. His face was drawn and his eyes looked as heavy as mine felt. "I'm so sorry," I said. "I'm so sorry for you, too," he replied. After the planes hit, the controversy surrounding the acquittal of the police officers involved in the forty-one-round shooting of unarmed African immigrant Amadou Diallo receded into the background. No one would have known from the way the community took care of its cops in south Brooklyn's 7-0 Precinct that police officer Justin Volpe had sexually assaulted Haitian resident Abner Louima in the bathroom a few years before. After 9/11, for a few months at least, the police and the public forgave their past and acted and felt as one.

Several months later, I joined an effort sponsored by the Department of Psychiatry at Columbia University to talk to NYPD first responders about psychological reactions to traumatic events. By then I'd had more than ten years of clinical training at the Psychoanalytic Institute, New York University Medical Center, and knew enough about trauma to recognize the dangers of the Mitchell method of one-shot group catharsis to which the program adhered.[13] I altered my approach accordingly so as to bolster the ego defenses of the cops who were there. I talked about the social world of the police and explained that some of the clinical signs used to assess pathology didn't precisely apply. The police tendency toward "normal paranoia" and hypervigilance, for example, changed the diagnostic criteria somewhat. Radical transformations in behavior might be a better indication of problems than the display of common symptoms devoid of social context. I gave the example of a police officer who released his gun from his holster when he stopped a car but, since 9/11, had started to take out his weapon and hide it in his hat and point the hat at the driver's head when he asked to see license and registration.[14]

The focus of these presentations was educational. I didn't try to solicit confessions or conduct group therapy. Nevertheless, the talks evoked a powerful response. One officer vividly described how he'd felt when he saw the dead body of a young girl with clothes blown off and no arm. "You could still see she was beautiful," he said. His eyes filled. "I wanted to kill them all." Men and women cops told me about the shame they'd felt as they fought their impulse to go in the opposite direction when they heard the rumbling sound of the towers coming down. Cops who had been on vacation when the planes hit were upset they weren't there to help and frustrated by the length of time it took to get home. Officers who worked in precincts in north Brooklyn were disturbed when they learned they couldn't go into Manhattan because somebody had to guard the bridge.

One officer confessed feeling wary patrolling a Muslim community. He thought every dark-haired, olive-skinned man was a terrorist and every veiled woman a suicide bomber. A lot of the cops recalled with utter horror seeing people jumping out of tower windows. When they let their minds wander while they were lying in bed, waiting to fall asleep, they could hear the ping-ping sound of the bodies hitting the pavement and smell that dreadful mix of fuel, metal, and flesh that clogged the hairs in their nostrils and clung to their clothing when they'd worked the pit. Some officers described their own near-miss encounters with dying and the grief and helplessness they'd felt when the buildings collapsed and buried their friends and the civilians whom they had sworn to serve and protect. Even eight years after the World Trade Center disaster, when I've interviewed New York City police officers about that time, their voices choke and their eyes tear up.

When the World Trade Center disaster occurred, I was a seasoned fieldworker. I had done my time on the street and had no interest in riding in patrol cars. Listening to their stories and understanding their world felt more important. Talking to these sad, brave, angry, worried men and women filled me with a renewed sense of purpose. Although I could not heal their wounds, I felt as though my presence had meaning. I realized then that I'd come full circle and found my way back home.

THE POLICE ACADEMY: ECHOES OF INSIDE AND OUTSIDE DOMAINS

After Ray Kelly appointed the late Jim Fyfe as deputy commissioner of Training, Jim hired me to work in the department with him on a variety of projects. Among them was a revision of the recruit curriculum and book of readings (the student guide). The social science chapters of the student guide were in a miserable state, constituting a mishmash of out-of-date material grounded in contradictory and often nonsensical theories that neither instructor nor recruit could understand. Bits and pieces of politically correct but scientifically questionable information were tacked on to various sections in order to appease some advocacy group from inside or outside the organization. I was not surprised to learn that recruits called the social science portions of their training "silly science" and that instructors taught lessons that didn't correspond to what their students were assigned to read.

To some degree, the 1970s cultural contradiction remained between the academy and street, inside and outside domains, formal and informal rules, computer-punching "bullshit" and real police work. These contradictions were heightened by the lack of recent patrol experience among instructors, the minimal use of simulations training, and the inclusion of materials that seemed only peripherally related to the job. Fyfe sought to address some of these issues in his reformulation of the curriculum. He added one day of simulations instruction in which pairs of recruits handled jobs involving mentally disturbed persons played by professional actor-trainers. Fyfe also added role-play training examinations that required students to engage in interactions with academy staff playing the part of civilians. Scenarios included domestic disputes and nuisance calls like a man pissing on a public building. He imported new instructors from precincts and increased the number of sergeants assigned to classrooms.

More controversial among the staff was his decision to dissolve the police science, law, and behavioral science departments and make every police instructor responsible for teaching all three areas. Uniformed cops are generalists who do not have advanced degrees, he argued, citing a document that linked the establishment of separate fields to an unrealized plan to employ university professors to teach recruits. Only the nonacademic portions of the instruction remained specialized, including tactical, driver, and weapons training. I was not around recruits enough to assess whether tactical and weapons training were attributed superior status by virtue of their perceived closeness to "real police work" on the street as they had in New York and Philadelphia in the 1970s.[15] I suspect this was the case and remains so today, although the increased use of simulations training has helped elevate the relevance of the academic curriculum in the eyes of recruits.

My first project in the Training Division involved researching and writing chapters of the new student guide that pertained to my areas of expertise. When I began to gather fresh data by talking to cops and detectives, I felt as though I was engaged in more meaningful work than I had for years. It felt good when a supervisor from the gang unit who had helped me with the chapter on policing children and adolescents told me my work "could save lives." I remember one black female instructor who was sitting in the outer office reading a draft of a section written by someone else. My door was open because I had the only air conditioner and the instructors' quarters were hot. The officer suddenly burst into a rant punctuated by curses, alleging the material was racist. I got up, walked to her desk, and asked her to tell me what was wrong. She pointed to the offending paragraphs and told me what she thought. I do not believe there was racist intent, but the phrasing was awkward and could be interpreted in ambiguous ways. I worked with the officer, deleting offensive sentences and altering words in the text to make its meaning clear. In making these sorts of editorial changes and writing materials that resonated with instructors, line bosses, detectives, and street cops, I opened a new chapter in my work with police.

My work with officers on the student guide helped me develop credibility and some degree of acceptance among academy staff as well as officers who worked outside, although my position as a civilian who reported to the deputy commissioner remained scary to some—no one knew whose mole I was, whether I understood and would respect cops' rules, and whether I was revealing what I saw and heard to him or worse, the much-loathed female chief whom Fyfe recommended to the police commissioner for appointment to the position of commander of the Police Academy, in a spurt of gender-equality politics run amok. It struck me then that rank-and-file cops aren't used to having their opinions heard by individuals who are in positions to get something done and who aren't afraid of making decisions that might offend superiors. Despite the rhetoric of empowerment preached during the birth of CompStat, the computerized mapping of crime statistics, in the 1990s police officers weren't accustomed to having the power to influence change.[16]

During my year and a half in the Training Division, I noticed another way in which the status division between inside and outside work continued to be reproduced in the minds of veteran cops, despite the modifications Fyfe introduced. Police officers who taught at the academy were viewed as out of touch not long after they left the street particularly if they'd spent only a few years on patrol or worked in low-crime precincts. The academy had higher status in street cops' minds than One Police Plaza downtown, because it functioned as a bridge between inside and outside domains even though the senior staff did attempt to isolate recruits from veteran precinct cops in order to instill in them the "right way" of doing their job. One Police Plaza was where the most powerful and highest-ranking "computer-punching" bureaucrats dwelled, including the police commissioner. Meetings that took place in its bowels resulted in new rules and procedures that burdened "real cops" with even more paperwork while leaving them vulnerable to getting hung out to dry if something didn't go right. "House mouse" is a derogatory term used in the NYPD for members of the service who spend most of their careers inside at One Police Plaza, although I've heard it used for some academy personnel as well.

The distinction between inside and outside domains, downtown and academy, and the academy and the street, seemed to echo up and down the ranks. Commanders and supervisors who led bureaus, divisions, units, and squads assigned to the street were attributed more status than those who managed officers who worked inside headquarters or other police facilities. The chief of Patrol, the chief of Detectives, the chief of the department, and their executives and subordinates who were dispersed throughout the city administration were generally viewed as superior to, for example, the chief of Personnel. The biggest source of shame for a cop, other than going to jail, is his or her placement on modified duty. It isn't so much the violation that brings discomfort but rather the stigma of wearing an ID tag that declares his or her status, lack of a weapon, and inability to be a real street cop on the street.

Today in the NYPD, the gender dynamic that linked outside work to masculinity lies latent, hidden in the mental imagery of individual officers but not manifest in the culture of policing at large. "House mouse" is a gender-neutral term, in contrast to "station queen," a phrase that has a similar connotation in the more machismo-laden environment of the Los Angeles Police Department.[17] Female NYPD officers are considered "real cops" if they have the prerequisite experience and competence. Women cops are no longer automatically assumed to be gay, bisexual, or promiscuous, although some may come to be thought of in that way by virtue of their demonstration of attributes and actions that are recognized as such beyond the world of the police.

The only officer I met while working in the NYPD who routinely couched comments in terms of issues of gender discrimination was the police academy chief, who had been among a group of women who were fast-tracked up the ranks to show that the glass ceiling had been cracked in New York. "She's not a cop," a street cop said, as if that would explain her difficulty making even minor decisions like what to have for lunch. "She's not a cop!" a detective exclaimed after claiming that he'd seen the chief wearing "only" a white dress and sandals while parading around ground zero, showing it to her friend, right after the World Trade Center disaster.

Cultural and political paranoia remains in the department but is distributed equally between the sexes. A detective pointed this out during a dinner we shared at a restaurant downtown. She confessed that she'd been surprised by my open, friendly manner during our first meeting at the police academy when she'd come to help out with the recruit student guide. She warned me that I should be closed and careful among cops. The department was a dog-eat-dog world full of envious men and women officers who would try to do me harm. Although I found the detective strange and excessively guarded, I understood that she was telling me something important while revealing a larger cultural truth. Several years later, I learned that she'd had to weather a storm of resentment as she'd successfully moved up the ranks during a distinguished twenty-year career that ended in her suicide. Later, as I learned about the internal dynamics within the world of police and how they influenced cops' perceptions about their work and sometimes made their lives miserable, I would realize that her experience was not unique. A few weeks after our dinner, I met Joe Dolan and Keith Ryan. A few years later, I began this book.

Acknowledgments

I am grateful to Joe Dunne, Lou Anemone, Bill Morange, Ray McDermott, Tom Scotto, Sam Katz, and Tony Rizzo for sharing their time, knowledge, insights, and experience. I would like to thank George Grasso for allowing me to use his unpublished memoir about his experience of 9/11. I am grateful to the many friends and colleagues I met while working in the Training Division of the New York Police Department (NYPD). They taught me a lot, and it was an honor to work with them. Although they have not read this book and are not responsible for its contents, they contributed to it in hidden ways. Thanks to Steve Silks, Jack Cambria, Joe Fox, Nicholas Estavillo, Frank Vega, Vincent DiDonato, Patrick McCarthy, Terry Riley, Joe Badalamente, Tom Mauro, and Jim McCabe. Thanks, too, to Edwin Young for his efforts on my behalf. In addition, there are a number of police officers who helped me on this project who requested that I not mention their names. They know who they are.

Writing a book is a lonely endeavor. As scholars, we often write for years without knowing whether our work will come to fruition in a publication. Acts of kindness on the part of friends and colleagues at different points in time help mediate the difficulty of the endeavor so we can overcome obstacles and push on. Thanks to Cary Federman, Satenik Margaryan, Jay Livingston, Jennifer Higgins, Brian McLaughlin, Jack Baldwin LeClair, Pat Kelly, Debra Davis, Jane Perr, Corey Zucker, Terry Wonder, Michael Baker, Sharman Mather, Amatzia Baram, and Rob Lambert for their support. Thanks to my brother Sam for letting me use his vacation house to work, to my brother Tom for his practical help, and to my sister, Priscilla, for her insistence that this book would someday bring rewards.

I owe a special debt to Robert Emerson and Gary Fine for their kindness and generosity. They read early drafts of this manuscript and offered advice and encouragement. They have also supported me at other critical junctures of my career. Thanks also to Paul Chevigny for his insightful reading of the chapters on the raid. Geoffrey Alpert was cheerful and encouraging when I was not. Peter Manning was hiding in the shadows rooting me on. Dave Klinger and Diane Vaughan gave me useful suggestions regarding bibliography. Peter Kraska responded immediately to my request for copies of his work. Robert Daley read an early draft of several chapters. His frank and honest critique of my work taught me what little I know about how to write. Maia Rigas bravely waded through the flood of grammatical errors to copyedit this manuscript. I am particularly grateful to Doug Mitchell and Tim McGovern at the University of Chicago Press and the anonymous reviewers who wrote such warm and constructive comments and encouraged the publication of this book.

Last and foremost, I want to thank Dave Martinez, Joe Dolan, John English, Rich Teemsma, and Paul Yurkiw for taking me into their world and sharing their thoughts. I hope that I have respected their trust by writing an honest book. This book is dedicated to them.

NYPD Organizational Chart, 1997

Police Commissioner

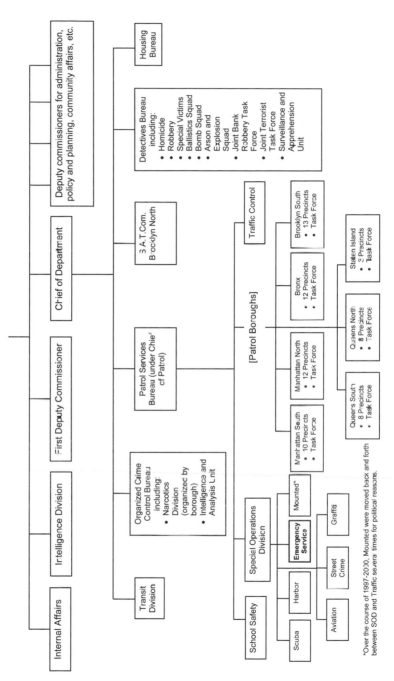

*Over the course of 1997-2010, Mounted were moved back and forth between SOD and Traffic several times for political reasons.

Rank and the Chain of Command

POLICE RANKS

- Police officer
- Sergeant
- Lieutenant
- Captain
- Deputy inspector
- Inspector ("full bird")
- Deputy chief (one star)
- Assistant chief (two stars)
- Chief (three stars)
- Chief of the Department (four stars)

DETECTIVE RANKS

- Detective third grade
- Detective second grade
- Detective first grade

MAJOR CIVILIAN RANKS

- Deputy commissioner
- Police commissioner
- First deputy commissioner

INTRODUCTION

ON JULY 31, 1997, A SIX-MAN EMER-
gency Service Unit (ESU) team raided the
apartment of two Middle Eastern terror-
ists who were in possession of bombs that they planned to detonate in
the New York subway that morning. Upon entering their bedroom, police
officers Keith Ryan and Joe Dolan fired their weapons, critically wound-
ing both suspects. A few minutes later, detectives Rich Teemsma and Paul
Yurkiw took X-rays of the bags found on the premises and confirmed they
contained bombs. In less than seven hours, one Muslim informant, six
New York Police Department (NYPD) Emergency Service officers, two
Bomb Squad detectives, supporting units, teams, and commanders narrowly aborted the nation's first suicide bombing.

One night when Keith Ryan and I were talking about the raid, he rose
to his feet. A big man at 6'1", his presence dominated the room. He then
began to describe what took place that morning. He bent his knees and
extended his arms in front of his face, pivoting just as he had done that
hot summer morning years before. I could almost see the suspects lying
prone on two twin mattresses, hidden in shadows on the other side of the
bedroom. Ryan was alone in the entryway. His partner, Joe Dolan, was
wedged outside, stuck behind the open door. Their sergeant, John English,
was a few feet behind. Ryan turned on the flashlight that was mounted
beneath the barrel of his gun. He could smell the sour odor of unfamiliar
bodies. Then he felt a rush of air and saw a dark figure suddenly lunge
toward him. The next thing he knew he was squeezing the trigger. He saw
the rounds hit but didn't hear a sound. At this, Ryan looked at me, then
sat back down. The trancelike expression that appeared on his face when
he'd relived the shooting had disappeared.

The incident lasted only a few seconds. Yet its personal and organizational consequences have persisted into the present day and altered the lives of the officers involved. Right after the raid, both cops and detectives emerged as heroes whose actions had saved hundreds of innocent lives. This all changed a few days later when the six men on the entry team let the police commissioner know that they didn't want to attend his press conference. They feared that publication of their names and pictures would result in retaliation by terrorists aimed at their families. Angered by what he viewed as a willful act of disobedience and disrespect, the police commissioner ordered the men to appear. They stood behind the mayor and the police commissioner at the press conference but refused to answer reporters' questions.

In the wake of these events, the conflict between the cops and top brass seemed to escalate and then spiral down the ranks, exacerbating nascent tensions in officers' squads. What should have been a victory marked by departmental rewards and promotions instead had a negative effect on the officers' careers. It is possible that some of the problems had begun before the raid, but none of the officers perceived it that way. Work opportunities that had seemed to be just on the horizon receded into the background. At first the officers faced the various obstacles and struggled to move ahead. In time, they grew frustrated, angry, and demoralized and made the decision to leave a job they'd loved for most of their lives, assuming, after twenty years in the NYPD, positions they saw as of lesser significance in other law enforcement agencies or private security.

Looking back on that fateful morning when he stood behind the mayor and the police commissioner at City Hall, Keith Ryan wonders where he'd be today if he'd just gone along and done what they'd asked. If he'd ignored his fears, lowered his eyes, and submitted to their will, he and his teammates would have moved up the ladder. Ryan imagines he would have made first-grade detective. Mounted on his mother's wall, displayed in a framed glass case, would be the Medal of Honor, the department's highest tribute, or at least the Combat Cross, to commemorate the day he and five teammates in the Emergency Service Unit led a raid that aborted what would have been the first terrorist bombing in the New York City subway.

Ryan has other thoughts every now and then. If they'd listened to him and his teammates, the police could have been better prepared for 9/11. Perhaps 9/11 would have been aborted, or more lives saved. The 1997 plot was a warning, part of the terrorist time line that began in 1993, when the World Trade Center was bombed, and culminated in that terrible day in 2001 when the towers came tumbling down. Ryan recognizes the absurdity of his fantasy, its grandiosity. He doesn't have the power to save the world. He's just a cop. He laughs, and then becomes somber again. He knows he should let go of the past. He's had an incredible career. A lot of the time, though, he still feels sad or angry. Strange as it seems, most of the officers involved in the incident feel much the same way.

While the raid involved a few seconds of fast-moving, nerve-wracking, adrenaline-pumping action, the fundamental social drama lay in the paradoxical events that occurred in the months that followed. The raid and its aftermath were significant because they threw into stark relief some critical features of contemporary policing in specialized units whose members are involved in dangerous, high-publicity, image-making police work. These features reflect on the police organization as an ongoing institution, on personal issues of career evolution, and on the complexity of emotion and thought that surrounds power, authority, and the use of lethal force.

This book provides a case study of the July 1997 raid and its aftermath as one multiphase incident that lasted for several years. It follows the lives of five officers in Emergency Service and the Bomb Squad from their participation in the 1997 raid until the attack on the World Trade Center in 2001, which forced them to revisit their past encounters with terrorism. Among the crucial issues the study illuminates are the psychological and social dynamics of lethal force, especially when directed at terrorist suspects in ambiguous situations that may threaten mass casualties; the internal culture and practices of the two specialized "first responder" units operating within the larger police organization; the question of danger and internal surveillance; the relationship between rank-and-file officers and bosses and their perceptions of leadership style; the jealousy and tensions that lie beneath the image of the blue wall of cop solidarity; and how police officers interpret and manage challenges to career mobility and their implications for morale.

This book has implications for issues of recruitment and retention of officers in specialized units as well as others within the police force, including officers in uniformed patrol and investigative detectives whose members have been more frequently subject to sociological research. In recent years, when economic times were good and alternative work was available, big city police departments have had difficulty finding qualified recruits who were willing to take on the hardships and risks of the current day, post-9/11 job. Despite the troublesome events that followed in the wake of the 1997 raid, the five officers featured here headed toward the World Trade Center on 9/11 along with most of their colleagues. Only a few police officers, whom no one talks out loud about, failed to respond to the mobilization. Initially everyone thought the disaster was manageable, and only a few cops and detectives expected the towers to collapse.

We continue to live in dangerous times. The wars in Iraq and Afghanistan have exacerbated international tensions and likely spawned new armies of terrorists, some of them hidden in pockets within the United States.[1] As recently as September 2009, a serious terrorist plot was discovered in New York City and Colorado by the Joint Terrorism Task Force. The arrest of those involved was nearly botched as a result of tensions between law enforcement agencies.[2] The potential for an accident resulting in mass casualties in high-risk organizational systems, such as nuclear power plants, also remains a cause for concern.

In the end, this book suggests that we shouldn't take for granted the commitment of our best and most highly trained officers. We cannot continue to treat them badly and then expect them to run in directions we flee and risk their lives to serve and protect. If we continue to ignore what they feel, think and say and do not address the issues they raise, we do so at our own peril. So do top-ranking members of the police organization. All of us may be courting catastrophe when the next disaster occurs.

LEARNING ABOUT THE TERRORIST RAID

During 2003 and 2004, I worked for about a year and a half in the Training Division of the New York Police Department as an assistant to the late deputy commissioner Jim Fyfe, assigned to various projects. I was immersed in writing chapters of the new recruit student guide when I learned about the events that are the subject of this book. A Police Academy sergeant told me about the raid and gave me the contact information of two of the Emergency Service officers involved. She knew I was looking for fresh material to include in the curriculum and thought the incident might be relevant. She had had a difficult time in a previous assignment with a boss who didn't acknowledge her training and skill. I think she identified with the problems some of the cops had had in the department and wanted to help them gain recognition for their heroic actions during the raid by helping to publicize events. She also wanted to have an impact on recruit training and felt stymied by her rank.

The prospect of talking to the officers intrigued me. I'd worked with cops in Emergency Service and was familiar with their role in the NYPD. Emergency Service shares with SWAT units in other cities the tasks of executing often warrant-based raids on criminal suspects, acting as tactical backup to the Hostage Negotiation Team, and responding to jobs involving lethal weapons. NYPD Emergency Service officers also deal with emotionally disturbed persons using verbal as well as tactical means and engage in other rescue tasks, including extracting people trapped in cars after accidents. Emergency Service work ranges from the most exciting rescue and special weapons and tactical jobs to such mundane service tasks as getting cats out of trees. In contrast to some specialized units, Emergency Service has an excellent reputation among other cops because its members are known to help them out. Emergency Service is also granted special status among commanders who call in ESU to deal with special tasks in ways that do not compound a mess or otherwise cause embarrassment. Emergency Service officers take pride in being the unit of "last resort" for cops and bosses alike. According to their motto, "When the public needs help, they call the police. When cops need help, they call ESU (Emergency Service)."

A few days after I learned about the raid, I arranged a meeting with the sergeant's two friends. The first thing I noticed upon seeing Joe Dolan and Keith Ryan was how different they looked from the average cop on the street today. Both were big, tall, and powerful men, throwbacks to another era before the height requirements were changed and women and minorities came on the job. Dolan was wearing a navy blue shirt and cargo pants and was accompanied by the black Labrador retriever he'd adopted when he transferred into the Bomb Squad several years before. Ryan was dressed in a white NYPD polo shirt and khaki pants. By then he'd also left Emergency Service and was working as a third-grade detective in the Intelligence Division ("Intel").

The officers talked like partners talk, which is why I prefer interviewing partners separately. They tended to finish each other's sentences, presenting a shared narrative that left me unsure of who thought and did what. Regardless, an intriguing story emerged in which the two officers appeared as heroes in a team effort that altered the course of New York history. The extraordinary set of events began one night in the late summer of 1997 when a Muslim informant approached some uniformed police near the Atlantic Avenue train station and alerted them to a plot to blow up the subway the very next morning. After the informant was interviewed by detectives, the Bomb Squad was called. Ordinance technicians detectives Paul Yurkiw and Rich Teemsma interviewed the informant and encouraged the duty chief to call Emergency Service. A meeting was held, and a tactical entry was planned.

More than two hours had passed by the time the officers finished presenting their account of the raid, and it was time for me to go home. When we said good-bye, the detectives gave me a hug that all but enveloped my 5'7" frame and made me feel small, young, and feminine. Dolan then concluded the conversation by saying, "That was the easy part." Curious, I arranged another meeting to find out what he meant. During several subsequent conversations, I learned about the paradoxical series of events that turned what they called "the perfect job" into a hotbed of conflict that seemed to cause a decline in their careers.

THE DECISION TO WRITE A BOOK

I didn't consider writing a book until after I left the Police Department and resumed my academic career. I was fascinated by the use of force during the raid and the paradoxical events that occurred in its aftermath. I liked Dolan, Ryan, and the other Emergency Service officers I'd met while attending some of their training. These cops seemed like skilled, tough-minded men who shared that mix of earnestness, warmth, and ironic wit that I'd come to link to some personal notion of "real police." I respected their expertise in areas that I knew nothing about, like plumbing, auto-body mechanics, electrical work, carpentry, and construction. I also appreciated their commitment to teamwork, rescue, and saving lives. In retrospect, I suspect that the raid and the officers involved were also interesting to me because they represented a last bastion of the traditional notion of the masculine real street cop that had been an enjoyable part of the fieldwork of my youth.

As I began to conduct in-depth interviews, my initial questions revolved around "fact," "truth," perspective, and interpretation. I wondered if all of the officers involved in the raid shared a similar understanding of the events. If the police commissioner had in fact been angry and vengeful, I wanted to know why and specifically what he did. I wondered what led the situation to deteriorate to such a degree that some of the NYPD's most dedicated officers began to feel ambivalent about a job they'd once totally loved. I was curious about what their experience revealed about the hidden world of policing in specialized units inside the NYPD.

After talking to a number of cops and bosses in Emergency Service who'd played some role in the events, I contacted Rich Teemsma and Paul Yurkiw, the two detectives who had dismantled the bombs found in the suspects' apartment. When they told me that their experience in the wake of the raid was similar to that of the Emergency cops, I was surprised. They were not involved in the conflict surrounding the press conference, had no beef with the police commissioner, and would have been happy to talk to reporters had they been asked. Nevertheless, they also encountered trouble in their squad and viewed the raid and its aftermath as the catalyst for the conflict and a negative turning point in otherwise promising careers.

Over the next few years, I interviewed officers of every rank who were involved in the raid, had knowledge of events, or who held important positions of power during the relevant period. I learned that the raid and its aftermath did, indeed, provide an open window into the department. Together, the officers' stories painted a multicolored mural that brought into relief important features of policing in specialized NYPD units whose members were tasked with dangerous work that had a high potential for violence. I discovered how the officers tried to nurture opportunities for advancement in their careers and manage the relevant challenges including problems with peers and bosses. I was witness as well to the frustration, anger, and demoralization that accompanied failure to meet their goals. I began to grasp the cultural dynamics of managing relationships within and up the ranks of specialized units with their particular rules of etiquette, and outside, in the larger police organization with its own. I also discovered new dimensions in the use of lethal force that seemed to pertain mostly to terrorist suspects.

OVERVIEW

Police Culture

Contemporary studies of policing emphasize the complexity and dynamic nature of police occupational culture. The police organization does not contain one monolithic culture but rather a "matrix" of subcultures whose members share different orientations to the job and in which different normative orders are dominant at different times.[3] Officers may use formal rules and law to guide behavior in certain situations and, at other times, invoke alternative principles, such as notions of masculinity and aggression. Even within occupational subcultures there is considerable variation in how individuals and groups of officers view traditional values, including notions of secrecy and loyalty, perceptions of the external environment as dangerous and hostile, conservatism, alienation from the community, and tension between cops and management.[4] While studies focusing on police organizations undergoing dramatic change recognize the varied and dynamic nature of occupational culture, they also note the persistence of traditional motifs.[5]

An analysis of the raid and its aftermath confirm the dynamic and varied nature of police culture and also the persistence of certain views, such as dichotomies in space, that are attributed differential value. Occupational norms that were once depicted in the police literature as rigid and nearly inviolate can be seen as flexible constructs that are subject to situational reinterpretation. A dramatic event like the raid that is remembered in different ways and repeated in stories also reveals how police occupational culture is continually redefined, reproduced, and articulated in ongoing political and social contexts.

The Warrior Subculture in Special Weapons and Tactical Units

In their exploration of Special Weapons and Tactics (SWAT) units, Peter Kraska and Victor Kappeler suggest that the increased militarization of U.S. policing, including the use of army and navy special operations units to train cops, has resulted in the development of a unique masculine, warrior subculture among the SWAT units, Kraska observed in training.[6] In support of the notion of a deeply embedded warrior subculture, Kraska suggests that cops join SWAT because they are attracted to danger. He notes that SWAT officers engage in mock combat paintball games during training and in their spare time. He mentions that snipers are trained to kill and that police who attain positions on sniper teams are attributed superior status in the eyes of their peers. Kraska goes on to suggest that incidents resulting in deaths among innocent victims appear to be frequent in SWAT units and blames this on the aggressive militaristic culture shared by the men.

In terms of Emergency Service, the notion of a deeply embedded and dominant masculine, warrior subculture does not really apply. It is true that the unit is heavily male in terms of its numbers and thus masculine interactional styles and ways of viewing the world are apparent. Nevertheless, I remain unconvinced that the masculine orientation of the unit leads to the development of a "malignant" attitude toward women or predisposes participants to the type of lethal aggression that Kraska describes. Cops in Emergency Service have varied attitudes toward female cops. Most of the men I interviewed believed that women could handle patrol and detective work, including dangerous undercover assignments, and jobs in specialized units, like Highway, that were heavily dominated by men. Some male officers had worked with women when they were in uniformed patrol or in the Detective Division. No man with whom I spoke claimed that women couldn't handle their job, although some didn't understand why women would want to do the work they did. In terms of the unit, the status division between inside and outside, real police work and computer-punching nonsense, is mediated by gender considerations but not dominated by views that exclude women from the domain of the street. Instead, it seems to replicate the distinction that soldiers make between REMFs (rear-echelon motherfuckers) who provide support from afar or "FOBits" who hang around the forward operating base, and combat soldiers who work outside the "wire" and fight "down range."

It is true that some of the officers in Emergency Service are attracted to risk and danger. Kraska links this personality orientation to war and combat, but these attributes may also be linked to participation in particular sports, emergency medicine, and even some anthropological fieldwork. Many officers are also aggressive in that they tend to prefer to utilize quick tactical solutions to lengthy verbal negotiations when dealing with difficult people. However, acceptance of rapid tactical options is mediated by a powerful cultural emphasis on competence, control, and minimal use of force.

Officers in Emergency Service do grant snipers special status because of their marksmen skills. However, I saw no evidence that officers placed value on killing or a high body count, although the decision to use lethal force was generally supported in the case of the raid.[7] No sniper in the NYPD has ever killed anyone in the line of duty, neither suspects nor innocent bystanders. In contrast to military snipers, police snipers mostly act as tactical backup and intelligence by providing information to hostage negotiators and other police about areas they cannot see. When NYPD snipers aren't involved in a special assignment, which is most of the time, they work in trucks alongside their peers. One of the reasons the sniper position is coveted is because it involves differential access to overtime pay. The sniper rifle is informally called the "money stick," a term that is commonly used but disliked because it ignores the skills involved and elevates the pursuit of money over commitment to the job. One former Emergency Service sniper told me he didn't like guns and avoided wearing one whenever he could. A supervisor, who was admired for his tactical and weapons skills, boasted that he'd only fired his gun once in his more than twenty-year career. The incident involved a "mercy killing" of a dog that had been shot multiple times.

Kraska argues that incidents resulting in deaths among innocent civilians appear to be frequent in situations in which a SWAT unit is involved. In the NYPD, there have been several incidents in which innocent civilians have died during raids by Emergency Service. One elderly woman had a heart attack after police used a "flash-bang" (nonlethal, minor explosive device) to disorient suspects prior to entering their apartment. As it turned out, the suspects weren't inside, and the woman who later died had refused medical care. Emergency Service officers had not prepared the warrant on which the raid was based, and were not involved in the flawed intelligence gathering that led to the mistake. On September 24, 2008, an Emergency Service supervisor, with an excellent reputation, ordered the use of a Taser to subdue a naked, mentally disturbed man who was standing on a ledge a few feet above the sidewalk, waving an eight-foot fluorescent light bulb at the cop who was trying to rescue him. Apparently, the crowd had been baiting the man and the cops when the supervisor finally decided to end the ordeal. When the man fell, his head struck the pavement and he died. The spectacle was caught on tape. The police commissioner publically faulted the supervisor, who took total responsibility for the incident and was put on modified duty in an isolated location away from his peers. A few days later, he snuck into Emergency Service headquarters, broke into a locker, retrieved a gun, and committed suicide rather than face the humiliation of a potential arrest and trial. The only controversial incident, known to the public, involving the use of lethal force by Emergency Service occurred in the 1970s, when an officer on an entry team shot a psychotic elderly woman who was armed with a kitchen knife. After Eleanor Bumpers was killed, new procedures were put into place and training developed on the verbal handling of barracked, emotionally disturbed persons.

Weapons and tactics expertise is hardly the only skill viewed as important by officers in Emergency Service. Police who can verbally negotiate with emotionally ill persons, including suspects, are highly regarded, and they are often called in to handle delicate jobs, such as talking down suicidal cops. So are officers with superior tool skills and similar technical expertise. The officers who are most respected by peers and bosses actively carry their load, are thoughtful and levelheaded, and competent in service and rescue jobs as well as those that demand special weapons and tactical expertise. Gung-ho behavior, thoughtless action, and overreaction to threats are viewed as dangerous because they suggest a lack of good judgment and common sense. Emergency Service officers thus appear to share a similar orientation to their work with the wild firefighters described by Desmond in his 2007 ethnography. They prize competence and control above all other attributes and view hypermasculine aggression, thrill-seeking behaviors, and thoughtless courage as negative qualities. By executing planned tactical entries at odd hours to maximize surprise, using distraction devices like "flash-bangs," carrying special tools and weapons, and wearing ballistic-resistant gear, team members attempt to minimize their vulnerability, reduce risk, and facilitate a minimal use of lethal force.

Differences in perception of the culture of Special Weapons and Tactics units partly relate to disparities in the location, size, and type of departments studied and the age and experience of the officers involved. Some researchers have conducted fieldwork among SWAT teams in small departments in politically conservative areas in which boys grow up shooting guns. I conducted my research among veteran Emergency Service cops in New York, a large, liberal city whose residents support firearms regulations and where private gun ownership is relegated to a small subculture of hunters and weapons enthusiasts. Police Department procedures regarding the use of force are stricter than those in state and federal law. Members of the top brass take procedural violations of the use of force policy seriously.[8] NYPD training and organizational culture emphasize the use of less than lethal means among officers in uniformed patrol as well as specialized units.

NYPD cops do not view themselves as soldiers although they admire the military and respect the special operations units from which they've borrowed some of their skills. Soldiers are trained to kill and also know they run a serious risk of dying in battle themselves. Their most coveted missions involve instances in which they can effectively use their killing skills. The police in the NYPD view the use of their guns in combat and lethal targeting as a last resort in situations of self-defense and protection of life. They are trained to control crime and preserve life and also engage in rescue and service work.[9]

Lethal Force

Lethal force was used in the 1997 raid on the terrorist cell. The suspects were not armed with guns, but bombs were found in the apartment close to where the terrorists had been sleeping. Most police condoned the officers' actions, although a few believed that a different team, alternative leadership, and another tactical plan could have reduced but not excluded the likelihood of deadly force. Nevertheless, I do not believe that masculine aggression and warrior subculture played a dominant role in the cops' decision to fire their weapons. Exploration of the events that occurred prior to the raid as well as the interaction between police and suspects suggest that the officers' decision was largely informed by situational exigencies accompanied by tension, fear, and the images of terrorists to which these emotions were linked. Of crucial importance in determining the officers' mindset was a series of conversations that took place during and right after the briefing, prior to the team's entry into the suspects' apartment.

Sociologist Randall Collins has recognized this phenomenon, noting that situations involving close-range combat may be filled with tension and fear, frustration, helplessness, and rage and that the outcome of such encounters is partly determined by how officers manage the heightened emotions involved.[10] British police have also recognized the importance of communications that occur during tactical meetings in determining lethal outcomes.[11] In situations involving the use of lethal force, police are also aware that outcome often determines the retrospective construction of right or wrong.

In the case of the raid, the formal parameters concerning the use of lethal force appear to have been temporarily lifted to accommodate the unusual circumstances in which the officers found themselves. In dealing with terrorist suspects in possession of improvised explosive devices (IEDs), the use of deadly force can be seen as a precursor to strategies that were only seriously considered in New York City after the World Trade Center disaster. If any single event has changed the culture of Emergency Service and created a more warlike orientation to particular aspects of their work, it has been 9/11, not the militarization of policing that began in the 1960s. This is not to say that militaristic images did not appear as part of the culture of Emergency Service and do not exist at the present time. They exist in latent form in Emergency Service and, to a lesser degree, in uniformed patrol. However, the incorporation of warrior motifs as dominant themes informing the thoughts, memories, stories, and actions of New York cops would require a number of significant changes in the social organization of the work. These would include a shift in job definition to exclude rescue and service calls and dedication of the unit to their SWAT role, a new emphasis on policing terrorism rather than crime and the violent emotionally disturbed, the lifting of cultural constraints that currently define notions of competence and limit the use of lethal force, and social and political change in the larger police organization that forces a shift in the unit's and possibly the department's dominant cultural paradigm.

Organizational Environment of the Raid

Police officers in specialized units exist within a larger organization and operate according to its principles. Formally, the Police Department is a hierarchical system in which power is distributed according to a chain of command. The police commissioner has the ultimate authority although he is appointed by the mayor and is beholden to him. The first deputy commissioner ("first dep"), a civilian title, is next in the chain of command, but this position holds more or less equal rank to the four-star chief of the department, who has the most prestigious position for a uniformed officer and probably any member of the service except the police commissioner. Other deputy commissioners, all of whom are civilians, mostly head inside bureaus, like Operations, Community Affairs, and the Training Division, and have the equivalent police rank of a three-star chief. Most outside street commands, like the Detective Division and the Patrol Bureau, are run by chiefs with three and sometimes two stars in the case of borough commanders. The Bomb Squad lies within the Detective Division, and Emergency Service is one of a number of small units in the Special Operations Division (SOD). In 1997, SOD was part of the Patrol Bureau, and its commanding officer reported to the chief of Patrol.

Cops and detectives are roughly the same rank, although detectives assume dominance in jobs that require their expertise. Detectives also make more money and have higher status, which increases as they move from third to first grade. Becoming a detective provides an alternative career path to officers who don't want to take civil service tests in order to move up from cop to sergeant, lieutenant, and captain. A first (top) grade detective makes the same amount of money as a lieutenant. Above the rank of captain, promotions are political and at the discretion of the police commissioner, who must choose from a number of officers brought to his attention by their superiors. Detectives must also gain the allegiance of bosses who have the incentive, opportunity, or influence to push their names up the list and gain the notice of the police commissioner. Officers are also sometimes promoted because they know top brass or do something extraordinary that makes the department look good.

Informal relationships play a strategic role in defining power and influence that can mediate, complement, and undermine formal rank. Starting at the very top of the organization, multiple political factions jockey for power and influence. Sometimes, the conflicts are ideological and involve allegiances to particular police commissioners and administrations whose members represent different leadership styles and policies. At other times, fights that emerge relate to personality issues and competition for the police commissioner's attention. Political neutrality is difficult to maintain as almost every individual is affiliated with one or another clique, all of whom are competing for limited resources. Every member of the service is therefore exposed to sometimes unsavory politics and is bound to get knocked about at some point in his career, regardless of skill, accomplishment, and formal rank.

Political divisions within a chain of command tend to follow organizational fissures as well as factions in loyalty to particular managers. The most powerful police are embedded in a web of relationships that transcend rank and reproduce a system of reciprocity revolving around the principles of who you know, what you owe, and what you have on participants. Police officers who have access to strategic information and resources and are owed a lot of favors often assume more power than befits their rank. When corruption occurs in today's NYPD, it is decentralized and involves relatively small numbers of officers who operate like gangs. As a result, it is no longer a bargaining chip in the system of exchange. "What you have on someone" is thus viewed less in terms of illegal activities than in relation to favors granted in the light of protection offered another officer who is discovered engaging in a "routine" indiscretion that could negatively impact his career, like the off-duty officer who is stopped while driving drunk and let go when he shows his shield and accompanied safely home.

Police brass, supervisors, detectives, and cops are linked in a thick web of relationships that deepens and expands with time on the job. Some of the relationships may involve negative value in the sense that one of the officers involved has "harmed" or embarrassed the other, creating a grudge that may be avenged in the future. For the most part, however, relationships have either positive value or none at all. An outsider who comes into the department as a deputy commissioner or other rank has not had the time to build a web and is therefore only as powerful as the strength of his relationship with the police commissioner and the depth of the networks and the loyalty of the officers he appoints or inherits from a previous administration. Although their interests sometimes collide, managers and cops are rarely completely at odds because of the personalized webs that bind them to people below and above their rank.

The police commissioner has control over almost every policy and personnel matter that falls outside civil service rules and labor contracts. Still, both union and nonunion issues tend to be informally negotiated and influenced by the principle of reciprocity, which reproduces and thickens the webs of exchange. Union presidents, for example, typically work with members of the top brass to iron out differences and come to mutually beneficial interpretations of contract rules. Precinct and unit commanders of the rank of captain or inspector negotiate in similar ways with union delegates, using them to solve problems in exchange for favors that make them look powerful in the eyes of the rank-and-file officers.

An individual who has connections to influential people of superior rank can progress through his career in ways that others can't. He can use his "hooks" to obtain choice assignments and maximize his opportunities for promotion to detective or deputy inspector and above. Officers who build alliances with police and civilians of every rank and status develop access to strategic resources and become part of the informal system of exchange, enhancing their individual worth. Officers who align themselves with bosses willing to try and promote them are also dependent on the bosses' pull with the police commissioner and who he believes should be recognized with an increase in rank and pay.

Cops typically view civilian members of the department as low in status by virtue of their decision to reject the police role and their permanent status as inside personnel. An exception is made for civilians who hold the rank of deputy commissioner and above, particularly those who were once police. Nevertheless, civilians, including janitors, technicians, painters, and others with access to special services and expertise also form part of the network. Formal, written requests for goods or "49s" (name of the form) put through "channels" (up the chain of command) can take months or years to obtain or never come through at all. Basic resources, from top-of-the-line street survival equipment, to toilet paper, pens, office telephone numbers, and computers and printers, are frequently procured through calling in favors or making trades.

The *Patrol Guide Manual* contains hundreds of rules that officers routinely violate in order to execute their jobs according to practiced recipes, live their lives with their families, work second jobs, and deal with personal problems and frailties. Bosses generally ignore minor infractions or let cops violate certain rules, regarding issues like overtime or conducting private business on duty, as a means of rewarding officers in a system in which pay is low, rewards are few, and resources are scarce. The fact that almost everyone sometimes violates rules also gives bosses power to hurt cops they don't like or who represent trouble or a political threat. In an uncertain world in which bosses can be vengeful, police of every rank need powerful patrons ("hooks" or "rabbis") who owe them a favor or are willing to fight on their behalf if they make a mistake, get into hot water, or need a boost in their careers. Officers who do everything right can suddenly find they are adrift when a patron retires and a promise is left unfulfilled. Race and gender intersect with politics as high-ranking brass look outward for approval or seek to quell internal unrest from minority police organizations.

Despite the existence of a network binding cops and commanders and reducing the conflict between them, rank-and-file officers do not assume they will come out equally or on top when push comes to shove and the alliance is put to the test. Cops assume that bosses are likely to steal the credit when a job goes right and hang them out to dry if the job turns bad. The higher-ranking the boss, the more he has to lose if he cannot deflect responsibility when a situation implodes. In *Wild Cowboys*, Robert Jackall implicitly points to this dilemma when he asks the question, "What kind of leaders are they that send officers into mortal danger, ask them to clean up ugly uptown messes . . . , and then pillory them or allow them to be pilloried, when they come out of the wreckage with dirty hands?"[12]

Internal Surveillance

Politics tends to get nastier as officers moved up the ranks because of increased competition and exposure to political factions vying for power and for the attention of the police commissioner. Higher-ranking officers also have fewer places to hide if they fall under the thumb of an opponent who has been empowered by the police commissioner or who holds a grudge. Internally generated paranoia is thus rampant among top brass who know they must move cautiously and be careful of whom they trust and what they put in writing, including private communications. Although they aren't usually at the political center of things, rank-and-file officers are also paranoid. Street cop paranoia has intensified in recent years in the light of advances in technology that have increased their exposure in the public domain. Cops thus see themselves as potential victims of the security systems that have been installed to monitor suspicious behavior on the part of criminals.[13] Hidden cameras record the activities of police as well as suspects. Helicopters carrying reporters watch the public and also the police. Even civilian "know-nothings" and "assholes" are armed with cameras and cell phones, recording events like the beating by Los Angeles police of Rodney King.[14] In preparation for controversial events, such as the Republican National Convention in New York City in 2004, police officers are explicitly warned that "the whole world is watching."[15]

Cops' belief that they are exposed and easily sacrificed is exacerbated by their sense that a double standard exists in the punishment of offenders. Chiefs and commissioners are largely immune from internal investigation. The word of the highest-ranking commander is likely to be taken over that of a subordinate unless the former's reputation is severely compromised. Only when a high-ranking scandal threatens to spin out of control or the police commissioner wants to neutralize a political enemy might he call on Internal Affairs to launch an inquiry into a member of the top brass. Although no one may be watching the top brass, cops are firmly convinced that everyone is watching them, including the police commissioner and his moles and deputies, the Internal Affairs Bureau, and the commanders and supervisors who lie within their chain of command and oversee their work.

The sense police have of living in a fishbowl in which they are constantly scrutinized and second-guessed is heightened by the way in which information is distributed and shared. Gossip and rumor run wild and rampant within and up the ranks. Individuals carry a load of narratives attached to their working histories wherever they go. A simple phone call to a "friend" regarding a transfer to a new unit can reveal a litany of negative or positive stories that tell how the officer was viewed in his former command, what he did, and why he decided to seek a transfer. Officers entering new units often come with labels like "rescue" (a boss in the new unit did a favor by rescuing the officer from a superior and/or colleagues with whom he was having problems), or sometimes something more favorable, depending on the hidden baggage that accompanies the transfer. Once a reputation is compromised, it's difficult to reverse and start afresh. Cops learn they can't trust civilians and they also can't trust cops. Some of the practical jokes that they play on each other provide informal instruction regarding these principles. The oft-repeated NYPD statement, "The job isn't on the level," refers to the belief that there's a hidden script in everything that happens in the department and that the script is heavily informed by politics.

In summary, physical danger, the uncertainty of the environment, the overwhelming sense of being scrutinized, the chronic threat of lawsuits and political violence, and the presence of the twilight zone of fantasy and speculation about who did and said what, combines to increase the paranoia that surrounds officers' daily lives, including those in management. Rank-and-file street cops know they have a lot of discretion to bend particular rules. Still, they feel that they are constantly on display and must monitor their every appearance, including issues as insubstantial as wearing their hat when they get out of their patrol cars. They believe they must be on the alert and prepared to account for their actions in ways that protect them in the face of various critical audiences, including supervisors, superiors, the press, the public, and judge and jury if the matter ends up in court.

Inside One Police Plaza:
Street Cops' Perspectives on Downtown

While power is based on a combination of rank and informal alliance, status is also determined by an officer's position in a spatial division that mediates the police construction of their world. Officers who have risen through the ranks as cops, supervisors, and commanders in the outside sphere of the street are granted higher status than those who have spent most of their careers inside. A collection of stories and characteristics are attached to inside and outside domains, particularly those that have achieved prominence in police history as a result of the crime, case, job, event, and people who are linked.

Cops call One Police Plaza in downtown Manhattan, where top brass have their offices, the "Puzzle Palace." From their perspective, computer-punching bureaucrats act like typical "house mice" and make decisions inside its walls that bind cops' hands, limit their ability to do their jobs, multiply paperwork, increase their vulnerability to punishment, and exacerbate the uncertainty in their lives. The center of power at One Police Plaza is the commissioner's suite on the fourteenth floor. Cops view the police commissioner as somewhere between God and a distant father who controls their lives like puppets on a string.

Officers in specialized units like Emergency Service are linked to the police commissioner more intimately through the street commanders who utilize their services as well as their chief. Most rank-and-file officers don't think about the police commissioner unless he makes a public statement that makes them look bad or he gets into a feud with the unions over their contract. Officers also often look on the commissioner with awe and want his approval if they have worked hard or taken serious risk. The unusual respect granted officers in Emergency Service may give them more power to negotiate up the ranks than the average uniformed cop. Some cops in specialized units may share a sense of entitlement to better treatment than other cops because of their training, skills, and involvement in dangerous jobs. Even cops in a team-oriented unit like Emergency Service can't help but want some internal acknowledgment of their accomplishments. Officers who strive for but are denied the police commissioner's recognition when they think they deserve it may suffer the kind of anger, deprivation, and abandonment as children experience when deprived of a loving father. Such reactions result from the intensely personal nature of the police organization, which often seems to echo family life.

A police commissioner does not discuss controversial issues directly with low-ranking subordinates. This would violate etiquette and could put him at risk of being quoted by officers who are not part of his loyal cadre. If he needs to communicate with members of the rank and file, a commissioner will talk to their highest-ranking chief, often his appointee, who transmits the information down the chain of command without compromising the boss. Sometimes a cop in the commissioner's security detail, his driver, or other trusted subordinate will transmit the boss's message to officers of his own rank. Still, the word that trickles down is always secondhand and often vague or imbued with the affect and intonation of the interpreter, not the source. The result is that an empty space exists in communications between cops and brass. This void is pregnant with meaning and breeds rumor, speculation, and fantasy as officers try to make sense of microscopic cues to minimize the uncertainty they feel. Personal and cultural transferences also flourish and illuminate the cultural themes and assumptions that mediate cops' perceptions of management.

Within this framework, the actions of the police commissioner and his deputies, particularly those that are negative, are often perceived as personal and intentional. Cops thus imagine the mayor, the police commissioner, and other top brass are thinking and doing things they may not be engaged in at all. Motives may then be attributed to actions that occurred simply because someone forgot. An insignificant message or "threat" from someone who works in the office of a high-ranking member of the brass may be imbued with special power when it's based simply on personal grudge. Some of the messages that come out of the offices of high-level commanders may not always have come from the big boss, as cops often assume. The effects of the real or imagined actions of high-ranking superiors may be intensified if they trigger uncomfortable images from individuals' pasts.

Outside Bosses

The status distinction between inside and outside police helps cement the ties between officers of different rank who occupy similar categories of space. Police who work "outside" in the Patrol Bureau, the Special Operations Division, or the Detective Division are generally viewed with more respect than those who spend the bulk of their careers in administrative positions, "inside." Inside personnel and administrators are believed to be out of touch with the real world of policing and sometimes afraid to be real cops. Inside/outside, petty bureaucrat/cop's cop, micromanaging/empowering, fear and intimidation/respectful, selfish opportunist/protector—these are dichotomous personality attributes and managerial styles that are linked to bosses associated to the relevant spheres, although a range of people and leadership types actually occupies each sphere.

"Cop's cop" is a term that is applied mostly to outside bosses who understand the world of the street and the working recipes that cops use to accomplish their jobs. Implicit in the notion of cop's cop is a boss who knows that the job demands flexible and sometimes creative interpretations of law and procedure. A cop's cop is willing to back up his officers when they are right or make an honest mistake. A midlevel or high-ranking boss who is not afraid to get his hands dirty when cops are in a tight situation and need his help is admired. This typically means supporting cops who made reasonable decisions that might have resulted in ambiguous outcomes. On occasion, it may also involve taking police action in a street encounter that arose spontaneously when rank-and-file manpower is short. Regardless, the cop's cop bosses know their place, don't forget they aren't cops, and concentrate on doing their jobs rather than those of subordinates, including negotiating with superiors and cushioning subordinates against negative fallout. A cops' cop is thus a kind, honest, and courageous leader who goes out of his way to help and protect good cops even if it means putting his career on the line. Although on occasion a cop's cop may reprimand recalcitrant subordinates, he is not punitive or vengeful. He also empowers his supervisors to do their job and leaves his officers alone as long as they get their work done, stay out of trouble, and treat the public with the respect they deserve.

Good and Bad Bosses

Cops recognize that they will only work for a limited number of cops' cops during their careers and that most of their bosses will fall along a continuum, ranging from good to bad, depending on how they relate to subordinates and superiors, understand cop culture, and interpret and enforce the informal rules that guide behavior. Every rank in the Police Department has a role to play that goes beyond what is written in the *Patrol Guide*. As line officers, sergeants tend to be close to their cops and not only supervise but help them handle jobs. Some sergeants tend to overidentify with their men and inadvertently fail to protect them by, for example, encouraging or allowing them to violate laws such as using "excessive" force or pushing the boundaries allowed in a search warrant. Others understand that part of their role involves protecting their officers against themselves.

Although lieutenants sometimes also take active roles on jobs, they should have sufficient distance from the rank and file to advise superiors, keep their secrets, and control cops from engaging in unnecessary violations of law and procedure. Lieutenants also handle administrative issues and paperwork not assigned to their sergeants. Even more than sergeants, lieutenants should ensure that cops do their jobs without "excessively" and dangerously violating suspects' rights or otherwise abusing their authority. Some lieutenants take this responsibility seriously, and some do not.

The principles surrounding role and rank in Emergency Service are illustrated during tactical entries. In these types of jobs, cops always go in first, while the highest-ranking line supervisor is last in the stack and is often assigned to guard the door or other open space that could leave the officers' backs exposed. One supervisor explained, "There's a saying in ESU, the higher up you go in life, the further you go back in the line. So when I was a cop, if I wanted to be the first one through the door, I could be the first one through the door. When I made sergeant, I'm the fifth one through the door, that's my position. That was my job. When you make lieutenant, if there's a sergeant there, you may not even be coming through the door. If you're a captain, you're not coming through the door at all. It's just not an issue."

Captains thus do not typically execute jobs with his cops. Instead, they stay nearby and manage and organize from above. Captains also act as cushions, mediating between subordinates and superiors from different units who may try to intervene on a job in troublesome ways. A sergeant compared the role of a captain to that of a rodeo clown who diverts the bulls so the cowboy can safely climb out of the ring. "A captain is like a rodeo clown, keeping the bulls off the cops' backs" so they can do their jobs and go home.

Cops perceive good bosses as officers who understand the roles and responsibilities that go with their rank. Cops respect active bosses who get out of their offices and observe them at work, as long as the bosses do their job and don't try to act like cops. Cops don't begrudge a good boss's efforts to exert control over what they do and stop them from taking action that could result in a negative outcome and individual or group embarrassment. One highly respected boss explained, "I had a thing [when I was a precinct commander]. I always took care of the good cops and I always made sure that I walked the streets. . . . I was on 125th [Street] if something happened there. You can't let these cops think that you are going to stay in the office. Once [they start thinking] he ain't coming out here, you lose all kinds of control. I got the respect of the cops because I went out there. That was my job. My job was to make sure that they were doing their job and at the same time, rewarding the ones that are doing the job. . . . I used to say the job [of a precinct commander] was to keep the cops happy, to keep the community happy, and keep downtown happy."

Of course, control is a balancing act on the part of a boss if he wants to maintain the loyalty and respect of his cops. As Elizabeth Reuss-Ianni notes in her 1983 study of street and management cop culture, there is a difference between a boss who makes sure his officers are doing their job and one who is "always breathing down your back (or) . . . looking to catch you up short. . . . It's OK if he (the sergeant) looks for you once on a tour to give you a scratch (initial your memo book) but when you know he is out there looking for you . . . then that's out and out harassment . . ."[16] Along the same lines, a good boss may punish a cop for an infraction once but doesn't keep going after him again and again. Good bosses also don't fan fires but instead put them out. In the words of a detective, "a bad boss makes a mountain out of a molehill. A good boss makes a molehill out of a mountain."[17]

In specialized units, some bosses don't have the training and skills of their cops. These bosses, in particular, must be aware of their limitations and leave certain safety and tactical decisions to their experienced supervisors and cops. Good bosses shouldn't attempt to go above their superiors' heads or take on their jobs unless they are advised to do so or the superior isn't available. Good bosses supervise but don't micromanage their cops. In general, they leave their cops alone to spend their time on patrol as they please so long as they stay out of trouble, are available when they are needed, make smart decisions, and handle their jobs well.

Good bosses of every rank protect their officers in a variety of ways. This may involve writing up reports that are consistent with the facts but omitting details that could give the appearance of impropriety. Protection also involves keeping cops from getting involved in situations that could put their lives at unacceptable risk, isolating them from unstable peers, preventing the execution of tactically unsound jobs, insulating them from superiors who demand that they take action that could endanger their lives, and doing whatever it takes to protect them from engaging in behaviors that could get them "jammed up" (disciplined).

Types of Bosses

While there are a few police bosses, legends in their time, who are loved and respected among nearly all peers and subordinates, most bosses develop good relationships with some but not all of their cops, depending on fit and preferred personality and leadership styles. My research with police revealed a number of basic types. "Control freak" bosses who micromanage subordinates are generally disliked, particularly in units like Emergency Service, whose members are highly trained, motivated, take pride in doing their job, and, as a result of their status among peers and superiors, feel entitled to a reasonable degree of trust and freedom. Also loathed are "fear-and-intimidation," authoritarian, manipulative, sadomasochistic types who "kiss up and kick down," ingratiating themselves with superiors while treating subordinates like miscreants or ignorant children.

While some cops experience a smothering sense of helplessness and rage at the hands of control freaks and/or fear-and-intimidation types, a few cops would prefer to work for them than deal with "wishy-washy" bosses who give vague and contradictory commands and then punish their cops when the result turns sour. At least control freaks tell cops what they can and cannot do and make it clear how a job should be handled and how they want information to flow, in most cases directly to them so they know all that is going on, can report to superiors alone, and take the credit for every success. Most cops would agree that the most difficult bosses are moody and inconsistent, demonstrating Jekyll and Hyde personalities that make it difficult to develop strategies to manage them. One cop explained, "What I hate most in a boss is a guy who doesn't know what direction he is going. You come in a happy guy one day and then you're a scumbag the next. If you are going to be a scumbag, be a scumbag 365 days of the year. If I have to worry about what kind of mood you are going to be in for today, I have no use for you because you are just making my life tough." Almost as troublesome as unpredictable bosses are those who are "spineless," never question superiors, and won't protect or fight for their cops. Wishy-washy, Jekyll and Hyde, control freak, spineless, and fear-and-intimidation types of bosses all take considerable flexibility and skill to manage effectively.

Managing Up

Most police officers develop an awesome ability to manage some of these difficult bosses. Cops who have the ability to humanize and, to some degree, empathize with the weaknesses of troublesome bosses tend to be better able to find saving graces in almost any human being and get along. There are also cops who identify with the often inflated notions of self-importance and superior knowledge of control freak and fear-and-intimidation bosses and are happy to flatter them and submit to their will. There are also cops who are not able to develop an empathic understanding of or identification with difficult bosses but can analyze their behavior sufficiently well intellectually to get along. Cops learn early in their careers to recognize bosses who interpret differences of opinion and politely stated directness as insubordination or a political threat. Even some well-regarded and generally competent bosses give orders using no-nonsense authoritarian interactional styles that rub some subordinates the wrong way. Other bosses who are also highly respected and better liked have a more tolerable, easygoing manner and couch their orders with terms like "Please" and "I would appreciate" that are easier for most adults to hear.

To protect themselves and survive in a world with diverse and difficult management styles, cops develop a variety of strategies to manage up. Evident among some cops when dealing with bosses who use fear and intimidation is unquestioning obedience coupled with blind admiration that is partly unconscious. Deliberate attempts to flatter and appear admiring, coupled with overt submission, constitute a successful strategy used by cops to get on the good side of narcissistic bosses, in particular. More frequent is a passive-aggressive approach, which allows cops to keep their dignity ("I'm not kissing ass") while maintaining the appearance of submission. They "'Yes' the boss to death" to his face and ignore what he says behind his back. Kowtowing, eye lowering, and shoulder-slumping gestures may be used in conjunction with "yeses" to appease authoritarian bosses who demand total obedience. Some cops can thus be seen adopting a similar posture as the "meekly insane" that author Jack Henry Abbott described for prison inmates when they are passing through a gauntlet of "redneck" prison guards looking for an excuse to beat them up.[18] The passive-aggressive strategy that may be accompanied by gestures of appeasement is sufficiently pervasive among the ranks to constitute a part of the police occupational personality that hasn't been recognized in the scholarly literature.

Cops also manage difficult bosses by avoidance, even if it hinders the execution of their job or involves lying on paperwork and withholding the facts to reduce the frequency of interaction. In serious situations cops also deal with micromanaging control freak bosses by delaying action and calling their captain or chief for support. Officers in specialized units who possess knowledge and skills not shared by their bosses may ignore commands that they believe are unsafe and proceed as they please, hoping superiors will come to their senses and ignore subordinates' passive disobedience if everything goes well. Some skilled officers also use chitchat and warm humor to defuse a boss's tension and pave the way to negotiate, using logic to explain why an alternative action makes more sense.

Other officers may sneak behind the commander's back and not reveal certain information in a modified version of the passive-aggressive approach that will be seen later in this book. As a last resort when dealing with troublesome bosses within a squad or unit, cops may appeal to others of same or higher rank, although this may violate the chain of command and is likely to have negative repercussions. It's unusual for cops to lodge a formal complaint against a boss even when grounds exist. By filing formal charges, they know they may win the battle but lose the war. Once-friendly bosses may view them as dangerous. At some point down the line, the boss they hoped to defeat may be in a position to take revenge.

When difficult bosses push cops to the brink and their efforts to manage them fall short, cops can resort to behind-the-back sabotage by slowing down their response to jobs, going out sick when they know they are needed most, and taking the maximum number of days off (which most think only makes sense anyway), complaining of bias to a minority police organization, spreading rumors, and on rare occasions, "dropping a dime" to Internal Affairs, accusing the boss of a violation in order to start an investigation. A central dilemma for cops in terms of dealing with fear-and-intimidation and control freak bosses, in particular, is how to maintain their dignity, maximize autonomy, and feel like adults in the face of disempowering and often crushing, irrational, arbitrary, and intimidating authority.

Reciprocity and Loyalty

"Loyal" and "loyalty" are terms that are frequently heard in the NYPD in the context of relationships with peers, supervisors, and high-ranking bosses. Loyalty can be understood as part of the system of exchange when positive values are attributed to the actions that are involved. Officers typically demonstrate loyalty to each other by limiting the flow of information to superiors regarding infractions, backing each other up on jobs, handling disputes among themselves, taking responsibility for partners' mistakes, and ignoring or denying knowledge of others' misdeeds. Doing the opposite by, for example, knowingly and overtly contradicting statements by peers or engaging superiors in matters that belong only to cops, if discovered, can initiate a cycle of negative reciprocity that may include more than one individual.

Rules are flexible constructs that are interpreted strategically, depending on the larger social and interactional context and the people involved.

Sometimes rules related to loyalty and reciprocity may be used retrospectively to excuse or justify past actions. Rules may be broken with impunity and neutralized in circumstances that are mundane. When two rules come into conflict, one or both may be nullified. Cops may discreetly go above peers' heads and use bosses to control or punish another cop by subtly or inadvertently alerting the boss about a violation or problem in the squad. Cops typically rat on each other when they think a peer's behavior is dangerous or otherwise troublesome, for example, by rolling their eyes when the sergeant brings up his name. Repetition of such gestures by more than one cop at different times is likely to give the boss a reason to investigate why.

A corollary of the oath of silence and loyalty cops share among themselves extends to relationships between bosses. Disagreements do occur among supervisors regarding how to handle problem cops and whether to cover for them when they are drunk, for example, utilize excessive force, or violate another point of law or procedure that could expose others to danger and embarrassment. Regardless, supervisors generally deal with disagreements amongst themselves and do not involve superiors. Even more than cops, supervisors thus stick together and provide a united front when it comes to dealing with their affairs. Sometimes this works in subordinates' favor. At other times, it works to their detriment.

One of the reasons that supervisors stick together is that they know that the threat to their careers doesn't just come from jealous peers, easily threatened superiors, and complaints from the public if a job goes amok. It also comes from cops. Bosses were once cops and know the games they sometimes play to manipulate bosses, settle disputes, maximize freedom, and sometimes avoid work. The code that bosses once observed as cops is thus reinterpreted in the light of new concerns about self-protection and the heightened responsibility that comes with supervising armed men of various temperaments who have the power to kill.

Officers demonstrate loyalty to bosses when they give them credit for their accomplishments, make them "look good" to those above, never go over their bosses' heads, control colleagues' behaviors that threaten to undermine the boss's success, help ensure that their bosses' desires are carried out, and alert bosses, directly or indirectly, to problems that need their attention or could damage their career. Officers generally prefer bosses who view loyalty as a two-way street such that positive values characterize both sides of the exchange. This means that the boss rewards cops' loyalty by recognizing their accomplishments; protects them when they make an honest mistake; allows them to handle personal matters on department time when the need arises; and tolerates minor infractions or administers only verbal reprimands when more troublesome indiscretions occur.

Bosses show loyalty to subordinates by their willingness to confront peers and higher-ranking superiors from outside their chain of command even at the risk of creating animosity that could negatively impact on their careers. Most Emergency Service supervisors were cops in the unit, know the work, and share their cops' skills. In other specialized units like the Bomb Squad, this isn't always true, with the result that threats to detectives' safety may come from the sergeants and lieutenants within their commands. This can increase the tensions between detectives and their bosses because there may be no informed intermediaries to whom a rank-and-file officer can appeal without going over his boss's head and violating the chain of command.

Instances in which cops feel betrayed by bosses involve the use of fear and intimidation tactics to threaten subordinates, cursing cops out in public, and otherwise embarrassing them and treating them with disrespect. Cops also feel betrayed by or angry at bosses who refuse to recognize and apologize for mistakes and blame cops instead. A superior who abandons loyal officers at a crucial time to pursue his or her personal interests is universally scorned. Even authoritarian, narcissistic, or opportunistic bosses tend to understand that loyalty involves an exchange, although they may be stingy in terms of what they give back to their cops, with the result that their officers are likely to withhold valued behaviors that could make their bosses look good.

Demonstrations of loyalty occur in the context of the fishbowl effect and help minimize negative exposure by keeping compromising information out of the hands of critical audiences inside and outside the department. At some point in their careers, almost every police officer has heard a boss threaten, "Don't you ever embarrass me again!" Cops can also be seen reassuring a frantic boss that he doesn't have to worry; they *will* make sure he looks good in front of the relevant audience. Officers thus gain the trust, loyalty, and protection of superiors when they demonstrate that they are there when the boss needs them, get him arrests and claim them versus giving them to cops in another command, and downgrade the category of recorded crime to its lowest denominator in order to show that the boss has deployed manpower effectively and has control of the streets.

The biweekly CompStat (comparative computer statistics for crime mapping) meetings in the "War Room" provide a metaphor for the public embarrassment both cops and bosses fear and loyal cops help their boss prevent. During CompStat meetings, members of the top brass sit in big leather chairs around a large donut-shaped table, flanked by rows of folding chairs reserved for other members of the service. Precinct or unit commanders stand up behind a podium and defend their crime statistics or other productivity data. The commissioner sometimes sits in while deputy commissioners, the chief of the department, and three-star chiefs bombard the commander with comments, questions, and, on occasion, suggestions to help resolve problems the data reveals. CompStat meetings may be kinder now than they were in the past, when they were viewed as degradation ceremonies designed to make precinct commanders look bad in front of peers and top brass. Still, CompStat remains a painful ordeal that must be endured, made better only because "everyone knows that they'll probably get beat up so there's not so much shame when it happens to you," explained one veteran commander.

Individualism and the Team

Emergency Service officers work trucks in pairs and handle "routine" jobs together with backup, depending on the call. The officers are also trained to handle certain kinds of jobs in teams of six to eight officers or more in coordination with backup teams assuming additional roles. Executing warrants, for example, typically involves a team of six to eight persons whose members follow a well-practiced tactical plan that has been discussed in advance. Each officer is assigned a specific role and tasks that are linked to entering a premises in a particular order in the stack (entry line), carrying particular tools and weapons, searching certain areas, and dealing with whomever and whatever is there.

Emergency Service officers all go through the same training and share equal skills. Roles on a team are therefore interchangeable, and any officer should be able to substitute for the others. Individual assignments on a team are then based less on expertise than on other informal rules revolving around, for example, territorial rights. Officers who regularly work the sector where a job takes place are assigned to the team and may choose to go in first. In practice, some officers have better skills in some areas than others, such as the use of special tools and negotiating with the mentally ill or even making rapid tactical entries, although few would admit deficiency there. In situations in which rookie officers are involved, experience and seniority may play a role in the selection of position on a team. In theory, the highest-ranking supervisor has the right to decide regarding such crucial matters as personnel and tactical plan, although a boss who violates traditional recipes for choosing teams, assigning responsibility, and discussing tactical issues is likely to meet disapproval.

The team orientation that pervades the culture of Emergency Service derives from tried and proven formulas for handling dangerous jobs. Officers on a team are dependent on each other for the safe and successful execution of the mission. If one officer makes a bad decision or doesn't handle the task assigned, he puts himself and his colleagues in jeopardy. The cultural emphasis on teamwork in routine matters reflects and signifies deeply embedded beliefs about life, death, and survival. Related to the notions of role interchangeability and the importance of the team is an emphasis on conformity among officers in the unit. Difference sometimes is interpreted as dissidence and/or individualism and, as a result, may be subject to punishment by the group. Emergency Service officers look down on peers who stand out or are seen as seeking the limelight and trying to "self-promote." Notions of good and bad cop revolve not only around skill, competence, bravery and common sense, but also the individual's willingness to put the interests of the team before his own.

The police organization shares a similar team orientation, which can be seen by the frequent use of sport metaphors to describe participation in particular jobs, including those that take place "inside." A similar team ethic pervades the subculture of specialized units like the Bomb Squad, in which officers work as individuals or sometimes in pairs, although partner involvement in the dismantling of bombs is discouraged because of the risk involved. Stipulations against individualism and opportunism thus appear to serve purposes other than reinforcing practical recipes for getting jobs done that link interdependence and sameness to survival.

Team Ethic and Bosses

The team ethic appears to be particularly beneficial to bosses because they are allowed to take credit in the wake of a victory while individual cops are not. Rules against self-promotion also give bosses the power to determine who gets what according to principles of their own choice, like loyalty. Jobs in the Bomb Squad are distributed according to a rotation. More often than not, it is a matter of luck when officers get the most desirable jobs, although willingness to work can play a role. Self-promotion when a "good job" is involved is discouraged because it can exacerbate jealousy and conflict in a squad and create an unpleasant working atmosphere for cops and bosses alike. Other principles, such as seniority, thus come to replace criteria like hard work and expertise exhibited in dangerous jobs in determining the distribution of important rewards. The leadership style of a commander sets the tone in small units like the Bomb Squad, with the result that alternative norms of behavior may dominate during the tenure of different bosses who choose alternative ways to manage conflict and do the job.

Rules prohibiting "self-promotion" raise an important question. How do cops, detectives, and police above the rank of captain move ahead in their careers when they are supposed to lie low and wait their turn? This issue is made particularly complex in view of the dominance of an informal system in which upward mobility is partly related to the favors and connections officers develop and in which performance and even seniority may play secondary roles, although a combination of all these factors generally increases the likelihood of moving ahead.

Career Management and the Dynamics of Morale

In *Danger, Duty, and Disillusion*, Joan Barker provides a qualitative account of the occupational socialization of patrol officers in the Los Angeles Police Department, highlighting a five-phase process that marks the transition in attitude and feelings about the job from the time police graduate from the academy to their retirement. While Barker's findings may be relevant to officers in uniformed patrol, they do not account for the problems in morale that arise in specialized units in the NYPD. There, disillusionment is rarely the result of the external issues cited by Barker, such as court decisions that limit the police or free guilty men, on-the-job injury and lawsuits against cops, or even personal matters such as divorce.

When officers in specialized units become demoralized it is largely because they feel victimized by forces within the department itself. These officers often still love "the job" but feel beaten down by a variety of circumstances that intensify with the passing of time. Of special significance to some are repeated interactions with bosses whose leadership styles conflict with their personal needs, desire for autonomy, and their professional sense of themselves as veteran cops. The techniques these officers once successfully used to manage career mobility begin to fail. Not only are the officers unable to gain rank, but they continue encountering difficult bosses who deplete their energy and add pain to their work. Not that every one of their bosses is troublesome. Rather, the chronic nature of interactions with those that are undermine the officers' ability to cushion themselves socially and psychologically. The difficult bosses then get under their skin and live "rent-free" in their heads long after they've left work and gone home to sleep.[19]

Officers who are continually promised rewards by superiors who then forget, withdraw, or fail to deliver them may experience disillusionment accompanied by the uncomfortable sense that they have been teased, abandoned, or betrayed. Officers may also feel entitled to promotion when they have participated in jobs that involve a lot of physical and/or mental risk and feel betrayed when such awards do not materialize, particularly when the officers believe they have continued to work hard. Money also plays a significant role that increases in importance with time on the job and intensifies the desire to gain a promotion. Even officers who consistently experience good relationships with superiors may not receive the recognition they feel they deserve. This situation is made more difficult because they often see junior colleagues who have done less move up because they are visible or have "pull" with someone who is connected with the police commissioner. In some cases, a combination of conflict with bosses and isolation from peers, lack of opportunity for advancement, and perceived injustice in the distribution of punishment and reward are instrumental factors in leading to demoralization. In others, the simple fact that a good officer cannot get promoted when others can results in low morale and the decision to leave the job.

Retirements among officers in the top brass are usually political. Three- and four-star chiefs (in other words, the chief of the department) typically retire before reaching the mandatory retirement age if a new police commissioner is appointed with whom they disagree and their positions are threatened or their authority compromised. Then and only then, for these loyal and highly committed leaders, does an outside position in the public or private sphere seem more desirable than their usually less lucrative police careers. The five rank-and-file officers who are the main characters in this book left the job while young and in their prime for a mixture of the reasons cited above. Most of their top-ranked senior officers left even earlier, shortly after the appointment of the new administration in the wake of 9/11.

1

ROOKIE

KEITH RYAN DIDN'T ALWAYS PLAN TO be a cop. He didn't know Emergency Service existed until after he joined the force. It wasn't that police work didn't interest him. He'd grown up mesmerized by TV shows like *Dragnet* and *Car 54, Where Are You?* After Ryan graduated from Brooklyn College, he tried several jobs before joining the department. He followed his mother's wishes and tried being a teacher. He didn't want to disappoint her by pursuing his secret dream of becoming a cop. She had no love for the police.

A left-leaning equal rights and antiwar activist, Mrs. Ryan shared the views of a lot of the youth who came of age in the 1960s. She also had personal reasons for distrusting police. When Ryan was a boy, the screaming inside the house would sometimes get so loud that the neighbors would call 911. Time and again, his father would open the door, welcome the cops into the kitchen and offer them a drink. Together they would sit nursing wine or beer and commiserating about the moodiness of women. In those days, domestic violence wasn't viewed as a crime but a private matter between husband and wife. Besides, the police could see from the furniture built with his fine craftsman's hands that Mr. Ryan was a hard-working European immigrant who provided for his family. So the cops didn't pay much attention to the little boy locked in his bedroom or the bruised face of his small, young Puerto Rican mother.

Keith Ryan was the firstborn of four children. He has one brother and two sisters, all of whom have families and successful careers. Ryan was the only one of the siblings who was routinely beaten by his father. This puzzles him still. He imagines his father was jealous of his mother's love for him. Ryan thinks his father was ashamed of the craterlike scar punched in the side of his son's face, just above his cheekbone, a remnant of a tumor he barely survived at birth.

Ryan grew up in a blue-collar neighborhood in Sheepshead Bay, Brooklyn, among hard-working families of Irish, Jewish, and Italian decent, with a few wise guys and their brash young children peppered in. He did well in school, excelled in sports, and had plenty of friends. Focused and self-contained, he didn't get into fights like some of his peers. The only time he might challenge some guy was if he threatened one of his siblings.

Grandparents from both sides of his family were generous people who helped him grow strong and survive the battles inside the house. Ryan recalls with fondness a kind and beautiful aunt. He remembers the rich, musty smell of her perfume and the warmth of her dark brown eyes. His mother was the backbone of the family. When he was small, she'd dress him up in a suit and take him to the park. He recalls the cool breeze and the warmth of the sun on his cheeks. A loving, intelligent woman, she tried to take care of her children and instill in them a sense of self-worth and independence. "I am what I am because of her," Ryan explained.

A smile lights up his face when he envisions the kindly eyes of the neighbor who raised pigeons, not the noisy pests that litter the parks and contaminate the city's air conditioners, but the sleek multicolored homing pigeons that are born and bred to race. He loved watching them spiral up into the sky, free of any encumbrance but the band they wore on their leg. He liked their loyalty, their long flights home from anywhere. He got a kick out of watching them lay their eggs and seeing the babies emerge. When he was eight years old, Ryan approached his neighbor and asked if he could buy a pigeon. The man told him no but offered instead to take him on as an apprentice. From that day on, he treated the boy like a son. Keith sat with his neighbor's family at dinners to celebrate racing events. When one of their pigeons won, Keith proudly stepped on stage and picked up the trophy.

Ryan recalls the first pigeon he owned, a half-blind, banded bird from Holland that he rescued from the steeple of the church. He named the bird the Dutchman and nursed him back to health until his father took him away. Keith thinks his father let the bird go but deep down knows that he killed him. A bird with compromised vision can't survive alone.

His parents divorced when Keith was eighteen. By the time he was twenty-one, he had built his own pigeon coop in the garage behind his mother's house. "I would go and get lost for hours. I felt safe there," he explained. I saw a film of Keith as a young man working in the coop. The camera caught him at his best angle, highlighting his bone structure and unblemished left check. His body was long and lean, like a runner in peak condition. His face looked intense, solemn, and fiercely handsome.

○ ○ ○ ○ ○ ○ ○

In 1986, Keith Ryan took the test to become a New York City police officer. He graduated from the Police Academy in 1987 and was sent to the 7-9 (79th) Precinct in Brooklyn, a neighborhood that was so bad that "people with guns were afraid to live there." After his probationary year was complete, he transferred to Coney Island. It didn't take more than a few weeks on patrol before he realized that policing was a natural calling that would always claim his heart no matter how bad things got or what fate had in store.

I know cops today who view such devotion as a symptom of the Stockholm syndrome. The department holds its officers hostage for a twenty-year term with the promise of benefits and a pension. In time, the cops become attached to their keeper, forming a painful bond. Uncertainty, petty tyranny, and punishment come to be viewed as signs of caring; the smallest gesture of human kindness is mistaken for love. I don't mean to suggest that love and kindness do not exist in the New York Police Department. There are plenty of wonderful bosses who treat their men with warmth, dignity, and respect. The men respond with loyalty, working hard to make their bosses shine in the face of superiors. The problem mostly lies in the system. Few curbs exist to stifle the actions of bullies who "kiss up and kick down." One bad boss can wreak havoc with a cop's career. A group or consecutive series of them can tear his life apart.

I am insufficiently cynical to believe Keith Ryan was a hostage victim. In some ways, the job set him free so he could become the man he'd always wanted to be. On the other hand, there are ways in which the department did hold him captive. It took only a few months on the street for the job to become as much a part of who he was and how he defined himself as the image he saw in the mirror when he shaved in the morning. A lot of the best cops in the NYPD share a similar burden. They cannot imagine their lives without a shield and gun, the keys to city history, a front seat to world events, and the special bonds they share with their partners.

After a few good years in Coney Island, Ryan began to think about changing assignments. Emergency Service was appealing. He liked the type of jobs the unit handled, the SWAT work, requiring special weapons and tactical expertise. The rescue work also interested him, as well as answering calls for help from other cops. Emergency Service cops respond to the most dangerous events, including natural disasters and terrorist incidents.

Ryan's thoughts of a transfer percolated unnoticed for several years. Few secrets are kept long within the NYPD. Spies lurk in unexpected places. Rumor and gossip, some of it unfounded, transcend the boundaries of rank. It was only a matter of time before the captain of the precinct got wind of Ryan's interest in pursuing a new position. Some bosses would refuse to give up productive officers and quash their hopes for a transfer. Ryan's captain believed that good cops should be rewarded in the little ways he could: choice vacation picks and days off; the most lucrative overtime gigs; and if they so desired, transfers to alleviate personal stress or advance their careers. The captain knew that Ryan had no red flags by his name, pending investigations, civilian complaints, or command disciplines (a type of formal reprimand). He was an active cop with stellar evaluations and good relationships with his bosses. In recent months, he'd made two collars (arrests) for homicide. He'd fired his gun once in the line of duty, grazing the suspect and stopping a rape in progress, Ryan recalled when I asked him about his activity and firearms experience.

He remembered the day the captain called him into his office and said, "Keith, you're one of my best cops. You don't complain and you do your work. Why didn't you tell me you wanted Emergency Service?" Emergency Service falls within the Special Operations Division, and the division chief was the captain's friend. With a phone call and good recommendations from additional bosses, Ryan was on his way to his new command.

It didn't take long for him to gain a reputation as an active cop who carried his load and excelled in certain kinds of jobs. He enjoyed using the Hurst Jaws of Life, a giant pair of hydraulic scissors that are used to cut people out of cars. He was also competent in other kinds of rescue work, including talking to "EDPs," police shorthand for emotionally disturbed persons, or "psychos," as they were once called. The work he liked best involved making the fast, fluid, tactical entries that Emergency Service cops use to executive warrants for crimes involving drugs or weapons.

It was during these often dangerous, tension-filled missions that Ryan once again became the competitive athlete he had been in high school. As soon as the job began, he got into the zone; his mind and body focusing on the action ahead. Knees bent, crouching slightly, positioned in the "SWAT squat," gun raised and extended in front of his face, he moved as gracefully as a dancer, stepping heel to toe, a perfect demonstration of the "Groucho" walk Emergency cops use to secure their balance and proceed into the eye of the storm. Once in the flow of the action, his mind and body as one, he could suspend the flurry of thoughts that often swirled in his head.

Of course there were occasions when he did dumb things, particularly during the early months when he was learning the job. His first week on patrol, he got a job involving a "jumper," a suicidal man, perched on the ledge of a window. Ryan rushed in, climbed up on the sill, and grabbed the man's hand.

"I'm holding on to this guy and he turns round and punches me in the face, three or four times and I'm hanging out the ledge of the window, no safety equipment, nothing. It's a hot summer night and my hand is sweating and the guy starts slipping. . . . I'm looking down at this guy and he doesn't say a word. . . . Suddenly "whoosh," he's falling twenty-eight stories and lands on the garage roof. I was black-and-blue, and my hands were shaking when I walked out of the room," Ryan explained.

When the lieutenant learned what happened, he checked to see how Ryan was doing, then gently reprimanded him. "Now I'm going to tell you this again, and I'm not going to give you a real hard time about it because I think you know that you are lucky you are standing here, but you gotta be prepared, Keith. If you want to be in the game, you have to think of your own safety first, more than anyone else. Your safety is paramount. Don't do what you did ever again. If he goes to the window, he goes to the window. That's his choice. I don't want him to take one of my men." The lieutenant patted Ryan on his shoulder and walked him down the stairs.

Never again would Keith Ryan jump on the ledge of a window without proper equipment. Nor would he ever feel again the same sense of amused chagrin when he heard the hysterical laughter of veteran peers and discovered the twenty Butterfinger candy bars they'd taped to his locker. Nevertheless, it would not be the last time he would find himself on the edge of a precipice, barely hanging on. In 1997, when he led a six-man team into the most dangerous job of their career, he would find himself there again.

10-1

PAUL YURKIW WAITED TO SEE IF THE ringing would stop before picking up the receiver. Crank calls and false alarms were the bane of Bomb Squad detectives' existence, and "If the phone don't ring, don't pick it up" was the philosophy of least resistance. The silence resumed, and he sunk his head into the pillow and went back to sleep. When the ringing started again and grew persistent, he reached for the receiver, which sat an arm's length away on a chair, next to a pen and notebook.

"Good morning. Detective Yurkiw, Bomb Squad, can I help you?" Yurkiw answered with the same ten words he'd used since he was transferred into the Bomb Squad in 1993, right after the World Trade Center was bombed. Now they were so ingrained in his head that he sometimes said the same thing when he picked up the phone at home.

It was 1:00 A.M. on July 31, 1997, and he and his partner, Rich Teemsma, were resting in "the Cave," a small room located next to the Bomb Squad's main office. The room, which doubled as a galley and a lounge, contained two sets of bunk beds, stacked foot to foot. A refrigerator and other kitchen appliances were built into the opposite wall. Teemsma and Yurkiw were working a double tour in the squad's 6th Precinct quarters in Chelsea and had been there since 2:00 P.M. the afternoon before. Both were looking forward to 8:00 A.M. when Yurkiw would go home and Teemsma would report to the range to shoot for his annual pistol qualification test.

At 6'2" and 250 pounds, Yurkiw retained the powerful build of the defensive tackle he'd played on his high school football team. His head was upholstered in short red hair. He had a red mustache, an oval-shaped face, and puffy cheeks that were burnt pink from playing outside with his two young sons. Before he'd left for work, he had tenderly kissed their faces, a gesture he would repeat throughout their college years.

Paul Yurkiw joined the NYPD in 1982 after he'd earned a college degree and almost completed an M.A. in special education. He, his wife, and two children shared a modest home in a suburb of Long Island not far from Jamaica, Queens. The kitchen, living room, dining room, master bedroom, and a den were on the first floor. The walls in the den were lined with Yurkiw's awards and medals, including the Medal of Valor. Recently, he expanded the attic, adding a new bedroom for the boys and an office for his wife. The sun shined through the skylight and brightened the blond wood of the bedroom furniture.

Yurkiw met Teemsma at the Midtown South Precinct, where both were assigned after they graduated from the Police Academy. During their first few months, they walked a foot beat. The opportunity arose to get a seat in a car when their boss announced he needed two cops to work the midnight to 8:00 A.M. shift in the 9th Precinct, known then as the "Fighting Ninth" because of heavy crime. When no veteran officers volunteered, Teemsma and Yurkiw grabbed the gig and became steady partners.

They enjoyed the routine, even the trips to take the prostitutes to Central Booking to be fingerprinted and locked up. After a long, dull night downtown, on their way back to the precinct, they stopped at Yurkiw's Ukrainian grandparents' apartment on East Seventh Street. As soon as the cops entered the building, they smelled the butter and cinnamon of his grandmother's freshly baked bread. Once inside, Yurkiw and Teemsma sat at the kitchen table and talked as the elderly couple prepared them a breakfast of eggs, kielbasa, and babka.

A few years after they started working together, Yurkiw transferred to Emergency Service with the help of a well-placed "rabbi" (connection). Teemsma got in later, using the names of the two Emergency Service cops the partners had met on patrol. The night Yurkiw nearly got killed, he was working alone.

Yurkiw was running late when he got in his patrol car and headed toward Queens, where he was assigned as fourth man in one of the unit's trucks. It was 1:30 A.M. the morning of June 21, 1989. Not far from a sign to JFK Airport, he saw a car parked on the shoulder of the Van Wyck Expressway. He pulled up behind, thinking the driver needed help. Yurkiw put his radio on the front seat and got out of the car but didn't call the job in to Central Communications, which broadcasts information to other cops.

"Are you stuck? Do you need a hand?" he asked the man, who had exited his vehicle and was approaching the front tire of Yurkiw's car. Before the man could answer, a call came over the radio and Yurkiw turned his head to listen. He heard a loud noise and felt the force of a sledgehammer smashing into his chest and thought he'd been hit by road debris. Then he saw the man's gun. At close range, it looked like a cannon.

Yurkiw used one hand to push the man's arm away from his face and, with the other, reached for his weapon, the Smith & Wesson 38 revolver issued at the time. The man fired two more rounds. Yurkiw struggled to push him away, fell back, and emptied six rounds, narrowly missing the man's head. He tried to reload his gun but dropped his speed loader. The man started to flee, then turned and fired again, hitting the ground below the officer's knees. Yurkiw leapt into the car for cover and started to load his gun, one round at a time. He grabbed the radio and called for assistance. The transmission was chilling. Yurkiw's frantic voice broke through, but his words were garbled. Every cop working that night recognized the choking sound of a "10-13."

"What unit's calling?" the dispatcher asked.

"Shots fired," Yurkiw responded, his pitch high and words muddled.

"Shots fired. What's your location?" the dispatcher asked.

"Van Wyck," Yurkiw responded, struggling to calm down.

"Van Wyck and where?" Yurkiw keyed the radio but his words were muddled.

"Unit calling, what's your location?"

"Rockaway. Past Rockaway."

"Rockaway Parkway and the Van Wyck. Shots fired over the air. Truck Nine Adam on the air?" the dispatcher asked.

"Adam Nine truck on the way, Central."

"Rockaway Parkway and the Van Wyck. OK, Lieu [Lieutenant]. You go. Rockaway Boulevard and the Van Wyck."

"He might have said northbound, Central."

"Central," Yurkiw said.

"What, Unit?" The dispatcher asked.

"2644, Central."

"2644, your location?"

"Van Wyck Expressway, just before Rockaway Boulevard."

"Van Wyck and Rockaway Boulevard. Shots fired. 2644 requesting."

"Highway, Lieutenant. You want us to respond?"

"That's affirmative, Lieu. Go!"

"Central, a white Maxima," Yurkiw said.

"OK. A white Maxima. 2644, are you injured?"

"Yes. Shot three times." His words blended together, and the dispatcher couldn't understand.

"10-5. Are you injured?"

"Yes."

"All right, we're in route. 2644 requesting. Stay off the air." The dispatcher ordered all units silent except for those with crucial information.

"Where is he, Central?"

"Rockaway and Van Wyck. 2644 requesting. Hit three times. We're looking for a white Maxima. First unit there please advise on the scene."

"Central, be advised it's a solo fly-man from Eight Truck."

"10-4. It's a solo unit from Eight Truck. It's a solo unit fly-man,"[1] the dispatcher said. Two sergeants announced they were on their way. Other units called in saying they were in the area but couldn't find the car and needed the dispatcher to reconfirm the address.

"Unit, I need your location."

"I think it's Van Wyck before Rockaway Boulevard. I see a truck unit." At this point, Yurkiw realized that he hadn't turned on the turret lights on the hood of the car and flipped the switch. A half-second later, a cop's voice came on the air.

"I see him now."

"OK, they're coming," the dispatcher said. The next sound Yurkiw heard was the squealing tires of the Emergency Service truck coming to a halt beside him and then the familiar voice of a cop he knew from the squad.

"Oh my God, Paulie. Take it easy and lie still. Everything will be all right."

Yurkiw's hospital stay was short. His vest saved his life and minimized injury. His arms were bruised in the struggle, and his chest felt like it had done time in a blender. Three large bullet holes were burned through his blue uniform shirt. Two penetrated his Kevlar vest to the white lining underneath. The third shot bounced off his chest and shattered the front passenger window, leaving pebbles of glass on the seat. The windows on both sides were smashed as well.

When he noticed the state of the car, Yurkiw was relieved Teemsma wasn't there because he might have been killed by the ricochet. Yurkiw also knew he was fortunate. Not until after the incident did his bulletproof vest become a regular part of his uniform. Scars remain. To this day he gets nauseated when he smells the scent of burnt black gunpowder.

Emergency Service cops camped out in Yurkiw's backyard for weeks after the shooting. They barbecued food, took care of his family, transported him to appointments, and celebrated together when they arrested the shooter, thirty days later, a drug dealer named Sean Boyd. Shortly after, Yurkiw rescinded his request to go to the Bomb Squad, delaying his transfer for several months. The first day he returned to work and opened his locker, he broke into a sweat and started to tremble. He wanted to make sure he still had the heart to do the job.

The morning of July 31, 1997, when he sleepily answered the phone in the Bomb Squad office in the 6th Precinct and started to jot down notes, he didn't realize he was about to face the sickening shadow of death one more time.

o o o o o o o

"We've gotta guy here who doesn't speak English but we think he's Middle Eastern. He's saying there're bombs in his apartment or something," the 8-8 Precinct detective explained, then started to elaborate. It was nice to hear a woman's voice at 1:00 A.M., and Yurkiw hated to interrupt.

"You want us to respond or you want to call us back? I mean, is there a package?"

"Well, he's saying they've got material in his apartment, some kind of bomb material." Yurkiw turned on his flashlight and grabbed the pad and pen and started to write down the answers to the *who*, *where*, and *what* questions that applied to the average bomb job.

"OK. Look, the longer I stay on the phone the longer it's going to take us to get there." Yurkiw hung up the receiver and announced the job to the other three cops in the Cave. He and Joe McGuire were supposed to be "catching" the call, according to the system of rotation established in the squad.

"Joe, you get that? Teemsma said from the top bunk across from where Jeff Oberdier, alias "Obie," was lying, listening to the exchange. McGuire was sprawled out with his eyes closed on the lower bunk opposite Yurkiw's feet.

"Tell him I don't make house calls," McGuire replied and pulled the blanket over his face.[2] The job sounded like the kind of unfounded "bullshit" that could last into the morning. McGuire—or "Fatty the Clown," as some cops called him—preferred to let detectives with less seniority handle the nonsense jobs while he waited for the "big one" to come along.

Annoyed, Rich Teemsma got down from his bunk and stood up straight. At 6'3", he towered over McGuire. Teemsma had a strong, muscular build from doing construction and yard work. His soft eyes, tan face, salt-and-pepper hair and graying mustache made him look like a Santa Claus minus the belly and beard. At forty-seven years old, he was mature enough to resist the desire to punch McGuire's face in.

"Goddamned shithead bastard motherfucker, please!" Teemsma said. The ringing started again and Yurkiw picked up the phone.

"We have a grenade over in Queens," he announced, noting the address.

"Yeah, I'll take that one," McGuire piped in. "I'll take Obie to Queens and handle the grenade. You guys take the one in Brooklyn." Most grenades are "a walk in the park"—unfounded and quick to resolve, and he knew he'd be back napping in quarters in no time. Yurkiw and Teemsma had been partners for most of their careers. They figured the night was shot anyway.

"OK. Paulie, let's just get this thing done," Teemsma said. The detectives called their supervisors to apprise them of the situation and get their consent to proceed. McGuire then headed to the parking lot, followed by Oberdier. A few minutes later, Teemsma and Yurkiw made their way past the desks in the front office and downstairs to the precinct door.

"Cocksucker rat bastard motherfucker, please!" Teemsma cursed when he got outside and saw that McGuire had taken the best car. Yurkiw laughed. Although he rarely used words grittier than "asshole" and "holy shit," he felt nothing but affection whenever his partner let out a torrent of curses. They were part of the complementary glue that had held them together for years.

Teemsma "breathed fire and blew smoke out of his ears" for fifteen seconds and then regained his composure. He and Yurkiw settled into their truck, revved the engine, and headed south. The last time they'd had a serious threat was in January, when four consecutive calls came in for letter bombs at the United Nations. Yurkiw and Teemsma had been working when the last three arrived. All were live devices, containing the military explosive Semtec.

As they were nearing Brooklyn Heights, they remembered their truck contained only one extra large bomb suit. They called McGuire over the radio to tell him they'd need him to bring them another. When he did not pick up after two tries, they let the matter drop until they got to the 8-8 Precinct. They didn't want to risk alerting "Central" if he was somewhere he wasn't supposed to be.

○ ○ ○ ○ ○ ○ ○

Rich Teemsma lived in Long Island further east from his partner of almost sixteen years. A talented carpenter, he designed and built the house he shared with his wife and two kids, a son and a daughter. Teemsma grew up in Manhattan, and then moved to Queens and Long Island, changing homes whenever drugs and crime began to submerge the neighborhood and the white, working-class families started to leave.

Teemsma's father was a cop in the late fifties, assigned to Manhattan's now-defunct 15th Precinct. Teemsma saw his first dead body when he was five years old. The corpse was laid out on a cement slab in the back of the station house. His father told him the man had fallen down.

"He didn't tie his shoelaces and tripped," Teemsma replied.

"Yes, son," his father said and patted him on the head. In retrospect, Teemsma wondered if the man had taken a swing at a cop and been beaten by the officers in the "house" or jumped off a roof and killed himself.

On another trip to the precinct, Teemsma got locked up by one of his father's friends who saw him exploring the cell and closed the door. His confinement was short in duration but made a lasting impression. He didn't want to see the inside of jail again.

Teemsma's Dutch-Belgium father and Irish mother were strict parents who believed that corporal punishment was the proper means to discipline their nine children. If one of the seven boys or two girls got in trouble, his mother would issue a warning and call her husband. Regardless of when he came home and how many days had passed since the infraction, he would always remember to take out the belt. Teemsma's father kept the street out of his home but the cop inside. Controlling and suspicious, he tended to treat his children like the people he policed. Teemsma recalled how he would order them to empty their pockets and pat them down when they came inside.

Teemsma spent most of his early years in Catholic school in Queens, which did nothing to enhance his interest in learning. A free spirit who didn't take well to harsh regimentation and humiliation, he rebelled by refusing to study. When the family moved to Long Island and he began public high school, his grades improved. The nine siblings were tight. They banded together and took care of each other, with the exception of their oldest brother, who tended to bully the others. "It was one for all and all for one," Teemsma said, with the same soft tone he used on the job. When the family was threatened by outsiders, even his older brother would pitch in to protect the group.

Teemsma tried several careers before becoming a New York City cop. Skilled with his hands and interested in auto mechanics, he built his own cars. At eighteen he joined the Marine Corps and was sent to Okinawa, although he'd wanted to go to Vietnam. In retrospect, he is grateful he didn't get what he wished for. Today, when he thinks of young men dying in another pointless war, his chest aches. After three years of military service, he began working for an uncle who was a vice president of a small airline. Teemsma explored the world. Africa, Europe, and South America were some of the places he traveled. On one trip to the Middle East, he visited Mecca.

In 1980, when he was thirty years old, he married a bright, twenty-four-year-old beauty named Kimberley, who worked for Estée Lauder. A year later, the couple had their first child, a girl, and soon after that a son. Neither of the children were physically disciplined or attended Catholic school. The Teemsmas believed in a merciful God.

Teemsma joined the New York Police Department in 1982. After he and Paul became steady partners, they leapfrogged through their careers, ending up working together, except for brief spells when their bosses decided they were too close for comfort and had to be split up. On January 25, 1986, Teemsma joined Yurkiw in Emergency Service. He remembered the date because of the newspaper headlines, announcing that the space shuttle *Challenger* had blown up.

Both cops enjoyed working in the unit. Interaction with the public on nonsense jobs was less than in the precinct, and there were opportunities for adventure. Shortly after Hurricane Hugo devastated Puerto Rico, the department initiated its first foreign rescue and recovery mission. Teemsma volunteered. He helped build roads through the rain forests, repair the water supply, and construct new houses.

In 1991, Teemsma decided to put in a transfer to the Bomb Squad. His reasons were simple. He'd been in Emergency Service a number of years and wanted to learn new skills. He liked working with his hands and didn't want to be trapped in an office writing reports. He also wanted a promotion.

"Well, they tell you if you're going to leave a good assignment you should move up, not down, so the Bomb Squad seemed like the logical choice. I also wanted to make detective. Cops in the Bomb Squad automatically receive a promotion to detective third grade."

For the first few years, Teemsma enjoyed the job, although he missed the camaraderie and team orientation of Emergency Service. Bomb Squad cops usually worked alone and were individualistic. The principle of "All for one and one for all" didn't apply.

o o o o o o o

Teemsma and Yurkiw pulled into the parking lot of the 8-8 Precinct and got out of the car. The 8-8 is housed in a prewar building expertly constructed in red brick with plaster walls, a high front desk and a staircase made of solid oak. Like most police facilities, the precinct was in bad shape. The station house walls were dirty and peeling, the plaster so full of stress fractures that it looked like it had suffered an earthquake. The floor hadn't been mopped with fresh water for years and the windows were cloudy with dirt.

The two partners headed past the dingy red-and-blue-painted foyer toward the stairwell in the back. As soon as they walked into the squad room, the precinct detectives launched into a graphic description of the "little monster" who was the duty chief that night. The "Tasmanian devil" himself had commandeered the precinct and had to be handled with kid gloves. Yurkiw understood. "You know a boss is a boss is a boss. He's got a job to do so sometimes you can't be everybody's friend. You got a job, and you do it the best way you see fit."

Teemsma and Yurkiw introduced themselves to the informant, then took him into a small interrogation room and sat down at the table. The informant, Mohammed Chindluri, was a small, thin, dark-haired man in his mid-twenties. He'd gotten his U.S. visa by winning a lottery in his native country of Pakistan. Shortly after arriving at JFK, a cabdriver had taken him to the Carter Hotel where he spent the night. The next day he went to a Brooklyn mosque to ask if anyone knew where he could spend the night. He'd been directed to the apartment at 248 Fourth Avenue, where three other Muslims were already living.

Two were Palestinian immigrants who had come to the United States

using Jordanian passports. The third man was another Pakistani who barely knew his roommates. Chindluri viewed the small, crowded apartment
as a temporary arrangement until he could get settled and find a more
desirable home. He had been in the apartment a few days when he began
to suspect that his roommates were up to no good.

The suspect, who called himself Gazi Abu Mezer, was intense and
angry. His frequent discussions of Middle Eastern politics were laced with
a fanatical rage that went well beyond the bounds of normal political
passion. Chindluri then began to notice the piles of anti-American propa-
ganda that littered the room, some of it calling for violence and jihad.

Concerned about their intentions, Chindluri began to ask questions.
Soon, the suspects showed him a bag filled with homemade explosives.
They also revealed their plot: they planned to detonate the device in the
Atlantic Avenue subway station during the morning rush hour.

The Atlantic Avenue station connects ten subway lines and the Long
Island Railroad. These include the 2 and 3 trains to the Upper West Side,
the Bronx and Harlem; the 4 and 5 to Manhattan's Upper East Side, east
Harlem, and the Bronx; and the N and R, which connect Brooklyn and
Queens through Manhattan. On weekday mornings, tens of thousands of
New York City residents and suburbanites are released into the bowels of
the transit system. An explosion could result in massive fatalities.

Around 10:00 P.M. the night of July 30, Chindluri made his escape,
claiming he had to buy cigarettes. Before he left, the suspects warned him
that if he wasn't back within a few hours they'd assume he'd gone to the
police. Frightened, he fled into the empty streets. He found a pay phone
and dialed the operator in hopes that she would recognize the crisis and
connect him to the authorities. Unable to understand his accent, she hung
up the phone instead.

Chindluri headed toward the subway station where he encountered
two Long Island Railroad cops, John Kowalchuk and Eric Huber. According
to the cops, the informant appeared agitated, gesturing wildly and talking
in Arabic and broken English that was difficult to follow. Every officer I
talked to agreed that they might have been tempted to dismiss his fears as
fantasy and send him on his way. Police routinely encounter people who are
emotionally disturbed, and as long as they are not a danger to themselves or
others and no one has complained, the cops can't do very much.

Huber and Kowalchuck decided to play it safe. They called an officer
at their headquarters who alerted the NYPD. Christopher Caruso and

James Christi, two officers from the 8-8 Precinct, were dispatched to the subway station to meet the informant. Although they saw that Chindluri was frightened and desperate, they weren't convinced he was crazy. When he repeated the word "bomba" and made explosion gestures with his hands, they decided to bring him to the "house."

Huber, Kowalchuck, Christi, Caruso, and the informant got into the patrol car and drove to the 8-8 Precinct. Once there, Chindluri was taken upstairs and handed over to the detectives. Joseph Palermo of the 8-8 Squad called the Operations Division and requested a translator. Meanwhile, he began to conduct an interview. Huber and Kowalchuck stayed in the precinct while Caruso and Christi went back on patrol.[3]

The Bomb Squad was alerted and the duty inspector, the duty captain, and duty chief called to the scene. When chief Charles Kammerdener arrived, he spoke briefly to the informant, then ordered detectives to conduct computer checks to assess the criminal status of residents of Chindluri's address. The results were negative. No one living at 248 Fourth Avenue had been arrested or was wanted on a criminal warrant.

Kammerdener was alarmed that some had Middle Eastern names. According to the informant, the ringleader Mezer appeared friendly with some of the residents, and so Kammerdener feared they might also be terrorists. He proceeded to take the next step, alerting detectives in the Intelligence Unit to use their access to the Immigration and Naturalization Service database to check the immigration status of Chindluri's roommates. That check also came back negative. None of the suspects were registered as legal immigrants in the United States.

Kammerdener was not convinced the informant was reliable. Nevertheless, he began to initiate the department's mobilization plan, securing the inner and outer perimeter around the building, and staging emergency personnel. He also implemented phase one of the evacuation procedure, securing transportation and a temporary base for evacuees. Police officers from the precinct Anti-Crime Unit were sent out to survey the block where the suspects' building was.[4]

"Now the remarkable part is that at that time of night these officers took it seriously and. . . . kicked it up to higher levels," explained Bill Morange, chief of the Special Operations Division. Keith Ryan echoed his sentiments, "Thank God nobody dropped the ball. Nobody took him for an EDP [emotionally disturbed person]."

o o o o o o o

The air conditioner coughed and rattled, emitting spurts of tepid air that barely cooled off the small interview room where Chindluri was sitting with Yurkiw and Teemsma. His brow was moist from sweat, and his hands were shaking. The police translator hadn't yet arrived. Teemsma handed Chindluri a cup of water, a legal pad, and a pen and gestured for him to draw what he had seen.

The informant sketched a cylindrical object with two end caps and a length of wire. Surprised, the two detectives looked at each other. According to Teemsma, a more precise drawing could not have been made by an engineer. "He drew the best pipe bomb I ever saw," Yurkiw explained. Convinced that they had to take the next step, Teemsma and Yurkiw took Chindluri outside and looked for the "devil chief" they'd been warned about.

Charles Kammerdener was sitting at a desk in someone's office, no one recalls exactly where. As citywide duty chief, he was responsible for any major event that occurred on his watch. A small, lean, wiry man with a graying crew cut, wrinkled skin, and perpetual tan, he'd been in the Housing Police Department for many years before it merged with the NYPD. An ambitious, serious, and hardworking boss in his early fifties, he'd reached the rank of assistant chief and probably hoped to add more stars.

After Yurkiw and Teemsma asked the chief permission to speak, the three walked into the interview room so they could talk in peace. Yurkiw and Teemsma schmoozed for a few minutes to pacify the chief. By the time they revealed the drawing, Kammerdener had retracted his "horns" and he seemed relaxed.

"Chief, take a look at this. What does it look like to you?" Yurkiw paused to give him time to reflect. "If it looks like to you what it looks like to us then we think we have a working job. What we could do is call Emergency Service and when they show up, we'll go through the numbers. We let them do their job and, in the event there is a working device, then we'll cross that bridge when we get to it. It's almost three o'clock in the morning. If we have to do an entry, we should hit them in the dark. We're from Emergency Service. We know how they work," Yurkiw said.

"And they know how we work. We've worked together a lot," Teemsma added. Kammerdener looked thoughtful. Then he told the detectives he thought it best to wait until daytime to execute an entry or other type of tactical solution. Bodies were scarce on midnights. Some rank-and-file officers believed that part of his hesitation also involved his career. He didn't want to take rash action that could get cops and civilians hurt and make him look bad to those above. Few officers of high rank would fault him for this sort of caution. Above the rank of captain, promotions are awarded at the discretion of the police commissioner. Kammerdener could get flopped four ranks if he made a call that embarrassed the department.

"The element of surprise is on our side between 3:00 and 5:00 A.M. before people are up and about. If we wait for daylight, we're talking seven o'clock. What if they wake up and see this guy is gone and they panic and grab the device and leave. It'll turn into a waiting game," Yurkiw said.

The chief listened but dug in his heels and insisted on postponing action until the day tour began. Just before Yurkiw and Teemsma gave up and started to leave, a blonde inspector walked in. She didn't look happy. Teemsma thought that maybe she'd just been reamed out by superiors or held responsible for making the call that brought the "Tasmanian devil" into the precinct and letting him take control. Regardless of the reason, Teemsma was awed by her nerve. "I've never heard anyone talk to a superior officer like that," he explained.[5]

"Chief, did I hear you right? What I'm hearing simply cannot be true. We've got bombs. We have to do this now. The only way we have a shot at stopping these guys is if we take them by surprise. We wait until tomorrow, we'll be picking up body parts," the inspector said, according to officers' recollection.

"It was like my wife yelling at me," explained a detective who was standing outside with his ear to the door and who did not want to be named. Yurkiw looked down, avoiding Teemsma's eyes and braced his shoulders, waiting for the fallout.

"Well, OK. We'll see what Emergency has to say," Kammerdener said, to the surprise of both detectives, who realized that maybe Chief K was more reasonable than they'd initially thought. Within four minutes, Ray McDermott, the executive officer of the Special Operations Division, was notified. Nick Mancini, the captain of Emergency Service, and his lieutenant, Larry Dwyer, were called as well as Emergency Service bosses and cops who were already working in Brooklyn and Queens.

Yurkiw and Teemsma dialed Emergency Service headquarters and told them they'd probably need the TCV, or total containment vehicle, depending on how the job materialized. They also called McGuire, who was back in "a reclining position" in the Cave and didn't answer the phone.

Jeff Oberdier was walking Rocky, one of the Bomb Squad dogs, and there was no one but Joe "Fatty" McGuire to handle calls. A few minutes later, Teemsma tried again but hung up after twenty rings. Finally, the third time around, McGuire picked up the receiver. Teemsma told him they needed an extra large bomb suit.

o o o o o o o

John English, a sergeant in Emergency Service, had been scheduled to work an 8:00–4:00 P.M. shift the day before. Another sergeant, who worked steady midnights, had requested the evening off but had been denied unless he could get another supervisor to take his place. The sergeant reached out to English, who agreed to the favor. He didn't mind working an occasional 12:00– 8:00 shift. It was always an education to patrol a sector late at night when another world seemed to inhabit the streets.

English was thirty-five years old, and at 5'6" he looked like a taller man. Although a few extra inches were beginning to creep around his waist, his build was solid and strong. He had the command presence of someone of senior rank. English enjoyed an impeccable reputation among both cops and senior brass in Emergency Service. Bright, honest, competent, open-minded, and reliable, people trusted him. A team player, he led by example. He knew when to rein in his men when they got angry and were tempted to do something they might regret. He did what he could to protect his cops when they made mistakes. Department rules and procedures mattered only as long as they kept his men alive. English listened but didn't believe every word of slander and gossip that circulated around the squad. Cops who worked for him started out with a clean slate.

A Brooklyn-born native who lived with his wife and small children in Long Island, English came from a police family. His father was a cop in the NYPD until he retired after being accidentally shot by one of the owners of Lundy's Restaurant. His mother was a nurse who was loved by kids in the neighborhood because she was easy to talk to and gave good advice. When her widowed sister-in-law passed away, she took in the three orphans and raised them as her own.

English's father was a firm but loving man who demanded a lot from his sons. English recalled his insisting the children help him paint and renovate their house when he'd rather have been playing outside. He also remembered the time his father caught him smoking cigarettes with a gang of his friends. English was punished, not because of the actual infraction but because he had failed to think for himself and act independently of the group.

English was proud that his father was a policeman and fondly remembers the day he picked him and his friends up from school and drove them the four blocks home in a patrol car. After finishing high school, English studied diesel mechanics and drove trucks for a while. In 1981, he decided to follow in his father's footsteps and become a New York City police officer. Before he graduated from the Police Academy, English requested assignment in Brooklyn's 7-5 Precinct, a high-crime house, notorious for tough cops and sometimes thuggish union delegates that rookies like English didn't yet know about.

His father was aware of the precinct's reputation and didn't want his son to work in a violent place loaded with troublesome cops. He quietly took the matter into his own hands and called a friend who arranged to send English to the 6th Precinct in Greenwich Village. The neighborhood had everything a young cop could wish for: different cultures and lifestyles, family disputes, the mentally ill, and enough violent crime to satisfy a young cop's lust for action, pretty women, and good, affordable restaurants.

It didn't take too many years of racing to "gun runs" before English developed a reputation as an aggressive cop who could handle himself on dangerous jobs. However, his nickname, "Johnny SWAT," was somewhat misleading. English was never a cowboy who thoughtlessly rushed into every incident, endangering peers and civilians or turning a molehill into a volcanic eruption. He liked talking to people and solving their problems. Even as a rookie, he knew there was more than one way to save a life.

After four years on patrol in Greenwich Village, English transferred to Emergency Service with help from his partner's well-connected policeman father. His training officer insisted he wasn't a teacher but gave English a word of advice: "If you want to learn to be an Emergency cop, shut up, listen, and watch how we do things." Like Keith Ryan, English learned early on that there were limits to how close to the edge competent "E-men" can push and still have support from their peers.

One late summer evening, police officer Jack Murphy, alias "God," a veteran with more than twenty-eight years on the job, walked, without safety equipment, onto the ledge of the Verrazano Bridge to rescue a suicidal girl. A few feet behind him, his partner was looking on, fuming.

"You can't do that, especially in front of these guys," he said, referring to the rookie Emergency Service cops who were tying themselves onto the bridge so they could help without risk to themselves. After the girl was safely on the other side of the bridge, God turned and faced the new cops.

"You saw what I just did?" God asked, looking at English.

"Yeah," English responded.

"Do as I say, not as I do. I'm serious. Do not EVER do that, because if I see you do that, you're done."

English loved Emergency Service. While he did not have the platinum tongue of some of the guys who could talk a crazy person into believing hell was a spa in the tropics, he could hold his own and get the job done. He also enjoyed other rescue work, from the mundane to the heroic, and was known as an expert in special weapons and tactical entries.

Several years later, when English was promoted to sergeant, he kept two things at the top of his list of priorities: keeping his cops safe when they went in on jobs, and making sure they didn't get "jammed up"—in trouble with the department.

o o o o o o o

On July 31, English had just turned out in Seven Truck when he received an order to call lieutenant Larry Dwyer. Dwyer, a chunky man of medium height with a double chin and a mustache, had come into Emergency Service in 1993 when the Housing and Transit Police Departments merged with the NYPD. Loud and brash, he embodied a Yankee version of a Southern good old boy.

Although it probably stung English and every other boss in Emergency Service when Dwyer made lieutenant and was sent right back to unit— one of many privileges granted to the cops who'd come from the smaller departments, English wasn't the type to begrudge another man's good fortune. So although they were different kinds of people—English was a family man and Dwyer a party boy—they got along.

"You got to get here right away," Dwyer told the sergeant.

"What's the matter?" English asked, sensing Dwyer's blood pressure was on the rise. He sometimes got excited about things that weren't worth getting excited about.

"We got something going with a bomb!" Dwyer responded.

So much for a quiet night. English put his foot on the accelerator, turned the corner, and headed toward the 8-8 Precinct. At this point, he wasn't convinced the job would come to much. It seemed an odd coincidence to get a serious job on a night he would have normally been at home asleep in bed with his wife. By the time English arrived at the 8-8 Precinct, half of the cops working midnights had already trickled in. English greeted the guys at the desk, then joined Dwyer upstairs.

o o o o o o o

Keith Ryan and Joe Dolan started their tour in Six Truck, patrolling their regular sector in Brooklyn, then "flew" to Queens because of a manpower shortage in the borough. Ryan was feeling uneasy because of a dream he'd had the night before. It had bothered him so much that he'd called his mother.

In the dream, he and his partner went into a room and encountered two men with dark hair and tan complexions. The men attacked the officers, and Ryan fired his gun, shooting them both. The two cops got in serious trouble as a result.

Ryan awoke from the dream soaked in sweat, his legs tangled in sheets. He ripped off the covers, jumped out of the bed, and looked around. "What the hell happened?" he asked himself, and then laughed when he realized he was alone in the bedroom of the basement apartment where he had lived for the last few months. His pulse was racing. He could feel his heart pounding against his chest.

"Joey, I had this really weird dream," Ryan said, as they turned onto the Brooklyn-Queens Expressway.

"Yeah?" Dolan responded and ripped off a piece from the lid of a cup of deli coffee.

"We were in this apartment and these guys assaulted us, and I shot 'em. Things got bad after that."

"Anybody we know?"

"I thought they were Spanish guys . . . olive complexions. But what would I be doing fighting Spanish guys? One of the guys had curly hair, fine features. You know I never dream about work," Ryan muttered, shaking his head.

Dolan dumped the empty coffee cup on the floor, shifted his weight and extended his legs to the floorboard. His seat was almost the size of a compact car but still the fit was snug. Ryan cast an affectionate glance at the big man beside him and pushed the dream out of his mind.

Joe Dolan was a muscular 6'4" Irishman in his thirties with a handsome face, a Mohawk crew cut, and tattoos blanketing the biceps of both enormous arms. Raised in a civil service family, his father was a New York City firefighter and his mother a housewife. He had one older brother, who spent a few years with the Housing Police before joining the Navy and becoming a cop in Rhode Island.

Dolan loathed school and had little interest in going to college, which left three major civil service options for a career; sanitation, police, or the Fire Department (FDNY). Police work seemed like the natural choice. After spending "the worst six months of [his] life" in training at the New York City Police Academy, Dolan was sent to Staten Island, not far from his home.

After a few months, he got bored by the slow pace of the precinct and wanted to go to a busier "house." An opportunity arose after he got the department's attention when he rescued a drowning victim in freezing waters. Dolan was rewarded with a medal and a transfer to the 5th Precinct in lower Manhattan.

Five years later, while driving to work one rainy day, he spotted inspector John Timoney, his former 5th Precinct commander, coming out of the subway. Dolan stopped the car and offered the man a ride to police headquarters. Timoney remembered Dolan as an active cop who cleaned up "conditions" in the precinct and made good arrests although his "summonses sucked."[6] So when Dolan confessed he was interested in another assignment, he asked him what he had in mind.

"Well, if you're offering me a helping hand, I went for an interview for Emergency Service a while back and they told me I wasn't on the job long enough, but that's where I'd really like to go. I've been watching them for years," Dolan explained.

"Call me at eleven o'clock," Timoney said, then opened the door and walked into the pouring rain. A few days later, Dolan was called in for an interview. Although he passed the required tests, his transfer was delayed for two years when a cop with a bigger "hook" stepped in and usurped his spot. Finally, in 1991, another place opened up, and Dolan's wish was fulfilled.

His first few months in Emergency Service were difficult. He loved the job but had to develop a new mental approach to handle the pace. Cops in busy precincts rush from job to job with little time to prepare in between. Emergency Service cops often handle heavier calls but are methodical in the way they work.

"Your job in Emergency Service is to show up and slow everybody down.

You arrive at the scene and grab somebody and ask what's going on. Once you have the story, you take the time to get your equipment off the truck and get on the right gear. It wasn't until I moved to midnights in Six Truck that I really started getting into their method of handling things," Dolan explained.

Dolan and Ryan met at a car accident in 1993 when both trucks responded to the same job. A few months later, they found themselves working together and, in time, became steady partners. Some of the chemistry of their partnership was captured in a motto coined by peers, "Keith will catch 'em and Joey will crush 'em." Ryan and Dolan were known as active cops who carried their load and sometimes more, picking up jobs for the occasional guy in the squad who preferred to sleep on midnights.

Little did they know when they started work that humid July morning in 1997 that their teamwork and tactical skills were about to be put to the ultimate test.

o o o o o o o

Their first job in Queens had involved a suspicious device in the basement of a supermarket on Northern Boulevard. Joe McGuire from the Bomb Squad was at the scene when they arrived. The device turned out to be an inert grenade. As soon as Ryan and Dolan got back in the car, they let the dispatcher know they were available. She issued a "10-3" to call Central Communications using Dolan's personal cell phone.

Their next order seemed odd. They were told to exchange their car with the men who were working Six Truck in Brooklyn, then pick up the truck's counter assault team car and drive it to the 8-8 Precinct on Classon Avenue. A CAT (counter assault team) car is an unmarked van that contains an assortment of weapons and tactical gear typically used to execute warrants and other types of entries.

Ryan and Dolan switched cars on the Brooklyn side of the Jackie Robinson Parkway, then headed to the 8-8 Precinct. When they arrived they knew that something serious was up; vehicles from all over the city were flooding the parking lot. Several were from the fleet of expensive department sedans reserved for chiefs and other high-ranking members of the brass.

As soon as Ryan stepped inside the precinct, he inhaled the pungent smell of cops at work, of fresh popcorn and ravioli, mixed with sweat and the odor of a hundred years of prisoners in holding cells. Although there hadn't been a major arrest or police-involved incident, a lot of cops were milling around and talking in groups.

The late tour sergeant was standing behind the desk, and Ryan greeted him with a hug and a warm smile. Before being promoted and transferred, they had been partners in Emergency Service. Since then they had remained devoted and loyal friends. After they caught up on recent events, Ryan asked him if he knew what was going on upstairs.

"I don't know, but it's heavy," the sergeant replied, and directed the officers past the cells to the stairwell. Ryan and Dolan headed toward the stairs. Halfway up, Dolan spotted John Reardon, one of the Emergency Service cops who worked out of Eight Truck, and asked him what was going on.

"There are these guys who say they are going to bomb the subways around Atlantic Avenue," Reardon explained. Ryan and Dolan looked at each other and started to laugh.

"Holy shit! That's Eight Truck's job, isn't it? Ryan said.

"Yeah," Reardon confirmed.

"Good. Then it's not ours. Glad it's your bag of shit! "

"Thanks a lot," Reardon replied. At this point none of the cops thought the job would turn into something serious.

When Ryan got upstairs, he saw Emergency police from Brooklyn and Queens waiting for the briefing to begin. Rich Teemsma and Paul Yurkiw were there as well as a handful of bosses including Dwyer and English, Emergency Service Captain Nick Mancini, Chief Kammerdener, and Inspector Ray McDermott, the executive officer of the Special Operations Division.

o o o o o o o

While Ryan and Dolan were catching up on the case, the police translator arrived. A young cop from the 13th Precinct, he spoke fluent Arabic and knew enough about Muslim culture and religion to understand the subtleties of the informant's speech. English and Dwyer took him into the interview room and sat down at the table. Ryan and the other cops waited outside, coming in every now and then to check on their progress.

Dwyer and English cared less about what the bomb looked like than gathering facts to help them develop an effective tactical plan to apprehend the suspects before they could detonate the device. They asked where the bomb was placed, and the number of people involved, if there were dogs on the premises, and whether the suspects had additional weapons. In order to assess the best time for a raid, they needed to find out what time the suspects woke up and where they would be hanging out.

"When is this gonna happen?" English asked

"Tomorrow morning after they finish praying."

"They're awake now?"

"They might be up praying."

"Did they say what time they're going to leave the apartment?"

"They plan to go early in the morning. They want to be on the train by rush hour."

"What time?"

"They'll leave around five."

"Was anyone outside when you left?"

"Some cabdrivers who speak Arabic and Spanish. They stay there all night waiting for work." English nodded his head in recognition. He'd worked in the area for years before transferring to Emergency Service. Although he couldn't recall the exact location, he remembered the Family Car Service, a twenty-four-hour storefront livery cab business.

"Do the suspects know any of the drivers?"

"I don't know. I've seen them talk to some of the people in the building." Chindluri's voice was calmer now than it had been when he first came into the station house. Although he appeared slightly anxious, there was nothing about his mood or manner that suggested he was mentally ill. English handed Chindluri a pen and paper and asked him to illustrate the layout of the premises.

He sketched a long hallway leading to a set of stairs. Behind the stairs, he placed the suspects' apartment. He noted that the building had three stories. Residential units were above and below where the suspects lived. At English and Dwyer's urging, Chindluri sketched a few items that marked the path through the building, including a bicycle, a tire, and a ping pong table that was folded at night.

On another piece of paper, Chindluri mapped out the interior of the suspects' apartment, depicting a rectangular space containing a kitchen and two bedrooms. Chindluri's bedroom was on the left side of the wall opposite the apartment entrance. The suspects' was on the right. There was a foyerlike space in front of Chindluri's bedroom containing a twin-sized cot where the Pakistani immigrant slept. The bomb was in the suspects' bedroom near the door.

English studied the diagram. Everything made sense except for one significant detail. He couldn't quite visualize how the apartment fit in the building at large. Under ideal conditions with few time constraints, the police might have gathered additional intelligence, by sending plainclothes cops to the scene to map out the site or contacting the building manager to get a copy of the floor plan. While confusion about the layout would remain until the cops were inside, some aspects of the situation were clear.

"The suspects are going to get on the train and blow themselves up and try to kill as many people as they can," the informant explained.

"Well, what do you think will happen if we go in and try to stop them?" English asked.

"If they can't kill other people, they'll kill you," Chindluri responded.

"Is that what they want to do?" English asked

"Yes, that's what they want to do. If they can't kill Jews, they're going to die killing somebody." This was the first time that English or anyone else in Emergency Service could recall a job involving suicide bombers.

In 1997, training in the fundamentals of terrorism was minimal, even for first responders. Although the police in Emergency Service received special training in the verbal and tactical means of handling persons with psychiatric disorders, terrorists were a different matter. There was no formal training in terrorist psychology. At the time, U.S. law enforcement officials still used negotiation techniques to deal with airplane hijackers in order to minimize loss of life.

Most severely depressed individuals have doubts about killing themselves. More often than not, they have an attachment to something or someone whom they love or who is dependent on them. Even criminals who do not have strong prohibitions against killing are attached to some part of their lives, their jobs, an activity, animal, family member, or friend to whom they are loyal. Cops can negotiate with people like this because they have something to lose and aren't motivated by a higher moral and religious belief that legitimates murder and suicide.

English recalled the carnage flashed across CNN, and the front page of the *Daily News*, when terrorists had blown themselves up in Israel. Bodies were scattered all over, bloody and broken. People, some of them bleeding, were screaming and running or helping the wounded. The flames in the background ignited the victims' eyes, revealing their shock and terror. He'd been repelled and mesmerized at the same time.

When New York City cops of English's generation envisioned the precedents in department history, they thought of organizations that were locally spawned. The Black Liberation Army (BLA), which split off from the Black Panther party in the 1960s, was one of the most feared terrorist organizations in New York. Members of the BLA assassinated police officers Waverly Jones and Joseph Piagentini in Harlem in 1971. The demise of the organization occurred in 1981, when the last of its leaders was arrested.

After that it was Puerto Rican nationalist groups that posed the biggest terrorist threat. In 1983, the FALN (Fuerzas Armadas de Liberación Nacional Puertorriqueña) set off four bombs in one day. The first was planted at Twenty-Six Federal Plaza, in front of the New York headquarters of the FBI. The second was disguised in a Kentucky Fried Chicken box and placed in front of One Police Plaza. Police officer Rocco Pascarella had his leg blow off and his face ripped up when the blast went off. A third device was discovered in Cadman Plaza in front of the Federal Court House in Brooklyn. Bomb Squad detectives Tony Senft and Richie Pastorella found the fourth bomb near the federal prosecutor's office at One Andrews Plaza. They secured it under a blanket and were starting to work on the secondary device. Senft was blown into the air when that bomb exploded. He lost an eye, half his face, and fractured his hip. Pastorella was also hurt.

At the national level, white right-wing groups soon took a strategic place in every cop's mind until the 1990s when U.S. policy abroad and the crisis in the Middle East finally brought the specter of international terrorism to the United States.

English knew that Israeli soldiers were taught to shoot at suspicious persons regardless of whether or not they saw a weapon. They were also trained to shoot for the head to neutralize the central nervous system. New York cops were taught to fire their weapons only in self-defense or to protect someone else from serious injury. They were trained to aim for the largest part of the body because it provided the widest target. The goal was to stop the offender, whether or not they killed him. Only snipers who used special rifles were trained to shoot for the head. English did not know how the rules of engagement applied to the suicide bombers they were about to encounter. He did know that he wanted his men to live.

o o o o o o o

English, Ryan, Dolan, and the other Emergency Service cops and bosses gathered around and began to discuss their tactical options. Chindluri's sketches were displayed, and Dwyer and English repeated the details of what they had learned. Two major proposals were put on the table and tossed back and forth.

"We could do a takedown on the street. Put snipers on the roof, set up a barricade and evacuate the building, then wait until the perps come out and take 'em down there," English suggested.

"They could be up praying. Even if they're sleeping, they'll hear us knocking on doors."

"We're walking into a fuckin' bomb factory. They're gonna blow up the building whether or not we're in there if they find out we're anywhere near."

"We could surround the building and wait until they come out. When they hit the street, if they don't stop, we take them out."

"We don't have a floor plan. There could be another way out of the building. What if they escape and head for the subway?" English said.

"We can't wait," Kammerdamer interrupted. "If they detonate the bombs when we're evacuating the building, they'll kill us and everyone else. We are going to have to hit them and hit them fast."

"OK. I want a six-man team because if they start detonating this device. . . . It's a small place," Dwyer said. Entry teams were typically composed of from six to eight officers. He'd settled on the smallest size in order to maximize speed and minimize casualties if the bomb went off.

In view of the fact that Dwyer was clearly worried about losing cops, it may seem surprising that neither he nor Mancini mentioned the option of hostage negotiation. The New York Police Department's Hostage Negotiation Team (HNT) was created in the 1970s by lieutenant Frank Boltz and detective psychologist Harvey Schlossberg after a series of incidents at home and abroad rendered law enforcement officials powerless to reduce loss of life using traditional methods. One terrorist situation was included amongst them: the massacre of Israeli athletes during the Munich Olympics.

One reason that the Hostage Negotiation Team was probably not mentioned involved the action-oriented perspective of many Emergency Service cops who relish the opportunity to use their tactical skills. Negotiation also contained the same problem as another option that was discussed and dismissed. Negotiators required the evacuation of the building. Only once innocent people were safe could detectives set up a system of communication and begin to talk to the suspects from a protected space. Another reason negotiation wasn't mentioned had to do with issue of command. Emergency Service bosses might have to relinquish control if "HNT" took over the job. The chief negotiator generally called the shots, subject to the agreement of the assigned duty inspector or chief, outranking even the Emergency Service captain.

Some bosses in Emergency Service did have reservations about the tactical plan but kept them to themselves. A few believed that they should have tried to negotiate. Assuming a successful evacuation, if the suspects "chose to die," no innocent lives would be lost. Others thought that a street takedown was preferable because it minimized risk to cops. In this strategy, the police would barricade the area outside the building then wait until the suspects emerged.

All the men who preferred alternative plans held senior Emergency Service bosses responsible for making a rash decision that put the officers at serious risk. "Mancini is a very impatient man. He was always rushing into everything, to his and others' peril. Dwyer's the same way. . . . We don't get paid to be reckless and lose the lives of our officers. I value my cops more than that," one boss explained.

Chief Kammerdener called the Operations Division to coordinate support. A job of this type demands a joint effort of units within and outside the NYPD. Brooklyn North and Brooklyn South Task Forces were needed to organize efforts to barricade the area and keep traffic at bay. The Transit Bureau, the Metropolitan Transit Authority and the Long Island Railroad had to be notified so they could suspend service and secure the trains and subways.

Ray McDermott walked to the window and trolled for a name on his cell phone. A striking man in his mid-forties, McDermott was six feet tall, with an average build that did not appear to have suffered from a more than twenty-year diet of "cop food"—pasta, meat, bagels, and donuts, although police are quick to dismiss the last as a stereotype. Dressed in a business suit, few would guess he came from a police family and had a father on the job. There was something about McDermott's manner that looked like he came from class or money or an Ivy League education. Although he spent most of his career on the street, his speech did not reveal a hint of the blue-collar lilt that permeated the talk of even the most educated cops who reached the senior ranks.

Prior to his current assignment, McDermott worked as the commanding officer of the Recruit School at the Police Academy. That job ended abruptly when Bill Morange was appointed the chief of the Special Operations Division and decided to take McDermott with him. "I think he felt bad for me," McDermott explained. Like Morange, McDermott had the street in his blood and was happiest working outside.

McDermott pressed a number on his cell phone but lost the signal, aborting the call. He went downstairs and stepped outside. Again he tried dialing Morange's home number. This time the call went through. Morange recognized McDermott's voice as soon as he picked up the receiver.

"We've got a situation," McDermott explained. "This guy claims that two men have bombs inside 248 Fourth Avenue in Park Slope over in Brooklyn. Dwyer wants to use a six-man team to execute a tactical entry." The chief raised his 5'10" physique out of the bed and reached for his clothes. He had spent most of his fifty-plus years as a cop in high-crime precincts before beginning a rapid ascent through the ranks. An old school Irish Democrat who liked people and respected diversity and civil rights, Morange was loved in the neighborhoods where he served as a cop and a boss. When he became a precinct commander, the community endowed him a royal title. They called him the "White Prince of Harlem."

Chief Morange pulled on his pants and tried to fasten his belt. The fit was tight. His gut had expanded since he'd become the "King of Toys" with Aviation, Scuba, Emergency Service, Mounted, and Street Crime among the units in his command. He knew his healthy appetite was part of the problem. The cops in Emergency Service also loved him too much. The ten squads, each of which was assigned a truck with a corresponding number, competed amongst themselves to see who could feed him better meals.

A glint of worry haunted Morange's dark-blue eyes, and extra lines bunched up the brow of his craggy face. His thoughts drifted from his cops to the tactical issues surrounding the current situation compared with jobs he'd known in the past. Morange had witnessed a lot of police entries in his distinguished career. Some were serious, involving barricaded suspects or people intent on killing themselves or getting the police to do it for them. Others were strange, even bizarre, like the tiger they once removed from a Harlem apartment. This job sounded different. Not since the World Trade Center bombing in 1993 had there been a major terrorist threat in New York City, at least not one that didn't involve one of the nation's "homegrown nuts."

He wasn't worried about any danger to himself. At this point in his career, he was more likely to be caught in the shifting terrain of depart-

mental politics than killed by a gun, knife, or bomb. He was concerned
about his cops. By the time the raid started, they would have been up all
night. The job required that they carry more than fifty pounds of gear on
a hot humid night. Part of a boss's job is to make sure his men are fresh,
comfortable, and have what they need to get the job done. Exhausted cops
are no different from surgeons who operate with no sleep. They're more
vulnerable to making mistakes that cost people their lives.

As the Emergency Service captain, Nick Mancini was responsible
for the welfare of his men. Morange wasn't always comfortable when
Mancini was working a serious case. Mancini's nickname, "Captain Chaos," underscored the bedlam that seemed to accompany his presence
on certain jobs. By acting like a cop instead of a captain, he sometimes
turned minor events into circus routines without central coordination
from above. At other times, he inflated his rank and acted the part of a
two-star chief.

Morange would chuckle several years later when he recalled the day
"Nicky" was bitten in the ass by a K-9 dog because he ran into a job ahead of
his cops and the handler. But on July 31, in the face of an incident involving terrorists and bombs, all humor escaped him. Morange shook his head,
recalling one incident that particularly galled him. After an Emergency
cop was shot, Mancini had failed to notify the chief. Instead, he'd gone
to the hospital to meet the police commissioner and greet the press. "It
wasn't Nick's job to be up the PC's ass. He should have been on the street,
coordinating efforts to apprehend the suspect who shot the cop, not politicking inside," another boss explained.

Morange knew that if Mancini had his way that morning he'd be breaking down doors with the cops on the entry team. Unnerved by the thought,
Morange aborted a case of indigestion by replacing Mancini's pockmarked
face with McDermott's smooth chin and sensible eyes. Morange trusted
McDermott completely to supervise the job, keep him in the loop, and
bring out the best in the men. Morange stepped on the gas and settled in
for the long drive from his home in Rockland County.

o o o o o o o

John English walked down the stairs of the 8-8 Precinct to stretch his legs
and get some space to think. He'd already memorized the sketches of the
apartment and started to review the tactical plan in his mind, looking
for cracks and omissions. Now he was putting himself in the suspects'

shoes, imagining what he would do if he was one of them and cops came charging in.

He envisioned a range of scenarios, depending on what the suspects were doing; sleeping, eating, praying, or better yet, taking a shower, defenseless and unprepared. All in all, English believed the strategy was sound. The only gap he could find was that it depended on the word of one man. Every intuitive inch of English's brain was convinced that Chindluri was telling the truth. The details of his story, the intonations of his voice, the expression on his face, the way his eyes moved when he talked, all confirmed that his story was valid.

Nevertheless, English had been on the job long enough to know that "things don't always appear to be as they appear to be." False or incomplete information can lead to deadly mistakes. He checked his watch. If they acted quickly, the cops could do a reconnaissance mission to check out the building. He walked to the squad room to talk to the other bosses. All agreed a drive-by was worth ten minutes of time.

Mancini was standing near the stairwell, eager to get started. Keith Ryan glanced in his direction, recalling the photographs the captain had passed around the squad a few months before: Mancini rappelling out of a helicopter; Mancini, dressed in full tactical gear, pointing his gun at something ahead.[7] The cops weren't impressed. They'd been there, done that, and didn't need pictures to prove it.

Ryan hadn't bothered to comment. He'd sat down at the table and put the palm of his hand on the indentation on his right temple. He'd placed his elbow on the table and rested his head. The photographs had stirred up images of other jobs when he and his teammates had gone crashing through doors, dressed like military commandos; of people scattering and children confused and scared. He recalled stories of jobs gone bad: bodies full of holes, no weapons found; no contraband; residents with clean records. Every incident had provided a valuable lesson, although it struck him as sad that some had been learned on the backs of other cops.

Mancini, Kammerdener, McDermott, Dwyer, and English headed downstairs, making their way to the lot where the counter assault team car was parked. Once he got outside, McDermott stepped away from the crowd and dialed Morange's cell phone number to give him an update and get his opinion on their plan. Their conversation was brief. Morange was mostly concerned about the time. More than five hours had passed since Chindluri had left the apartment, and the clock was ticking fast.

English got in the driver's seat with Kammerdener beside him. Dwyer, Mancini, and McDermott piled in the back. As English pulled out of the parking lot, McDermott called Division headquarters and requested that someone bring Morange's uniform to the Fourth Avenue address. The chief was heading to the scene and planned to change in one of the trucks.

As English turned off Atlantic Avenue, the look of the area transformed. The buildings turned squat and square, a contrast to the elegant brownstones in the gentrified sections of Park Slope. Some had fire escapes in the front, and graffiti marred the surface of brick and concrete. The zone was mixed, and warehouses, businesses, and residential apartments sat side by side.

The suspects' address was between President and Carroll Streets. An automotive supply store, a construction company, an after-hours club, and two bodegas shared the block. Nelson's Grocery lay just in front of the entrance to the suspect's building, across the street from Tania's Deli. Both were gated, adding to the dismal starkness of the block. English looked around, then turned to Dwyer.

"That's Six Truck's sector. It's Keith and Joe's job," he said. Keeping a steady speed, English passed by the location, then turned down a side street, circled the area, and drove by again. Chindluri's description of the exterior was accurate down to the last detail. The cops counted ten cabdrivers sitting or standing around outside. English and Dwyer would organize a second Emergency team to quietly take them down and secure them in restraints so they wouldn't slow down the six men on the entry team.

Back in the 8-8 Precinct, the cops were waiting restlessly for the bosses to return. Teemsma and Yurkiw were standing apart from the Emergency Service cops. Joe Dolan wandered over and said hello. He had great respect for the nerve-racking, gut-wrenching work they did. A good bomb technician must have the mental ability to master a delicate set of skills and use them in extreme situations. Focus and patience were important. Someday, he hoped to develop the expertise the job required. The Bomb Squad was the only job other than Emergency Service he'd ever wanted to work.

Ryan was sitting with a group of Emergency Service cops, thinking about the raid. He had begun the process of purging irrelevant thoughts from his head but paused to listen to their conversation.

"What's the time?" one cop asked.

"Almost four," another replied.

"This could be a very long night," the first cop said.

"Yeah. These cocksuckers are gonna fuck up my day job," the other remarked. Most cops hold second jobs to make ends meet or their wives work while they run home to babysit. Overtime gigs are usually welcome sources of additional income when they can be timed ahead not to interfere with previous obligations.

Ryan didn't care if the job lasted all day, because he needed the overtime and wasn't working his second job that week. Instead, he'd planned to visit his brother and sisters, fix things in his mother's house, and run errands requiring a car. She'd never learned how to drive. Ryan believed she'd earned every bit of help he could lend twice over. She'd sacrificed a lot for him and the rest of the family. Times had been tough after she and her husband split. She'd managed alone with four children and no money in a house he had deliberately gutted. Not even the kitchen appliances had been left inside. He'd also taken the photo albums, passports, and birth certificates. No one in the family ever saw them again.

Ryan looked up when he heard footsteps on the stairs, and conversations among the cops ceased. Dwyer walked in first, followed by the other bosses. They confirmed the accuracy of Chindhuri's description of the exterior of the building. There was no criminal activity outside, no prostitutes or drug deals going down. The block was quiet except for the livery cabdrivers standing around and waiting for work.

The time had come to select a team. Dwyer called for volunteers, emphasizing that the mission was dangerous and demanded the fastest cops. Ryan popped his hand in the air then stifled a laugh when he looked at his partner's face. Dolan looked reluctant, "like a little boy who doesn't want to go to school."

It didn't surprise Joe that his partner, "being Keith," had raised his arm. Since the moment Ryan stepped out of the front door of the Police Academy, he had been gung ho, ready and willing to handle any job that came his way. Dolan was more circumspect; preferring places and situations that were familiar and utilized known expertise. The job involved bombs. The only thing he knew about explosives was when to call the Bomb Squad.

Regardless, Ryan was his partner and he was his wing man. Joe Dolan would follow Ryan to the grave if that's what it took to protect him. Dolan slowly raised his hand. When Mike Keenan from Six Truck, Mario Zorovic from Eight Truck, and John English from Seven Truck followed suit, a rumble of voices erupted in the room.

Police officers work together, cover for each other, and fight among themselves when a colleague does something annoying, refuses to carry his load, or busts the going rate by, for example, writing too many tickets and making his peers look bad in front of their boss. As a result, cops know each other's strengths and weaknesses better than anyone else. No one in Emergency Service doubted that Dolan and Ryan were fast on their feet. Ryan was a natural athlete whose speed and agility were enhanced by his participation in endurance sports. He had no trouble maintaining mental focus and dismissing the kind of negative thoughts that can interfere with performance during stressful jobs. Dolan was tactically competent and physically strong and had the presence of mind or instinct to back up his fellow cops in the event lethal forced was used.

A good team isn't just composed of the strengths of each individual. Like baseball and other team sports, good police work depends on how officers work as a group. Familiarity builds knowledge, confidence, and trust. Zorovic, Keenan, Dolan, and Ryan had worked together for months in Park Slope. They knew the neighborhood and each others' policing styles.

Although they didn't work steady midnights, English and Dwyer had good reputations among the cops. English was viewed as a thoughtful, even-tempered, levelheaded, master tactician with years of experience under his belt. Dwyer was more controversial. Regardless, the cops had no doubt that he would back them up on a dangerous job.

Dwyer, not the cops, had concerns about the volunteers. It wasn't their competence that worried him. The problem was that almost all of the cops were married and most had children. The job was risky. A part of him believed that some or all of the men on the entry team would be killed. It is bad enough for a police commander to lose cops. Dwyer did not want to shoulder the guilt of making a fatherless child.

"Listen, like I said. If the bomb goes off, it's a small place. I want six men and I don't want guys who are married and have kids, or if you're married it's one thing, but not kids."

Teemsma and Yurkiw exchanged glances. "It was like a thought wave. We both were thinking the same thing. Are you kidding? What does one have to do with another? This guy is nuts! You've got this one lieutenant who didn't grow up in Emergency Service and wasn't taught the traditions by old-timers. It's 'I'm the boss and whatever I say goes'. . . . This will not work," Teemsma explained.

"I don't care what you do, but I'm going," John English said. His pupils had contracted, and his gray eyes looked small and dark.

"Well, dude, uh, you know—" Dwyer was interrupted midsentence.

"—I can't speak for anyone else, but I'm going!" English insisted. There was no way in hell Larry Dwyer or anyone else would oust him from the entry team. They were his men going in. English wasn't about to let them handle a dangerous job without him there to back them up. Dwyer caved in to his sergeant. He and English were too close in rank for him to put up an argument. The cops were a different story.

"Look, I'm telling you this is the way it's gonna be. I do not want cops on this job who have children." Dwyer's tone was firm. Ryan shook his head and suppressed a sarcastic remark. He usually bent over backward to give the imports from Housing the benefit of the doubt.

He'd felt bad for them after the merger of the Housing and Transit Police Departments with the NYPD. The NYPD veterans had been hostile. They resented the privileges that the Housing police had been granted; the transfers with rank and special assignment status intact that meant that they made more money than New York cops with more time and experience on the job. Ryan knew that Dwyer hadn't asked for the merger. He'd reaped the rewards but wasn't to blame for its terms.

Some cops thought Dwyer was a pretty good boss. He let them do what they wanted and covered for them if they got caught. If one of them came to work drunk, even a known alcoholic, he could rely on Dwyer to sign a "28" form, requesting time off, and send him home. Nevertheless, there were days, and this was one, that Dwyer swung his dick around, and even Ryan got annoyed.

"That's bullshit," Dolan said. "That's not the way this works. If it's in your area, you do it, no matter whether you have ten kids. That's always been this unit's protocol."

"Well that's not how it's gonna be," Dwyer replied.

"So what if guys go do my job and get killed? You're going to have me live with that the rest of my life? That's my job. If someone has to get killed, it's supposed to be me," Dolan said.

He understood where Dwyer was coming from—no boss wants to hand a folded flag to the widow of a slain officer. But still, the officers in Emergency Service worked as a team and took the same risks. When news of events later seeped up the ranks, police executives at the top of the organization thought Dwyer's objections were absurd.

"Yeah," one senior commander explained, "Let's say I wanted to send an unmarried guy in the door first—supposing he couldn't shoot straight, supposing his forte was electronics, not taking the door. You're dealing with a critical incident here and it's highly likely we were going to have a bloody confrontation if only a third of what this guy was saying was true and accurate, so I would want my most highly trained people in there and I wouldn't ask them if they were married or single, black or white, Catholic or Protestant or Jew.

"I would say, hey, listen, you're the best shot I got, you're in first and you got the best head and this is where you go. . . . Putting together an all-star team doesn't mean you are going to have an all-star performance. It's the sum of the parts, and everyone has something to offer. . . . You look for people who have worked well together before, who know each other's moves. You look for a unit's cohesiveness and skill level. . . . The cops are going to tell you that. Respect them. Listen to them. They know. You have the ultimate word, but they are the experts. That's what you trained them to be."

After Dolan said his peace, more cops jumped into the fray, creating the specter of mutiny and forcing Dwyer to hear them out. Ryan listened intently as one after another officer voiced his objections. He knew that Dwyer was scared and taking the situation seriously. But Keith wasn't afraid. Maybe if he was going in with someone whose moves he didn't know he might have felt doubt. "I guess it's a little pompous and cocky but it didn't faze me. I was fully confident that I would complete the task one way or another," Ryan explained.

It didn't take more than a few minutes for Dwyer to relent. There were bosses who would press an irrational point for no other reason than to prove they have authority. Dwyer wasn't one of those. He probably would have had to withdraw his proposal regardless of the actions of his men. There weren't a lot of childless men in Emergency Service. In 1997, the unit's demographics leaned toward white men of Italian or Irish decent. Few racial or ethnic minorities or women applied to the unit or made it to the final cut. The unit demanded street experience; as a result, most E-men were older than the average cop on patrol and had their own families.

All six members of the team needed to pool their maturity and experience and perform at peak capacity to survive this job. As the highest-ranking boss on the entry team, Larry Dwyer also had to assume a leadership role. A boss who makes one mistake at a critical juncture can undo a lifetime of doing everything right. By sharing his fears with his men, he'd chipped a hole in their armor, leaving a residue of unease in the air.

In contrast to the military, there is no acceptable casualty rate in polic-ing. There are no computer-punching number crunchers sitting in front of their downtown desks, calculating equations to determine how many men can die in a mission and still claim victory. If a police commander believes that lives will be lost in a job, he scratches the tactical plan and starts over again.

English was also scared but took it in stride. "I'd be lying if I told you I wasn't scared, because you're scared, but you work through it. Fear is a good thing. It keeps you sharp." He suppressed his fear and prepared him-self mentally by focusing on the job and how he would handle the "what ifs" that might arise.

Each member of the six-man entry team had an assignment, depend-ing on where he was in the lineup of cops through the door. Dolan had Chindluri's key to the apartment and was responsible for unlocking the door. He and Ryan would enter the apartment first and walk straight to the bedroom where the suspects were sleeping with the bombs. Mike Keenan and Mario Zorovic would go in next and subdue the Pakistani immigrant who was sleeping on the cot next to the kitchen. John English would enter fifth and veer right, following Dolan and Ryan in case they needed help. As last man in, Larry Dwyer was responsible for guarding the door to the apartment.

All officers would carry the standard protective equipment, a helmet and two vests. One vest was worn under the shirt and covered the vital organs, extending from neck to his waist. The "level-three tactical" vest extended to midthigh and was worn on the outside of the uniform. It contained ballistic ceramic inserts that were resistant to one or two shots of rifle fire.

Each officer was instructed to select a weapon from the arsenal in the truck, depending on his position in the stack.[8] As first man in, Ryan would carry the "bunker," a large bulletproof shield that weighed about fifteen pounds. He therefore chose a 9-mm Glock model 19, which was light in weight (20.99 ounces), and fired fifteen rounds per magazine and one in the chamber. He liked the Glock because he used it on patrol and in prac-tice at the range and it was familiar and comfortable in his hands.

Neither Ryan nor the other five cops were concerned about making the entry in the dark. Most raids were executed at night when suspects were least alert. Cops don't use night vision goggles, because they are expensive and require extensive training. Instead, they carry small flashlights, swinging their arms back and forth and turning the switch on and off to survey the area and guide their path.

Ryan's light was affixed to the bottom of his Glock. A piece of black rubber glad wire connecting to the light was sitting along the trigger guard. To activate the light, he need only squeeze the grip with his middle finger, freeing his index to pull the trigger. If he turned it on in the suspects' bedroom, he couldn't reverse course. His night vision would be compromised.

John English needed both hands to carry the heavy, steel-battering ram in case the team had to forcibly open the door. He therefore chose to carry a Glock and a backup gun, which he could keep holstered until his hands were free. Semiautomatic pistols do occasionally "jam" when, for example, the slide is blocked, resulting in a failure of the round to cycle or a "double-feed," when two bullets compete for the chamber at once. This possibility of malfunction was increased with the Glock, which had a design flaw that wasn't acknowledged and corrected until 2001.

In the event their gun jammed, cops were typically taught to clear the chamber rather than grab for a backup weapon. The officer who carried the bunker was an exception. If Ryan's gun jammed, he was supposed to keep the shield up, drop his Glock and reach for his backup gun. No one asked what he should do if he was alone in a room with a jammed gun, two suspects, and a bomb.[9]

On routine patrol, Dolan used a 9-mm Smith & Wesson that some cops informally coined the "BMF"—big motherfucker—because of its size and weight. The Big Mother weighed 37.5 ounces and, at 7.5 inches in length, was longer than the Glock. Dolan did not elect to use his service weapon for the job. Instead, he chose the Ruger Mini-14.

The Mini-14 is a semiautomatic rifle that weighs not quite seven pounds and holds a twenty-round magazine. It fires a 5.56-mm or 223-caliber round that moves at high velocity and can penetrate steel and concrete and can pulverize bone. The 223 round has a soft lead point at the end of a copper jacket. When the round is fired, the lead deforms and the projectile expands, leaving behind a big hole. The same "devastating" caliber was used by the military in the M-16 rifle during Vietnam. Dolan selected the Mini-14 because it was a powerful weapon that would likely stop the suspects. He was also concerned that the suspects might barricade themselves inside the apartment and thought the Mini-14 could penetrate the door.

Mike Keenan, Mario Zorovic, and Larry Dwyer all chose MP-5s. Each magazine in the 9-mm submachine gun contained thirty rounds that could be fired in rapid succession even when placed on semiautomatic. The MP-5 and the Glock both used "ball ammunition," fully copper-jacketed rounds that make a small hole in the target and usually exit on the other side. The cops saw this as a disadvantage. Ball ammo caused less damage than soft-point or hollow-point ammunition, which expanded on impact and stopped inside. Copper-jacked rounds also had a greater potential to ricochet; projectiles could bounce off a wall and hit innocent people or come back at the cops. Regardless of what kind of ammunition the men employed, it often took more than one shot to stop someone.

"There are very few things you can do to a human body that are going to stop a person instantly. What stops the person is generally loss of blood. His pressure goes down. The bigger the hole, the more blood is lost, the quicker the person succumbs. With ball ammunition the only shot likely to stop someone is one that hits the brain or spine and deactivates the nervous system or if you hit something skeletal, like breaking a leg, so the guy can't move. A lot of people have died from knife-wielding dead people," an NYPD weapons expert explained.

Before the cops headed downstairs, Dwyer told them to empty their pockets of items that might jangle and alert the suspects. Ryan removed keys, change, and a Swiss Army knife. Directing his words to Ryan and Dolan, English then repeated some crucial details of the intelligence information.

"The bag's in the corner of the room on the right of the door."

"When the time comes and they go for the bag . . ." Ryan didn't finish the sentence.

"They go for the bag, they get shot," English confirmed. Chief Kammerdener then made a remark that Ryan would never forget. "You go in the room and you do what you gotta do." Ryan explained, "he set the tone for the job. . . . Most chiefs won't stick out their necks like that." With those eleven words, Chief Kammerderner earned Keith Ryan's loyalty for the duration of his career. Some of the other cops felt differently. They'd heard of too many instances in which frightened commanders had gone back on their word to save their careers, leaving the cops to take the fall. Regardless, the chief's statement helped bolster the officers' confidence and undo the damage caused by Dwyer.

As first man in on the entry team, Ryan held the lives of the cops and civilians in his hands. If he failed to react fast enough or shot and missed the target, the suspects might detonate the bombs. If he responded too soon, he could unleash a chain reaction. All six cops would empty their guns and "light up the room." Ryan could also do everything right but win the wrong lottery. His Glock could jam or he could fire his weapon and cause the bomb to explode. "That job was a catch-22. Either they blow me up or I blow me up," a boss explained.

As the cops gathered their gear, McDermott received unexpected news. The commanding officer of the Brooklyn South Task Force had jumped the gun and prematurely cordoned off the area surrounding the building. Although the problem was quickly corrected and people and cars allowed back into the Fourth Avenue area, the mistake might have fueled a latent fear of several members of the team. Even unmarked vehicles rarely remained anonymous in high-crime neighborhoods where people were familiar with the comings and goings of cops. If the wrong person noticed police activity or the change in traffic patterns, he might alert the suspects. According to an article that later appeared in the *New York Post,* several neighborhood residents had been aware of increased police presence but thought it related to an impending drug bust.[10]

Ryan and the rest of the cops filed outside and loaded the van. John English made a call to his wife to tell her he was about to get involved and wanted to say goodnight. Although he did not elaborate on the details of the job, his wife understood the hidden script. "Anytime I call her like that, it's pretty much because it's something big."

English climbed into the driver's seat. Dolan sat next to him in the front. Ryan and one of the other cops sat in the two seats directly behind, next to the gun locker. A third cop was wedged in a small seat in the back. On the right rear side of the van was an equipment bench containing items like flash-bangs and tear gas. Chindluri, the police translator, and one Emergency Service cop squeezed onto the bench. The battering ram and the bunker were placed on the floor. The men cradled their weapons on their laps or kept them holstered up. The windows in the van were dark so no one on the street could see who and what were inside.

After all the men had settled in, Nick Mancini opened the door and gave them a parting speech. An intense man with high blood pressure, he seemed particularly strung out that morning. He warned the cops of what might happen even if they did everything right and told them to be very careful. He concluded his speech with "God bless you." Ryan exchanged a look with his partner.

"What's the matter with him? Why do I feel that I have just been read my last rites?" he asked.

"He did. That motherfucker just read us our last rites," Dolan responded. Although he was laughing, the muscles in his shoulders contracted and his eyes got wide.

"It's my birthday," Ryan said.

"This isn't good. This isn't fuckin' good," someone muttered under his breath.

"Keith, I can't die. I didn't kiss Jennifer. I never leave the house without kissing her," Dolan said. His daughter had been asleep when he left and he didn't want to wake her. Ryan looked straight into his partner's eyes.

"Joey, you aren't going to die. It ain't gonna happen. Nobody's dying tonight." Dolan's shoulders relaxed. The tension drained out of his face.

Dolan and Ryan were partners for a reason. There were jobs that pushed Ryan to the limits, like instances of domestic violence, which made him feel angry enough to kill the guy who beat up his wife or abused their child. In times like that, Dolan's eyes might get hard and beady but he would keep cool, soothing his partner and keeping his temper in check. Ryan, in turn, often took a leadership role, calming Dolan down when he got nervous or a little impatient. Sometimes, when Dolan got up on the wrong side of the bed, he would respond angrily to an irritation that others would let roll off their backs. Ryan's mere presence would serve to keep down the heat that bubbled inside and Dolan would restrain himself. When Ryan felt depressed or burdened by too much thought, he could count on Dolan to crack a joke or otherwise lighten his load.

John English turned on the ignition of the counter assault team car and backed out of the parking space. He shifted gears and stepped on the gas. Kammerdener, McDermott, and Mancini followed in an unmarked sedan. Teemsma and Yurkiw were fifth in the caravan. Halfway there, Teemsma stopped the truck. The cops in Emergency Service were carrying the heavy guns. The detectives in the Bomb Squad planned on going in after the raid was over and any shooting done. Yurkiw and Teemsma removed their guns and secured them in their equipment bag. "I was never a big fan of carrying a gun," Teemsma explained. Teemsma stepped outside, stripped down to his underwear and, protected by the darkness of the street, slipped on the fire-resistant jumpsuit he wore under his bomb suit. Teemsma zipped it up but left the collar open, seeking relief from the heat.

"It's showtime," he said, and put the truck into gear.

3

SEVEN SHOTS

CRAMPED, THE AIR HEAVY WITH sweat, gear, and unspoken fear, the six cops headed toward Fourth Avenue. Emergency Service cops usually talk when they band together on their way to jobs. In the early morning of July 31, 1997, there was none of the typical banter; no racial and ethnic jokes, no bitching about work or who was stealing their overtime, no muttering about "the two-faced man-hating muncher" who blew her way up the ranks in half the time it took their great Irish boss who spent his career on the street and earned every promotion.[1]

Each cop was lost in his own thoughts, preoccupied with his role in the entry. The ride over was quiet, so quiet you could have heard a raindrop falling on cotton. Ryan prepared himself mentally like an elite athlete, rehearsing the job in his mind, dividing it into a series of actions and triple-checking each one.[2]

He thought about everything that could go wrong and practiced what he would do if it did. "I must have run through the job at least fifty times before we actually got to the door. I knew what I would do if the door opened out instead of in, or if the key didn't work. I knew where Joey would be if I stepped to the right. I knew he would be right behind me."

John English was also rehearsing the job in his head, envisioning the informant's descriptions of the layout and sketching his moves, depending on those of his teammates. Every now and then, thoughts of his children made an unwelcome appearance in his head and he would fight to regain his focus. "I hoped they wouldn't have to hear from somebody else that I wasn't here . . ., but that's like a race car driver thinking about crashing," English explained.

They were half a block away when someone broke the silence. In one respect, they knew that the raid was "just another entry," like hundreds they'd done before involving suspects who had weapons or drugs or both. With only minor variations, they'd used the same tactical plan many times before on jobs and in training. On the other hand, they knew that this raid was different from the usual entry.

Two of their bosses had inadvertently upped the ante by suggesting that police might die. They were dealing with bombs, unpredictable weapons that could cause mass destruction, depending on their composition, strength, and the place of detonation. Despite all their precautions, the cops remained concerned about the informant. Not that they didn't believe his story. Most everyone did. They simply couldn't trust anyone who wasn't a blue-blooded NYPD cop with a shield and a red I.D. For all they knew, Chindluri could be allied with the suspects, preparing to set them up. Even if he wasn't intentionally lying, people often embellish the facts. The cops' lives depended on the accuracy of every detail of intelligence.

"You're lying, you're dead," Ryan said, looking directly at the informant, the cop from the 13th Precinct translating his words into Arabic.

"You'll be the first person we take out if one word of what you say isn't fact," Dolan added. One by one and sometimes together, the cops in the van descended upon Chindluri, like wasps attacking a person disturbing their nest. When John English pulled up next to the building and turned off the engine, Dolan turned around, and faced the informant one last time.

"You get out of the car. If you scream, talk, or even breathe too loud—"

"—I'll shoot you first," Ryan finished his partner's sentence. There wasn't a doubt in Chindluri's mind that the cops were serious. English turned around, looked at Chindluri, and felt mildly sorry. He seemed like a decent guy who happened to walk into a cyclone. Now he was stuck in a van, unarmed and vulnerable, hanging by a string between a bomb and six scared cops carrying rifles and MP-5s.

Ryan and Dolan opened the doors in the middle of the van and jumped out, followed by Mike Keenan, Mario Zorovic, John English, Larry Dwyer, the informant, and the translator. Chindluri was wearing a hood to cover his face so he wouldn't be recognized by anyone on the street. It was 4:45 A.M. and the Long Island Railroad train and the subway lines under Atlantic Avenue had just stopped running or were rerouted.

The eight men started walking toward the front door. Crouched down, knees bent, Ryan held the bunker in his left hand and the Glock in his right. His movements were as fast and fluid as a college swimmer propelling himself through water on the last lap of the best race of his life.

Dolan, who was walking behind his partner, paused, then landed a blow that flattened a livery cabdriver who had suddenly leapt to his feet. "One guy stood up quick and just got leveled, boom, we took control of that." Fifth man in the stack, English saw people flying and heard the dull thud of falling bodies as the second group of Emergency Service cops forced the cabdrivers to lie down and applied restraints to their wrists.

McDermott and Mancini got out of their car and headed toward the cops who were securing the front of the building. Mancini pointed his shotgun at a driver who suddenly found he was lying face down on the ground. The driver was not armed and didn't resist, which was fortunate because, unbeknownst to Mancini, the firing pin on his shotgun was broken.

Ryan and Dolan went into the building first, followed by the other members of the team, the informant, and the police translator. Once inside, the hood was removed so Chindluri could show the way. A single bulb in the ceiling cast a harsh light and illuminated the dingy hallway. The floor was littered with ash and cigarette butts. The air smelled rancid like spoiled meat.

As Ryan and Dolan veered right then left down the narrow passage, they started to feel uneasy. Nothing looked like what Chindluri had described. The muscles in English's arms cramped from the absence of sleep and the weight of the ram. He struggled to put together his mental map of the layout with what he saw and came out mystified.

Dolan looked back at the police translator who pointed left, indicating an area to the back of the stairs. Dolan nodded his head then looked in the informant's direction. The translator was pushing him down the hall while he was trying to take a step back and pointing ahead. "You kind of realize that you are in the right place because the guy is scared shitless," Dolan explained.

Ryan paused when he came to a door at the end of the hallway. He opened the door and stepped into an open courtyard. There, planted on the opposite side was another staircase. Everything suddenly made sense. A second building was hidden behind the first, divided by the courtyard. "That's one ballsy cop," English thought as he went through the courtyard door and realized the translator was wearing neither tactical vest nor helmet.

The smell of rotten food grew stronger as Ryan made his way across the yard, passing a row of garbage cans. A rat scurried near his feet and he swerved to avoid it, careful to maintain his position low to the ground and not cross his legs. Falling with the bunker was not an option he cared to think about. Once, while inside a dark room, Ryan had tripped on a glass table and accidentally fired a shot, creating a deafening noise and scaring his teammates who thought he'd been hit.

Ryan continued walking and stared straight ahead. Then he saw what they'd been looking for. There, under the stairs, he spotted a bicycle with no front tire and a laundry cart, just as Chindluri had described. When the other cops caught sight of them, their breathing evened out and their lungs felt clear. Then they saw the entrance to the suspects' apartment.

"This is for real now, guys," Dwyer said, stating the obvious. He turned back to Chindluri and the police translator and sent them retracing their steps, back to where McDermott and Mancini were waiting outside. The area around the first building was swarming with uniformed bodies. Snipers were lining up on rooftops. A helicopter from Aviation was waiting on standby, ready to go if a manhunt erupted on the street. Highway and Disorder Control had locked down an eighteen-block radius surrounding 248 Fourth Avenue.

The six cops on the entry team stacked up behind one another, in front of the apartment door, their only cover the bunker that Ryan was holding in his left hand. Had the door suddenly exploded, some or all would have been injured or killed. Emergency Service cops sometimes have to compromise one kind of safety for another. In this case, the name of the game was speed, surprise, and team strength. They had to advance directly inside as one compact, crushing wave.

John English looked around, searching for a place to put down the ram if he didn't need to use it. Keenan, Zorovic, and Dwyer held their MP-5s in a low ready position, waiting to breach the door. Mini 14 balanced in his left arm, Dolan reached in his pocket and removed the key. He put it between the thumb and index finger of his right hand, then turned toward his partner.

"Are you ready?" Dolan asked.

"Ready," Ryan replied. Dolan looked at the rest of the team.

"We're ready. Let's go," they whispered, nodding their heads once. Dolan inserted the key and turned the lock. He heard the cylinder move but his heartbeat seemed much louder.

"OK," he said. Ryan shifted his weight forward, ready to move. Dolan turned the knob and tried to open the door a crack.

"Son of a bitch," he muttered then looked at his partner. "I locked the fucking door," he said with a sheepish grin on his face. Ryan stifled a loud guffaw. Muted laughs echoed from the cops in the stack, and the tension went down a notch.

English exhaled. At that particular moment, he didn't care that the door was locked. The key worked, which meant that he could put down the ram. If he'd had to force the door open, it would have caused a near sonic blast, alerting the suspects and giving them time enough to launch a counter assault.

"Well, open the fucking door. Let's go," Ryan said. Dolan turned the key to the right, then gave the door a shove and tilted his head to the side. He squeezed his eyes shut and cringed. A bloody image of Waco swept through his mind. There in the Texas heartland, the suspects had learned about the raid by federal agents prior to its execution. Four agents were killed and more than twenty wounded in the gun battle that followed. Dolan recalled the words of one of the agents, "Hurry up! They know we're coming." Believing the door was booby-trapped, Dolan geared up for the explosion, not realizing he would have died without seeing a spark.

He kept his thoughts to himself. Communicating concern would not change the mission. The police in Emergency Service do not deviate from a tactical plan once it's in motion because that would entail additional risks. "You have five guys behind you committed to the plan. There's no time now. The key is in the lock. It's like you have your pants unzipped. You can't stop now and start a new tact [tactical] plan."

Ryan stepped inside, pushed the bunker in front of his face and extended his gun beyond. Near the center of the bunker was a four-by-five-inch ballistic portal, a bullet-resistant window that allowed him to see what lay ahead. Ryan headed across the apartment toward the suspects' bedroom. Dolan followed close to his partner's back, acting as his peripheral vision and another set of eyes.

Zorovic and Keenan stepped inside and started to fan out left, heading toward Chindluri's bedroom. The room was dark, and neither officer saw the empty cans of food on the kitchen counter as they passed the stove and sink. They dared not turn on their flashlights lest they illuminate the empty space between the floor and the suspects' door. Despite their bulk, Ryan and Dolan walked almost silently, then stopped in front of the suspects' bedroom. The only sound anyone heard was the rustle of Kevlar vests chafing against their shirts. English put the ram on the floor, unholstered his gun, breached the apartment door, and followed Dolan across the room.

Zorovic and Keenan smelled the odor of sweat and turmeric and knew they were near their target. When they reached the dark figure of a man lying on a twin mattress, one cop put his gun to the guy's head while the other applied restraints to his wrists. "He had no chance of getting to anything there. If he had sneezed he would have been shot, because no one is taking any chances of anyone getting to anything in the apartment," Dolan explained.

English heard the man scream once, then there was silence. Ryan looked at the thin, raw wood door that lay between him and bombs. He could feel the damp warmth of his partner's breath on his neck. Holding the bunker in his left hand, Ryan balanced his gun on two fingers, and grabbed the stained metal handle and pulled the door. It opened out instead of in so he had to step back and around the frame to get inside.

He pulled back on the grip of his gun to turn on his flashlight. The device contained 65 lumens of light, providing a thick stream of illumination accompanied by widening circles of diminishing radiance. Despite the light, Ryan's sense of distance remained distorted. He imagined the bedroom measured about twenty feet and he had space to maneuver. Later, when he returned to the scene, he would be shocked to discover the size of the room.

Most lethal confrontations occur at point-blank range or "short point," when the officer is barely inside an entryway, exposed and vulnerable until he repositions himself in a defensive stance. Suddenly Ryan noticed movement coming from the direction of the mattress on the far right side of the room. He felt a rush of warm air then saw a man lunging toward him. Ryan fired once.

"I didn't hear a sound but knew I got him because I saw the round hit his head but he kept coming." The shot penetrated the skin then tumbled around, missing the suspect's skull by a fraction. Crouched down, the suspect moved toward Ryan's leg and tried to grab his right hand. Ryan flexed his wrist and fired down, hitting the guy's hand.

"I'm thinking, what the fuck is wrong with you. . . . At one point I could have shot him point-blank in his head but I didn't want to kill him. . . . . I'm having this conversation with myself. . . . I wanted him to stop. He gave me a look like I've never seen. It was wild and at the same time focused and controlled. There was no fear. I fired a third time and hit him in the torso. I kept saying to myself, 'Stay down. Stay the fuck down. . . .' He was still crawling when he hit the ground and then he kind of like stops and leans over to one side." The last shot penetrated the suspect's body and went through the mattress and into the floor.

Still wedged behind the door, Dolan heard his partner yell, then the pop, pop, pop of the gun. A split second later, Ryan took a step forward and pivoted to the left, leaving just enough space for Dolan to squeeze past and enter the bedroom on his partner's right shoulder with the Mini-14 raised. Although he heard the sound of gunfire, he didn't yet know who, if anyone, had been shot. He looked down and around, and spotted the figure of the first suspect, starting to sit up on the mattress, balanced on his hip.

Peering through the sights of his rifle, Dolan saw the suspect's empty hands. He did not see the blood seeping into the mattress and congealing into a puddle on the floor. A few rays of early morning light were beginning to penetrate the darkness and, with the illumination from his partner's Glock and the tunnel vision and heightened perceptions that occur in a combat situation, he could clearly see the suspect's face.

His skin was light compared to the dimness of the room, his eyebrows thick and black. He had an oval-shaped face, short dark hair, and a trimmed mustache. His nose was large and thick at the base like a boxer's broken years ago. If it hadn't have been for the hardness of his eyes, he might have looked like a decent guy, Dolan thought.

"Don't move! Police! Don't move!" Dolan ordered. The suspect glared at Dolan, eyed the floor in front of him, and then glanced back in the cop's direction. Suddenly, the suspect lunged toward the corner of the room to the right of Dolan's feet. "At this point, I fired twice, hitting his hip and thigh," Dolan explained. "I heard the bolt move but didn't hear the rounds go off. I saw the sparks fly through his body." The suspect stopped, then curled up into a ball and lay still. Less than three seconds had passed since Dolan had entered the room.

While Dolan was busy confronting the first suspect, Ryan had taken another step into the room and was pivoting to the left. He noticed movement, then a glimpse of a dark cloud diving toward the other side of the room. Chindluri's words hung like a dead man in the back of Keith's mind. "The bombs are in the righthand corner near the door. . . . If they can't kill Jews, they'll kill you."

Time seemed to stop and everything started to move in slow motion. Although Ryan was aiming his gun as fast as he could he didn't feel his arm was moving fast enough. "I wanted the man to stop. I didn't want to shoot him. I thought I was yelling at the top of my lungs, 'What the fuck are you doing?' But no sound came out." Ryan fired two shots at the second suspect. "He goes right down. I heard the air forced out of his lungs but didn't hear my weapon discharge."

Ryan glanced at the second suspect. He was small and wiry with shoulders the width of a girl's. His dark hair was curly and his eyebrows thick. A dark brown mustache extended beyond the width of his lips. A morning shadow of heavy beard glossed his otherwise clean shaven chin. Lying prone and immobilized, blood and urine staining his clothes and seeping onto the floor, he looked like a child. If Ryan had seen him walking the streets, he wouldn't have believed him capable of committing a major terrorist act. "That little girl would kill you in a heartbeat," Ryan thought when he recalled the frailness of the suspect.

When English heard Ryan yell, "Get down! Get down!" and then the sound of the first shots fired in rapid succession, Dolan was still wedged outside the bedroom door. As soon as he squeezed inside, English moved to the left and tried to follow, then stopped to avoid a collision. Dwyer had abandoned his post at the entrance to the apartment. Impatient, he urged English ahead, pressing into his shoulders, pushing him into Ryan's back. "Hold it, hold it," English yelled at Dwyer. "I can't get through."

When the shooting stopped and Dolan stepped to the right, English moved around to the left and into the bedroom. By this time, both suspects were immobilized with multiple gunshot wounds. Gunpowder residue hugged the air like thick fog. Its rich, crisp scent mixed with the metallic smell of fresh blood. The odor was distinct but not unpleasant. The small window in the bedroom faced another building and added to the bleakness. Shadows bounced off the walls when the cops moved about. No one dared touch any light switches in the apartment lest they release a surge of electricity and set off an explosion.[3]

English stared at the suspects. A light-colored quilt bunched up on a mattress was stained a deep, wet crimson red. One suspect was holding himself in a fetal position. The other lay at full length, limbs twisted and bent. English could hear both men breathing. One was almost gasping, inhaling in short, shallow bursts like he'd been punched in the gut or broken his ribs. English took out a pair of handcuffs and leaned over, intending to cuff each man, then paused, wishing he had thought ahead to bring protective gloves. The suspects were bleeding out and the place was drenched.

"Does anyone have a spare pair of rubber gloves?" English said aloud.

"Come on. There's a bomb. Just get him cuffed," someone said. English bent over and cuffed both suspects.

"God, I hope there's a bomb," English said aloud, then glanced at Dolan. "How fucked up is that?"

"I hope we haven't shot them for reaching for some figs," Dolan responded. Two people were critically wounded and probably dying, and neither was carrying a knife or gun. He envisioned the headlines, "Two Emergency Service Police Officers Indicted by Grand Jury for Executing Two Middle Eastern Immigrants Reaching for a Pair of Socks."

"Sarg, come here," Dolan said. English walked over and shined his flashlight in the direction that Dolan was pointing. A black backpack lay in the corner of the room. English felt ten pounds lighter. "It was a black bag. That's all I cared about because, no matter what, these guys would have been OK. It was exactly as Chindluri had described so, as far as they were concerned, the shooting was good," English explained.

He bent down and looked at the backpack. The flap was closed so most of the contents were hidden but what he could make out was disturbing: a thin, black box and some metal switches. "That was all we needed to call in the Bomb Squad," English explained.

"I was never so relieved to see a bomb," Dolan recalled. He and Ryan weren't just concerned with whether the shooting was legally justified. Neither officer could easily live with himself knowing he'd killed an innocent man. "We are there to protect and serve. We aren't paid assassins," Ryan explained.

When Ray McDermott heard the first sound of gunshots, he ran through the first building and into the courtyard. By the time he got to the suspects' apartment, the shooting was over and English was dragging the bodies into the kitchen. McDermott looked at the suspects, suppressing all questions but one: were cops hurt? he wanted to know.

"We're OK, but I think we should get these guys out to the ambulance because if we let them bleed to death here, it's not gonna look good," English said.

"Yeah, you're right," McDermott responded, relieved that one less concern remained in his armory. He and English each grabbed an arm and carried the first suspect outside, into the courtyard. McDermott explained,

"There was like a screen-type door that we had to go through and I remember John and I slipped with the guy. I'm a little bigger than John and John is stronger than me, but carrying one guy out, we were sliding in the blood because he was bleeding and a lot of blood was on the floor."

English didn't shy away from confessing his anger at the suspect and admitting he treated him roughly as he and McDermott transported him to one of the ambulances parked on the street. McDermott viewed the events through the lens of a commander intent on presenting his men in a light the public would understand. "But to show what kind of men they were, they tried to treat their wounds," he explained.

"What have you got?" one of the emergency medical technicians (EMTs) inquired when he saw the first bleeding suspect.

"They're shot," English replied, then dropped the man on a stretcher that was lying on the ground. He and McDermott turned around and went back into the building.

o o o o o o

Richie Teemsma and Paul Yurkiw had been sitting in their truck waiting for Emergency Service to call them on the radio. When Ryan first fired his gun, they heard a popping sound and saw muzzle flash coming from inside the building.

"Is that shooting?" Teemsma asked.

"I think so," Yurkiw responded. A few second later, they heard more shots fired in rapid succession.

"Why are gunshots going off?" Teemsma asked.

"Bomb Squad, Bomb Squad!" someone yelled over radio.

Teemsma dove inside their equipment bag to look for his gun, bumping heads with Yurkiw, who was doing the same thing. Teemsma found his Glock and started to run toward the building. Figuring Emergency Service had more than enough heavy weapons, Yurkiw followed unarmed. Both detectives were wearing fire-retardant jumpsuits and no body armor.

Teemsma ran through the front door of the building, into the hallway, then opened the door to the courtyard. He stopped to avoid a collision with the second suspect, whom Ryan and English were dragging into the street.

"Richie, there's something there," English said. Teemsma didn't hear. He felt as though he'd mainlined a quart of adrenaline. "What you see and hear when you're in the thick of it is almost delusional. . . . Everything changes. I don't know if your mind speeds up or what, but everything around you slows down. Too much is going on for you to absorb so it omits things that won't help you survive. . . . At first, I thought that shots were still being fired and I'd run into one of the suspects who was running away," Teemsma explained.

Yurkiw passed Ryan and English in the hallway and caught up with his partner. Emergency Service cops were swarming the courtyard, pointing their weapons up at the people in the first building who were leaning out their windows. The sight of their faces and the smell of burnt gunpowder made Yurkiw uncomfortable. He felt like his chest was on fire and wished he'd taken more time to find his gun.

"Who do I shoot?" Teemsma asked.

"You don't need no stinkin' bullets," Yurkiw said, then laughed to reassure himself. Teemsma lowered his gun and looked toward the opposite side of the courtyard. Mario Zorovic was standing behind the stairway, gesturing with his hands.

"Bomb Squad, get in here!" he yelled. Teemsma and Yurkiw made their way toward the suspects' apartment, grabbing the large portable light which was parked near the door. The residue of gunpowder in the air was dense and pungent. Yurkiw suppressed a wave of nausea and continued inside.

In the righthand corner of the room, Teemsma and Yurkiw saw the black backpack, lying upright against a red crate. The top flap was closed. On top of the crate were a TV and a few odds and ends. Surrounding the bag were a box of Champ trash bags, an empty bottle of Gatorade, a deli coffee cup, a pack of Marlboro cigarettes, some papers, and a large pile of clothes.

Teemsma looked at the mattress that was resting in the far corner of the room. It couldn't have been much more than an arm's length away from the backpack, an easy reach for even a child. The detectives squatted down and looked. "We didn't want to get too personal with it," Yurkiw explained. Protruding from one side was a small rectangular box attached to four toggle switches. One switch was set in the opposite direction from the other three. Neither officer was sure what this meant. It could have been inserted at a different angle or else it was turned on. Teemsma and Yurkiw backed out of the room.

o o o o o o o

"What's up with him?" the paramedic asked when he saw Ryan and English with the second suspect.

"He's shot. He's bleeding out," English replied. They dropped him on the stretcher.

"Let him die," Ryan muttered under his breath. He felt as though he was rolling around in an ocean of fluctuating emotions. When he'd fired the first shots, he'd felt bad for the guy. Then he realized, "The guy wasn't just trying to get away but wanted to get my gun and kill me." Then he wished he'd taken the head shot. Had a bomb gone off, all that would have remained of him was his vest and a chunk of red flesh.

Ryan looked around. The street was exploding in barely organized bedlam. Police vehicles were parked at odd angles all over the block. The Emergency Service officers, who had been positioned outside during the shooting, were holding their ground in case other suspects emerged and tried to escape. The snipers were still poised on the rooftops, looking sweaty and hot. The police helicopter was hovering above their heads with its searchlight on, illuminating the frenzy of uniformed bodies knocking on doors and trying to clear the block.

English and Ryan walked back inside to begin evacuating the rest of the suspects' building. Some residents had already fled their apartments and were wandering in the hall. "There were a lot of people walking around, wearing these light-flowing robes. . . . Many were Arabic. They were just scared. We were scared, too," English said. The cops still didn't know if additional terrorists were hiding inside.

Assuming their same positions in the stack, the six cops climbed the stairs and breached the door to the apartment on the second floor. A man who had been asleep abruptly awoke as the stampede of armed men, looking like commandos, entered his bedroom. Frightened, he jumped out of bed just as Ryan thrust the bunker with the full weight of his body in his direction.

"I levitated him right off his feet, knocked him right out. I didn't know who he was. I felt really bad for the guy." I believe the man's name might have been Masood Mughal. An American citizen originally from Pakistan, he recalled his experience of the raid in an interview in the August 1, 1997, edition of the *New York Times*. "They treated me like a suspect and put me in jail. They asked me my nationality and wouldn't tell me why I was there. I am a peaceful man. I've never heard of such a thing. They took me in only because I am a Muslim."[4] Mughal wasn't alone. Four other Pakistani residents would also be taken to the 8-8 Precinct, interrogated, and later released.

Next door at 234 Fourth Avenue, Maria Ortiz heard the commotion outside and ran to the window and saw the flashing lights, trucks, cars, and more cops in one place than she'd ever seen before. Then she heard her mother's voice calling the family to rush to the street. "A policeman was standing there at our door, telling us to get out of the building because it was in immediate danger," Ortiz explained.[5] She and the other families in the building were loaded on buses and sent to the YMCA.

While the block was being evacuated, the entry team headed down to the basement. By this time the cops had calmed down. The flood of adrenaline that had pumped through their bodies during their first two entries had dwindled to a steady drip. Ryan breached the door first and ordered a terrified couple who were standing in the foyer to get on the floor. Mike Keenan and Mario Zorovic secured them while Ryan and Dolan continued walking to the back of the apartment and entered the bedroom on the right.

Inside, two terrified children were huddled on the bed, wide-eyed and tearful. Ryan moved the bunker out of the way, bent down, and picked up a four-year-old boy and pulled him into his chest as if he were his own. Dolan held on to the second child, a little girl a few years older than his daughter. Ryan spoke Spanish, trying to comfort the children and diminish their fears. "I hugged the shit out of the kid. . . . It was like when you yell at your own child then hug him because you feel so bad," Ryan explained. When both cops walked into the other bedroom and handed the children to their parents, Ryan apologized.

"Lo siento. Toda esta bien. No te preoccupes. Somos la policia." "I felt guilty about having to do this to innocent people," he explained.

"I've never seen anything like it," Ray McDermott told Bill Morange a few minutes later. "Ten minutes after they shot two men, they're holding these kids in their arms and comforting them. . . . You talk about big rough guys. There was a Spanish-speaking family that was being evacuated. A child was crying, a little girl, I believe, and here you have Joe Dolan and Keith Ryan holding the baby, like very calm, doing their job, but making a point to take the time to talk to the children to calm them and calm the family down and reassure them."

o o o o o o o

Before Teemsma and Yurkiw could get to their truck, they were intercepted by McDermott.

"There's no firearm involved," he said. Implicit in his statement was a question they all understood.

"Well, it looks like a working device. So, as far as we are concerned, the device was the weapon. Right now we've got wires and four toggle switches. One is turned in the opposite direction from the others. So it looks like a perp hit the switch and tried to detonate," Yurkiw said.

"It's a good shooting. It could have been shovels and rakes and coffins in there," Teemsma added. Yurkiw went on to explain the cops' rules that helped define who he was. "You know, if it was an empty shoebox or there was nothing in it but flares or it was a hoax, we still would have gone to the wall for them."

Relieved, McDermott began to consider loose ends. He hadn't seen the informant and the cop translator since they'd emerged from the building before the entry went down. He couldn't remember where they were or what he had told them. He sent some cops to look for them but they came back empty-handed. Finally, one of the cops recalled that they'd told them to wait in the counter assault team car. McDermott walked to the van, opened the door, and informed them what had occurred.

Lieutenant Jim Black, the commanding officer of the Bomb Squad, had only been at the scene a few minutes when he saw Yurkiw and Teemsma heading toward their truck. A small, thin, nervous man under normal conditions, his anxiety level had heightened considerably since he'd made rank. Cops are merciless when it comes to mining weakness, and Black was a perfect target. His fears manifested themselves in twitches and ticks, which fueled their imaginations. Some detectives had gone so far as to nickname him "Ricochet Rabbit" because he looked like he was bouncing off walls. "Black was like a super ball in a shoebox," Yurkiw said.

When I found out that Black's boss was inspector John Bajek, I understood his nervousness. Bajek was the type of demanding, high-maintenance superior officer who would fray most cops' nerves. On the positive side, he didn't take kindly to "bullshit" and liked to hear the straight story. The down side was that a lot of cops resorted to lying, cheating, and distorting the facts if it served to limit the amount of time they had to deal with him. Early in his career, Bajek had earned several advanced degrees, which heightened his sense of superiority and set him apart from a lot of his peers whose formal education was limited to a B.A. and a street degree. A smart, slim, handsome man in his prime, Bajek could have had his choice of bright, gorgeous wives or even a harem of beautiful women if he had been a little less shy or self-centered or whatever it was that led him to seem so aloof.

That and some lack of social skill set him apart from the kind of boss that cops tend to appreciate. In terms of officers who were below him in rank or didn't count in his world, he sometimes ignored them as if they weren't there. At others, he burst into angry tirades, and cursed, screamed, and threatened to "do them," that is, kill their careers—if they didn't live up to his expectations. A lot of people hated Bajek. He also had friends, even among subordinates, who idolized him, perhaps, or agreed that he was indeed the smartest man in the department. Regardless of what a lot of cops and commanders thought, most felt a twinge of concern when they saw the dark, misty shadow that haunted his eyes. Beneath his bravado, arrogance, and need for perfection, he sometimes seemed like a sad, lonely man.

When lieutenant Jim Black saw Rich Teemsma walking with a gun in his hand, he cringed and, some claimed, his right eye began to twitch as he worried that he'd have to explain why a Bomb Squad detective, packing a pistol, killed someone. Stranger things had occurred in the NYPD, but not in the squad while he was in command.

"Did you shoot anybody?" he asked.

"No," Teemsma replied. "I'm just going to put this away because I don't have a holster right now. It looks like something is in there, so we're gonna get the camera." Reassured, Black walked to Bajek, groveling, and told him the news.

Teemsma crawled into the front seat of the truck and secured his gun in the bag. He grabbed the Polaroid camera while Yurkiw put in another call to McGuire requesting the extra large bomb suit. The camera and a few tools in hand, the two detectives returned to the suspects' apartment where Teemsma snapped five photos.

"We got some pictures," he said to Black when they got outside. "These are what it looks like now. I don't know what it's going to look like in ten minutes. But these should give you an idea of what the place looks like and what we can see at the moment." Teemsma handed Black three of the Polaroids, furtively palming the other two. Black took the photos to Bajek. That was the last time either detective saw them.

Yurkiw and Teemsma sat in their truck and studied their photos. They had sixty minutes to think while they let the bomb "cook." Most home-made explosives used a sixty-minute kitchen timer to time the detonation.

Bomb technicians therefore usually waited an hour before handling an explosive device. While property might be lost if a blast took place, lives and limbs would be spared.

The extra light from the flash of the camera highlighted something that neither detective had seen in the dim and cluttered space inside the bedroom. What looked like a string of colorless fishing line was extending from the backpack over the carton of trash bags to beneath the pile of clothing and papers.

"We've got a second device," Teemsma said out loud.

"A booby trap," Yurkiw confirmed.

∘ ∘ ∘ ∘ ∘ ∘ ∘

While the bomb cooked, the six Emergency Service cops stood outside on the opposite side of the street, waiting to go to the hospital. Ryan and Dolan were leaning against a car, a few feet away from the other cops. Cops involved in a shooting are typically examined for trauma immediately following the incident regardless of whether they are injured. This policy is part of a union strategy to protect the men from saying too much in the event the incident was ambiguous.

"I don't think they fuckin' know we're here," Ryan said after forty-five minutes of waiting around.

"No. They forgot about us," Dolan confirmed. The shooters were giddy with fatigue, relief, and excitement. The chaos outside seemed hilarious and bizarre. Bosses were talking on cell phones and ordering cops to carry out various tasks, sometimes contradicting each others' directives or duplicating efforts that were already under way.

Between jokes and spasms of laughter, Ryan was beginning a mental process that he would continue for days, replaying the shooting in slow motion, rewinding the tape, and watching it pass through his head again. Like a movie director, he assessed his actions and revised the script, not to change events but to explain to himself and others how and why he'd taken the steps he did. "As a cop you play God out there, deciding who can live and die. You have to be able to handle that. The interaction forges the path . . . what they do . . . that is what helps you make your decision. So it's up to them whether they live or die," Ryan explained.

Dolan spotted a sergeant walking toward them and nudged his partner. The brass on the boss's collar indicated he was from the 7-8 Precinct.

Although the team had met at the 8-8 station house, the job had turned out to be in the 7-8.

"You're the shooters?" the sergeant asked, surprised that no one had yet attended to them.

"Yeah, Sarg," Ryan replied.

"What are you doing here? You shot these guys and nobody's taken you to the hospital?" Both cops burst out laughing, then regained control.

"No. We're just watching the show."

"Get in my car. We're taking them to the hospital," the sergeant said to his driver, who led the way to the parking spot. They piled in the sergeant's car and drove to New York Methodist Hospital on Seventh Avenue in Park Slope, leaving the other members of the team standing alone.

o o o o o o o

A little before 7:00 A.M., Joe McGuire showed up with the extra large bomb suit. He approached Teemsma first and said that he wanted to help handle the job. Teemsma looked at McGuire.

"Tell me you're not serious?" he said, incredulous.

"I've had a lot of experience."

"Where were you at 1:00 in the morning when the job came in?" Teemsma asked, then walked away. "Holy Mary mother of Christ, fuckface Fatty [Joe McGuire] wants his fucking picture in the paper!" Teemsma said.

With the help of Jeff Oberdier and some cops from Emergency Service, the detectives began to suit up. They put on their thick army-green pants. The shoes came next, then the bulky green jackets, which extended from the back of their heads to their thighs. The suits were made of Kevlar with ceramic inserts, and lined with a fire-resistant material to provide the best protection available. Only their hands were exposed.

"Paulie, you don't have to do this," Teemsma said.

"Eat shit! You're not going in without me," Yurkiw responded. Jim Black saw them gearing up and approached the pair.

"There's only one of you going in," he said.

"OK," Yurkiw responded, then surreptitiously told Oberdier and the Emergency Service cops to keep up the work. They helped slip the ballistic helmets over the detectives' heads and make sure they were tucked in under the ceramic epaulets, lining the detectives' necks. In the front of the helmet was a large three-quarter-inch clear-plastic blast-resistant face shield that allowed them to see. Fresh air was pumped in the mask through a hose connected to a small, battery-operated motor affixed to the shoulder of each suit.

The bomb suits weighed about seventy pounds and could get hotter than 115 degrees inside, depending on the intensity of the sun and the temperature. When Teemsma and Yurkiw gathered the X-ray equipment and walked back into the building, it was already 80 degrees outside. Black looked at the officers geared up and heading inside, threw up his hands, and walked away.

Back inside the apartment, Teemsma looked around the small bedroom, trying to figure out where to put the X-ray plates without disturbing the backpack and mound of clothes. He gingerly lifted some shirts off the pile, exposing a large black rectangular bag. He pointed out the monofilament that connected the two devices and carefully stepped around.

Yurkiw stuck a plate in the back of the booby trap. After taking several X-rays, the detectives started to work on the backpack, securing the plates where space would allow, catching its back and sides. They took the X-rays to the courtyard and held them up to the light. The booby trap contained a dark heart-shaped shadow that they couldn't identify. On top or below were a cylindrical canister, coils, small metal springs, and an assortment of wires. Thousands of freckles were sprinkled in the bag. The X-rays of the backpack revealed two or more pipes with a jumble of wires sticking out the one end. Some pelletlike objects were clinging to the stem and accumulating in bunches at the tops. As X-rays are black-and-white and do not reveal depth, they could not tell the color of wires and where most were attached.

The detectives returned to the bedroom and knelt down next to the backpack. They needed a better look to assess the situation and determine how to safely dismantle the device. Teemsma opened the blue plastic clasp attached to the pack and lifted the flap, revealing a closed drawstring on top. Teemsma started to cut the string so they could see inside, then paused with his hand suspended in midair. Yurkiw whacked him with the scissors.

"Cut it," he said. With the noise of the air pumping into his mask, Teemsma couldn't hear but saw him mouth the words. Since 1982, when Senft and Pastorella had been injured, the department had discouraged detectives from working together on the same job. Yurkiw insisted on stretching the rules. "The one thing about Paul is he stayed with me the whole time. I told him to leave. If this goes off then only one of us goes. I didn't want to hurt him. At the same time, I was glad he was there," Teemsma explained.

Teemsma cut the string, and the officers pulled the bag open and looked inside, bumping heads in the process. A web of black wires was extending from the bombs, which were solidly packed with nails. Four extra-large square batteries were wired up and wedged inside. The bomb was in "hang fire," momentarily jammed so any vibration could set it off.

"If you can picture two guys in the vicinity of 250 pounds each and we are kneeling over this package in a bomb suit and we open up the top to see what we are working with. Then we looked at each other, like, 'Oh, shit!' We realized then that we had a live device. We knew as well as anyone else in the Bomb Squad that the bomb suit offers just enough protection so they can find most of you in the event that they are going to have a funeral. That's the bottom line. So we were thinking that we'd better get the hell outside," Teemsma explained.

The detectives walked out of the apartment watching their every step. By the time they reached the street, the temperature inside their suits had raged to 100 degrees, creating pools of sweat in the vacant space at their ankles and wrists and soaking their suits from the inside. They took off their helmets and jackets and dried themselves with a towel. They found a shady spot on the fender of the truck and sat there. A paramedic gave them bottles of cold water and wiped down their foreheads with icepacks.

They rested for fifteen minutes and talked about how to proceed. Initially they wanted to handle the materials remotely, using one of the department's two robots. The battery of the first robot died in the hallway. They couldn't fit the other inside the apartment door. They then decided to rely on the old-school methods that they'd been taught in training and successfully used in the past.

o o o o o o o

Chief Morange, who'd arrived shortly after the shooting and changed in the truck, was standing next to Ray McDermott on the perimeter. He was not happy about the way events were unfolding but was powerless to do anything. A careful by-the-book approach to getting the job done safely had become a rushed event and "people were walking around half-cocked." Suddenly, the beads of sweat that had been accumulating on his brow turned into a stream, flooding his neck and chest and drenching his clean, white uniform shirt. The mayor and the commissioner were getting out of their car and walking up the street.

"This is not good," Morange said, then repeated the words again. He'd seen the Polaroid pictures and been briefed regarding the status of the bombs. The last thing the chief wanted was police commissioner Howard Safir and mayor Rudy Giuliani blown to hell in a blast. Morange asked an Emergency Service cop who was standing nearby to give the pair tactical vests.

A few minutes later, John English saw Safir and Giuliani leaving the Emergency Service truck, parked on the opposite side of the street. Both men were wearing their vests backward. Neither one had on a helmet. The cops standing by the truck were laughing, and English knew that they'd taken revenge for the contract dispute between management and the rank-and-file police union regarding a slew of issues, salary primarily. He took out his cell phone and called his wife, repeating words that she'd heard many times before.

"I'm involved. I might be late."

"Yeah, I'm watching the news."

"I didn't know what it was going to be, but it turned into something big."

"Yeah. Well, I knew when I turned on the news this morning that it was you."

"I'm gonna to be here a long time."

"OK," she said and hung up the phone, relieved. John English would call his wife several more times that day to let her know what he was doing and when he would be getting home.

A herd of brass was flanking the mayor and the commissioner. Mancini was in the middle, eagerly pushing his way to the front. As the captain of Emergency Service, he wanted the brass to know he was "the man" that day. Bajek moved in next, inserting himself beside the mayor. Yurkiw and Teemsma watched as Bajek and Giuliani pulled away and walked to the front of the building. A few minutes later, the detectives got up to look for Jim Black.

"We have to take care of the secondary device first because it's in our way," Teemsma explained.

"No, I want you to take care of the pipe bombs first," Black responded.

"Look, Lieu. We've got a booby trap, a second bomb, and if we don't deal with that first, when we move the first device, it could set the backpack off," Teemsma explained.

"Just do the first device," Black insisted.

"Can't do that, sir. I don't know how it is working exactly, but we're going to do the other one first," Teemsma said.

"Well, if that's what you want to do," Black said.

"OK." Teemsma turned around and rolled his eyes in Yurkiw's direction. "Thank you very much, you ignorant, ass-kissing, motherfucker, please!" Teemsma said once out of earshot. An 8-8 Precinct detective signaled to Teemsma. He was talking on his cell phone and held it out.

"Paulie, I've got one of the guys in the squad on the phone. He's at the hospital talking to one of the perps. The guy wants to talk to you," the detective said.

"The cop?" Teemsma replied.

"The perp. He wants to tell you how to take the bombs apart."

"You're kidding?" Teemsma replied.

"He's fucked up but alive and ready to talk." Yurkiw looked at Teemsma.

"We don't need to have this asshole help blow us apart," Yurkiw said.

"We'll put him on the phone," the officer said.

"No. It's better I don't talk to him. The last thing I need is for this guy to tell me how I am supposed to take this apart because he is just going to fog up our minds," Teemsma said.

He and Yurkiw put on their helmets and jackets and made their way back to the suspects' apartment. Their first task was to disconnect the monofilament so there wouldn't be a "sympathetic" explosion. Teemsma traced the line from the backpack to the secondary device, then carefully cut the line. He hooked a rope to the booby trap, walked outside into the courtyard and upstairs, rigging the line over the banister, across the courtyard to the foot of the first building. After he walked twenty-five feet away, he pulled the bag. It moved a few inches then got stuck.

Teemsma went back inside, gently lifted the bag, then reattached the line, went outside, and started pulling again. When the device got wedged in the frame of the bedroom door, Yurkiw cut up an orange traffic cone and placed it in the crack, providing a cushion to help slide the bag through. The same method was used to ease the way through the door of the apartment. Once the secondary device was in the center of the courtyard, Teemsma pulled again from inside the hallway. The bag flew up, turned upside down, dumping the contents onto the pavement. "You let gravity do your work for you, separating the source of ignition from the explosive device," Teemsma explained.

When the dust settled, Yurkiw and Teemsma walked into the court-yard to examine the materials. The freckles they'd seen in the X-ray were thousands of kitchen matchstick heads that had been broken apart. The canister contained sixteen ounces of explosive powder. The wiring used to heat the device was made from the coils of a hair drier. The heart-shaped object was a padlock someone had tossed inside. It had no explosive value except as a "frag." Dozens of 9-mm bullets were distributed around the canister. Yurkiw and Teemsma stored the pieces of the bomb in a corner, then walked outside.

The temperature had risen inside their suits to 115 degrees. Both detectives were hot and dehydrated and had to take a leak. They took off their helmets, jackets, and pants. They used the bathroom inside a store, then sat on the bumper of the truck. Sweat poured off their faces and burned their eyes. Their jumpsuits stuck to their ribs and legs. The salt made their balls itch. They drank bottles of cold water and paramedics applied cold packs to their foreheads.

Jeff Oberdier stayed by Teemsma and Yurkiw during each break, helping to keep them focused and upbeat. Prior to joining the department, he'd been in the military, on the Explosive Ordinance Disposal Team, and understood the mental aspects of the job. "Obie was dressing and undressing us, asking us questions: What type of firing mechanism was it? What type of wires? Were they speaker, braided, single strand? How are you feeling? Are you feeling weak, sick? He made sure we were in a good frame of mind and knew what we were doing so we didn't go in there thinking, now we're tired, let's just get this thing over with," Yurkiw explained. When McGuire tried to join the three detectives so bosses could see that he was involved, Oberdier blocked his path.

By this time, the situation on the street had calmed down. English, Dwyer, Keenan, and Zorovic had gone to the hospital. The mayor and the commissioner had gone to their offices downtown. Morange felt relieved. The only people around the building were cops and bosses. Only the Bomb Squad detectives were working inside.

A well-built, young female paramedic walked up to Yurkiw and Teemsma and gave them two bottles of cold water, which they promptly poured over their heads. She walked away and they followed her back with their eyes.

"You'd rather be doing that?" asked an Emergency Service cop who was staring in her direction. The detectives looked at each other and laughed. At 9:30 A.M., they were ready to go back inside. The temperature outside had risen to almost 90 degrees.

The backpack was heavier than the secondary device, and every time Teemsma pulled it a couple of inches, it snagged. "I tried to spend the least amount of time with the target but it kept getting hung up and I had to walk in and fix it," Teemsma explained. Eventually, he was able to slide the device around the last orange cone and pull it into the courtyard. Then he stood in the hallway and spun the pack upside down, spilling the contents on to the floor. Four pipe bombs, taped with nails, a canister of black powder, and four large batteries tumbled out, creating a cacophonous echo in their wake.

The detectives moved the second robot into the courtyard and manipulated its arms to separate additional materials. When McGuire butted in, Teemsma handed him the controls. "We'd already done everything, anyway," he said. Teemsma and Yurkiw walked into the courtyard and looked at the bomb. The wires that had extended from the toggle switches to the pipes were long enough to run from the backpack through the sleeve of a man's shirt to his hand. All he had to was flick his fingers to detonate the device. The pellets that had been scattered around the pipes were 9-mm rounds, which would have acted as additional "frags" had the bomb exploded.

Blasts behave differently in open and enclosed areas. In a confined space like a subway car, the damage from such a device could be extensive. Although both devices only contained low-grade explosives, the nails alone would have heated up and been thrown somewhere around twelve hundred feet per second. The bones and body parts of people standing nearby would have turned into frags themselves, causing additional damage.

Yurkiw and Teemsma began to collect the evidence and move it piece by piece to the total containment vehicle (TCV), which was parked outside in front of the building. When they picked up the rectangular box that was attached to the toggle switches they didn't notice a piece of paper that was taped to the inside. Further dismantling of the bombs would have to wait until they got to the range.

Still wearing their bomb suits, the two detectives made several more trips into the courtyard to gather the materials and load up the TCV. They got into their truck and accompanied the bombs to the firing range at Rodman's Neck in the Bronx. The bombs would later be taken further apart and labeled as evidence for future legal proceedings. After they dropped them off, Teemsma and Yurkiw drove to City Island to get something to eat.

"When I bit into the sandwich, my wife and kids came into my head and I just, like, choked and stopped, and I had to hold back the emotion because it hit me all at once. We were almost killed," Teemsma said.

All in all two bags containing explosive devices were found. The primary device consisted of four 9-inch pipes packed with gunpowder and nails and wrapped together. The bombs lacked a timer or remote control detonator, confirming Chindluri's suggestion that the suspects planned to execute the mission in a suicide. One of four redundant switches had been put in the on position but had not gone off. Judging from this evidence, it did appear that the suspects had tried to kill the cops.

According to a front-page article in the New York Times appearing on Friday, August 1, 1997, "Police Commissioner Howard Safir said that the material was powerful enough to kill anyone within 25 feet of detonation in an enclosed space." FBI sources indicated the damage might have been more extensive.

An ominous echo ripped through the streets, unnerving the police as well as the public. The week before, thirteen people had been killed and 170 wounded in a suicide bombing in a Jerusalem marketplace. The same type of terrorist act was nearly unleashed in New York.

The Joint Terrorism Task Force began its investigation immediately. While the final reports would take months to complete, some facts emerged in the first few hours. Abu Mezer had been arrested previously in Israel and accused of being a member of a terrorist organization. Although Hamas denied involvement in the Brooklyn plot, no one knew if the suspects were acting alone or attached to a different terrorist organization. In the wake of the incident, security was boosted at public buildings, including police headquarters and several courthouses.

A thirty-one-year-old nanny interviewed by the New York Times after the raid expressed shock when she learned of the events that had made her late to work. "There are some things you just put out of your mind," she said, trying to process the notion that suicide bombers had tried to attack the subway. "It's almost like death, you don't think about it."[6]

The reaction of civilians and police at the highest ranks of city government was similar. Crime, not terrorism, had been the basis of Giuliani's platform for mayor and remained his major focus of concern. Since the introduction of CompStat (comparative computerized statistics used in the mapping of crime) a few years before, crime had become easier to understand, manipulate, control through the strategic deployment of troops, and present in a positive light in terms of a downward trend.

Only the six cops on the Emergency Service entry team and the two detectives in the Bomb Squad remained preoccupied with the subject of the raid. Keith Ryan and Joe Dolan had seen the icy hatred in the suspects' eyes. John English had felt the warmth of their blood on his bare hands. Rich Teemsma and Paul Yurkiw had shared the same shimmer of fear when they'd opened the bag and realized the bomb was live.

THIS IS GOING
TO HOLLYWOOD

UNDER ORDINARY CIRCUMSTANCES, everything slows down in the wake of a police shooting. Injured parties are taken to the hospital. The crime scene is cordoned off, and detectives are called in to interview witnesses and gather evidence. The Police Department then focuses attention on the cops involved. A boss from the unit, in this case Dwyer, Mancini, or another Emergency Service supervisor, accompanies the team to the hospital and ensures they are properly treated.

The job at 248 Fourth Avenue was anything but ordinary. The crisis seemed to extend for hours. The cops on the scene were busy working sniper details, searching for other terrorist suspects, evacuating buildings, and dealing with bombs. The 7-8 Precinct sergeant who'd transported the officers to Methodist Hospital had returned to the scene, leaving Ryan and Dolan to deal with the medical staff themselves. The officers walked into the emergency room and headed toward the desk where the triage nurse was filling out paperwork. She looked up when they approached.

"Yes?"

"We just shot somebody," Ryan said.

"OK," she said, then resumed processing forms. The two cops stood there, waiting for direction. Five minutes later, she raised her head and gestured toward the row of half-empty chairs.

"Well, sit down over there and wait, and we'll get you registered."

"Registered? We're not patients," Ryan responded.

"What are you, then?" the nurse asked.

"Patients?" Ryan laughed, and turned to his partner. The nurse returned to her work. They didn't sit down. It would take a shoehorn to fit Dolan in one of the hospital's puny plastic chairs, and they didn't want to mingle. It seemed that everyone had a story to share about some cop somewhere who'd been rude or written them an unfair ticket. It had been five years since the beating of Rodney King in Los Angeles, but strangers would bring up the incident as if it had happened yesterday, and in New York. Worse was the love-crazed look of the cop buff and that inevitable question, "Have you ever killed anyone?"

Twenty minutes more of standing around and Dolan's annoyance had reached a fever pitch. A part of him wanted to grab the nurse by her frizzy brown hair and nail her face to a television screen so she'd see what they'd done and why they were there.

"Do you believe this shit?" he asked.

"We're patients," Ryan said, shrugging his shoulders.

"They don't know what to do with us."

"No. They don't have a fucking clue." The hospital was in Brooklyn South, a police borough command that was composed of a number of high-crime precincts in which police-involved shootings sometimes occurred, and so the officers couldn't understand why the medical staff didn't have the protocol down. In response to my inquiry, a commander explained that Methodist wasn't a level-one trauma center and a lot of its surgeons had never handled a bullet hole unless they'd done a residency at King's County, St. Vincent's, or Bellevue hospitals. For that reason, the police didn't usually bring wounded suspects there or go there themselves when police-involved shootings occurred. The commander also suggested that the unusual nature of the raid and the fact it involved terrorists and bombs might have absorbed resources that might otherwise have been devoted to facilitate the medical processing of members of the team.

"I can't believe this shit!" Dolan crossed his arms. Ryan looked at his partner's face and started to laugh. A shadow had seeped into Dolan's eyes and his pupils contracted to pinholes like they always did when he was getting impatient and angry. Ryan glanced at a young black man, seated in the waiting area, wearing a T-shirt and worn pair of jeans. Open in his lap was a tinfoil package of cooked roti, a Trinidadian specialty. The scent of goat or lamb mixed with some putridly sweet-smelling hospital disinfectant poisoned the air.[1]

"She don't give a shit. Why are we here, anyway?" Dolan asked, glaring at the triage nurse.

"We're traumatized. It says so in the *Patrol Guide*."[2] The union rules regarding the hospital visit seemed just short of ridiculous at times like this. They were veteran Emergency Service cops involved in a "good shoot-ing" and didn't need time to collect their thoughts and get their stories together in preparation for the investigation. It irritated them to be stand-ing around, twiddling their thumbs, waiting for an examination they didn't need.[3] Ryan and Dolan waited another ten minutes before a nurse came out and directed them into a small office. She dropped the shades to cover the windows and took down their names and a brief medical history. When she left, the officers squeezed into the seats and waited for the doctor there. Soon, other Emergency Service cops began to drop by to say hello and give them the latest news. The first one to arrive came with a request from the Bomb Squad.

"Richie wants to know if either of you guys touched the backpack," he asked. "No," Ryan responded.

"No," Joe confirmed. "Why? Someone tamper with the bomb?"

"They think that one of the toggle switches was put in the on position," the cop responded.

"Yeah? Does that mean what I think it does?" Ryan asked.

"They don't know why it didn't go off," the cop confirmed.

"Holy shit! Holy fuckin' shit!" Ryan replied.

"It looks like there are two bombs. They found a trip wire extending from the backpack underneath a pile of clothes."

"Holy fuck!" Ryan said.

"Jesus Christ, I must have been standing on top of it," Dolan said. Two more Emergency Service cops entered the room, wide grins expanding their cheeks making them look like blowfish.

"What the hell did you guys do in there? You really fucked them up good! How many rounds did you guys let off?" one asked.

"Five and two from the Mini-14," Ryan responded. He had to stop and think how many times he'd pulled the trigger because he couldn't use sound to measure. *How did I only hear a small pop-pop from a Mini-14? Even on the range when they wore ear protection, the noise of the rifle was deafening.*

"When was the last time you looked at yourselves in a mirror?" another cop asked. Ryan looked down at his shirt and noticed the stains for the first time. Blood had spilled from his vest onto his uniform shirt. "Remember those light-blue shirts? I wonder what genius at One PP came up with those. Good thing Bratton came along or we'd still be in light blues, pack-ing six-shot revolvers."[4]

"You're walking pathogens. They ought to quarantine you guys. God only knows what those shit bags are carrying in their blood." Ryan thought of the suspect he'd first shot. "He [Abu Mezer] had no fear. Cops lose their edge when there is no fear," Ryan told me later.

"Yeah, boss?" One of the cops pulled a vibrating cell phone out of his pocket and answered the call. "That's affirmative. 10-4." He put the phone away and announced that he and his partner had to leave. They'd just been assigned to King's County Medical Center to guard the suspects, who had come out of surgery and were lying, restrained, in the hospital prison ward. Doug Connolly and his partner, Lou "the Chief" Piazzo, came in shortly after the other cops left.

"Hey, Baba, how's it goin'?" one of the cops asked. Ryan smiled. Everybody liked Doug "Baba" Connolly, although they wondered how a sweet guy like him could put up with his overbearing partner five-plus nights a week. Not that Piazzo wasn't a competent E-man, but his attitude grated on a lot of guys' nerves.

"Good, we're good," Ryan responded, then noticed the mortified look on Piazzo's face and gave him a reassuring nod. He and Connolly had been working the midnight shift but hadn't been notified about the raid. Not until after the shooting did they realize what they had missed.

"I should have been there, damn it! You're my guys," Piazzo pleaded.[5]

"Ahh, nice of you to show up. I hope you got a good night's sleep," another cop said.

"What are you saying?" Piazzo replied, jaws clenched tight and his neck red as a bell pepper. He felt bad inside, like a kid excluded from a party or a freshly trained Marine who stays on base when the rest of his company's going to war.

"Lou, it ain't your fault, and everybody knows it ain't your fault. He's just breakin' your balls," Ryan intervened. He loved Emergency Service, but some of the things that the guys did to each other sometimes got under his skin. God help the cop in the unit who was different or who displayed even the tiniest weakness. They would prey on him like sharks in a feeding frenzy.

Forty-five minutes later, a nurse came in and announced that the doctor was ready to see them. The other officers scattered when a tall Pakistani doctor walked in, wearing a stethoscope around his neck. He introduced himself and proceeded with the examination, wrapping the blood pressure device around Ryan's biceps and pumping it up.

"What is your blood pressure normally?" he asked

"117 over 70," Ryan replied.

"It's 117 over 70. Is this normal?" the doctor asked.

"Yeah, I'm like this all the time."

"You're 117 over 70?"

"Yes."

"That's what it is now." The doctor shook his head, surprised that it wasn't higher, then checked Ryan's pulse.

"54?" the doctor said, an incredulous look seeping into his face.

"I run," Ryan said, explaining why his pulse was lower than average.

"You feel faint?"

"No, I feel normal."

The doctor picked up an instrument and put it into each of Ryan's ears. "Can you hear OK?"

"Yes."

"Any ringing? Unusual sound?"

"No."

"I've never seen such clean cars."

"What?" Ryan replied, confused.

"Your ears are so clean."

"I bathe, Doc. I've got good hygiene, what can I tell ya? My mother raised me right." The doctor put down the instrument.

"OK, you're fine," he said, directing Dolan to give him his arm. "He's fine, too," the doctor said after the examination. He put away his instruments and left the room, closing the door behind him. Dolan pulled out his cell phone and called his wife to give her an update and see how their daughter was doing. Ryan remembered he hadn't yet spoken to his mother. He figured she might turn on the TV and get alarmed. He decided to call his sister so she could reassure their mother that he was OK. His sister answered on the first ring.

"Hey, sis, everything's fine. But I wanted to tell you before you heard it on the news. We shot somebody."

"Where are you?" she asked.

"Methodist Hospital."

"Why are you there?" his sister asked. He heard his mother's voice in the background, but he couldn't make out her words.

"No reason. It's routine. They check you for trauma."

"We're five minutes away."

"You're kiddin'?"

"Mom has an appointment with the doctor, remember?" Oh shit, he thought. Just my luck. The same day I shoot someone, my mother's at the hospital. He could feel the sharks circling and looked over his shoulder, glanced at his partner and pointed to the door.

"I'll meet you in the parking lot," Ryan said to his sister, and hung up the phone. He put on a thin navy-blue NYPD jacket to cover his shirt and walked out into the daylight. He started to sweat and wiped the moisture away from his eyes, then looked down to avoid the sun, which had bounced off the car mirror and struck him in the face. He waved when he spotted his mother and sister walking toward the hospital entrance.

His sister was a half-foot taller than his mother and slim, with long legs, shoulder-length brown hair, and a face that ended up implanted in the brain of every man she met. He'd had to run interference more than once to protect her from the Neanderthal cops who came sniffing around, ready to impale anything wearing a skirt. How's your sister? they'd ask. Don't even think about coming near my sister, Ryan would say with an icy look in his blue eyes.

"Ma, I'm OK. I'm really OK."

"Yeah?" his mother asked, wondering why he was telling her this.

"I'm here, and I'm OK," Ryan repeated. She stood stiffly, preparing for the worst and waiting for him to explain. "Joey and I were involved in a shooting. These guys had bombs. I shot them both. Joe shot one guy too. No one was hurt." Her face started to crumble.

"It was you? I knew it was you. Are you OK?" she asked.

"Mom, don't cry. I'm talking to you. Everything's fine. We're both doing all right."

"What are you doing here then?" she asked.

"Routine check, ears, blood pressure. They do that when you've been involved in a shooting. We're done now. We're waiting for someone to pick us up and take us to the precinct." Ryan thought of the examination and started to laugh.

"This isn't funny," she scolded, but her eyes had dried and her face looked put together again. They talked a few minutes more before Ryan said good-bye and rejoined his partner inside. Not long after he left his family, the police commissioner's driver, a former Emergency Service cop, opened the door and gave them the heads up.

"The commissioner's coming," he said. Ryan and Dolan tucked in their shirts and waited. A few minutes later Howard Safir walked in, followed by his driver. The rest of his security detail waited outside. The commissioner looked different that day. His lips were turned up at the edges, inflating his cheeks and creating wrinkles and pits on either side of his mouth, signs of pleasure in an otherwise sometimes unreadable, perpetually taciturn face.

"You guys did a great job. You're real heroes. This city is safer because of what you've done." The two cops stood frozen at attention, barely absorbing the words from the department Top Cop who was as close in their eyes to God as they expected to get in this lifetime, regardless of the ambivalence Safir provoked as their leader and a person. As soon as he left, a few minutes later, the rumors began to fly. Nobody is sure where they started but people think that they began with a nod from Chief Morange, who had spoken to the police commissioner several times. The rumors soon took on a life of their own as cops swallowed them whole and spit them out in sometimes new form; rank-and-file officers on the entry team were getting promotions to detective; bosses and cops were all getting medals; Mancini was going to be appointed deputy inspector. Private photo ops were being scheduled with the commissioner, the first deputy commissioner, and the chief of the department. Hopes were high and expectations spiraling to the moon.

Keith Ryan, Joe Dolan, John English, Mario Zorovic, Mike Keenan, and Larry Dwyer had woken up that morning intent on doing their jobs. Now they were standing victorious, looking out at a clear blue sky, like high-altitude climbers perched on the peak of Mt. Everest. In all the excitement, no one thought how quickly the weather can change.

o o o o o o o

Ryan's cell phone rang and he answered, expecting a message from a cop telling them to come outside because they were ready to pick them up. Instead, he heard the voice of a buddy who'd once been on the job and now worked freelance for the "Agency," the Central Intelligence Agency (CIA).

"Hey, Keith. I heard what happened. You OK?"

"I'm fine. We're still at the hospital but should be leaving soon."

"Look, I don't have a lot of time to talk, so I want you to listen and listen good. There's more to this than those guys. You don't know who is watching all this. So whatever you do, don't go out there gloating, like you enjoyed hitting these guys."

"You know that's not me."

"There are guys out there who will kill you for looking at them cross-eyed, you and your whole family. We don't know who else is over here."

"This isn't a personal thing," Ryan protested.

"Not for you it isn't. These guys aren't any different from those Israeli psychos who whacked anyone caught eating pita and pine nuts after the Munich massacre. The guys you shot don't have squat. They must have had help to get here and buy those bombs."

"I'll watch my back," Ryan said and hung up the phone. He didn't realize his pulse had jumped to eighty and that a worried look was paving a road in his face. Not long after, John English got a similar call from a government operative "with direct involvement in the Middle East," informing him that the suspects were linked to a terrorist group there and had come to the United States with financial support from the organization for "the purpose of causing harm."[6]

o o o o o o o

Meanwhile, while Ryan and Dolan were talking to their families, English, Zorovic, Keenan, and Dwyer were in another room in the hospital being examined for trauma. All of them checked out fine except for Dwyer, whose blood pressure was camped in the stratosphere.

"Let's get outta here," he said as the doctor unwrapped the blood pressure device from his arm.

"You can't leave. Your blood pressure is high," the doctor said.

"It's always like this," Dwyer replied. The doctor shook his head and put his hand on the lieutenant's shoulder.

"You need to lie down. Your blood pressure is dangerously high," he said.

"My blood pressure is always high. That's normal," he said, struggling to get on his feet.

"Look, this is serious. You need to stay here for observation."

"Observation? Forget it. I'm fine."

"I want you to lie down. You need to be on medication. One of you, please, go get a nurse. We need a nurse here. Your blood pressure is incredibly high. You have to lie down."

"Lieu, you gotta lie down like he says. We won't leave you, I promise," one of the cops teased. Dwyer gave him a menacing glower and maybe the finger as well.

"No, I'm not doing it," Dwyer said and popped off the table like it was a hot plate. The doctor shook his head, made a notation in his chart, and left the room. Just as he was closing the door, the cops burst into hysterical laughter, which echoed down the halls.

o o o o o o o

The 8-8 station house is located on the corner of Classon Street and DeKalb Avenue across from a large brick housing project that looks like every other low-income public housing project in New York City.[7] Dolan and Ryan got out of the car and walked toward the American flag flying near the door. Ryan looked up at the tower that soared above the brown cinderblock base of the building. A small round window was etched into the red brick, close to the top. "All you need is a moat to keep out the assholes," and the building would look like a small-sized medieval castle, a cop explained.

Ryan nodded at the desk sergeant as he made his way through the entrance, passed the locker room, and into the muster room straight ahead. The latest legal and procedural bulletins from the *Patrol Guide* were attached to clipboards hanging from one of the walls near an assortment of sector maps depicting arrests for larceny, narcotics, assault, and homicide. A small black-and-white television rested on a shelf spewing a steady drone of talk show conversation to empty rows of blue plastic chairs. The bulletin boards that laced the walls were pasted with mug shots and wanted posters. Adjacent to the muster room was a bathroom. A used hospital glove and crumpled papers littered its floor and a garden of greasy, brown crud and green algae was growing at the base of the toilet.

Ryan opened the door, went inside, splashed water on his face, washed his hands, and then walked back out to the front desk. Two cops escorting a handcuffed prisoner were talking to the sergeant. Maybe the suspect was crazy or stupid or stoned because he was shouting in a high-pitched voice and fat-mouthing the cops. His curses echoed up the back stairwell until one of the officers pulled the suspect's handcuffed arms up behind his back and threatened to throw him into the East River if he didn't shut the fuck up.

A few minutes later, they accompanied him down a hallway to the left and into holding cells that looked like people-sized versions of the cages that house monkeys in research laboratories. They stuffed the prisoner inside one and locked the gate. He pressed his face against the metal grating, creating a Swiss cheese pattern on his face. Further down the hall, to the right, was a room that contained the original 1930s cells with their old wrought iron doors still intact. Not long before, it had been closed by OSHA, the Occupational Safety and Health Administration, because of problems with ventilation. Now the room was used for storing junk that cops had scavenged but didn't want to bring home to their wives.

Ryan and Dolan headed up the steep flight of stairs in the back of the precinct. When they reached the squad room on the second floor, they saw some of the Emergency Service cops on the team, standing around, mingling with the detectives. The detectives, some of whom were old-timers in their mid- or late forties, were sharing stories about the history of the precinct they'd been told when they were rookies.

"I'm telling you they were collared right here," one detective explained. "They lived over in the Fort Green projects. Yeah, the perps who died in the Attica prison riots. Three out of the forty guys who died were from the 8-8." In more than twenty years on the job, the detective had watched as gentrification continued to alter the face of north and south Brooklyn while the housing projects seemed to remain the same; a bureaucrat's fantasy of affordable homes for the urban poor turned into felony breeding grounds that helped train police recruits and keep the prisons in business.

Ryan felt something hit his head and looked up beyond the crown moldings. The white paint that covered the patterned tin ceilings was peeling in sheets like snakes shedding their skin. He combed his fingers through his short hair and brushed out the flakes. Despite its cramped interior and austerity of furnishing, the room looked warm and inviting in the daytime with the sun shining brightly through the oblong windows. At night, it looked different because the rectangular blocks of fluorescent lighting emitted a surgical glow that highlighted the shabbiness of the linoleum floors and the paint peeling off the window frames.

"Clinton wants us in there," Dolan said, referring to the officer assigned to interview the officers and write the incident report. He and Ryan made their way through the desks that were arranged back-to-back and used by several detectives who worked different shifts. Lawyers from the district attorney's office were starting to mill around. One detective alerted Ryan that agents from the FBI and the Bureau of Alcohol, Tobacco and Firearms (AFT) were somewhere downstairs, waiting to talk to the cops on the entry team. Ryan and Dolan squeezed in the tiny interview room, which contained a table, two chairs, and a hand wrought iron bench. A water pipe extended from the ceiling to the floor in the corner. The squad detectives had used it to anchor handcuffed prisoners during interrogations until a lawsuit was filed alleging that the pipe was too hot. Now the bench was the officers' hitching post.

The interrogation that deputy inspector Francis Clinton was required to conduct of Ryan and Dolan is called a GO-15. This refers to general order 15, a section in the old *Patrol Guide*, which stipulates the rights of police officers questioned in departmental proceedings: a union delegate must be present, and if requested, an attorney; questions must pertain only to the officers' employment; and statements made during a GO-15 cannot be used against the officer in the event of a criminal trial.

The interview was short and to the point. The officers told Clinton what happened. They identified themselves as cops and fired their weapons in self-defense. All the rounds missing from the cops' weapons had been accounted for, and bombs had been found in two bags. Before he terminated the interview, Clinton learned that the officers had been admitted to the hospital under their own names. Apparently, Chief Morange had requested the incident be treated like an undercover operation. Concerned about exposure, Clinton left the officers in the 8-8 and drove to Methodist Hospital.[8] He discussed the matter with hospital administrators, who agreed to delete the cops' and bosses' names from the medical charts and computer records.

A few hours later, when he began to write up the "49" police incident report, Clinton used position numbers to refer to the officers. "Because of the sensitive nature of the ongoing investigation regarding suspected terrorist(s) in possession of explosive devices, all information identifying Law Enforcement Personnel will be deleted from this report."[9] Ryan was referred to as position one, Dolan as two, and so on down the stack. Only three of the bosses who played roles in the raid were identified by name: Nick Mancini, Charles Kammerdener, and William Morange. Ray McDermott did not appear in the credits under Emergency Service, probably by his own humble volition. His name did appear among the group of high-ranking bosses, starting with the mayor and the police commissioner, who eventually came to the scene.

o o o o o o o

Lou Anemone, the chief of the department and the highest-ranking uniformed member of the service, wasn't on the list of those present during or after the raid. Not because he didn't want to be there. He was thousands of miles away, enjoying a hard-earned vacation with his wife and friends on the sunny beaches and high-rise hotels of Cancun.

When he heard the news, he was sitting on a bus on his way back to the hotel after eating breakfast. A fit, slim man about six feet tall in his late forties, Anemone was dressed in a red-striped polo shirt and hand-pressed chinos. He had a youthful appearance, slightly weathered skin, vibrant eyes, and short, kinky brown hair that was beginning to gray at the temples. Even in the morning, his tan face bore the shadow of the heavy beard he sometimes had to shave twice a day. An infectious smile covered the width of his narrow face whenever he thought about the days when he was a cop on the street or a four-star "super chief" during the tenure of former police commissioner Bill Bratton.

Feared, loathed, loved, sometimes by the same people at the same time, Anemone was known as a no-nonsense commander with a deep love for cops. Impatient, blunt to the point of abrasive at times, he was a gutsy leader—or detractors would say a "loose cannon"—who was willing to speak his mind, even to superiors with whom he disagreed. An intelligent and well-read man when it came to academic studies of the police, he wasn't afraid to entertain new ideas that didn't come from inside the ranks. Whatever his flaws, no one had any doubt that Anemone had made a significant contribution to the department at a critical time in its history when police were developing new tools to fight crime.

Anemone's rise through the ranks began when he was assigned the task of ending the Crown Heights riots in 1991. After three days of looting and multiple injuries, Mayor David Dinkins said he had "had enough." The riots were sparked by a hit-and-run traffic accident. A car driven by a member of the Hassidic Orthodox Jewish community sped through an intersection and killed a seven-year-old Guyanese boy, igniting racial tensions that had been festering for years. Anemone arrived with fresh troops and joined his men before the burgeoning crowd. Speaking through a megaphone, he assured the demonstrators that their rights would be honored but warned them they would be locked up if they broke the law. "That first night we made twenty or thirty arrests, and broke up the groups that were engaging in illegal activity. That ended the riots," Anemone explained. His cops loved his fearlessness. According to popular legend, he led them through the neighborhood, reclaiming the street "block by block."[10]

When Bill Bratton was appointed police commissioner in January 1994,

Anemone became the chief of Patrol. Retirements and promotions soon resulted in an empty spot in the position of chief of the department, and Anemone's name came up. Bratton's plan to appoint someone else was aborted when Mayor Giuliani intervened on Anemone's behalf. "That was the best decision I never made," Bratton told Anemone several years later.

NYPD politics becomes tougher as cops move up in rank. Each new administration appoints their own top commanders and flushes out those they fear have conflicting loyalties. When Giuliani forced Bratton out of the department and appointed Safir police commissioner, the ball kept rolling, as it often does with a change in administration, knocking down a generation of respected commanders. First deputy commissioner John Timoney was forced to retire, and Tosano Simonetti took his place. At this point, the sands had begun to shift, and Anemone was increasingly vulnerable as he and Simonetti didn't get along.

To Anemone's relief, Simonetti retired in 1998. According to journalist Leonard Levitt, Giuliani urged Safir to appoint Bernie Kerik to take his place, but in a rare act of rebellion, Safir declined, referring to Kerik as "a thug" who didn't belong in a position of power; or, according to a well placed commander, Safir said no because "Bernie Kerik has too much baggage." Instead, Safir appointed the chief of Detectives, Patrick Kelleher, as first deputy commissioner of the department.[11] At first, Anemone was pleased by the appointment because he thought that he and Kelleher were friends. Some said Kelleher had a Machiavellian leadership style, while others claimed he was a smart politician with some personal flaws who did what he had to do to protect himself and the commissioner. Certainly Kelleher was "fiercely loyal" and willing to do whatever he could to please his boss. At some point, the demands of politics appeared to nullify those of his friendship with Anemone, who would soon find himself out of the loop.

o o o o o o o

Anemone was moving slowly through the mass of Mexican traffic, which was creating a cloud of pollution that made Los Angeles smog look like morning dew. The bus had been under way for less than ten minutes when a travel companion asked what was happening in New York. He'd woken up early that morning and heard the news on CNN. Anemone had nothing to add. He hadn't been notified.

When he arrived at the hotel, he and his wife retired to a quiet corner of the lobby. At this point, he didn't know if there'd been an explosion. It was 10:00 A.M. when Anemone dialed his office on his cell phone. Inspector Jessie Peterman answered the call.

"Jessie, what's going on? I heard there was a shooting and bombs were involved."

"Chief, there was no explosion. There was a plot to blow up the subway, but it was aborted. The perps were caught prior to leaving the apartment."

"Who's involved?"

"Chief Kammerdener, Nick Mancini, a team from Emergency Service, and the Bomb Squad. Emergency Service entered the place early this morning. The perps got shot. The cops are fine. Clinton's either at the scene or at the 8-8 Precinct. He's the duty inspector."

"Frank?"

"Yeah?" Peterman responded. Anemone sighed. "Has everybody been apprehended?"

"As far as we know, yes, but the investigation is still going on." Peterman recounted the details of what transpired, which were a matter of public record. Shortly after they finished talking, Anemone telephoned Clinton.

"Frank, it's Lou Anemone. I want you to fax the "unusual" [the 49 incident report]."

"I can't do that, Chief. We got a security issue here," Clinton replied.

"There's nothing confidential in that report. Now fax me the 49!"

"We're talking terrorists here."

"Are the cops' names on the 49?"

"No."

"Is the informant's name on the 49?"

"No."

"Then send the fucking fax!"

"I'm not gonna do that, Chief."

"What are you talking about? It's all over CNN. The whole fuckin' world knows what happened!"

"The investigation is ongoing. I don't think it's a good idea."

"You're being ridiculous. Now I'm telling you to fax me the 49." Exasperated, Anemone's voice got shrill and caught his wife's attention. She raised her eyebrows.

"Lou, what's going on?" she asked. Anemone held up two fingers, signaling for her to wait.

"Can't do that, Chief," Clinton repeated.

"What the fuck is wrong with you? You want to end up a duty captain in Brooklyn North?" Anemone uttered an empty threat he knew he'd never follow up.

"Well, that won't get me to fax that thing," Clinton responded.

"Asshole!" Anemone muttered and put down the phone. His fists were clenched, and his suntanned knuckles had turned pearl white.

"Tell me what's going on?" his wife asked.

"This fuckin' jerk doesn't understand this is not a secret anymore and he's refusing to fax the 49." She put her hand on his shoulder and looked him in the eye.

"Lou, it's over with, anyway. We'll take care of it when we get back," she said. She was his anchor when the seas got rough, and his anger started to dissipate. There were other people in his career who knew how to sooth the tempest that raged inside when he felt frustrated and out of control, his secretary for one. When he was starting to go "bonzo" and raise his voice, she'd stick her head in his office and tell him his cursing could be heard in the halls. In seconds, he'd calm down.

Bill Bratton was another. The only time he ever took Anemone "into the woodshed" and dressed him down was after a bad joke backfired during a CompStat meeting. Inspired by Jack Maple in the 1990s and introduced by Bratton during his first months in office, CompStat utilized statistical mapping techniques to examine patterns of crime so bosses could target particular spots and bring the numbers down. Once every few weeks, a police commander would stand up at the podium in the "War Room" at One Police Plaza and explain to a circle of top brass what he was doing to reduce crime.

Anemone and Jack Maple's prank, which resulted in Anemone being verbally disciplined by Bratton, involved projecting a cartoon image of Pinocchio on the giant screen behind the podium. When Borough Commander Tosano Simonetti opened his mouth and tried to explain the "stats" in his precincts, Pinocchio's nose grew long and thin. Seeing the odd expression on the faces of superiors, Simonetti turned around and saw what was going on. Irate, he spoke his mind, then stormed out of the room. Most other times when Bratton heard that Anemone was getting wound up, he would tell him to put on civilian clothes and take him out for an informal breakfast. They'd talk about what was going on in the department, and Anemone would cool down. Several years passed before he learned that the timing of their meetings wasn't coincidental.

Anemone put away his cell phone and looked out into the hotel lobby. He and his wife took the elevator up to their room, put on their bathing suits under some clothes, and joined their friends on the beach. Every now and then someone would reveal a hidden detail about the raid that Anemone hadn't heard, from the number of men on the entry team to the names of the cops involved, and ask him what he knew.

"The only thing I know is what you're hearing on CNN. It's in good hands. No need for me to get crazy," Anemone would respond. Most of the time, he was able to maintain his equilibrium, stop thinking about police business, and enjoy his vacation. But every now and then when he was stretched out in front of the vast blue sea in Cancun, he would start to think about the bikini-baring, radio-blasting masses packing the beaches of Coney Island. Then his mind would wander north into the heart of Brooklyn. A shadow would pass over his eyes and the sun would disappear in a cloud of ominous memories.[12]

He had been on the Brooklyn Bridge in 1994 right after an eighteen-year-old Hasidic student was shot in the head by a Palestinian extremist. The boy had been in a van with fourteen of his friends when the suspect pulled up alongside and opened fire with a 9-mm semiautomatic pistol. Although the shooter was caught, Anemone wasn't sure the investigation had gone far enough. "Was there a link between the shooting and other terrorist incidents?" he wondered. "Were the participants tied to an organization?"

The year 1990 had brought alarming events as well. Rabbi Meir Kahane, founder of the Jewish Defense League and leader of a militant anti-Arab movement in Israel, had been assassinated. The murder took place during a Zionist conference at the Marriott Hotel in midtown Manhattan. The chief of Detectives said the assassin, El Sayyid a Nosair, was acting alone. Anemone wasn't so sure and, as a result, was less than satisfied when they closed the investigation shortly after Sayyid was shot and apprehended.

Anemone put down his book and walked to the edge of the beach. He dove in the crystal clear ocean and stood waist deep with his feet on the sand. New York shores weren't nearly as pleasant. Masses of jellyfish invaded Coney Island in August and condoms always littered the shallow waters where people swam. Reiss Park looked better because the water was too dark to see the bottom. Distance swimmers who raced in the river waters around Manhattan once braved an endless series of needles to fortify themselves against the mounds of pollution that raged more formidable than the currents. Now the water was clean enough that all they needed was a pair of goggles and a tetanus shot to do the twenty-eight-mile swim. Still, even if Anemone had been a swimmer, he doubted he would have done the marathon. He'd seen too many floaters—ripe, bloated human bodies with their eyeballs half-eaten by fish or the rats that infested the rocks along the riverbanks.

His thoughts shifted to the rats he saw in the basement after the World Trade Center bombing in 1993, big fat scavengers guzzling the food that had been blown out of the building's commissary. Anemone recalled trudging through the filthy puddles that had flooded the area after the water pipes broke in the blast. He had been at a meeting at One Police Plaza about the new riot plans when the terrorists drove the van into the parking garage and the bomb went off, collapsing floors and creating a huge pit. He'd quickly headed toward the Operations and Command and Control Center on the eighth floor to find out what was going on.

"Chief, I'm glad to see you!" the desk lieutenant said when Anemone walked inside.

"What's happening?" Anemone asked.

"It looks like a transformer explosion. There's a lot of smoke." Anemone began to set up parameters and assign cops to traffic control. Then he got an order from his friend and mentor, Mario Selvaggi, the chief of Patrol.

"The guy who replaced you in SOD doesn't know his ass from his elbow," Selvaggi said. "I want you to handle this and coordinate with the Fire Department."[13]

Anemone's first order of business was giving the commander of the Special Operations Division (SOD) tasks he could handle, like controlling the landing zone on West Street so the helicopters could fly in. Next, Anemone talked to the Emergency Service cops who wanted to execute a rescue but needed clarification and clearance from a boss.

"OK, so I understand the elevators are out?"

"Yeah, Chief. They're out."

"Is somebody there from the elevator company? Do we have mechanics?"

"They're on their way, but, yeah, we have a whole team of mechanics."

"Can we put them on the roof?"

"Well, yeah, but the thing is, Chief, we gotta practice."

"We do have a high-rise rescue plan?" Anemone asked.

"We do, but we never practiced it. We never did."

"OK. Well, now is the time. We'll fly up a sergeant and a cop to rappel from the helicopter onto the roof." Anemone turned to the sergeant. "You and [Rodney] Gillis cut the antennas and prepare a landing zone on the roof of One and Two World Trade Center. Then we'll airlift a team of ESU and Otis mechanics up to the roof. We can put up rescue teams on the choppers and evacuate anyone who can't use the stairs." After the mission got underway, Anemone joined the police commissioner and deputy mayor and gave them a briefing. Then he met with the Fire Department. Just as he was leaving the meeting, he felt a tug on his sleeve and stopped. An Emergency Service sergeant had grabbed hold of his arm, trying to get his attention.

"Chief, you got to help us," he said.

"Hold it. Wait a minute," Anemone said. The sergeant let go of his sleeve. "Now tell me, what's going on?"

"You gotta help us! The fucking Fire Department is screwing around again. We have some bodies downstairs in the basement. The Fire Department is giving us shit about moving the bodies to the temporary morgue."

"OK, let's go." Anemone slipped on boots and walked into the garage. The fire battalion chief was standing around, surveying the wreckage. Cars had been blown apart and upside down, and busted pipes were sticking out all over the place. Some dust-covered red chairs were lying on the ground next to a mass of debris and plastic dishes.

"What's going on, Chief? What's the issue here? My sergeant is tellin' me he wants to move bodies to the temporary morgue," Anemone said.

"Well, we're in charge here. This is a collapsed building. That's our responsibility. We'll handle this *our* way," the fire chief replied. Anemone jerked his head back and then gave him a piercing look.

"What are you, a fuckin' dope? Look around. What do you think this is, a transformer fire? You have to be kidding! Smell it! This is a crime scene."

"Now, look. We've got this all worked out. We're gonna—"

Anemone interrupted the fire chief midsentence. "—No. This is what we are going to do. We are going to take these bodies to the temporary morgue, and we're doing it now."

"All right, all right! My guys are here, too. They'll help."

"So you carry the stretchers with us then. Come on," Anemone said, struggling to overcome the impulse to tell the chief he was an imbecile. Soon, cops and firemen loaded the bodies onto stretchers and headed toward the morgue. Anemone and the fire chief led the way. The firemen stopped just short of making the left turn that opened into the morgue.

"These guys want to go out in front of the cameras," the fire chief said, pointing to his right, where a group of reporters had gathered outside. Anemone positioned himself nose to nose in front of the fire chief.

"No. This is not about getting your picture in the fuckin' paper! The bodies have got to be photographed, searched, and identified. What the hell is the matter with you guys?" Anemone demanded. After the Emergency Service cops bagged the bodies and lined them up on the floor, he headed toward the Fire Command Station to coordinate the evacuation with the battalion chief.

"Chief, I got the helicopters ready to go. We've set up the roof on both towers so we have a landing pad. You want to split the rescue teams? I'll put your guys on two choppers, and we'll take one. We can work our way down the floors," Anemone said.

"No, we're not going to use *your* helicopters. We're climbing," the battalion chief spat out as if he'd been asked to blow a cop. Anemone's neck got hot, his mouth pursed up, and he did an about-face and walked away, heading back to where the Emergency Service and Aviation units were coordinating the first high-rise rescue in department history. Despite moments of obvious tension, Anemone thought he'd managed a successful rescue and done his best to avoid fanning the flames of the wildfire that had blazed out of control for years between the FDNY and NYPD—until a few days later when he got a telephone call. Then he learned that Fire Department brass had complained to Mario Selvaggi that the police had refused to cooperate. The firemen's union wrote a letter alleging the same thing. Over the next few months, the New York City Fire Department met quietly with the Port Authority and convinced them to lock the doors at the top of the World Trade Center towers. The year 1993 was the last time the New York Police Department would ever be able to execute their high-rise rescue plan at the World Trade Center.

o o o o o o o

After completing the last of their interviews, Ryan and Dolan joined the rest of the team for the debriefing. Dwyer, who was talking in an excited voice, paused when the two officers entered the squad room. He acknowledged them with a smile and a handshake, then walked to a strategic location and started to lecture his men. Dwyer's hair was cut short and uneven in the front, which made his jowls appear plump and pronounced. Average in height, his arms and shoulders were fleshy and full, making him look like a pint-sized sumo wrestler, standing on a soapbox delivering a sermon to a crowd.

"Dude, listen up. This is a big job. Tomorrow we'll be on the front page of every newspaper in the country. They make movies out of shit like this. We play this right, and we'll have money like you never dreamed."

"What's he talking about?" Ryan mumbled to Dolan, who shook his head.

"Me and Nicky, we've been talking about this. We stick together. We'll get a book out of this job, and movie rights. I'm telling you we'll be on every talk show from New York to California. We'll be on *Oprah* and *Larry King*. I'm telling you, this is going to Hollywood!" Dwyer was jumping around and waving his arms like a puppet, and it occurred to English that he should tell him to sit down. Maybe the doctor was right. The last thing English wanted to do was get down on his knees and breathe air into Dwyer's lungs.

"Larry, what are you talking about?" Ryan asked.

"I'm talking about us all signing a contract and splitting the profits on a book. Nicky has the connections. We get on the news and write a book about this, and I'm telling you, we're on our way to Hollywood."

"Are you crazy? I don't wanna be on TV. I don't want to be in a fuckin' movie," Ryan said. His voice was firm but soft, as it often was when he was struggling to keep his anger under control. A few of the other cops were making similar comments and voicing discontent.

"But this is the ticket. We've got an opportunity here and we don't want to blow it. I'm telling you, this is big, very big," Mancini piped in.

"We don't know who these guys are," Ryan said.

"Don't you get it? This book comes out, and we'll be on every talk show from here to California. The movie would be a huge hit! This is our ticket. We all gotta stick together."

"Wait a minute! This is not what Emergency is about. We do our jobs and be quiet about it and go home," Dolan said, citing generations of protocol and echoing the comments of other cops on the team. Part of the reason Emergency Service was respected by cops and bosses was because they did their jobs, didn't ask for special recognition, and let ranking officers claim the glory for the work they did.

"You don't get it. I got a phone call from a buddy in the Agency who's retired from the job. He's telling me we don't know who these guys are. We don't know who else is in this country. I am worried about my family. We make too big a deal of this and they could retaliate," Ryan said.

"Aw, your friend doesn't know what he's talking about," Dwyer said.

"The hell he don't. We just shot two terrorists. Whoever did that in this country before? What makes you think they are the only guys here? We don't know that. We don't know if they're part of a terrorist organization."

"We can ride this wave to get promoted. We can ride this wave and make money. We're gonna be kings. Hell, we're kings now. Just listen to—" Dwyer's face and neck were red.

"—No, Larry, you listen! You want to go on TV. Then go. I got nothing to say about that." By then, every one of the cops was talking at once and almost all were saying the same thing, John English included.

"This is an incredible opportunity," Mancini pleaded. Dolan leaned over to his partner and whispered.

"What do you want to do?"

"I told you what I want to do. Joey, I'm not telling you not to talk to anybody. You do what you want to do, the same as everybody else, but I'm not doing it," Ryan said and turned to English.

"Johnny?" he asked.

"I'm not talking," English said. Mike Keenan and Mario Zorovic were equally vocal and adamant.[14] While they hadn't been the shooters and didn't share all of Ryan's concerns, neither were interested in a fast track to fame and fortune.

"Dude, listen. You sure about this? We can make this happen," Dwyer pleaded.

"Larry, shut the fuck up," Ryan said. As the meeting broke up, Ryan and Dolan headed toward the stairs. That is some crazy shit, making a party out of shooting someone, Ryan thought as he opened the front door of the precinct, stepped out into the afternoon heat, and got in his car. Dolan followed Ryan out of the parking lot. The debriefing had also rubbed him the wrong way. He understood that he and the other officers on the team were being pulled in two directions. Four cops and their sergeant were trying to downplay the raid like it wasn't any different from any other entry, even though everyone knew that it was because bombs and terrorists weren't everyday jobs. The problem was that a couple of the bosses were stirring the pot and making more out of the situation than they should. They were all in Emergency Service, and if the incident had come down on someone else's sector when another shift was working, a different team would have been mobilized with the same or different results. He felt a knot form in the pit of his stomach, so he stretched and inhaled. Although everyone had agreed to present a unified front, the team was divided in sentiment. At some point down the line, someway, somehow, the opposing sides were going to collide.

5

BLOOD TRAIL

IT WAS LATE IN THE AFTERNOON
when Keith Ryan and Joe Dolan drove
back to Fourth Avenue to pick up the gear
they'd left behind. The block was empty except for a few police vehicles:
an Emergency Service truck parked a few yards down from a van and two
unmarked cars that were sitting in front of 248 Fourth Avenue.

The crowds were gone, but evidence of the shooting was spread
across the pavement. Streaks of blood extended from the street to the
building entrance. A black jacket, two pairs of latex hospital gloves, and
a blood-drenched shirt lay a few yards from where the officers parked.

Ryan stepped out of his air conditioned car into a wall of 97-degree
heat. The humidity had lowered since morning but when he inhaled
the thick, dry air, his throat felt parched and he wished he'd thought to
bring a bottle of water. He stood beside his partner, looked around, and
noticed the bloody clothes on the street. The emergency medical technicians must have cut the clothes off the suspects and patched them up so
they wouldn't bleed out before putting them in the ambulance.

The façade of the building glistened in the afternoon sun. The doorway looked too narrow to fit six big men wearing tactical gear, and every
cop on the team had to have been focused and fluid when they went
in, adjusting their shapes like ocean water flowing into a stream. He
observed the light affixed to the top of the door and recalled the dim,
shadowy glow that had been cast on the doorstep. This was the first time
that he'd noticed there was a fire escape in front. Ryan glanced at the
Family Car Service, which was located to his left, facing the building
entrance. A huge sign above the storefront window announced the name

and telephone number. Two large gray cans, brimming with trash, were resting in an enclave next to the storefront door.

The cops standing around 248 recognized Ryan and Dolan and greeted them with congratulations and high-fives. An Emergency Service cop was guarding the entrance, his powerful presence softened by the sight of the strap on his Kevlar helmet dangling, unfastened, beneath his chin. Holding his MP-5 loosely in one arm, barrel pointing down, he patted Ryan on the back and shook Dolan's hand.

"Good goin', boys. You lit those towel heads up good. It's amazing these scumbags aren't in the morgue. They must've lost ten quarts of blood between them! Cocksuckers deserve a coffin in hell," the officer said, supporting the shooters' actions and toasting their victory.[1]

Ryan grinned, concealing what he was feeling inside. His body ached with fatigue. He still wasn't sure if he wanted to celebrate. He felt good about what he'd done. Still, the only reason he'd fired his gun was because he saw no other choice. "Everybody makes a big deal about getting into a shooting and they kind of glorify it, and I don't think there's anything glorified about it. I was lucky because it was a good shooting, but it could have gone the other way. It could have been a bad shooting. I don't feel remorseful. I did what I had to do. People say, you should've killed them. I say, you know what? It was a wash. They didn't blow us up, and I didn't kill them. God looked down and said, today's a wash," Ryan explained.

"You guys want to see the apartment?" the Emergency Service cop asked.

"Nah," Dolan replied. He'd seen enough in the past twenty-four hours. He thought of his daughter, Jennifer, toddling around on her stubby legs, exploring every inch of the house as if it were a brand-new universe. He wanted nothing more than to take her in his arms and ruffle her bright blond hair, immersing himself in the smell of her velvet skin. He imagined telling his wife about the raid. They got along well that way.

Nancy had been a cop in the Highway Patrol Unit, so she understood what he did and who he was. They'd met when both responded to an accident on the Gowanus Expressway. Joe started to follow her around on jobs after that, eager to ask her out but uncertain as to how she'd respond. He smiled inwardly when he recalled how she looked in her Highway uniform with the high boots and oversized hat. She wasn't a big woman, and most of the cops in the unit were twice her height and weight. He'd found her irresistible and feminine, and he also respected her as a cop. In a command dominated by men, she carried her load and didn't take shit from the guys. The feelings between them were mutual. His sardonic half-smile, rugged good looks, and strong physique had melted the stalwart façade she had worked to cultivate since day one in the academy.

"Come on, Joey. We need to see it again," Ryan said. He knew his curiosity was morbid but the pull was strong, like wanting to see a body in an open casket to verify that a person remembered as living was dead. He wanted to view the apartment in the daylight, to see the proof of what he knew had happened there. In his mind the entry replayed itself like a clip from a film. Even as the shooting had gone down, he had seen it in slow motion, watching it from the outside, as if there were two of him in the room.

The Emergency Service cop led the way. Not that anyone had to. Ryan and Dolan knew the path from muscle memory. It was also clearly marked by two parallel trails of blood. They walked past the faded red staircase and through the hall. Blood had pooled in spots and dried to a crimson brown. Periodically he looked down, trying to avoid the sticky stains. He was taken aback by how primitive the interior looked. The floor was covered in panels of raw pine. The ceiling was crumbling from a busted water pipe or a bathtub that had overflowed from the floor above. Behind the stairwell, there was a heel print in the puddle of blood. Someone—most likely a cop or a boss—had been walking toward the bedroom after the suspects had been dragged out.

Ryan and Dolan followed the blood trail into the middle of the courtyard. Ryan turned around and looked back. A door was open to a first-floor apartment that had been evacuated hours before. He felt vaguely uneasy, recalling, perhaps, an image of shots fired, no one guarding the apartment door, and their backs exposed. He had been pissed off by Dwyer's Hollywood fantasies but couldn't otherwise fault him. Better that he leave his post at the door and run toward the blast than away. Other bosses would have likely done the same thing if they thought their men needed help.

Adjacent to the garbage pails he'd passed that morning, Ryan saw a bright pink pile of toys. The toys looked incongruous, like the Raggedy Ann doll some officers had seen whole and untouched in the pile of flaming debris and body parts at the site of the Flight 800 crash years before. He envisioned the faces of the children he and Dolan had taken out of the basement apartment. It had pained him to see the fear in their eyes. He didn't like to think about the squalid condition of their home.

Jobs with children crushed his soul and left him feeling bruised and broken. He'd been a rookie the first time he'd held a dying child in his arms. Ryan and his partner had arrived at the scene to find a six-year-old boy had fallen into the bathtub while his father was sleeping in the next room. Ryan had done mouth-to-mouth, to no avail. After work, he'd changed into civilian clothes, got in his car, and drove upstate to see his sister. Halfway there a state trooper had pulled him over driving 120 miles per hour. Not thinking straight, Ryan got out of the car trying to save the trooper a walk but causing alarm instead. The trooper screamed at Ryan to show his hands and get back in the front seat, then kicked the door closed. Ryan apologized and showed the trooper his shield.

"I'm sorry, I'm really sorry. I'm on the job," he said.

"Are you all right?" the trooper asked as he looked at Ryan's sunken eyes and quivering mouth.

"No, I'm not," he said, and his face started to disintegrate and his eyes overflowed as he struggled to contain himself, then he told the trooper what had happened with the child.

"Your dying won't do that boy no good," the trooper said. "Now get back in your car and go up to your sister's and do not, and I mean do not, go faster than seventy miles per hour. You understand? There are too many people dying tonight. I don't want a cop on my hands." The trooper escorted Ryan to his sister's doorstep, then turned around and headed back to the highway.

On Christmas Eve the year before, Ryan had had another bad job. Dolan was off that night and Ryan was working with another cop. He and his partner had seen a sanitation truck carelessly weaving in and out of the street and predicted an accident. Still, they'd been surprised when they'd gotten the call two hours later and seen the devastation. The truck and a car collided with such force that the car had been crushed like an accordion and then exploded. Ryan and his partner had tried to pull out the passengers but they were pinned inside, welded to burning leather. It wasn't until after the Fire Department put out the flames that he realized there was a fifth person trapped in the back; a little girl who was missing half of her face and was glued to her car seat. Ryan started to sob.

He touched the scar on his right temple and took a deep breath as he recalled what he saw. "It just horrified me," he explained. "They were all dead. They died on impact. The guy was pinned, melted into the seat. All of them were. . . . You know as cops we're like the court jester. On the outside we're laughing and joking about the weirdest things. Inside, our hearts are like shattered glass."

o o o o o o o

Ryan continued walking through the courtyard toward the second building and behind the stairs until he stood in front of the door to the suspects' apartment, which was painted an institutional green, the color of jails and some city hospitals. When he, Dolan, and the Emergency Service cop started to go inside, an FBI agent approached and blocked their way.

"Hold on, you can't come in here," the agent said

"All right, whatever you want," Dolan replied and turned around.

"Wait, Joe," the Emergency Service cop said, then turned to the agent.

"So what do you mean they can't go in there?"

"They can't go in. We're doing a crime scene."

"These guys are responsible for your fucking crime scene. They were in here before it was a crime scene!" the cop replied.

"OK, well, just don't touch anything," the agent said, shrugging his shoulders and moving out of their way.

"Does he think we're fuckin' morons?" Ryan cursed and shook his head as he and Dolan walked inside. The kitchen caught the cops' eye first. They'd barely noticed the mess in the morning. Some of the disarray was caused by the officers when they'd tossed the place, looking for evidence. The suspects had also left unwashed dishes in the sink and a pot of sauce sitting on a burner of the stove. A plastic bag of paprika was lying on the greasy, red-checkered countertop. A container of rice, a bottle of corn oil, salt, hand lotion, dish soap, and a coffee cup were lined up in the corner against the wall. The cops walked by a small table and paused in front of the door to the suspects' bedroom. For the second time that day, Ryan felt the moist warmth of his partner's breath on his neck. He realized he was sweating profusely and chalked it up to the temperature in the airless room.

"Holy shit," Ryan said when they breached the entranceway.

"The room's only 8 by 10 feet," Dolan responded in a barely audible whisper.

"Holy fuck! Holy fuck! It's not even the size of Nicky's office," Ryan said.

Dolan laughed uncomfortably. "I thought the room was 10 by 12 feet at least. Shit. I thought it was a fucking mansion. I don't know how they lived there. I guess coming from where they came from, here is still better than what they had over there, but they were living in shit," he explained. Stunned, Ryan squatted down next to the two mattresses, which had been folded and jammed against the wall. "I realized that the bombs were no more than two feet away from where these guys had been sleeping. That was when it really hit me how close we'd come. . . . It shows you how the mind compensates to make the situation better than it is," Ryan told me later.

Two spent 9-mm cartridges were resting near the center of one mattress. A rifle casing from Dolan's Mini-14 was a few inches away, marked by a small ruler the detectives had used when they photographed the scene. Three more cartridges and casings were lying on the floor. A seventh round had penetrated the mattress and burrowed into the wood below. A large, expanding circle of red and brown blood covered the mattress. A sticky mass was drying on the floor where the mattresses had rested before the cops turned everything upside down. Four large black pillows had been thrown on the top of the second mattress.

A red crate had been tossed onto the mattress with the TV, a pile of clothes, and a blood-stained quilt. An empty box of Champ trash bags was lying nearby. A large hunting knife, housed in a brown leather case, was within reach of the second mattress and might have been kept underneath. Leather topsiders, cigarettes, matches, and a pair of wire cutters were resting on the floor not far from a torn brown suitcase. The clock on one wall looked new compared to the raw pine floors. Some of the walls were unfinished. Others were painted a dull white but had beams with nails still exposed. One corner wall was discolored by smoke or chemicals or spilled food. Some dates and numbers were written on the opposite side of the wall.

The bedroom contained a crudely made closet composed of planks of raw wood and a metal bar to hang clothes. A pair of crutches and a large spool of heavy wire was stored inside. Some airmail letters addressed in Arabic and a copy of *Webster's English Dictionary* rested on a table in another part of the room. A decorative relief of a gilded shrine with columns was suspended from one wall. A large, gaudy, yellow and green scroll containing quotations from the Koran hung opposite. Taped beneath the scroll was a page from the Koran. On the floor below, an empty drawer had been turned upside down and shoved against the wall, creating a table. A large hardcover edition of the Koran was resting on top in an ornate wood frame.

The bedroom smelled acrid and meaty, like hot dogs and urine in the subway station at Coney Island on a summer afternoon. Ryan wiped the dampness from his brow with his sleeve and got a whiff of the stink of all-night sweat that was brewing beneath his arms. "Let's get outta here," he said.

Later, perhaps even then, Dolan reflected on why he'd done what he did. "The point of my shooting this guy was to stop him from moving. He started moving after I got in the room. . . . I caught a glimpse of a black bag out of the corner of my eye. . . . Maybe you would have done it that way, maybe you wouldn't. Maybe you would have stepped to the side and hit him in the head or maybe you would have fired the Mini-14 and missed him completely and the guy would have set off the bombs. Anything could have happened. You had to have been in that room. It's over in a very short time. It's like a car accident. You are getting into it and you are skidding and you know what is going to happen and you are just waiting for it and it seems to take forever, but time gets distorted. It really takes only a few seconds."

Inside the sunlit courtyard, Ryan used his hand to shield his eyes from the glare. He recalled his thoughts drifting back to the man who had been in the apartment on the second floor. "I wanted to go back upstairs. I still felt bad. I'd laid that fucking guy out. I hit him hard with the bunker and he went right down." Right before he and Dolan got outside, they spotted lieutenant Sean Crowley, a former Emergency Service cop, who now worked in the Office of the Deputy Commissioner, Public Information (DCPI), whose members act as the department's spin machine and filter information between the press, the public, and the police.

"Hey, Sean. How ya' doin?" Ryan asked.

"Keith, I'm really sorry about this," Sean replied, according to Ryan's recollection.

"Sorry about what? Sean, what are you trying to tell us?" Ryan said.

"They released your information to the press."

"Why? How the fuck could you do that? They released our names?"

"Yeah, they did. They released your names. I'm sorry. There wasn't anything I could do."

"Jesus Christ. Do you know what we've been through? I don't get this. They deleted our names from the hospital records and now they're just gonna give out our shit like that?"

"I'm sorry."

"What the fuck is wrong with these guys?" When Crowley didn't reply,

Ryan shook his head and walked away. "I was so fucking pissed. I was overwhelmed. It seemed like no one was looking out for our safety. No one was protecting us. Their answer to my security was to give me a radio and tell me, 'Don't worry if anything happens, just call us.'"

"By releasing our names to the press," Dolan explained, "they opened the floodgates for calls from reporters who could easily find out our telephone numbers and where we lived." He thought that had DCPI just left it alone, then maybe Ryan wouldn't haven't gotten the telephone call that night from the reporter. A source familiar with DCPI denied that the department released the names to the press. "We don't release police officers' names until maybe a few days after a shooting if we are going to do it but the press inevitably gets ahold of the names a few hours after. Some police buff or someone else always releases the names. If Sean approached Ryan, Sean might have said that we were not going out of our way to convince the press not to use the names," the source explained.

A high-ranking boss in the Special Operations Division agreed that DCPI did not release the names of the officers after the raid. He believed that information about the men on the team was leaked through someone in Emergency Service and thought that Nick Mancini might have been the culprit. "Nick had multiple contacts with the press and liked to promote himself. I think he was the one who first told reporters the [officers'] names."

"Nice job, guys," Ryan heard Six Truck lieutenant Tony DeLuca say when he saw Dolan and Ryan leaving the building. A solidly built man of average height, DeLuca had unusually small hands, a physical attribute of which he was acutely sensitive, providing the many officers who loathed him ample fodder to spice up a conversation and make him mad. "Keith, you still want that sniper rifle, don't ya?" DeLuca asked.

"I guess this proves I can shoot," Ryan whispered under his breath. DeLuca knew he wanted the rifle because he'd applied and been denied the year before. Ryan not only wanted the expert marksman status the position entailed but also the overtime pay. Nevertheless, he'd be damned if he was going to get down on his knees and beg or let DeLuca jerk him around anymore.

"Those are my guys," he said as Ryan was walking away.

"Now we're his guys!" Ryan said to Dolan with contempt in his breath. Wired and weary, a bad feeling was beginning to gnaw at his gut as he got in his car and drove home.

○ ○ ○ ○ ○ ○ ○

If the terrorist incident happened in 2010 in the NYPD, crime scene detectives would collect all kinds of additional evidence. Sections of the stained wall would be removed and tested for chemical vapors. Samples from the rim of the toilet seat would be examined to see if explosives or drugs had been dumped inside. Dolan and Ryan would be photographed, then stripped of their clothing, which would be tested for blood and gunpowder residue.

Nevertheless, the evidence collected at the scene in 1997 still told an interesting story that was supplemented by interviews and computer-generated data shared among different law enforcement agencies. Gazi Ibrahim Abu Mezer was born on October 2, 1973, in the West Bank town of Hebron, a location considered a breeding ground for terrorists. On July 6, 1993, he obtained a one-year travel document from the Israeli government. On September 19, 1993, he was granted a Canadian student visa, which was set to expire on April 4, 1994. Mezer was admitted to Canada on September 14, 1993. On September 23, he applied for but was denied a nonimmigrant U.S. visa. In February 1996, Mezer was observed "acting suspiciously" on the U.S-Canadian border, near Vancouver. Four months later, he attempted to enter the United States twice, was arrested, and voluntarily returned to Canada. Six months after that, he entered the United States illegally, was apprehended, and deportation hearings begun. Mezer procured the $5,000 bond with money sent to a friend from his uncle in Saudi Arabia and was set free pending resolution of his case.

Lafi Khalil was born on October 24, 1974, in the West Bank. On June 26, 1995, he obtained a Jordanian passport, which was valid for two years. On November 14, 1996, he obtained an Ecuadorian visa. On November 25, 1996, he received a US C-1 transit visa that entitled him to enter the United States for up to twenty-nine days en route to Ecuador. Using the visa, he entered the United States on December 7. The immigration inspector mistook the document for a B-2 tourist visa, which was valid for six months. Upon arrival in the United States, Khalil flew to Syracuse, New York.

According to newspaper reports, Rudolph Giuliani was "seething" when he learned about the suspects' immigration history: "I think it is appropriate to question why this person [Mezer] was allowed into the country announcing that he was part of a terrorist group in Israel."[2] In the wake of the team's actions, it's hard to believe that Giuliani wasn't also secretly pleased. Since he'd ousted Bill Bratton as police commissioner and intensified enforcement of quality-of-life offenses, Giuliani had continued to lose public support. The raid presented a coup for the administration that he wanted to capitalize on.

o o o o o o o

When Paul Yurkiw and Rich Teemsma finished working at the crime scene, they followed the total containment vehicle to the range at Rodman's Neck in the Bronx. Although the ignition had been separated from the explosive materials, the pipes still had to be further dismantled and bagged as evidence. When they got to the range, Yurkiw and Teemsma used the robot to help them place the four pipes in an enclosed sandpit so they could be safely and methodically taken apart. The detectives then carried the bombs' remains into the office and began to catalog the evidence. When they started working on the switching device, they discovered an eight-by-eleven-inch piece of paper was folded up inside the plastic box that had been attached. Teemsma opened the note and read it out loud. An edited version of one of the paragraphs is reproduced below.

> *In the name of God, this message is for the U.S. citizens and the United States of America. We want you to understand that nobody can win the war against Islam and we are warning all U.S. citizens, U.S. embassies, and Jewish Americans in the United States and around the world that we are going to bomb the ground under the American and Jewish States. . . . We demand you stop the starving of Iraqi Muslims, pull American troops out of the land of our prophets, and release all Islamic prisoners . . .* [several terrorists housed in American prisons were named, including those implicated in the World Trade Center bombing in 1993]. *We are ready to hit everywhere with suicide bombs.*

"Flight 800? Paulie, look at this!" Teemsma said, pointing to a barely decipherable sentence at the bottom of the document in which the terrorists suggested that they had something to do with the disaster.

"These guys are claiming responsibility for the TWA Flight 800 crash?" Yurkiw asked, reading the letter over Teemsma's shoulder.

"Bullshit!" Teemsma said. He did not believe that the terrorists had anything to do with the Flight 800 crash, which had occurred almost exactly one year earlier, on July 17, 1996. Images of the disaster floated around in the back of his head. Not until he'd picked up the boot in the sand had he realized it still contained its owner's foot. The officers in the

Scuba Team had the worst detail that day; diving in zero-visibility water, trying to salvage body and airplane parts without cutting themselves or their dry suits and hoses on sharp pieces of metal.

The phone rang, interrupting Teemsma's thoughts. When he picked up the receiver, he was greeted by Jim Black, calling from the Manhattan office.

"Yeah, Lieu. We'll be finished in a while. We found something, a note attached to the switching device, a threat to blow themselves up if we don't meet their demands," Teemsma said.

"Put that back and don't say nothing to nobody about it. The guys from the FBI want to handle this. There are some things we shouldn't know about. I'll be at the office when you get here. I want you to bring the evidence so these guys can take a look," Black said.[3] Teemsma folded the paper three times and put it back in the box. An hour later, the Crime Scene detectives arrived and started to photograph the evidence. Around 5:00 P.M. Yurkiw called his wife to tell her he wouldn't be home until late. "I can barely type with one finger, so paperwork takes a long time."

After completing a nearly thirty-hour tour, the two detectives drove back into Manhattan. Jim Black was waiting on the first floor of the precinct when they arrived. They gave him the toggle switch device and showed him where the note was placed. Teemsma and Yurkiw made their way upstairs into the Bomb Squad office and joined the detectives on the evening shift who were sitting at their desks, reading newspapers, sipping coffee, and talking among themselves. They had heard different stories about the case and were eager to find out what happened firsthand. Teemsma and Yurkiw shared the details, beginning with the call from the 8-8 Precinct squad.

"Nice work, guys! You lucky bastards!" one officer said and shook their hands. Most of the detectives sitting around were senior guys who'd spent years in the unit without seeing a job like this. The conversation stopped ten minutes later, when Jim Black walked into the room, accompanied by two federal agents. Black was carrying the switching device. He pulled the note out of the plastic box, held it in his hand and walked straight up to Teemsma, who was leaning against a desk.

"Do you guys know what this is? Look what you missed! This was with the switching device," Black said.

"What?" Yurkiw whispered. He couldn't tell if Black was serious, making a joke, or promoting himself at their expense. Teemsma kept his mouth shut, but his fists contracted and he stood up straight. One punch and I could wipe that smirk off the asshole's face, he thought, and then glanced at his partner. Yurkiw shook his head and struggled to turn his confused frown into a smile of trouble-avoiding contrition. Fed up with their boss's bullshit, Teemsma turned around and headed toward the Cave, followed by Yurkiw, and a senior detective a few minutes later.

"He's gotta be jerking us around," Yurkiw said.

"Richie, you know when Jim is lying because his lips move," the senior detective said.

"Gutless, skinny-assed son of a motherfucker, please!" Teemsma hissed. Yurkiw sat down on a bunk. The detective gave them both a sympathetic glance and returned to the office. Working for Jim Black was like scuba diving with a barracuda. You never knew where he stood. One moment you looked over your shoulder and there he was, suspended in space, sporting a toothy grin. The next second he disappeared.

"Paulie, let's finish up and get outta here," Teemsma said, closing the door to the men's room.

"A cross between a barracuda and a weasel," Yurkiw said.

"What?"

"Jim Black."

"He's not a bad guy. Get rid of the white shirt and blue shield and he'd make a good neighbor," Teemsma said. The detectives walked downstairs to their cars.

o o o o o o o

Yurkiw's house was empty when he arrived home around 10:00 P.M. School was out for the summer and the boys were playing ball with their friends. His wife was working late or visiting her family. Yurkiw put away his gun and walked into the kitchen. He opened the freezer and pulled out a bottle of vodka. He poured himself a drink and sat down at the dining room table. The ice-cold liquid cooled his throat and created a warm sensation in his chest. After a few more sips his muscles relaxed, his mind felt pleasantly numb, and he had to struggle to keep his eyes from closing. He put the empty glass in the kitchen sink and walked into the bathroom to brush his teeth. He turned on the TV and lay down on the bed. The last thing he recalled before blacking out was a newscaster talking about the "terrorist bombing plot that was foiled by the NYPD."

○ ○ ○ ○ ○ ○ ○

Teemsma pulled his car into the garage and walked into his house through the side door. Kim was waiting in the living room with the two kids, who had eaten dinner a few hours before. Teemsma gave his wife a hug, then lifted the kids off their feet and kissed them each on their forehead. While Kim warmed up his dinner, Teemsma chatted with his son and daughter, then sent them off to bed.

Teemsma and Kim sat at the kitchen table. She sipped Zinfandel while he ate salad and leftover lemon chicken. Teemsma had married a bright, attractive wife. Although she didn't have a college degree, she'd moved up the ladder to become an invaluable member of the human resources staff at a Long Island hospital. She also shouldered the bulk of the responsibility for their children's care. Nothing new, the kids were fine, she told him when he inquired about her day. Their daughter was already talking about going to Columbia University, which Teemsma was ambivalent about because he believed the school was full of communists, although her ambition and intellect thrilled him.

"So tell me, Rich, what happened?" Kim asked. Teemsma told her the story, leaving out only a few details, like that terrible moment when he and Yurkiw had shared the almost certain knowledge that they were going to die. She wasn't fooled. She knew from the look on his face that he'd been scared; that he'd left something out of his account so she wouldn't worry or perhaps so he wouldn't relive the anxiety. Not that she'd really worried about him getting hurt anyway. He'd been in tight spots before in Emergency Service and the Bomb Squad. Even during the dark days after Yurkiw got shot and Teemsma was half-blaming himself for not being there, she didn't think he'd get injured or killed on the job. Teemsma felt the same way. "It wasn't that I was tougher than anyone else, but I just knew and she knew that nothing was gonna happen to me," he said.

"Who *are* these guys?" she asked.

"Well everyone's saying they're Hamas, but I don't know. My guess is that they're serious, but not hardcore. Maybe they have an uncle who's connected. It seemed more like, I'm gonna impress the family and be somebody by doing this. But who knows? They were going to kill themselves, for sure. They tried to do that when Emergency went through the door."

Teemsma left his wife with the dishes and went into the bedroom. He stripped off the covers and lay down, enjoying the breeze from the air conditioner and its calming white noise. The sheets felt clean next to his skin, and as soon as he buried his head in the pillow, he dropped off to sleep. He woke up a few hours later, his body clock turned inside out from the thirty-hour tour.

Kim was sleeping soundly on her side with one knee bent. The smooth curve of her hip was visible underneath the blanket. Her curly hair straddled her shoulders. He looked at her with affection and also a little guilt. He knew she felt abandoned by his job. I have to quit acting so selfish, he thought. I have to stop taking my wife for granted. I've got to make time to give her what she needs.

Not wanting to wake her, he went into the living room, lay down, turned the TV on low, and closed his eyes. He thought about what would have happened if the terrorists had gotten into the subway. In terms of fatalities, it would have been worse than the 1993 bombing of the World Trade Center. What a hellhole that was, he thought, recalling the last body they'd dug out of the basement. The man was lying face up with his arm extended over his chest. His eyes were swollen shut, his nose and lips so bloated and bloody he didn't look human except for the dirt-filled ear protruding from his burial ground, and the long, black bush that sprouted from his head. Twenty or thirty plastic cups surrounded the body. The man was wearing a white shirt and might have been a restaurant worker.

He hadn't smelled bad, even after lying there decomposing for six weeks. The meat that had been blown out of the commissary freezer had stunk much worse. The temperature had plummeted in the days that followed the blast and had frozen the corpse. It was hard to tell the man's age. The seventh casualty, counting the fetus of the pregnant woman they'd found lodged in the ceiling, he looked like he was somewhere between thirty and fifty years old.

Teemsma had just gotten home from work when the explosion occurred. His kids were parked on the couch in front of the TV when suddenly the screen went blank. Teemsma remembered walking in the door and hearing them crying. Oh, shit. Not now. I don't want to buy a TV now, he'd thought. He'd squatted next to the television and tried another channel. The screen stayed blank. Maybe it was an antenna failure, he thought. At the time, the city's signal equipment was housed at only two places, the World Trade Center and the Empire State Building.

Teemsma turned to channel 2 and got sound and a picture, which meant that the problem wasn't in Midtown, so it had to be in the towers. Then he heard an emergency bulletin. According to the announcer, there had been a transformer explosion in the building. The number of casualties wasn't known. Teemsma reached for the phone and called his commanding officer.

"This is Rich. You want me back in there?"

"I do," he said.

"See you in fifteen minutes."

"Are you home?"

"Yeah."

"There is no way in hell you will be here in less than three hours!"

"I'll see you in fifteen minutes." Teemsma hung up the phone and called his brother-in-law who worked in the Aviation Unit of the Nassau County Police Department. Kim and the kids piled into her car and drove Teemsma to the Coliseum parking lot, where the helicopter was waiting. A few minutes later the cops from Emergency Service were waving the chopper in for landing on West Street in downtown Manhattan.

"Who do you think you are?" the cop said when he saw his former teammate stepping out onto the tarmac instead of a dignitary.

"I's *impotant* and I's gonna stay *impotant*," Teemsma joked. The cop grinned. A disappointed press shook their heads and put down their cameras.

"What do you need?" Teemsma said to the detective who was running the investigation on behalf of the Bomb Squad.

"I just scraped this off the ceiling. Can you take this to the lab and find out what it is?"

"Not a problem." Teemsma took the plastic bag of ashes, jumped into a truck, and drove to the lab on Twentieth Street. He handed the package to Jim Black, who was a boss in Crime Scene then and, according to rumor, chief Lou Anemone's eyes and ears.

"Jim, I have to know what this is now," Teemsma said.

"No problem," Black said. Ten minutes later, he came out of the lab with an analysis of the contents. "It's O3 nitrates," he said. O2 nitrates are nitrate explosives that haven't yet been deployed. O3 are nitrates that have been burned.

"We got a bomb for sure, we can say that?" Teemsma asked.

"Yeah, we can say that for sure," Black confirmed. Teemsma took the report and got in the truck. He stepped on the gas and drove downtown. He passed one swell of paralyzed traffic by driving onto the sidewalk with sirens and flashing red lights. He parked the truck across from the World

Trade Center, in front of the Merrill Lynch Building, where a meeting with the brass was taking place. When he got inside, he handed the paper to his commanding officer.

"Bomb?" he asked.

"Bomb," Teemsma confirmed. The lab report was passed from chief to chief until it got to the deputy mayor. Teemsma walked downstairs, across the street, and onto the sidewalk in front of the World Trade Center. He and his partner put on helmets and stepped into the B-2 level where the blast had occurred. He noticed the cadaver dog, a German Shepherd, was crawling around beneath the broken beams, sniffing debris.

When the sergeant saw the two detectives, he pointed out some long tubes that were lying adrift and exposed on top of some crushed cars. He said they were fiber optics and warned them not to touch them. If they did, the New York Stock Exchange and Kennedy Airport would go down. Teemsma walked past rows of mangled cars, some of which were lying with their tires face up. It looked like a scene from a horror movie: giant dead roaches lying on their backs with tires as legs extended in the air. Some of the large red metal beams that supported the building were standing up straight. Others leaned heavily in one direction like they were going to tumble. The floor rose and fell like waves foaming with dust and debris.

The ground around what had been the commissary was layered with plastic dishes, broken glasses, paper, and cement blocks of broken wall. Teemsma made his way across a section of pavement that had cracked and split apart like arctic ice in a swell of 100-degree heat. A large, gaping hole lay below where the concourse of the north tower had caved in and plunged down several levels. A fireman, attempting a rescue, had run blindly across the floor and had fallen into the pit and suffered serious fractures. He's lucky he didn't die, Teemsma thought.

"Transformer fire, my ass," he said. A few weeks later the police opened the sidewalk above the blast between the two towers. Teemsma recalled standing around with fellow cops, looking up into the open air.

"They tried to knock this building down," he said.

"Holy fuck!"

"Yeah, they did. They really did. Take a look at the structure and the support beams. If you want this building to go down, all you need to do is hijack a 747 and kill yourself and everybody with you and you'll knock it down." Years later, Teemsma's words would come back to haunt him.

○ ○ ○ ○ ○ ○ ○

"Nancy, are you upstairs?" Dolan said when he opened the door to his house in Staten Island and went inside after returning from the crime scene in Brooklyn. It was getting dark, and he turned on the light in the foyer. Inhaling a sweet-sour aroma, he realized his wife was cooking up ribs in the slow cooker. His mouth watered and stomach contracted. He couldn't remember when he'd eaten last.

"We're here," she shouted. His calf muscle cramped from fatigue when he started to climb the stairs. He pressed down on the heel of his foot, took the last four stairs two at a time and sauntered into their daughter's bedroom. Nancy was holding the baby and snapping her into a pair of pink-footed pajamas. When she saw her father, she squealed and reached out her arms.

"She didn't want to go to sleep until you got home," Nancy said. Dolan pulled his wife and daughter against his chest. For five minutes, he held the embrace, his muscular arms creating a warm, protective circle around them. "It was intense. He'd been involved in other shootings when I was on the job and he wasn't that emotional afterwards, but they happened before we had the baby," she explained.

Dolan stepped back, took his daughter, and cradled her against his collar bone. Wisps of her hair stroked his chin, and he buried his face in the flowery scent of baby shampoo. A wave of tenderness engulfed him, and he gently lowered his arms and pulled her to his chest.

"I gotta shower before we eat," he said. Nancy nodded, took Jennifer from her husband, and tucked her into bed, pulling the blanket up to her chin to shield her from the central air, which she'd turned on high when he had called to say he was on his way home.

The hot water pelted his back and shoulders, massaging away the sweat and fatigue that had been accumulating since morning. After he rinsed off the soap and dried himself off, he put on a T-shirt and the dark gray flannel pants he wore around the house. He rubbed the mirror with the palm of his hand to clear off the steam and looked at his reflection. His cheeks and chin were bristled thick. Too spent to pick up a razor, he turned off the light and walked downstairs. He made two frozen margaritas, handed one to Nancy, and walked into the living room. He stretched out in an oversized chair and turned on CNN. He watched the news until Nancy called him to dinner.

Savoring the rich, succulent taste of the pork, he picked the rogue tomato from his salad and put it on Nancy's plate. He poured on bottled dressing and then started to talk about the job, beginning with the entry, then retracing their steps to when they were first notified. The phone rang more than once during the conversation but neither he nor Nancy bothered to pick it up and no one left a message behind.

Dolan left Nancy in the kitchen and went to bed. As soon as his head hit the pillow, he plunged into a heavy sleep. Toward morning he woke up and thought of the job and felt thankful that he was alive. Maybe an image appeared in his head of the scroll he'd seen in the suspects' apartment as he drifted off to sleep. Months later, he would get a half-sleeve tattoo, inked around his bicep, depicting Archangel Michael and the seven deadly sins, commemorating the raid and reminding him that his life had been spared.

o o o o o o o

"There were four redundant switches. I don't know why the bomb didn't go off. I think it was the hand of God, like in a cartoon; he put his finger on the fuse. That was the closest I ever came," John English said to his wife, who was squeezing his hand and wiping the single tear that had leaked into the dark circle beneath one eye. She'd been waiting up for him after putting the children to bed. He'd called her twice in the evening to let her know he was delayed with bosses asking questions and endless piles of paperwork. Around 9:00 P.M., when she heard the familiar sound of his car in the driveway, she'd opened the front door and stepped outside.

English greeted her with a hug and pulled her inside. He kissed her lips, held her tight, and then led her into the living room. They sat on the couch, each holding the other while he told her about the job. He spared no detail. She was his best friend and lover and there wasn't anything they didn't share. When he finished the story, they went upstairs. English undressed, showered, and lay down next to his wife in bed. She rested her head on his shoulder, then took his hand and placed it on her bulging abdomen. He felt their baby kick and smiled, then drifted into sleep. "It was when I was talking to my wife that I realized how close we had actually come to dying. You don't realize it until later when you have time to think about it. Then the next day you put it out of your mind and go back to doing whatever you're doing—but the next day didn't turn out that way," English recalled.

o o o o o o o

Keith Ryan went home to an empty apartment in the basement below his mother's house on East 21st Street in Sheepshead Bay, Brooklyn. He walked into the kitchen, washed his hands, and then took a bottle of sparkling water out of the refrigerator. Exhausted but not quite ready to sleep, he went into the living room and turned on the TV to channel 1, the local New York City news station. As soon as he collapsed on the couch, he had to fight the urge to close his eyes. He got up, grabbed the keys to his mother's house, and walked upstairs. He wanted to let her know he was safe before he went to bed. She'd seemed worried and frail when he'd bumped into her at the hospital. His imagination, he supposed. His mother was anything but frail.

"Ma?" he called out when he walked into the house filled with the memories of his youth. The furniture was new, since his parents split up. It was the smell of the plaster and wood floors that brought to mind a past he didn't like to think about. It struck him as odd that, when he would stand by the fireplace at Christmastime, he'd suddenly catch a whiff of his father's breath—stale wine and rancid sweat bludgeoning the sweetness of his aunt's perfume.

Ryan smiled when he saw his mother sitting on the couch with the television on but the sound muted, reading a book. Her curiosity was insatiable. She read anything and everything, but philosophy and psychology appealed to her most. When she heard his footsteps, she put the book face down on the table and stood up. Ryan gave her hug and, glancing over her shoulder, read the cover of her book.

"Nietzsche?" he asked.

"A casual stroll through the lunatic asylum shows that faith does not prove anything," she said, then reached up and folded her fingers over the top of his powerful shoulders and looked into her son's face. Her eyes started to well up with tears.[4]

"Mom, don't cry. I'm fine. Really, I'm fine. It was just an entry."

"Don't lie to me, Keith," she said, and he felt ashamed that he couldn't tell her the truth—that the cops had been scared, that one second of hesitation and he, Joe, John English, and maybe the other three cops would have been killed. "I have some chicken in the refrigerator." He sat with his mother at the kitchen table and picked at the food, unable to garner much hunger in the wake of more than thirty hours of no sleep. He asked her about her hospital visit, then started to talk about his day, skipping the details of the shooting and dwelling instead on what happened during the trauma examination.

"The doctor did find something," he said.

"What?" she asked, with a wary look on her face.

"I have clean ears. I told him you raised me right," he said and laughed. His mother smiled, but there wasn't much joy in her face. Sometimes, when he stood in front of the mirror, he saw that same dark look in his own reflection.

"Ma, everyone's saying we're getting promoted," he said and got up from the table. This time her smile looked real. He said goodnight and headed out the door and down to his apartment.

He glanced at the news before turning off his TV. The camera had captured an image of the street in front of the entrance to the first building after he and Dolan had left for the hospital. The two detectives were putting the pipes in the truck. For the umpteenth time that day the suspect's eyes flashed through his mind, and he thought about the shooting and the dream he'd had the night before. "The crazy motherfucker didn't give me a choice. It couldn't have lasted more than ten seconds, and I never heard the gunshots. All I remember is seeing the muzzle flash. It's so weird. I screamed but don't know what I said. The interaction forged the path . . . When he moved, I had to act. It was up to him whether he lived or died," he recalled.

Ryan envisioned the suspects' bedroom with a spooky sense of déjà vu. "I was in that room before," he thought, "whether you believe in God or Buddha, there was some sort of divine intervention there because as real as I'm sitting here now, I know I had been in that room before. I don't understand why. Why did they want to kill us? Why were they there in that room when I was there too? What was the connection between us?"

The loud ring of the phone startled him, and he grabbed the receiver. He didn't recognize the voice until Larry Celona introduced himself. Celona was a reporter for the *New York Post*. Ryan said he didn't really want to talk to a reporter, but Celona insisted that Mike Collins from the Office of the Deputy Commissioner, Public Information (DCPI) had given Ryan permission to talk. Later, when I called Celona, he remembered talking to Ryan but not the details of their conversation. He also claimed that he knew Ryan from before. The one thing that was apparent from our brief telephone conversation was that he was one of those reporters who put the story before the interests of the people involved, including perhaps his informants, barring a specific request from DCPI.

"That was some day's work," Celona might have said, or something similar.

"Yeah, I guess it was."

"So what happened?" he probably inquired at one point or another.

"I mean, I'm glad we stopped them. They could have killed hundreds of people, children, mothers, people they don't even know. I don't know why we were called to handle that job. It's a good feeling to know, in some way, that you, you know the team, we helped change the future."[5] After describing a few additional details, Ryan said good-bye and hung up the phone.

Sources inside the Office of the Deputy Commissioner, Public Information, denied that Collins had given Ryan permission to speak to Celona or provided Celona with Ryan's number. Instead, they suggested that the reporter might have caught Ryan off guard by calling him when he was at home. "Rarely do reporters lie. They wouldn't be long in the business, and Larry Celona has a good reputation. But reporters are quick to move in and try to talk to people who are anguished and upset and maybe that is what Larry did, calling Keith," suggested a high-ranking boss in DCPI.

I heard from other officers in Emergency Service that Larry Celona made it his business to cultivate cops, frequenting their parties, and acting like he was their friend. It didn't take long before cops would forget who he was and let him into their lives. He seemed like a regular guy. Joe Dolan defended his partner and viewed the matter as one of happenstance. He didn't think Ryan sought out Celona or wanted to have an on-the-record conversation with a member of the press. "I could have probably made the same statement as Keith. I was just lucky enough not to pick up my phone. I had a couple of rings and hang-ups on my answering machine, but I didn't pick it up so I don't know who it was and nobody left a message."

After Ryan lay down on his bed, a jumble of disconnected images passed through his mind as he drifted on the edge of sleep. As soon as he opened his eyes and tried to make sense of the thoughts, they disappeared.

RICOCHET

RYAN WOKE UP FRIDAY MORNING
feeling preoccupied. The events of the
previous day seemed to dwarf all the other
work he'd done in the NYPD. About twelve years before the day of the raid,
he was standing in Madison Square Garden getting ready to graduate from
the Police Academy. He and the other recruits listened with pride and excitement to the recording of Frank Sinatra singing "New York, New York."
Then, in what seemed like a single motion, the hundreds of newly made
rookie cops threw their white gloves into the air, creating a cacophonous
blizzard of joy and relief. The raid seemed like the culmination of a lifetime of preparation—the suffering and sacrifice of his childhood, months
of training at the Police Academy and Floyd Bennett Field, twice yearly
visits to the range at least, his work ethic, his love of action and commitment to the job—it all came down to eight seconds inside that dark, seedy
bedroom. It might have scared him to think that luck played a role in the
victory. It felt better to attribute the outcome to teamwork, skill, training,
courage, and the grace of God.

Ryan got out of bed and looked through the window at the sun shining
outside. As he started to look away, he caught his reflection in the glass
and felt blessed to be alive. He spent the day running errands and visiting
family. Around 5:00 P.M. he went up to the pigeon coop above his mother's
garage and passed several hours there. He cleaned cages and fed his birds,
then watched them comb their feathers and waddle around. He found
their cooing soothing. At 10:00 P.M. he walked downstairs and lay in the
dark on his living room couch. He sipped a cold bottle of sparkling water
and sunk into the peace of the quiet Brooklyn night. He was starting to

drift to sleep when the telephone rang. Startled, he sat up and reached for the receiver.

"Hello?"

"It's John English."

"Hey."

"The PC wants us all in his office tomorrow morning. There's a press conference with him and the mayor at ten and they want us there."

"At a press conference?"

"Yeah. They want us to answer questions."

"But our names aren't on the 49."

"Keith, I don't know why they changed their mind. I just got notified."

"Joey knows?"

"Yeah."

"OK, thanks." Several telephone calls and an hour of speculative gossip later, neither Ryan nor anyone else on the entry team had come up with an explanation for why the brass had changed their minds and opted to publicize their names. At this point, the cops viewed the matter mostly as an inconvenience. They figured the police commissioner would come to his senses when he heard their concerns.

o o o o o o o

Around the same time that Ryan received notification from John English, the police reporter Larry Celona was talking to Inspector Mike Collins on the phone, confirming what he'd just been told: that the cops on the entry team were going to attend the press conference and answer questions. Yes, Collins likely assured him, cops, bosses, the mayor, and the police commissioner would all be at City Hall.

An odd-looking man whose head seemed too large for his short plump body, *New York Post* reporter Larry Celona was probably feeling good. Maybe he sometimes took flak because he worked for a newspaper that fed an audience that didn't like to read lengthy pieces in the press. Still, the *Post* wielded a lot of influence as the main source of news for the city's cops and firemen, which made his job easier. He knew how to talk their language and write the kind of stories they liked.

I imagine Celona looking at a blank page burning through the computer screen and thinking about writing a piece about the raid. He could write a generic rendition without using names or quotations from interview notes, or he could scoop the *New York Times* and the *Daily News* with a firsthand account. The choice wasn't particularly difficult.[1] A high-ranking boss who worked in the NYPD's Office of the Deputy Commissioner, Public Information, explained, "I don't know if Larry said that he was going to keep names out of it. I don't know whether he had a confidentiality agreement with Keith or not. I guess he thought he didn't and when he heard there would be a press conference, he decided to release the information and get the scoop."

o o o o o o o

Keith Ryan got up when the alarm went off at eight on Saturday morning. Although he'd slept five or six hours, he didn't feel rested. He put on a T-shirt and shorts and brewed some coffee. He opened the door and stepped into the driveway and picked up his copy of the *New York Post*. He glanced at the front page headline, which read "Inside the Terror Nest" and boasted of several exclusive stories. The headline "Hamas Connection: U.S. Had Bomb Boss Jailed But Let Him Go" struck him as the most alarming.

Ryan spread the *Post* on the table, poured himself a cup of coffee, sat down, and turned to the second page. There in big, bold, unexpected letters was his name: "Quick on the Draw: ESU cop Keith Ryan says he can't believe the enormity of the bomber's scheme."[2]

"Fuckin' dick!" Ryan cursed out loud. A hot sense of alarm flushed through the pit of his diaphragm to his chest and then turned into angry shame. He felt exposed, like he was walking into a firefight unarmed or taking a test unprepared. His eyes burned, and his cheeks flushed pink. Later, he told me he thought he could almost feel the "heat from the red dot" of a terrorist's sniper rifle, piercing his forehead. Then whatever he was feeling, fear or concern about his family or something else, changed to rage.

A photograph that accompanied the article fueled his fury. There he was, in black and white, standing outside the Emergency Service truck holding a Mini-14. At first he thought the picture had been released by the department. Then he realized that the *Post* might have had it on file. At the time, he'd been assigned to a dignitary protection detail, guarding the prime minister of Israel. The prime minister's driver had suddenly stopped and let the prime minister get out of the limousine to greet the crowds who were pushing against the barricades. Dolan had braked, and Ryan jumped out of the truck and positioned himself as the prime minister's bodyguard. The reporter snapped a picture of Ryan's stern face, scanning the crowd for weapons. The next day, the *New York Post* ran a story that featured photos of Ryan with the Israeli prime minister and his caravan. Shortly after Ryan signed in to work the next evening, he had received a telephone call from a chief who was blistering mad.

"You idiot! What the hell were you thinking of? Why did you let him get out of his car? All we need is another Jew shot by an Arab fanatic! What are you, stupid? Don't you know he was safe in that bulletproof car? It says here you live near Coney Island. The next time you pull a stunt like that you're gonna be doing day tours in the Bronx. You should have stayed in your fuckin' truck!" he screamed. Ryan rolled his eyes and stifled his irritation. When he thought about that now, he wondered if the chief who yelled at him was the same one who balled out another cop in the wake of a similar incident with the U.S. president. Bill Clinton had also stepped out of his bulletproof car to greet the crowd, leaving his Secret Service agents inside. So no one intervened when a bystander handed him a small pizza box. Clinton had already opened the lid of the box and discovered the aborted fetus inside when a cop ran up. Later, the cop got in trouble for not getting there soon enough. According to Joe Dolan, it bothered Ryan that now he was probably going to get yelled at for the same picture twice.

"Near-certain disaster—thwarted twice in the space of a minute. . . . Two cops from an elite unit who stared death in the face and captured the accused bombers through sheer bravery and quick reflexes. . . . After creeping through a foyer, two ESU cops—Keith Ryan and Joseph Dolan—heavily armed and clad in body armor, burst into the bedroom and began yelling, 'Police! Down!'"[3]

Ryan cringed when he got to the sections of the article that quoted him. He slammed the paper shut and folded it so only the sports section showed. He got up and washed the empty coffeepot and put it in the sink to dry. He took a shower and then got dressed in civilian clothes, put his gun in his belt, and walked to his car. On his way into Emergency Service quarters, he stopped for a cup of coffee and something to eat, and then at a newspaper stand, where he picked up copies of the *New York Times* and *Daily News*.

The *Times* ran a story about the suicide bombing at a marketplace in Israel that Hamas had claimed responsibility for. Another story discussed the Brooklyn plot and mentioned ongoing speculation that the terrorists were also tied to Hamas. The *Daily News* contained similar statements by officials as were cited in the other newspapers. In the *Post*, Giuliani was quoted as saying, "[There is] no question part of the motivation here was to attack the United States, to attack Israel, and to attack Jewish interests in New York and possibly globally."[4]

∘ ∘ ∘ ∘ ∘ ∘ ∘

Ryan and the five other officers on the entry team met at Emergency Service quarters and changed into their uniforms. Some of the men had seen the article in the *Post*. It probably wasn't hard for some of them to imagine Celona worming his way into Ryan's head and conducting an offhand interview. Maybe some believed that Inspector Collins had strongly encouraged Ryan to talk. English didn't recall the matter except that it didn't faze him. Ryan had done a great job. Nevertheless, I suspect that some of the guys were bothered by the report because it made it seem that Ryan was going against a team decision. It also appeared to violate informal etiquette surrounding the issue of team equality, that no single individual deserved special recognition. Regardless of who thought what about how the article came about, I suspect it spawned a lot of gossip behind Ryan's back.

English, Mancini, Dwyer, and Zorovic piled into one car and headed into Manhattan. Ryan, Keenan, and Dolan were still standing around looking for a ride when Cliff Masab showed up. Masab was the Six Truck delegate to the Patrolman's Benevolent Association (PBA), the rank-and-file union. He'd been with the officers when they'd done their GO-15 interviews and understood what they were going through.

"How ya doin', guys?"

"OK, I guess. Cliff, ya got something going right now?"

"Whaddaya need?"

"Can ya maybe give us a lift to One PP? We're supposed to meet the PC."

"Sure. I'll take you down there." The four officers squeezed into the car.

∘ ∘ ∘ ∘ ∘ ∘ ∘

They took the Brooklyn-Queens Expressway into lower Manhattan, cruised through the security gate at One Police Plaza, stopped to chat with the cop in the booth, and then proceeded into the parking lot. "The Puzzle Palace" loomed ahead, a tall, red-brick monster of a building wedged in the back of a courtyard a few blocks north of the Brooklyn Bridge. Ryan, Keenan, Dolan, and Masab walked through the rear entrance, using their identifications to get through the turnstile, and got on the elevator head-

ing upstairs. As soon as the door slid shut, they felt the walls close in and
the air get thin.

Although the building was largely abandoned on weekends, the stench
of power politics lingered like fumes from a diesel truck. From a street
cop's point of view, One Police Plaza is the home of deputy commissioners,
super chiefs, and white-shirted "house mouse" bosses who scurry about,
ever eager to please. The commissioner's suite lay on the fourteenth floor
on the opposite end of a wide hall from the bathroom used by civilian and
low-ranking police employees. The waiting room was nicely furnished
with upholstered chairs and a coffee table. A police officer was manning
the front desk and the security gate, which divided the foyer from a conference room and a row of offices in the back. The largest, with the big picture
window overlooking Manhattan, belonged to the police commissioner.
The officers were still standing around in the waiting room when Tommy
Martin, a former Emergency cop, joined them. Cops who become drivers
to chiefs and commissioners sometimes absorb, in vicarious fashion, the
attitude of their boss. Martin was Safir's driver.

"The boss sent me out to talk to you guys. We got word that you don't
want to do the press conference. I'm telling you, and I quote the boss,
'You don't go to this news conference, I'll disband the unit and you'll all
be suspended.' Sorry, guys. This is big politics now, and politics is a dirty
game," Martin said, and turned around and walked back toward the police
commissioner's office.

"Did he just threaten us? He did. Safir just threatened us. I can't believe
he did that," English said.

"Son of a bitch!" Ryan exclaimed.

"You know, the chief is going to put his career on the line for us," English
said. Later, English told me that Safir's way of handling the situation was
as unnecessary as it was alienating to the officers who had just risked their
lives to serve him and the department. "You know he didn't have to say that.
He could bring us into his office and talk to us. I mean, if he tells us our
post for the day is the press room in City Hall, that's a lawful order. We can't
disobey. He doesn't have to resort to making exorbitant threats. There's
never been a situation where cops are worried about terrorists killing their
families." Despite himself, English stood up straight when he saw the police
commissioner coming toward them from the back of the office.

"Good to see you again," Safir said, shaking their hands. A few seconds
later he disappeared.

"What was that?" Ryan asked.

"Politics. Big politics," English replied. When Bill Morange walked in from the hall, he could see concern written all over his cops' faces. He'd talked to the commissioner that morning and knew that the news wasn't good. Several officers recalled that Morange made three round trips from the waiting room to the commissioner's office to plead their case. No one knows but Howard Safir and Bill Morange the exact words that were exchanged, but I talked to one top commander who had overheard.

"Bill [Morange] knew that politically it wasn't the right way for him to go but he couldn't turn his back on his cops because he was committed to them as much as they were committed to working for him and Ray [McDermott]. He [Bill] believed they had legitimate concerns. They were worried about their families because it was terrorism, and we didn't know a whole lot about it. The Puzzle Palace had different concerns. They felt that there wasn't a problem showing the cops off. Safir was upset. He was really upset. There were things said. Bill knew what they did day in and day out and understood their concerns. Maybe Safir never did understand. Bill always felt that loyalty is a two-way street. He understood why his men were worried. Upstairs may not like it, but the chief had to keep them informed and give his opinion, too. He told Howard that he really didn't think their names should be released. He said that we were stepping into a new era. It wasn't as if cops hadn't been targets before. Bill knew the history. Everybody said that nothing happened between 1993 and 2001, but a lot of things happened." The commander mentioned the case of Edward Leary, the unemployed computer technician who took a firebomb into a Lexington Avenue number 4 train in 1994 and injured forty-eight people. He was holding the device, a mayonnaise jar filled with flammable liquid, when it went off. When police picked him up in Brooklyn, they saw that his arms were burned and the skin on his face was peeling off. "Now all anyone talks about is al-Qaeda, but there was Hamas and a lot of other jihad organizations. New York has a big Jewish community. There are targets all over the place. We didn't know what these terrorists were capable of doing," the commander explained.[5]

Ray McDermott's impression of Bill Morange was similar to the commander's quoted above. "It was very easy for me to say I was also going to do the right thing because Morange is my boss and when he says, we're going to do what's best and right, that's what I do. It shows you the kind of man he was and how much he loved and respected his people because [with the press conference] he put his own reputation and career on the line for his men. It reminded me a lot of my father, and I followed suit because you follow your boss. I still follow him."

o o o o o o o

Morange shook his head when he came out of the commissioner's office for the last time. He glanced at Mancini with suspicion in his deep blue eyes. Morange didn't know if Mancini spoke to the "PC" earlier that night and made some special deal. He was convinced that Mancini had few qualms about jumping the chain of command when an opportunity arose to get in the limelight. "Mancini would have put his name on a marquee if he could," a chief explained.

"Whatever you decide to do, I will be behind you 100 percent," Morange said to his officers, mustered a warm smile on his weathered face, straightened his shoulders, and lumbered out of the room. He headed toward City Hall, where Ray McDermott was waiting to hear the news.

Keith Ryan stood there quietly seething, too numb to realize what he felt. He was angry at Safir for ignoring the chief's advice. He hated himself for putting Morange in a position where he felt compelled to put his career on the line. He was ashamed that he'd talked to Celona, regardless of whether DCPI was involved. Ryan feared that his actions would hurt other cops by intensifying retaliation on the part of the department. Rage bubbled like lava beneath the veneer of his solemn eyes and the muscles in his shoulders tensed like a coiled snake. It was at that very moment that Mike Collins happened to walk into the police commissioner's waiting room.

Collins's tall, once-lanky frame had filled out since his days as a cop patrolling the streets. The curly brown hair of his youth was sheered short, and streaks of gray were invading the meadow above his ears. Only his warm jovial eyes remained exactly the same as they had in his youthful days as a cop.[6] Although Saturday was his regular day off, he'd driven into Manhattan especially to greet the officers and see if they needed his help with the press conference. He'd brought his son along so he could enjoy a taste of the job. The boy was standing next to his father, looking admiringly at the Emergency Service cops in their dress uniforms when Ryan exploded.

"Do you guys have any questions?" Collins asked.

"Yeah. What is wrong with you people? What the fuck is going on here?

You put our names out there, and now my picture's in the fuckin' paper!"
Ryan raged. The other cops exchanged looks and cast their eyes down.
Stunned, Collins put his hand on his son's shoulder and steered him into
another room. The boy had never heard anyone yell at his father like that.
Then Collins stepped back into the waiting room. "What the fuck is the
matter with you people? Why would you release our names to the press?
What is it with you people? What are you going to do when they kill my
brother and his kid? My mother, she lives alone!" Ryan continued.

"I'm sorry," Collins said.

"What are you gonna do when they kill my whole family? Are you gonna
give them an inspector's funeral, and you think I'm gonna be happy with
that?"

"Keith, I'm sorry that things happened this way." Collins's tone was
so sincere and gentle that Ryan was taken off guard. Then it dawned on
him that he was acting crazy, talking to an inspector like that, and he was
completely mortified.

"Boss, I'm sorry. I'm really sorry. I crossed the line. I know it's not you.
I owe you an apology. I'm just worried about my family." The other Emergency Service officers were standing there, shocked and dumbfounded.
Although Ryan has never forgiven himself, Dolan defended his partner
and understood where he was coming from. "Keith was the one who was
saying it so I wasn't going to stop him. You know if he didn't say it, I was
going to say it or any one of the guys was going to say it. It just happened
that Keith was the one who came out with it. I would never tell him to
shut up. I love that guy and he can say whatever the hell he wants," Dolan
later explained.

Mike Collins had spent enough time on the street to know that even
the best cops can lose their cool in situations in which they should show
restraint. He'd been there once or twice himself when confronted with
certain kinds of people while policing the public, although his humor and
instinct for self-preservation had kept him from stepping over the line,
and maybe his partner had helped. He'd read the papers that morning and
suspected that Ryan was feeling bad about talking to the reporter. It occurred to me that maybe the shooting was also testing Ryan's nerves. Any
time a cop fires his weapon and hurts someone, lingering like a stalker in
the background is the fear of being second-guessed.

Ryan didn't hear English call his name after Collins left the room. The
only sound he heard was the echo of his own angry voice bouncing inside

his skull. "I really admire Mike Collins . . . He's not out to hurt cops," Ryan explained. "He could have suspended me on the spot. He is one of the most stand-up guys I ever met. He let me do that whole tirade. He was a gentleman. He could have cut me into twelve pieces and left me in twelve parts of the city."

"Nick, what do you want to do? You were the boss on the job," Ryan asked, collecting himself.

"I can get up there and say something," Mancini volunteered.

"A synopsis, something generic."

"Yeah."

"OK, guys. When you go across to the press conference with the mayor, make sure that you look good," Masab said as the cops and their bosses made their way down to the lobby and marched through the revolving doors, into the front courtyard, past the security booth, and onward to City Hall.

∘ ∘ ∘ ∘ ∘ ∘ ∘

"Square your hat," Cliff Masab said to Dolan, whose hat was tumbling down his forehead. The cops were lining up outside the press room, getting ready to greet the mayor, when Marilyn Mode, the deputy commissioner of Public Information, walked in. Mode was in her forties, about 5'6" in height, and slim enough to carry her tailored suits with a certain degree of elegance and authority. A head of bright blonde hair crowned the perpetually frazzled look she wore on her face, which was echoed loudly in the behavior of her dog, a little white pedigree named Lil who accompanied her to work—to the consternation of her uniformed peers. Mode had managed the press for Safir years before when he was fire commissioner. For reasons few chiefs and deputy commissioners understood, he treated her word as gospel regardless of what others said.

Indeed, a number of top brass, including those loyal to Safir, viewed her as a cancer undermining his administration. "She didn't always have command of the facts and had no compunction about running to the police commissioner or Kelleher or Anemone with any wild accusation. She ruined a lot of reputations that way, hurt a lot of people. Once those things are out, it's hard to take them back," one chief explained. "She was a loose cannon and a bit of loon," noted another. "She wasn't great to be around in a crisis. She panicked easily. . . . She never could take responsibility," a third confirmed.

"What are you doing here?" Mode asked when she saw Masab standing next to Mancini, Dwyer, English, and the cops.

"I'm Cliff—"

"—I know who you are," she interrupted. "You're not supposed to be here. You weren't invited to this meeting. You know, you are doing a great disservice to these guys by coming down here, waving your union placard," Mode said in these or similar words, according to several officers who were there. They recalled she was shouting or talking in a loud, piercing pitch.

"I have every right to be here," Masab responded defensively.

"So you think you can just do whatever you please? Where the hell do you get off telling the commissioner what to do?" Mode continued.

"I'll do my job. You do yours," Masab countered.

"Who do you think you are? You're cops. You're just cops. You go in there and you stand behind the good Mayor and you answer his questions. You *will not* embarrass me. You *will not* embarrass the police commissioner! You think you can pick and choose what orders you're going to follow? If you don't go in there and answer questions, you will be suspended on the spot, and there won't be any more Emergency Service!" she screamed, according to the cops, and stormed out of the room.

"What the fuck just happened?" one cop asked.

"She thinks Cliff is here because it's a contract thing."

"This is not lookin' good!"

"Heads up, guys. The mayor's coming in," Masab said. By the time Giuliani entered the room, the cops were lined up and standing at attention.

"All right, you're going to file in the way you are and we are going to call you up to the podium. Then we'll have you make a statement to the press," Giuliani said, and then glided into the press room, leaving them reeling.

"He's pissed, he's really pissed," English said. Less than five minutes later, they were called into the press conference and he, Nick Mancini, Larry Dwyer, Mike Keenan, Mario Zorovic, Joe Dolan, and Keith Ryan joined Safir, Giuliani, and Charles Kammerdener on the stage. Kelleher was also there, standing next to Safir, hiding his broken arm from his wife who was away and hadn't yet heard that he'd gotten injured. After the short meeting, Giuliani began his closing remarks.

"The point is, they prevented a major terrorist attack from taking place," he said, and then gestured to one of the reporters who had his hand raised.

"Mr. Mayor, can we talk to some of the guys who actually went in?"

"Would you like to speak to one of the reporters?" Giuliani turned to John English.

"No, thank you," English replied. Safir likely fumed at the politely stated affront, and Marilyn Mode's naturally ruddy cheeks turned crimson. Then Mancini walked up to the microphone, identified himself as the Emergency Service captain and started talking.

"I don't think anybody was prepared to go in with an explosive device. We certainly have the tools that can prevent bullets from piercing us, but at the speed that shrapnel would come out of an explosive device, all the tools and barricades and body bunkers that we had wouldn't have done anything—and they realized that. It was almost as if they were going in naked, and that was a frightening thought. I think everybody was frightened. We left just before dawn, and that was it. My wife is eight months pregnant, I have two small children at home, and she was quite annoyed that I had to leave the house at two o'clock in the morning," Mancini said.[7]

"They didn't hesitate," Safir added when Mancini was going into the details of the story. Shortly after their captain's speech, the cops were ushered out of the press room.

"You know, we just blew our one opportunity. We just blew it!" Dwyer muttered as they left.

o o o o o o o

Perspectives varied about how the officers on the team had handled themselves in the face of the conflict of interests. English remained convinced that they'd done what was necessary to protect their families, even if it meant political suicide. "They didn't know. . . . Who knew? They didn't have the intelligence-gathering knowledge or ability to know in that amount of time. Not one person there knew if there was a connection between the Brooklyn terrorists and a larger organization or if there were other terrorists in the U.S. We had legitimate concerns. We honestly believe that they were part of a terrorist group, which it turns out they absolutely were. They weren't just two fanatics that were here on their own. I was disappointed. I didn't have anything bad to say about Safir until that day. They could have made it an even bigger story if they said, 'Listen, we don't want the team to appear because we're not sure who these people are.' It came down to ego. They weren't going to be told what to do by a bunch of cops."

In retrospect, Dolan wondered if they'd made a mistake. "Trying to turn down doing that press conference put a nail in the coffin. Telling the mayor that we weren't going to do the press conference was the worst thing we could have done. We shot ourselves right in the foot. A reporter [Larry Celona] from the *Post* started this whole thing. . . . Actually, this thing was on its way down the toilet right after the shots were fired. You could tell by the end of the job because the calmest people there were the people involved in it. Everybody else was running all over the place, bosses running past bosses, trying to do this and that at the scene."

While some supervisors understood where the cops were coming from and would have supported the decision had they been in command the night of the raid, others agreed with Dolan's assessment. "It was the lead story. NYPD Emergency Service Unit stymies a terrorist attack. Safir wanted the officers to stand behind him while he was giving this wonderful account of what they had done, which was a tremendous positive shot in the arm for the department. Keith Ryan and Joe Dolan weren't willing to do that, and they had some legitimate concerns. Safir was livid. He had people speak to them on the side, but they still didn't want to do it. Then they wind up in the *Post* with an extended interview. So, you know, that enraged Safir even more. There was a lot of talk that Dolan and Ryan could have gotten anything they wanted but, because of their actions, they would never get anything now. I think I might have handled it a little bit differently. If the police commissioner had asked me to stand behind him and say what I had done, I would have obliged. A lot of other people feel the same way. Keith chose not to and, to his credit, he stood his ground. But the longer-lasting effects of this decision are just coming to light now. He angered the police commissioner and, when you anger the police commissioner, guess what? You lose."

Most of the brass at One Police Plaza, including a few who had once been street cops and street commanders, didn't understand what got into the cops. "Downtown viewed it as a positive thing," a respected chief explained, "They could have easily done it around them, which they had to do anyway, but to give them their opportunity to take a bow and publically congratulate them for their heroic act, saving hundreds, if not thousands of lives. . . . who knows what it would have done to the economy. I mean, you could roll this thing out and get an idea of the potential devastation that could have occurred had the attack gone off."

Looking at the larger picture and knowing "the job's not on the level," some of the cops figured there was a hidden script they didn't understand. Certainly the growing rift between Giuliani and his adversaries was deepening. Many members of the public viewed his crackdown on quality-of-life violations or "zero-tolerance" policing policies that led to stopping and sometimes arresting people for minor infractions as an excuse to discriminate against racial minorities. Early on, Howard Safir had laid the ground for a battle with the police unions when he refused to cater to top police union officials, appointing the task to lower-ranking deputies. Union presidents consider themselves equal in rank to the police commissioner by virtue of the power they muster among the troops. Problems between management and the Patrolmen's Benevolent Association (PBA) were probably inevitable. But by showing what was perceived as disrespect to the more cooperative unions, Safir was sticking his nose in a hornet's nest.

One chief, assigned to a street command, recalled the course of events. "At first it seemed Giuliani would be the best-loved mayor in police history. I mean, if a cop got a hangnail or was hurt in a car accident, the mayor was at the hospital to see him. Then the contract happened with PERB [Public Employment Relations Board] handling the arbitration. The cops felt a claim to why New York was turning around [and therefore deserved a raise]. This started in 1996, and Giuliani wanted to stop it. There was an immediate soft job action [minor reduction in activity, small demonstration, or similar types of protest] on a Friday. Throughout my history job actions were always treated with the same level of apologist policing as disturbances in the street, you know. You let people vent. That's smart management anyway. You just can't come out with a hammer. The unions have real power. You can't go out there and dictate every summons to write or every collar to make. So Chief Anemone calls all the commanders down to headquarters and goes into this, 'We're not going to tolerate this.' The job action ended, but the talks continued and, maybe a year later in 1997, the union was able to get a modified job action going, 50 percent guerrilla warfare. The confident arrogance of Mayor Giuliani was the problem. He wouldn't schmooze the issue with the press, and neither would Howard Safir," the chief concluded.

"Well, Rudy is like a pit bull. He's nice to have around when someone is breaking into your house, but otherwise you're afraid he might eat your kids," comedian Chris Rock said in response to a question by Bill Moyers, capturing the ironies of the Giuliani-Safir administration in terms of public perception. Despite the department's problems with the press, the public, and the unions, many members of the brass considered Safir a decent commissioner. He was tough but loyal to those whom he chose to serve directly under him. Crime had been falling and continued to keep pace with the downward national trend.

But Safir's flaws would come to haunt him. He was not comfortable with the press and preferred to govern in secrecy. Appointing a woman as deputy commissioner of Public Information who could not compensate for this weakness didn't help. While loyalty is important in any administration, it should be balanced by willingness on the part of subordinates to respectfully speak the truth and advise their bosses accordingly. Some who were deeply loyal to Safir suggested that maybe he tried too hard to please the mayor. "Howard was loyal to a fault," a high-ranking chief explained. Safir was willing to be Rudy's shadow, fall guy, and servant and do his bidding without question or compromise.

There is a hubris and arrogance that can accompany power even among good men and women. Cops and civilians who reach high office sometimes become enamored of their rank, are quick to take offense, and are unforgiving in their perception of how subordinates should act in their presence. I'm not suggesting that Safir was this kind of man. Perhaps all he demanded was the respect that came with the office, and he would have listened to Morange's appeal on behalf of the cops, if the story naming two of the officers hadn't appeared in the *Post*. On the other hand, Safir and Giuliani wanted to use the raid to promote the success of their administration and might not have been willing to listen to the fears of some unruly white shield cops. From the cops' perspective, the issue of safety was involved, and Safir was willing to throw them under the bus to profess his loyalty to the mayor and make his administration look good.

o o o o o o o

On Monday morning Lou Anemone met with the police commissioner to discuss what had been going on in the department while he was in Cancun. When Anemone learned the details of the investigation of the suspects, he cautioned Safir against moving too fast because there had been other incidents in the past. Just six months before, a Palestinian man, Ali Abu Kamal, had opened fire on the observation deck of the Empire State Building. One person was killed and six more injured before the suspect turned the gun on himself. When the police recovered his body, they found a note blaming the United States for Israeli aggression against his people.[8]

Anemone believed that other terrorists, acting alone or as part of a group, might be standing by, preparing for an attack. "It's not out of the realm of possibility that cops would be targets. They do everything we ask them to do at work; the least we can do is take a little bit of extra time or effort to make sure they are OK. We have to be absolutely certain there are no loose pieces before we bring the cops forward," Anemone said. Safir told Anemone they'd already had a press conference on Saturday and that other events were being planned. "We argued about that [but] he was the police commissioner. . . . I was always trying to convince them that we were the target and we would always be the target, so we had to keep the bad guys guessing," Anemone explained.

As soon as he returned to his office, Anemone had his secretary schedule a meeting with the six members of the entry team. Then he sat down at his desk and studied the incident, calling the ranking officers involved to get their stories and studying relevant documents. "I looked at it all, the short time span that they had to gather as much information as they could and then proceed forward. It was a great idea to take along the informant and the translator because they had to go in the back of the building to find the apartment. All the steps they took, stopping the trains that went underneath the place just prior to the execution of the raid, the people they had on standby from the Fire Department, EMS, their ability to keep this all under wraps and quiet and confidential. I was impressed. They had it all covered. I was just pissed I wasn't there," Anemone explained.

When the six officers sat down in his office, Anemone congratulated them and said he was proud. He did not pick out particular officers but treated them as a team. Neither Ryan nor Dolan felt comfortable during the meeting. "He didn't make eye contact with me and Joe," Ryan explained. Anemone denied treating either cop differently from the rest of the team. He felt nothing but admiration for what they'd done and certainly didn't mean to slight anyone. "I think they transferred some of the feeling they had for Safir onto me," he said.

By this time, rumors were beginning to circulate among the top brass regarding the existence of tensions between Safir and Kelleher and Anemone. While Giuliani had once protected Anemone, the latter's outspoken and confrontational style was emerging as a problem for Safir, who didn't appear to have Bratton's ability to manage certain types of creative people. For his part, Anemone believed that Kelleher acted unprofessionally in a variety of matters that were important to him. That Anemone sided with the officers on the issues surrounding the press conference probably didn't help their case in view of his standing with the first deputy commissioner and the commissioner. Thus, the fissures that were beginning to emerge between the department, the press, and the unions were reverberating within the highest levels of police management. Regardless, the cops didn't know what was happening above their heads and assumed that Anemone, Safir, and Kelleher were aligned.

○ ○ ○ ○ ○ ○ ○

Around Wednesday, August 6, Keith Ryan and Joe Dolan drove into Manhattan for separate appointments with two psychologists from Psychological Services, the internal unit responsible for fitness of duty evaluations of recruit and veteran officers. Trauma assessment and counseling in the wake of a shooting were mandated for cops and bore no stigma for officers involved.

In theory a clinical interview in the wake of a critical incident makes sense. In practice it doesn't appear to accomplish much except to screen out extremes of mental instability and protect the department legally. In-depth clinical interviews are rarely practiced. The questions psychologists ask officers who have been involved in a shooting are not designed to get an overall clinical picture but to weed out suicidal depression, psychosis, and violence-prone behavior. Male cops, in particular, view seeing a shrink with skepticism and as a sign of weakness and femininity. The police psychologists in Psychological Services are also seen as dangerous because they owe their allegiance to the department and have the power to seize cops' guns.

"You realize you are in a catch-22 situation when you go for the trauma counseling because they might take away your gun, which is like taking a car away from a race driver. So what are you now? You are an Indy 500 driver without a car. You don't know what you are. Your law enforcement status is connected to your ability to have a gun and the responsibility that comes with it. Now we are saying that we don't trust you with that gun. It's not like we are going to send you back to something you know. We are going to put you on modified duty and send you some place where you don't do law enforcement. Once people find out you don't have a gun, they won't respect you as a cop. There are a lot of expressions, like rubber gun squad. All have very negative connotations," a police commander explained.

Neither Dolan nor Ryan had any intention of revealing their thoughts to the department psychologists. Keith Ryan plastered a pleasant look on his face when the psychologist ushered him into her office. She gestured toward a chair, where he sat down and surreptitiously checked her out. She was heavyset and wore an ill-fitting suit that bunched up around her hips. Her hair was dyed a uniform blanket of brown like from a do-it-yourself Clairol kit. She carried herself with an air of authority but little warmth, which didn't add to his sense of comfort. It didn't help that she went through her list of questions like a telemarketer reading a script.

"So tell me why you're here?" she began.

"I was told to be here."

"Why?"

"I shot someone. You know better than I do."

"OK, well, I'm going to ask you a few questions. How are you sleeping these days?"

"I slept like a baby."

"Have you noticed any change in your eating habits since the shooting?"

"No. I eat when I'm hungry."

"What about drinking? Are you drinking more than you usually do?"

"Well, I'm drinking a lot of water," Ryan said, trying his best to hide the sarcasm that was lurking inside.

"You know what I mean."

"No. I'm not."

"Drinking?"

"Yes."

"Are you dysfunctional?"

"Dysfunctional? I'm functioning just fine."

"I mean, you know, are you OK sexually?"

"Miss, I never had a problem shooting these guys. I still don't have a problem shooting these guys. I shot two fuckin' scumbags that were trying to kill me. That's the bottom line. I didn't shoot a child. I didn't hurt anybody that was at the wrong place at the wrong time. I shot two people who made a real good attempt at killing me and that doesn't bother me one bit. I didn't lose an ounce of sleep over this; if I had to do it again, I'd do it again!" Ryan recalled saying, dismissing her inquiry and justifying the shooting in one punch while establishing the absence of internal conflict.

"Well, OK then. We're done here. I'm going to give you a few days off. That's the routine. You can go back to work next Monday."

"I can go?"

"Yes." Ryan got up and walked out of the office, glad the interview was over but feeling annoyed. "I was like—what did you even call me in for? Are you going to ask pertinent questions? I don't even know what a pertinent question is, under the circumstances, but if you're going to call me in there, at least ask pertinent questions. She didn't ask me anything that pertained to what exactly happened," he explained later when he reflected on the interaction.

There were a number of issues the psychologist could have raised. If he did in fact appear defensive and irritable and she pointed that out, he might have confessed that he was annoyed by her questions, pissed off at the police commissioner for ordering the cops to appear at the press conference, angry at himself, perhaps, and furious at Larry Celona for exposing him in the *Post*. Had she taken a clinical history, she might have discovered a well of rage was hidden beneath the events surrounding the shooting. Ryan had a lot of things to be angry about, some of which weren't visible even to himself. He was also afraid. He didn't know what the future would bring but sensed it was something ominous. "This is America, not Israel, but it's starting to happen here. We were just in our infancy stages in understanding what terrorists were willing to do. I kept telling everyone that this guy was different. The suspects weren't afraid to die," Ryan explained.

o o o o o o o

On August 9, 1997, the bottom dropped halfway out of the Police Department when a police officer assaulted Haitian immigrant Abner Louima in the 7-0 Precinct in south Brooklyn. All eyes turned from the raid to the shameful events that occurred in the first-floor bathroom when Justin Volpe committed the single most heinous act of police brutality in the history of American policing—with Charles Schwartz or possibly another officer guarding the door.[9]

Keith Ryan and Joe Dolan were working the midnight shift when the incident began to unfold. A fight broke out in front of a club. Justin Volpe, Charles Schwartz, and some other officers from the 7-0 Precinct responded. Volpe tried to break up the fight and was "sucker punched" by one of the participants, whom he misidentified as Louima. Louima was arrested, handcuffed, and put in the back of a patrol car, where the beating began. When he and the officers arrived at the station house, Volpe dragged Louima into the bathroom and sexually assaulted him with the handle of a mop or broom, or plumber's helper. The crime was not reported until after Louima had been admitted to the hospital, where surgeons spent hours trying to mend his mangled gut.

The next day, when Ryan and Dolan heard about the incident, they were relieved they hadn't responded to the job. "Thank God we didn't get sucked in and they didn't call us to do an evidence search. . . . It started as a bullshit fight and, if it came over as a 10-13, they probably cancelled it right away. Believe me when I tell you that God works in funny ways, because I was so grateful that we didn't get pulled into that whole mess because my buddy was the patrol supervisor that night and they raked him over the coals," Ryan explained.

Few of the more than 37,000 officers in the NYPD believed the allegations against Volpe were true. Only later, when the facts mushroomed into a cloud of indisputable horror, did they finally admit the truth, and most waited until Volpe confessed during the trial. "There is no way that this guy could have done that; nobody could be that sick. How could you be a cop and do that? Volpe worked midnights. We used to run into him all the time, and let me tell you, he had a reputation for being a fucking hothead, a shit bird, a loose cannon, but still I couldn't believe that," Ryan said.

Morange had a similar reaction. "I told Charlie Campisi (chief of Internal Affairs) that I would bet everything I owned that it didn't happen and, when Charlie knew the facts, he said, Billy you are going to be shocked. Man was I wrong. I would have been standing there in my socks if they would have let me keep them. If you do your homework on guys involved in things like this, you'll find out later on that they were doing a lot of things wrong. Volpe had a reputation, all of them did. They were heavy drinkers. They were out partying. There was even a rumor that they were shooting at one another out on the street one time."

Initially headquarters shared Morange's disbelief. Lou Anemone, beloved Brooklyn borough commander Pat Brennan, and one or two precinct commanders were some of the few who didn't think Louima's story was a lie. Another street commander explained,[10] "I was CO at [another] precinct when it happened. I was sitting with the chief in a community meeting, and he had a very calm way about him. He said, 'There's a report they put a broomstick in this guy's rectum.' Chief Brennan is not saying it's crazy. You could see by the way he just kept eating his sandwich and saying what happened, that he thought it was something. He said the guy was in Coney Island Hospital. Next thing you know, it's in the papers. It was like a hand grenade, Diallo too, like there is a moment or two before it explodes. . . . No community unrest at first. . . . Then the media. There's a picture of him coming out of the hospital . . . First you hear this guy got injured in a homosexual club . . . but I sensed that something happened here and I realized that so, maybe it was a gay club, but they aren't bad people. You're starting to hear things about his injuries and you realize it could have happened. I was ashamed to be a cop. After Safir dumps the precinct commander, he starts this committee [on police use of force]. I get on the phone and it's from an inspector in the press office, 'They were going around the room and some guy was saying you can't feel safe and be a black man and walk the streets in the 7-0 Precinct and you're not afraid of the criminals, you're afraid of the cops. Now [the name of the commander who's telling the story]. . . . We know him. He walks around with us. You leave him there. Don't take him out of Brooklyn.' I call my guys in because I knew they'd be ashamed to be cops, and I tell them the story that the press inspector told me. He [the community leader] is talking about you. . . . The guy doesn't know me. . . . He's talking about the way you react to the community and you should be proud and you shouldn't be ashamed. Then we had someone in the community talk to the cops."

Lou Anemone recalled the initial briefing with Charles Campisi. "I was sitting there listening to the same thing that Safir, Kelleher, and a couple of other people were hearing. What was remarkable to me was that I think there was a lot of skepticism in the room, but to me it had the ring of truth, sitting there listening I could believe it a little more. I knew a little bit of the history in the 7-0. It was a precinct that had given us trouble in the last couple of years. They had a wild PBA (Patrolmen's Benevolent Association) delegate there. At this point in time I was thinking he was still there or he might have been under investigation, disciplined, or on suspension. It was a tough place, with cops fighting the department, doing things off on their own," Anemone said.

Regardless, everyone at the debriefing agreed that the accusation had to be handled as if it were true. "It was decided that the sergeant on the desk and other supervisors on that night would be held accountable and their actions investigated," Anemone explained. The Internal Affairs Bureau was given carte blanche to pursue every end of the investigation. Just as Safir was getting ready to adjourn that first briefing, Anemone spoke up.

"You have to do more than that," he said.

"What do you mean?" Safir replied.

"There's the CO [commanding officer] and an XO [executive officer]. You can't leave this place the same. We have to take steps."

"Well, they were off. Quinlin's still on vacation," Safir said.

"The XO was in that morning. The safest measure here is to remove that whole management layer," Anemone insisted, although the commanding officer, Jeremiah Quinlin, was his friend. Not long after the meeting, Safir replaced Quinlin with Ray Diaz, an ambitious inspector who was known for his even temperament and hands-on approach to policing.

The assault took place in one of two open stalls in the unisex bathroom located off the hall, opposite an office space, enclosed by a plasterboard and glass partition that didn't reach the ceiling. Rust and a thick mix of vacuous grunge layered the water pipes and floors surrounding the toilet where the crime occurred. The toilet bowl looked like it had never been cleaned. Brown stains of blood and feces were smeared in isolated spots on the dark blue walls.

Prosecutors, federal agents, Internal Affairs, and Crime Scene detectives lit on the 70th Precinct like locusts. Lockers were taped off as part of the crime scene. Volpe's gloves and shoes were photographed and bagged. The suspects' lockers looked similar to those of other cops. Inside one door was posted *Penthouse* photos of naked women; above and to the left was the face of Jesus Christ on a prayer card. Justin Volpe had a picture of Bob Marley pasted on the inside of his locker door. Schwartz had a blood-red Marine Corps placard on the outside of his.

More revealing, perhaps, was some graffiti in the locker room. Next to Volpe's black locker with an arrow pointed toward his door, was a cartoon image of a man with the puffed up chest and arms of a competitive body builder. His legs and torso had been drawn as sticks. Although Volpe was not tested for drugs, Charles Campisi was convinced that the crime was committed during a bout of "'roid rage."

By the time the case went to trial, most of the brass were convinced that Volpe was guilty, but the cops still weren't ready to yield. They'd rather believe the ridiculous—that the victim had harmed himself by engaging in rough, consensual homosexual sex—rather than feel the shame that came with the recognition that one of their own had committed the heinous assault. Rich Teemsma recalled the investigation lasting for months and permeating every division and borough. Internal Affairs detectives absconded and tested every mop, broomstick, and plunger owned by the City of New York in search of the weapon. Eventually the detectives in the

Manhattan office of the Bomb Squad were forced to bring in their own cleaning equipment and hide it in quarters so they could do the floors.

Meanwhile, sometime after the incident, the police commissioner convened a committee to explore the use of force. Anemone was not asked to attend, although he was the highest-ranking street commander in the department. Later, when the committee released its findings to other members of the brass, Anemone wrote a number of comments, which were apparently ignored, and there were no revisions to the report. This increased Anemone's frustration, and tensions at the top mounted.

Meanwhile, Volpe's crime hit New York City like a tsunami, submerging the raid, the press conference, and issues of terrorism under a giant swell of anguish and pain. "It's ironic but what saved us was fuckin' Abner Louima. But it was a double-edged sword. It took us out of the limelight, but people forgot about the terrorist threat, that we'd aborted a disaster. But another would come," Ryan said.

Abner Louima hadn't really saved them.

7

TOP COPS

IN THE WAKE OF THE RAID, THE COPS and detectives began receiving invitations to events honoring their accomplishments. They started in the fall with a banquet sponsored by the FBI and culminated in an award ceremony in Washington, D.C., and a meeting with President Bill Clinton in 1998. Recognition came from state and national law enforcement agencies, businesses, and religious and cultural associations—everyone but the upper echelons of the NYPD.

James Kallstrom, assistant director of the FBI, announced in a letter to Howard Safir dated September 17 that the officers had won the Prevention of Terrorism Award. Kallstrom requested that the police commissioner or other top-ranked member of the brass accompany the recipients to a ceremonial dinner at the Waldorf Astoria Hotel on Manhattan's East Side: "I believe you will join me in noting the prevention of any terrorist act is of the utmost importance to police work. . . . It is my hope that you or an appropriate command official can be present to take part in the presentation." Listed among the recipients were Charles Kammerdener, Ray McDermott, Nick Mancini, John English, Keith Ryan, Mike Keenan, Mario Zorovic, Joe Dolan, Jim Black, Paul Yurkiw, and Rich Teemsma. The police commissioner didn't attend the October affair, nor did any of his deputy commissioners and three- and four-star "super chiefs."

A few weeks later, Chase Bank organized an elegant banquet for the officers and their wives. Joe McGuire, Jeff Oberdier, and Eddie Hayes, a sergeant in the Bomb Squad, were included in the invitation. The Emergency Service cops and Bomb Squad detectives sat at separate tables. A photographer, hired by Chase, took pictures of each. The glossy postcard photo that the detectives received as a memento captured the jealous tensions erupting within the Bomb Squad. It was easy to pick out McGuire in the crowd. Even men as tall and strong as Teemsma and Yurkiw looked petite standing next to their sadly overweight peer. McGuire's wife was a pleasantly plump woman of average height, short brown hair, rosy cheeks and bright red lipstick. She was wearing a conservative round-collared blouse that reached above her clavicle and would have made a poster girl for good Catholic wife—that is, if she hadn't been giving the finger to the camera. Yurkiw and Teemsma were convinced the gesture was intentional; that she wanted to spoil their memory of the occasion to get back at them for "stealing" her husband's case.

o o o o o o o

By the time Teemsma and Yurkiw were summoned downtown to meet the commissioner, the internal feud in the squad had blossomed into full-scale war. Neither detective had firsthand knowledge about the fiasco surrounding the press conference with Emergency Service. They'd heard but largely ignored the rumors that floated like flatulence, poisoning reputations and careers: the Emergency Service cops were fighting among themselves; supervisors were trying to steal the show; the mayor was irate.

The two detectives got in their car and headed south on the West Side Highway, east on Chambers Street, around the block, past the security booth, and into the parking lot behind One Police Plaza. As soon as they opened the door, they started to feel the weight of the building's embrace. They viewed the Puzzle Palace as a vertical dungeon where rank-and-file police transferred in to work and came out different men, having lost their street cop identity.

A police commissioner's aide greeted the officers and escorted them into the War Room. Yurkiw and Teemsma sat down in two huge chairs surrounding the oval table with the hole in the center where top brass sat. Although neither officer had been in the room before and didn't know it was used for CompStat, they felt its grand and intimidating mood.

When Eddie Norris walked into the War Room, neither detective stood up. They knew each other from the old days when they'd been rookies together in Midtown South. Yurkiw and Teemsma assumed Norris was still close to them in rank and sentiment. Norris was shorter than average but had a strong, solid build. His head was shiny and bald, and he had the same vibrant eyes and bad boy sex appeal as the character Vic Mackey in the FX

TV series *The Shield*. Indeed, even in the NYPD, he was known for attracting beautiful women whom he enjoyed showering with expensive gifts.

"You guys are still together and doing good things!" Norris said, grinning.

"Eddie, how ya been?" Yurkiw responded.

"Good, I'm good. By the way, you guys did a really nice job with that Brooklyn bomb! I heard all about it."

"Eddie, where you been? You know you look like a doctor, dressed up in that suit like that. I heard you made sergeant. So which boss are ya' driving?"

Norris threw back his head and laughed. "I'm the deputy commissioner of Operations."

"You what? Holy shit! You're jerking me around. Really?" Yurkiw pulled his knees out from under the table and started to get up. "OK, well, I'm halfway up now. Ya' want me to genuflect?"

"You guys haven't changed. I'm glad to see things are going well. It looks like there's some plans in the making. Everything is looking good for both of you. Hey, anytime you want to talk, my door is open. Just give me a call." Norris turned around and left the room.

"He's still a regular guy," Teemsma said.

The aide returned and escorted the detectives into the commissioner's office on the fourteenth floor. Yurkiw barely saw the room's interior. "I was in awe, trying to make visual contact with the commissioner and not look around too much." Being honored by the police commissioner in his office was like being on top of the world.

At a trim 6'3" tall, Howard Safir was an imposing figure. In a different way, Patrick Kelleher was as well. His cheeks radiated a ruddy glow. His eyes were cool. A short, thin, wily man with gray hair and a windswept face, the first deputy commissioner reminded Yurkiw of Willie Shoemaker, the Texas jockey.

"You're going to have a very good Christmas," Safir said, and then shook their hands and posed for pictures. He looked so content that his frown seemed irrelevant, usurped by the almost warm glow in his eyes.

"You guys did a great job. You will have a good Christmas," Kelleher echoed Safir's words.

After the photographic session concluded, Teemsma and Yurkiw were escorted outside. Both men were feeling high. "One PP" suddenly seemed like a friendlier place. They were convinced that they had not misinterpreted the hidden message contained in the commissioner's words: they'd been promised promotion to second grade.

"I refused one promotion," Yurkiw said to Teemsma, recalling the week after he got shot.

"You what?"

"I told you. Chief Johnson sent me the new vest and said I'd be getting a gold [i.e., detective's] shield. It didn't feel right. There were guys in Emergency Service who'd been in line for detective for more years than I'd been on the job. I said no."

"You didn't know any better," Teemsma said. Cops rarely refuse a promotion because there's no predicting when or if it will ever be offered again. Still, Teemsma understood why Yurkiw did what he did. Sure, the guys in Emergency Service might have congratulated him to his face. Behind his back, they might have been resentful, spawning gossip to undermine his character. Teemsma predicted that similar trouble would emerge in the Bomb Squad if he didn't handle it right. Under Bajek and Black, advancement in the Bomb Squad had followed the system encouraged by McGuire, with seniority ahead of hard work and accomplishment. There were senior detectives in the squad who deserved a promotion. There were also others who felt entitled because of their place in line. Teemsma liked the Bomb Squad. Joe McGuire was the only guy who really got under his skin. Teemsma wanted to keep relations cordial and not lose friends. He thought it was better to approach the matter directly rather than have it come through the back door when the orders came down. He chose that weekend to break the news. He was visiting his father, who lived next door to a fellow detective named Tommy McBride. Teemsma was in his father's backyard when he saw Detective McBride outside.

"Hey, Tommy, how ya doing? You got a beer? I want to talk to you about something anyway," Teemsma said.

"Sure. Meet you out here." McBride went inside and came back out a few minutes later carrying two cold beers. He and Teemsma sat down in the shade and talked about the job.

"Tommy, look. I wanted to let you know out front. I'm getting promoted. Me and Paulie met with the PC last week. I don't want no backstabbing, so I wanted to tell you man to man, face to face."

"Hey, Rich, that's great. Good for you!" McBride replied, but his smile was half-hearted and his words bounced off Teemsma's ears with a hollow ring. McBride was younger but had been in the Bomb Squad longer, which put him ahead seniority-wise.

By the time Teemsma and Yurkiw returned to work the following week, news of their promotion had spread around the squad like a virulent disease. Conversations ceased when they entered the room. Lips were pursed, heads were bent over desks, and hands were flipping uncomfortably through the *New York Post*. "If you walk into a room and it's full of people and as soon as you walk in everybody shuts up, then you know they are talking about you, so you know something is up," Teemsma explained.

"It would be a helluva lot friendlier in here if we'd both been blown to Mars," Yurkiw said as he and Teemsma glanced at each other and then headed into the Cave to fill their coffee cups. When he got back in the squad room, Teemsma sat down at his desk and tried to dismiss the chill in the atmosphere as a figment of his imagination. The guys could have been talking about anything, he told himself. But, as the days passed, the hostility increased, and he was forced to admit his perception was real. McBride had relayed their conversation to guys in the squad, who told McGuire, who then fueled the flames among the other detectives.

McGuire also had Black's ear. As a first-grade detective and a high official in the International Association of Bomb Technicians and Investigators, McGuire traveled throughout the United States, making friends with people who had favors to give, increasing his worth among bosses and peers. McGuire was known as the go-to man if an officer needed something, like tickets to a ball game or an upgrade on an airline. He also provided information. "You know boss, I heard _____. You might want to check that out," McGuire would say when he learned something of interest to superiors whom he saw when he went upstairs at One Police Plaza distributing Bomb Tech T-shirts. By creating a web of debt among peers and superiors, he upped his rank and built a powerful domain.

Black was new in the squad. He didn't understand explosives, wasn't familiar with the personnel, and didn't know the informal rules governing the distribution of resources. McGuire became Black's institutional memory. His status as a veteran detective and the president of a prestigious organization made him the logical choice. So it wasn't hard for McGuire to convince Black that Teemsma and Yurkiw were arrogant upstarts who were moving in on the senior guys. There was some degree of tension between Teemsma and Black anyway, given that Black sometimes acted like a spineless inside boss as far as Rich was concerned.

Soon new rumors spread: Teemsma and Yurkiw were soliciting publicity from outside contacts. It wasn't a secret that Yurkiw worked security for a Jewish philanthropy on his days off. The detectives in the Bomb Squad assumed the partners' names were in local papers because of Yurkiw's "Jewish connection," that neither officer would be getting awards if they weren't promoting themselves. Suspicion in the squad was confirmed when the Jewish War Veterans nominated Teemsma and Yurkiw for an award. When Black learned about the award, he issued a command. Neither detective would be allowed to attend an event unless a boss and other team members were also included.

"Anytime there was a dinner or invitation to anything pertaining to the Brooklyn job, it was either we all go or you're not going. . . . When the bosses weren't on the itinerary, we were told to make phone calls to get them invited; finally I told Black that I wasn't responsible. I didn't ask people to ask us. 'You call them up or contact DCPI and have them get in touch. It's not my place to do that,'" Yurkiw said.

Gossip about the two detectives spread from the squad's Manhattan office to the range at Rodman's Neck to bosses at headquarters until there was no place the two officers could go that wasn't soaked in venomous wrath. "I could feel it when I walked into a room, the sudden silence. It was like I am looking around, and I see all this blood, and I say, who is bleeding? Then I look in the mirror behind me and I've got thirty nines [9-mm automatic handguns] in my back. That was me bleeding there; I didn't even know it," Teemsma explained.

On October 20, 1997, the Jewish War Veterans awarded Public Service plaques to Yurkiw and Teemsma for "Outstanding Heroism in the Line of Duty." Oberdier and McGuire received awards for "Americanism and Patriotism." Teemsma was happy that Oberdier was recognized. He had been there during the critical stages of the job, helping them think through the task and manage their fears and keeping McGuire at bay.

Michael Julian, a former NYPD boss and current head of security at Rockefeller Center, announced the next major award. In a letter addressed to Ray McDermott on October 21, 1997, Julian invited Yurkiw, Teemsma, and the six men on the Emergency Service entry team to the Christmas tree lighting on December 2, 1997. Prior to the event, RCPI Trust, the owners of Rockefeller Center, were going to honor the officers and their families at a dinner in the Top Room at Hurley's, an elegant restaurant.

Meanwhile, the atmosphere in the Bomb Squad was starting to get under Teemsma's skin. Sometimes he'd doubt himself. Maybe he and Paul hadn't done anything unusual and the Fourth Avenue job was no different from the routine others they'd handled before. Then he'd rehash the incident and realize that he was right. The job was unnerving and dangerous. He and Yurkiw had picked up the job that McGuire didn't want when he thought nothing would come of it. They'd played key roles from beginning to end. When all was said and done, Teemsma had let McGuire play with the robot to get him off his back.

Just after the tree ceremony, when Teemsma was running an errand at One Police Plaza, he dropped in to speak to Ed Norris at his office. Norris welcomed him in, and they spent a few minutes shooting the breeze. Then Teemsma got to the point.

"Listen, I got a favor to ask."

"Whaddaya need?"

"Tell me, do you think the Brooklyn job is worth a promotion?"

"Absolutely!" Norris replied.

"OK, then, do you think you could back us up and help us get this promotion? We won't say anything."

"Absolutely, I'll speak to Anemone and the commissioner," Norris said. Teemsma left One Police Plaza feeling more optimistic than he had in weeks. With the "PC," "the first dep," and the deputy commissioner of Operations on their side, the promotion seemed like a done deal. Teemsma's confidence was bolstered several weeks later when, in separate conversations, Black told him and Yurkiw to make sure they had their dress uniforms in order. They were going to headquarters to get a promotion to second grade.

They didn't know that Black might have been playing two roles; responding to messages from above while campaigning against them behind their backs. It was common knowledge that Anemone had gotten Black his current position in the Bomb Squad. So it wasn't a surprise when he paid Anemone a visit to convince him the detectives should not be given special consideration. "This is part of what they do. These guys were not a paragon of virtue because they did what everybody else does on a daily basis. . . . We were also concerned that the two were politicking for the promotion, rather than letting it happen in due time," Anemone recalled. "But, it's true; the department does promote some cops for meritorious police work," he added in response to my question.[1]

It's no secret that promotions are sometimes based on things other than excellent police work. The drivers of top brass are routinely promoted for taxiing their bosses around, although some do more, acting as administrative lieutenants and organizing their superior's working life. Officers also get promoted because they have a friend in the right place at the right time who owes them a favor and is willing to fight on their behalf. Make no mistake about it; women are sometimes promoted over more-qualified men because the police commissioner wants to prove that his department doesn't discriminate. A pretty face and little charm, coupled with cautious flirtation and an understanding of politics, can go a long way in manipulating weak-kneed members of the brass.

Anemone gave his opinion about the detectives' promotion to Safir and Kelleher, who may or may not have considered it when they reviewed the list. A high-ranking member of the brass close to Kelleher denied that he was influenced by Black and involved in any decision that compromised Teemsma's and Yurkiw's efforts to move ahead in their careers. "Pat never had a conversation with Black. In fact, he never had a conversation with Black about anything. This is the first time I've heard any down side to that situation, and I know for a fact that Kelleher wasn't involved."

Sometime later, Teemsma was outside the police commissioner's office when it dawned on him that something had gone awry. He had been summoned to headquarters to receive the Centurion Award. Although recipients were chosen by an outside organization, the police commissioner bestowed the gift of a three-hundred-dollar check. Teemsma was standing in the waiting room near the front desk when Safir and Kelleher walked in, accompanied by a slew of top brass, Eddie Norris among them. Teemsma looked at Norris and noticed the uncomfortable look on his face. "I could see him backpedaling like he wanted to walk back through the door he just entered. I said 'Hello,' but I knew, at that point, he wasn't on my side either," Teemsma said.

Still, it was disappointing when promotions came and went and neither Yurkiw nor Teemsma was on the list. Despite his anger, a part of Teemsma understood. "Inside the NYPD, there is an unwritten rule. Bosses don't go against bosses. Black was a boss. He did not want us to get promoted because he would have had a mutiny on his hands. Jim Black was afraid to go to bat for anyone. He was a nice person, but he had no backbone," Teemsma concluded.

Teemsma and Yurkiw waited until after the holidays to talk to John Bajek. They told Black first so he wouldn't think they were secretly going over his head. Black turned pale and looked scared when he heard what the men were planning to do. Yurkiw assumed that something about their partnership unnerved Black. "Bosses always said they couldn't handle us together. I guess we were intimidating. They assumed we were so tightly knit that they couldn't trust us, I guess, like one lies and the other swears [to it] and vice versa."

I doubt that Black was afraid of the two detectives. Bajek was a far more dangerous threat. If he wasn't already informed and in agreement with Black's interpretation of events, the officers' actions might force the lieutenant to explain why he was sabotaging two of his men. If Teemsma and Yurkiw happened to rub Bajek the wrong way, he could also blame Black for not controlling his men. Bajek wouldn't think twice of serving Black's "balls up on a platter" if he had a reason and no one higher ranking intervened.

Teemsma and Yurkiw waited for more than an hour outside Bajek's office while the inspector marched in and out, looking important. Several times, he walked right past the detectives but avoided eye contact and acted as though they weren't there. I can't say for sure if Bajek's behavior was intended to demonstrate his superiority or if it reflected an oblivious interactional style or preoccupation with other affairs. Regardless, when he finally saw fit to call the officers in, Teemsma approached the matter directly and didn't waste any time.

"Inspector, we understood we were getting promoted, and we're wondering if you could tell us why our names weren't on the list."

"Well, there have been times in my career that I have felt I have been overlooked too," Bajek said what was probably true in a tone as cool as marble inside an igloo. The message was clear. Suck it up and quit complaining, because that's how things work in the Police Department and that's how they work around here. Self-serving asshole! Teemsma thought, figuring that Black and McGuire had gotten to Bajek, too. "I made a big mistake, trusting the guys. I never should have told Tommy McBride. I never should have told him. I should have just let it pop up in the orders. You dangle money in front of cops' faces and all bets are off. I'm number ten in line, according to their pecking order, because I got there after ten guys, and Paul after that," Teemsma explained.

On January 8, 1998, Yurkiw and Teemsma were happy to learn that the Board of Trustees of their union, the Detectives' Endowment Association, had awarded them, Oberdier, and McGuire Detectives of the Month.

After the names were published in the union magazine, the nomination was amended to include two detectives from other squads. One had interviewed Chindluri when he was at the 8-8 Precinct. The other had talked to Gazi Abu Mezer in the hospital about how to dismantle the bombs and telephoned Teemsma at the scene, suggesting he talk to the suspect.

While the union recognition felt good, it didn't replace the increase in status and pay that would have come with a change in grade. It also couldn't substitute for formal acknowledgment from the department. "You know, Rich, everybody that wants to tell us we did a nice job is completely outside the New York Police Department," Yurkiw surmised, amazed.

o o o o o o o

The trial of the two terrorist suspects began on June 4, 1998, with Judge Reena Raggi presiding. The United States of America versus Gazi Ibrahim Abu Mezer and Lafi Khalil took place in the U.S. District Court, Eastern District of New York, in Cadman Plaza in Brooklyn Heights.[2] Zachary Carter and Bernadette Miragliotta were the prosecuting attorneys. Michael Padden and Jan Postal represented defendant Gazi Ibrahim Abu Mezer, and Bruce McIntyre represented Lhafi Khalil.

Khalil and Abu Mezer had both been indicted on one count of threatening to use a weapon of mass destruction and one count of conspiring to use a weapon of mass destruction. Mezer was charged with using and carrying a firearm and Khalil with possession of a fraudulent green card. The prosecution's case was based on testimony from Chindluri, the two Long Island Railroad cops, the FBI agents, and the NYPD officers involved, including Charles Kammerdener, Keith Ryan, Joe Dolan, Rich Teemsma, and one of the 8-8 Squad detectives who interviewed the informant.

Defense attorneys for Abu Mezer argued that he hadn't planned to detonate the bombs. He was only a petty criminal involved in a scam to obtain a reward advertised by the government for the prevention of a terrorist attack. Khalil's lawyer claimed that his client was not involved in the buying or building of weapons of mass destruction and had no knowledge of a plot. Mezer confirmed Khalil's account at trial, claiming that he had acted alone when he purchased the explosive materials in North Carolina.

When he was in the hospital, Abu Mezer had confessed to the FBI before consulting with an attorney. He said he was with the terrorist organization Hamas, and had planned to detonate the bombs in the B train at

8:00 A.M. because "a lot of Jews ride that train." In his opening statement, Mezer withdrew his confession and claimed his intention involved the scam. During preliminary hearings to suppress the confession, defense attorneys Padden and Postal argued that the police lacked a warrant to search the suspects' apartment. They claimed that the officers used excessive force during the raid and, as a byproduct, procured the evidence against their client. The defense attorneys also argued that the use of excessive force compromised Mezer's mental state in such a way that he confessed to something he didn't do. He was interviewed first before he went into surgery when he thought he might die or lose his leg. The second interview was conducted postoperatively when he was in a drug-induced haze. The defense argued that the FBI agent had manipulated their client into making a false statement by presenting him as a soldier on the opposite side of a righteous war. Thinking he might die, Abu Mezer took to the flattering image because he preferred to be remembered as a martyr than a petty thief.

Judge Raggi dismissed the defense's arguments. Her logic revolved around the difficulty of establishing excessive force and its weak link to the procurement of the evidence. "The fact that your clients were shot and their physical and mental conditions as a result may be probative of whether they were competent to make statements . . . but this hearing is not about whether they should or should not have been shot, so I don't think that's going to be particularly relevant. . . . Given the nature of (the) black athletic bags. . . . You'd be hard pressed to argue to me they didn't have probable cause to search the entire apartment for those bags. . . .

"We're not dealing with an anonymous telephone call, we're dealing with an informant who goes to the scene, who says he personally within 24 hours of that entry saw two bombs in that location. . . . This is not an *Illinois v. Gates* situation, . . . If I thought that your clients had competently waived their rights in the hospital after being shot, I'm not sure I would suppress on this ground even if I found it was excessive force . . . This is a tough excessive force case in any event," Raggi said.[3] Based on testimony from the operating surgeon and other medical personnel, Abu Mezer was found "alert" and "mentally competent" when he was questioned by the FBI, and his confession was admitted into evidence.

Additional documents in support of the prosecution's case included photographs of Khalil and Mezer together in North Carolina and a picture Khalil had taken of Mezer, brandishing a shotgun, wearing garb associated with violent militants, and assuming a posture of martyrdom. The district attorney presented a threatening letter that Abu Mezer sent to the State Department two days before the raid. The letter contained a matchstick and a copy of the suicide note that Teemsma had recovered at the scene. The FBI also introduced a video of a mock–up explosion replicating what would have happened had the primary device gone off. It showed the bomb detonating and fragmenting into small pieces, spewing nails and shrapnel in every direction.

Chief Charles Kammerdener was called to the stand early in the trial. During direct examination, an exchange took place aimed to clarify questions a jury might have about the legality of the entry.

"After making the decision to enter the location, did you attempt to contact a prosecutor to obtain a search warrant?" asked the district attorney.

"No," Kammerdener replied.

"Why not?"

"Two factors; the main factor was to expedite the entry because of the exigent circumstances . . . It was now well after 3:20 when I decided the witness was credible. It was my determination that this person . . . would hit the morning rush hour on a train or bus. . . . it was not my intention to conduct a search, it was only to secure these individuals inside and I could apply for a search warrant later on . . . [The informant who resided there]. . . . had a key to the location."

Ryan was called to testify next. When he sat down in the witness chair, he felt his pants tighten uncomfortably around his waist. He'd stopped running sometime after the press conference and was starting to gain weight. The direct examination was cut-and-dry. Ryan answered questions about the visibility in the apartment and then described what went down in the bedroom, reliving those critical seconds in his movements and tone of voice.

". . . Maybe a second, millisecond, two seconds [later]. . . . The individual kept moving and kept holding on to my leg and I discharged two more rounds into him. . . . I kept yelling: Police. Don't move. Get down. Get down. Stay still. Get down. . . . I pivoted toward my left side, at which point I observed what appeared to be a black bag or duffel bag. The individual on the left was crawling and attempted to lunge toward the bag. . . . I discharged my weapon twice . . ."

The two suspects were sitting in the courtroom watching Ryan testify. Khalil looked gaunt and tense and was hardly moving at all. Abu Mezer was constantly fidgeting and his eyes were darting in every direction until they found their focus on Ryan's face. Then Abu Mezer began nodding his head as though he recognized himself in Ryan's description of his struggle with Lafi Khalil, the suspect he shot. Twenty minutes into Ryan's testimony, an aside took place.

Judge Raggi and the attorneys acknowledged that Ryan and Dolan didn't know which suspect was which when they barged into the bedroom. Noting Mezer's odd behavior, Raggi expressed concern that the jury might mistake him for his roommate, Lafi Khalil. Lafi Khalil, not Abu Mezer, had grabbed Ryan's hand and the back of his leg. Later, he would recall that he'd shot Mezer first. The confusion might have resulted from Mezer's behavior in the courtroom and the fact that he had been cast as the mastermind of the plot. I suspect that this way of remembering helped Ryan neutralize any residual conflict surrounding what he did. It's easier to rationalize firing the first shots at someone who is imagined as totally evil than someone who's not. It's not as if Ryan woke up in the morning with the desire or intention to kill someone.[4]

All in all, the cross-examination by defense attorneys Padden and McIntyre went smoothly. Ryan cautiously danced around their questions, giving brief, precise answers to avoid confusion that might diminish the prosecution's case. Padden and McIntyre argued that Ryan was afraid when he entered the room; that he'd learned in the tactical meeting that they would be confronting terrorists armed with bombs; the low lighting increased his tension, resulting in his instantaneously squeezing the trigger when Khalil moved instead of using less-than-lethal means to block the suspect's actions.

"Did you see anything that would lead you to believe that you were going to be called upon to do something out of the ordinary that night?" Padden asked.[5]

"No. . . ."

"You were told something about individuals in an apartment in Brooklyn with devices that were possibly explosives . . . ?"

"Yes."

"Were you also told in the course of the meeting that there was an alleged terrorist plot involving bombs going on in Brooklyn that night?"

"Yes. . . ."

"Do you now recall . . . that you were told there was an alleged terrorist plot?"

"Yes."

"Were you also told in the course of that meeting that the individuals that were involved in this plot were Arabs?"

"Yes. . . ."

"Now, if you will, Officer Ryan, would it be fair to say that you felt nervous about heading to a location where there is an alleged bomb that evening?"

"I really didn't think about it much."

"Were you apprehensive in any way?"

"No."

"Have any fear for your safety or what might happen there?"

"No."

"You were pretty much doing the job that you were being told to do, right?"

"Yes."

"And that job was to go into that location and neutralize the situation. Is that fair to say?"

"Apprehend," Ryan corrected.

"And do you recall whether he [Dolan] uses the key or not, or whether the door [to the apartment] was locked?"

"We were standing at the door. Joey puts the key in the door. He turns the key. He looks at me and says, Oh shit, I locked it. . . . So I said to Joey, pardon my profanity, but I said, Open the fuckin' door so we could get in. So he turned the key and we went in. . . . ."

"Does that cause a little concern among you, a little more apprehension about the situation you are walking into?"

"Truthfully, I thought it kind of lightened the moment."

Padden swiftly switched tactics and tried to create an impression of Khalil as a small, helpless victim of a home invasion who was shot while kneeling below a big cop's waist. Padden questioned Ryan repeatedly about Khalil's movements; how he went from a prone position lying face down on the mattress to a low crawl.

"When you say he [Khalil] moved, did he get up and start moving, or did he move as he was lying down?"

"He began to lunge in my direction. He never fully stood up erect."

"Did he get to his knees?"

"I don't know what the definition of a lunge is. I don't know if his knees touched the ground. I was just watching him."

"You saw a form moving, but it was moving in your direction. Is that how you remember it?"

"Yes."

"But you are pretty sure he wasn't up on his feet?"

"He definitely was up on his feet."

"When I say you are above him, his entire body is still somewhere below your waist. Would that be fair?"

"Yes. . . ."

"You didn't hit him or smash him with the body bunker in anyway. Right?"

"No."

"You started to shoot, and you fired two shots in rapid succession. Right?" Padden rested his cross-examination after questioning Ryan further about his interaction with Abu Mezer and Ryan confirmed that he had not actually seen Mezer touch the black bag when the suspect lunged in its direction.[6] Rewording some of his colleague's questions, McIntyre continued to try to construct an image of Khalil as the victim of an overreaction on the part of a frightened cop who could have easily warded off the threat by using the bunker instead of his gun.

"And he [Khalil] was kneeling at the time [that you fired downward]?"

"I can't say he was kneeling. I knew he was moving. I don't know if he was on his knees or a definite description of what he was doing. I refer to it as a lunge. He was coming at me. . . ."

"Can you show us with your hands how big the shield [bunker] would be?"

"It wouldn't be an accurate description."

"Well, as best you can, Officer. I mean, is it something that goes from the floor to your chest, is it something that's approximately two-and-a-half feet?"

"I would rather give you an accurate description."

"Just give us . . . a rough idea of the size of the shield," Judge Raggi intervened.

"If I were standing, it would probably reach from my feet to about the midportion of my thigh. . . ."

"You say the person was trying to bring you down, is that by dragging your legs and bring it out from under you, or how was that?"

"Pulling [my leg]. . . ."

"So his head then was below your waist and there was a hand on the back of your left leg, there was a hand on your right hand, correct?"

"Yes."

The prosecuting attorneys covered the same ground when Dolan was called to testify. No contradictions emerged between the accounts of the two partners. Dolan did admit that he'd been afraid but denied it played a role in the decision to use deadly force. He explained that he fired his gun when the suspect moved toward the bag that he believed contained bombs. He also mentioned flipping open the cover after the shooting, confirming evidence that there were bombs inside.

Rich Teemsma's testimony, which came several days later and was backed up by evidence from the FBI's video of the mockup bomb, left no doubt in the jury's mind that the primary device had been functional and would have caused extensive damage and loss of life had it detonated in the subway.

o o o o o o o

Ryan, Dolan, and Teemsma were relieved when the trial concluded almost a year after the two Palestinian terrorists attempted to blow up the New York subway. Abu Mezer was convicted on two counts of conspiring and threatening to use a weapon of mass destruction and one count of using and carrying a firearm during and in relation to those crimes. He was sentenced to two concurrent terms of life imprisonment to be followed by thirty years of imprisonment.

Lafi Khalil got off lightly, compared to what might have happened in the wake of 9/11. The prosecution couldn't prove beyond a reasonable doubt that Khalil had participated in the construction of the bombs or been involved in the plot. As a result, he was only convicted of possession of a fraudulent alien registration card and given the harsher than usual sentence of thirty-six months in prison, followed by a three-year term of supervised release.

After the verdict came in, Keith Ryan celebrated with a quiet dinner with his girlfriend. He and Caroline had met at a funeral less than eight months before. A tall, strikingly beautiful woman, she had short blonde hair, fair skin, lively eyes, and an effervescent personality that provided a welcome antidote to Ryan's solemn demeanor and the anger and sadness he sometimes felt. Although he didn't know who she was until they were introduced, she recognized him as one of the officers who had come to visit her father, a retired Emergency Service cop, when he was sick. She also remembered his face on the television coverage of the press conference. He'd intrigued her then. Noting his scar and not knowing his name, she'd called him "the man without a face." For a month after the funeral, Caroline furtively "stalked" Ryan, attending events where she knew he'd be and arranging opportunities to engage him in conversation. It didn't take long before they started to date and then fell in love. Her presence lightened his moods and warmed his heart. She took his side in the struggles at work and made him feel understood. But even Caroline, the woman who would soon become his wife, could not soften the impact of what was in store for him inside the unit he'd loved more than any assignment in his career.

○ ○ ○ ○ ○ ○ ○

One day in the middle of a nasty winter, detective Michael Corr of Emergency Service was sitting at his desk.[7] Not a lot was happening, so he checked his e-mail and then began surfing the Internet, until he came across the website for the National Association of Police Organizations (NAPO). There he saw highlighted in colorful ink the listing for the Top Cops Award. He doubleclicked "Top Cop" and read the requirements for nomination. The 1997 raid on the Brooklyn terrorist cell seemed like the perfect case to submit. Corr typed up a summary of the Fourth Avenue raid and included the names of the men on the Emergency Service entry team. He also included Nick Mancini, partly because it was protocol to include the boss. He attached some supporting documents, stuffed them in an envelope and mailed it to the Washington office of the National Association of Police Organizations. He forgot about the package until several months later, when he got a call from a boss downtown in the throes of a serious hissy fit.

○ ○ ○ ○ ○ ○ ○

Sam Katz was sitting in the Thomas Street office of the Detectives' Endowment Association in lower Manhattan, rummaging through her 1998 files, searching for cases to submit to the Top Cops award. A tiny, vivacious woman with short, dark hair, Katz had been hired in September as the union writer and executive assistant to the president. Her boss, Tom Scotto, was president of the Detectives' Endowment Association and also the National Association of Police Organizations (NAPO). The result was he walked around with the weight of a lot of union issues on his shoulders, and he relied on Katz to help him carry the load. This included her taking an active role in handling NAPO matters, in particular the annual Top Cops award.

Scotto, along with other executives, had developed the Top Cops award in 1993 to elevate the image of the national association and honor law enforcement officers throughout the country. Since then, Top Cops had taken on a life of its own, becoming the most prestigious honor a North American police officer could receive. Sonny Grasso, a retired NYPD detective turned Hollywood consultant and producer and one of the two detectives who'd investigated the famous French Connection drug case, had coined the name "Top Cops" for a television series. Scotto liked the name and contacted Grasso to ask permission to use it for the NAPO award. Grasso agreed, and the Top Cops award was spawned.

Any sworn law enforcement officer in the fifty states (Puerto Rico was recently added) could make a nomination by mailing in a description of the case with the names and roles of the officer(s) involved. Award candidates could include officers of any rank from any state, county, or local law enforcement agency in the United States. The annual award was given for incidents that took place the previous year.

To minimize the role of politics and facilitate funding, Scotto and Robert Scully, a retired union official who was hired as executive director of the national association, enlisted the sponsorship of several outside organizations concerned with law enforcement. The judging committee for the Top Cops award included a list of representatives from these agencies and police departments across the country. Several committees reviewed the applications until they were narrowed down to ten cases involving one or more officers. The ten winning officers or groups of officers were then invited to Washington, D.C., for three or four days. Their second night in town, they went to a black-tie award ceremony attended by an assortment of corporate sponsors, political dignitaries, and Hollywood actors involved in police-related movies or shows. The People's Choice award for Top Cop(s) of the Top Cops was announced then. The high point of the affair involved an invitation to the White House to meet the president and attend a public relations event in the Rose Garden.

Sam Katz kept a file of major police cases in a drawer in the event something arose that merited further investigation to determine if it fit the requirements of the Top Cops award. The Brooklyn job had piqued her interest immediately. "What struck me was that had anybody screwed up along the food chain, the whole of Brooklyn would have been blown sky-high underground. . . . thousands of people could have died. I was flabbergasted," Katz explained.

When the deadline for the Top Cops award drew near, Katz reached for the file and began to prepare the material for submission of the case. She proceeded with care to ensure that all the major players were included. "I was very cognizant not to cheat anybody out of submission," Katz said.[8] After triple-checking the names, she interviewed several officers to verify facts. Years later, she would recall what Yurkiw said during their conversation. "In an underground subway car with the problems of the back draft and difficulties of the rescue mission in such a confined space, the devastation would have been even worse . . . it would have been a 'bag and broom job.'" Had the bomb gone off, the police would have been left sweeping up remains and putting them in a body bag.

Not long after the Washington office of the National Association of Police Organizations received the submission, Katz was informed that Michael Corr had also put in the names of seven Emergency Service officers who were involved. When the folks at the National Association of Police Organizations received the nomination that included the names of the detectives, they decided to combine the two submissions into one. The final Top Cops nomination for the whole Brooklyn case included twenty-six officers, including the two Long Island Railroad cops and twenty-four others from the NYPD.

Weeks before she submitted the documents, Katz had described the incident to Scotto, who agreed that it was worthy of consideration for the award. He trusted Katz's judgment and saw no reason to micromanage a loyal subordinate who worked her job 24-7. Buried in other concerns, he put the conversation out of his mind, knowing the Top Cops' business was in good hands. "They were very respectful of me," Katz explained, describing her relationship with her boss and the other police officers with whom she worked. "As the head of NAPO, Tom also didn't want to seem like he was fixing the competition, so he wasn't involved in the prescreening of the hundreds of candidates. I didn't even have him sign off on the paperwork. He wanted to stay out of it. I worked on the NAPO submission with Victor Cipullo, one of our union officers, and he signed his name."

o o o o o o o

Independently of NAPO and the union, the names of sixteen of the officers involved in the Brooklyn case were also submitted for departmental honorable mention in 1998. Officers who were granted honorable mention earned a Silver Star and became eligible for one of the department's three medals. The police on the entry team were nominated for their role in executing the tactical plan, apprehending the suspects, and aborting a terrorist strike that could have killed thousands of people. Teemsma and Yurkiw were cited for their part in interviewing the informant, assessing the bomb threat, conducting a radiographic examination of the primary device, discovering the secondary device, and using a hand entry technique to render the bombs safe.

The paperwork on their submission noted that "the removal of the two explosive devices created an imminent and personal danger to the lives of Detectives Teemsma and Yurkiw," that one of the toggle switches on the primary device had been "activated by a perpetrator in an attempt to detonate the bomb," and that, according to tests conducted by the FBI, "all of the individual components of the 'Primary' explosive device were tested and functioned properly." Oberdier and McGuire were credited with "utilizing a robot, from a safe vantage point, [and separating] the components of the bomb."[9]

The nominations for recognition were sent "through channels" and endorsed by superiors. Yurkiw and Teemsma's were signed by John Bajek, Captain Gin Yee, Inspector Bruce Smolka, and Chief William Morange. I don't know who signed the paperwork for the Emergency Service police but assume that Morange and McDermott were among the names. Several months later, the Bomb Squad detectives and police in Emergency Service learned that they'd been awarded the Silver Star. Their names were then forwarded to a special committee for consideration for medals.

Teemsma had been told that he and Yurkiw were up for the Medal of Honor, the highest award; although this communication could have involved several indirect conversations resulting in the creation of the type of rumor that runs rampant in the police organization and often disappoints. Another possible scenario might have involved a top-ranked member of the brass who agreed to grant an award or promotion but then changed his mind after further consideration when political pressure was applied. The Medal of Honor is reserved for acts of "gallantry and valor performed with knowledge of the risk involved, above and beyond the call of duty." This medal was a long shot. More often than not, the Medal of Honor is given, posthumously, to an officer's family after he or she has died or been seriously injured in the line of duty.

In early September 1998, the Emergency Service cops learned that they were going to receive the Medal of Valor. The Medal of Valor is awarded for "outstanding acts of personal bravery at imminent personal hazard to life or for outstanding community service." Yurkiw and Teemsma were notified that they weren't receiving a medal at all. They weren't the only officers disheartened by this turn of events. Ryan and Dolan were as well. While English was surprised that his cops had received a medal at all, in view of the flack surrounding the press conference, he was disappointed that Dolan and Ryan didn't get the Combat Cross, at least. The department's second-highest honor, the Combat Cross is typically granted to members of the service who "successfully and intelligently perform an act of extraordinary heroism while engaged in personal combat with an armed adversary under circumstances of imminent threat to life." When Ryan heard the news, he was taken aback.

"I'm not going to Medal Day," he told his partner, "I'm just not going. You aren't gonna give us the medal we deserve, and I'm gonna stand there and kiss your ass and shake your hand? I'd rather shake the hand of a dead fish."

"Keith, you've gotta go," Dolan said. "You gotta go. It's for your family. Let's go. You'll take the medal they're gonna give you and be happy we survived this fuckin' thing together, all right?"

Medal Day took place in the courtyard of One Police Plaza on a cool, sunny day, the 15th of September. The deputy commissioners and the department's high-ranking chiefs were seated in rows on a portable stage in front of the audience full of medal recipients and their families. Safir stood up at the podium next to Giuliani and gave a speech.

"Today we recognize the heroic acts of the men and women who were recently called upon to exhibit selfless courage and valor. Whether in uniform or civilian clothes, on-duty or off-duty, each of these officers unhesitatingly acted to preserve the safety of others. That courage and bravery which we salute is the hallmark of true heroism," Safir said.[10]

The police commissioner went on to announce the awards. The Medal of Honor was given to the family of one officer who had been slain in the line of duty. Fifteen others received the Combat Cross, and thirty-three, the Medal of Valor, including the six men on the Emergency Service entry team. Seven police commands were recognized for outstanding service, a tribute that would help propel their commanding officers' careers.[11]

One by one, the audience watched the award recipients march up on stage and shake the police commissioner's hand. Then Rudy Giuliani did the honor of pinning the medals on their chests. The cops from Emergency Service were sitting in the back row in dress uniform, waiting for their names to be called and watching the events unfold. English recalled the ceremony with pride and a sprinkling of resentment. "I would have preferred to get the medal from somebody that was worthy of giving it out, like Bill Morange or Ray McDermott. But it was a great day for my family. . . . You know, you're in the company of heroes, I mean, guys that did things— I look at what we did and it doesn't—there were things that other guys did that didn't save as many lives immediately, but they were in just as much danger and they did just as much as we did, so it was a tremendous honor to be there with them. . . . I remember standing up there and looking at the two boobs up on the stage. Giuliani was falling asleep, falling asleep! I'm looking up on stage and I'm watching him nod out. It goes to show you how much this guy really cares. He doesn't. He cares nothing. And Safir, I don't know. I think they grudgingly put those medals on us."

Ryan and Dolan were swept up in the same sort of paranoid feelings they experienced a year before in Anemone's office. "I see the mayor and I see these chiefs and everything," Dolan explained, "they're all sitting up there, and the mayor's looking around, and Safir's looking down, and I swear to Christ, they're staring at us. It may have just been an optical illusion—I'm sitting there wondering, what the hell did we do?"

"Are they fuckin' staring at us?" Ryan asked, seeing the same thing as his partner.

"Yeah, what the fuck is going on?" Dolan replied. When his turn came to greet the mayor, he recalled squeezing Giuliani's hand as hard as he could to give him a "handshake from hell." Ryan tried to be gracious when he went on stage. Still, he couldn't help but get a fleeting sense of satisfaction when he thought he saw Giuliani wince because he'd apparently pinched his finger while pinning the medal on Keith's chest. "I got that prick good, mothafucka! But I was a gentleman. 'Thank you, Sir,' the whole bit," Ryan related, recalling his effort to play the game in the face of his most senior boss.

After the ceremony, the officers and their families milled about in the courtyard, sharing stories and exchanging observations. Morange and McDermott soon joined them. The officers listened attentively while their chief uttered his heartfelt congratulations. His words felt like a cool breeze on sunburned skin.

"We were sitting in the audience, I think they were staring at us," Dolan confessed.

"What? They were what?" one of the cops said.

"They were waiting to see which one of you people was going to throw themselves on the grenade for the cause. You know, give the medal back," Dolan said, recalling McDermott's reply. "Why would I give it back? We survived this fuckin' thing, you know, they may be breaking my balls, but I'm here to have my balls broken, that's the beautiful thing," Dolan later explained.

Two hours after the affair began, the officers dispersed and headed toward their cars. Some of the men in Emergency Service planned to celebrate the occasion by going out to eat with their families. Ryan headed home. He wanted to tend to his pigeons. Racing season was approaching fast, and he needed a victory. By the time he pulled onto the Brooklyn-Queens Expressway, Ryan had begun to feel like a weight had been placed on his chest. He felt responsible for damaging the chances of his teammates to get what they deserved from the department.

"Deep inside, I felt that everyone in little ways was mad at me because of my obstinacy about not speaking at the press conference. I think they were pissed. It wasn't like Joey wanted to go on TV. It was more like we blew a golden opportunity to get whatever we wanted from the PC." Although he didn't tell me this, I suspect that the business with Larry Celona also continued to weigh on his mind.

o o o o o o o

A few days after Medal Day, Rich Teemsma was working in the Manhattan Office of the Bomb Squad when the phone rang.

"Bomb Squad, Teemsma," he said, omitting his title. He didn't have much regard for titles.

"Teemsma? Rich Teemsma? You must be mad at me," said the voice on the other end of the line.

"Who's this?" Teemsma asked.

"Inspector O'Donnell."

"Inspector, I don't even know you. I don't see how I could be mad at you."

"We were gonna give you the Medal of Honor, but I spoke to Jim Black."

"To tell you the truth, Inspector, that and my shield gets me on a bus," Teemsma said, then transferred the call to Black, at O'Donnell's request.[12]

Ricochet Rabbit, that two-faced, no-balls motherfucker! Please! Teemsma thought. For weeks, he'd suspected that Black was responsible for quashing their chances for a medal, and now he had proof. Annoyed as he was, Teemsma understood the logic of the lieutenant's decision to sabotage individual honors in view of the dynamics of the squad. "Jim Black was put into a command full of prima donnas, not everyone, but certain ones. He was protecting himself. He was only in the Bomb Squad a short time. McGuire was an instrumental part of this. He wanted recognition for the job, but Paul and I weren't going to give it to him. It was his job and we wound up doing it and, all of a sudden, he wanted recognition for a job that he wouldn't get out of bed to go to. That pissed me off, so I was not gonna help him. I was gonna do everything I could so he didn't get the recognition, and that's why it happened. There was a fight going on. Jim Black was impressed with Joe McGuire because of his position in the International Association of Bomb Technicians and Investigators and all his contacts at One PP. Whatever Joe said, Black did. Joe poisoned the Bomb Squad into thinking, look at these two guys—they are getting all these awards, and who do they think they are . . . breakfast, lunch, the Waldorf, the FBI, guests at the Christmas tree? We were getting a lot of recognition from outside the agency, and they were going to make sure that, inside, we were going to get squat. It was Giuliani, too. He painted everybody with a big brush. The Emergency Service guys said they weren't talking at the press conference. We were the same in his eyes. The Emergency Service cops got medals because they were in the Special Operations Division under Ray McDermott and Bill Morange. They don't come better than them. We were in the Detective Bureau in the Bomb Squad with John Bajek and Fatty [Joe McGuire] controlling Jim Black."

o o o o o o o

On September 3, 1998, the National Association of Police Organizations (NAPO) announced the winners of the Top Cop award. Weeks before, Executive Director Bob Scully had sat in his office, contemplating the submissions involved, including the Brooklyn case. He thought that twenty-six names were too many for one case. Perhaps he consulted members of the Executive Board of the National Association of Police Organizations. Whatever occurred informally, the decision was made to narrow the NYPD winners down to the six officers on the Emergency Service entry team and their captain, Nick Mancini. "I was pissed off—the beauty of the case was in the teamwork—but what can you do?" Sam Katz explained.

When Teemsma and Yurkiw got the news, they, too, were annoyed. Once again, it seemed their contribution had been swept under the rug. "Richie, tell me if I'm wrong. It *was* a bomb job, no?" Yurkiw said. At this point, it seemed their only recourse was to talk to Tom Scotto and see if he could help. Teemsma made an appointment to meet Scotto the following week. Unbeknownst to them, a flurry of backroom political activity was already taking place. Mike Keenan and another officer from Emergency Service were in the union office talking to Scotto in the polite and deferential tone appropriate to addressing a union president.

"Tommy, this is a great honor. We can't thank you enough," Keenan said, according to one officer present.

"I had nothing to do with it, actually. You know my executive assistant, Sam Katz? She's the one who deserves the credit."

"Well, it's really an honor, and we certainly appreciate everything you've done. But we're here for a reason. We got seven guys here on the list going to D.C. You see, there's this one person. He played a major role in the whole thing, and we believe it would be unfair to leave him out. So we're wondering if you could include him. You know, it would be the right thing to do."

"It's not my decision to make. There's a process here."

"Well, he was with us through the whole job, beginning to end," Keenan said.

"Well, listen. Why don't you give me the information? I can send it out as an amendment to the original inclusion.

"His name is Ray McDermott. He's our boss, a deputy inspector. That would be great. We really appreciate it." After Keenan left, Scotto braced himself with a cup of coffee. Then he picked up the phone and dialed Bob Scully in the Washington office. It wasn't a pleasant call. Since Scotto had replaced Scully as president of the National Association of Police Organizations and become his boss, their relationship had become more strained than before.

"You know you're overriding the Executive Committee," Scully said.

"I'm making one modification as president. Ray McDermott was an important part of that team and should be included," Scotto said. Scully muttered something that Scotto couldn't hear.

"I'll present it to the board," Scully said and then hung up the phone. I don't know what transpired after that except that McDermott's name was added to the list.

On August 11, Scotto met with Rich Teemsma and Paul Yurkiw. It was the first time either detective had been in the Thomas Street building, and they were impressed. The small 1940s structure had been renovated, modernized, and made into a plush, spacious, and tastefully furnished lobby and set of office suites. "I wouldn't mind living here," Teemsma said when he stepped into the elegant conference room.

A few minutes later, Tom Scotto walked in and greeted the two detectives. Standing next to Yurkiw and Teemsma, Scotto looked small and squat. At not quite 5'9" tall, he had the square, solid build of the boxer he'd once been, with a few extra pounds around the waist. Scotto's salt-and-pepper hair was slicked back with mousse and naturally styled so that a thick wave seemed to erupt above his forehead. He looked like a stereotype of an NYPD detective from a Hollywood movie in which police and mobsters look alike. Teemsma and Yurkiw presented their case to the union president. They told him about their involvement in the Fourth Avenue incident, from their appearance in the 8-8 Precinct to the dismantling of the bombs at the crime scene.

"We've already had one modification. I can't keep adding modifications," Scotto said, partly because he dreaded another confrontational conversation with Scully. At the same time, Scotto felt he should try and represent his detectives as best he could. "All right, look. I'm sorry about this; I do want you guys down there. Let me see what I can do. We can take care of the money if it comes down to that. I'll give you a call tomorrow."

"Thanks, thanks a lot," Teemsma replied. Teemsma recalled Black's name coming up at the end of the conversation and thinking, well, that takes care of that. Scotto didn't recall any mention of Jim Black and said he didn't know who Black was until he called the union office later that day. Meanwhile, Scotto asked Sam Katz to draft a letter and fax it to Bob Scully in Washington, D.C. The letter was written on Detectives' Endowment Association stationery, reflecting Scotto's position as union president rather than NAPO executive. The letter recounted the substance of the meeting and requested modification of the Top Cops award to include the two detectives. "These two Detectives played a major role in this event, from the initial interview of the informant, to the dismantling of the bomb. . . . Not recognizing these two officers would be inappropriate. Therefore, I think the best way to resolve this matter would be to add them to the current list from New York, with the New York City Detectives' Endowment Association picking up the cost of their inclusion."

That afternoon or the next day, Jim Black called Scotto and identified himself as the commanding officer of the Bomb Squad and Teemsma and Yurkiw's boss.

"Tom, I gotta ask you a question," Black said as Scotto recalled.

"Shoot."

"Did Paul Yurkiw and Rich Teemsma come up to you about this NAPO thing?

"Yeah, they did. I talked to them a few hours ago."

"Those motherfuckers! Don't do shit for those guys! They're going around here self-promoting themselves to the media, getting awards. They didn't do shit! They did exactly what all my men do every single day. We don't get publicity. That is what being part of this unit is," Black said.

"Look, I put in a request. I haven't heard anything yet."

"I'm telling you, these guys didn't do any more than anybody else on the team."

"Well. I hear what you're saying, but it's up to the NAPO Executive Committee at this point."

After Scully received the request for the new modification, he and Scotto spoke. Apparently Scully complained that Scotto was overriding the board and not doing things the right way. There was a process involved and the composition of awardees was the decision of the board. He also told Scotto that eight guys were already going to Washington and they couldn't keep adding new people like that. At this point, Scotto gave up and told Scully to "forget about it." In the wake of the phone call from Black, Scotto decided the battle for Teemsma and Yurkiw wasn't worth fighting about.

Several days passed, and Teemsma heard nothing about the Top Cops award, although he did field a mysterious phone call from someone from Washington, D.C., asking to speak to Jim Black. Before taking the call, Black told Teemsma to shut the office door. Although he couldn't hear the conversation, he could see into Black's office through the large glass window next to the squad room. Teemsma noticed that Black's neck and face turned beet red and he kept biting the nails of his left hand while holding the receiver with his right.

"We're getting fucked right now," Teemsma whispered to Yurkiw, who was standing a half-foot away. The next day when Teemsma still hadn't heard any news, he decided to give Scotto a call.

"It's a dead issue. It's not going anywhere," Scotto said.

"What happened?"

"I can't tell you that. But it's over with. All I can say is you should watch your back, and you watch your bosses," Scotto said, according to Teemsma's recollection.

"All right, well, thanks, thanks anyway," Teemsma said and hung up the phone.

"No good?" Yurkiw said.

"I guess it's too late to start kissing ass now," Teemsma responded. Something clicked inside that wouldn't fully register for months. Men who had once been his friends had succumbed to the pressure of politics and turned their backs on him. In the last eight months his feelings about the job had begun to change. Worst of all, he'd watched himself become a person he didn't like or want to be around. "You turn into an angry person. I guess I realized that I'd turned into a person I'm not, and that's when I started thinking it was time to pull the pin [retire]," he explained. Although Teemsma would stay in the Police Department another few years, the idea of retirement took seed in the wake of the news that Black had sabotaged yet another move by Teemsma and Yurkiw to gain recognition and move ahead in their careers.

o o o o o o o

Detective Michael Corr had just been ambushed over the phone. He thought he'd seen and heard everything; that no change in leadership, maniacal boss, and perturbation in department politics could have surprised him. But nothing had shocked him more than the insane tirade that had just been aimed in his direction by someone he hardly knew. He'd typed up the Top Cops nomination months ago, thinking he was doing something good for Emergency Service that the department would appreciate. Now he was being threatened by a high-ranking boss who was screaming at him, insisting he had no business submitting names for the Top Cops award without going through the commissioner's office. No one I interviewed knew the name of the boss, but rumor had it that it was someone close to Howard Safir.

o o o o o o o

It was Tuesday, August 21, 1998, and Tom Scotto was sitting at his desk, sipping coffee, and sorting through his inbox when he heard a knock on his door. He recognized Katz's voice and told her to come in. The conversation was brief. Patrick Kelleher, the first deputy commissioner, was on the line and wanted to speak with him right away. Scotto picked up the phone and signaled Katz to close the door. Scotto recalled that Kelleher assumed an angry tone, peppered with expletives that Scotto found insulting. Several high-ranking members of the brass who knew Kelleher well denied that he'd talk like this. While he might curse in jest or fun, they'd never heard him using the "f" word to dress someone down.

"Hey, how are you, Commish?" Scotto said in a warm tone of voice. He was one of Kelleher's friends and had been for years.

"Who do you think you are?" Kelleher said, according to what Scotto remembered.

"Is this Pat?" Scotto replied, convinced some cop was playing a practical joke.

"Yeah, this is Pat Kelleher. *Commissioner* Kelleher."

"Is there a feather in your ass or something, Commissioner? What's wrong with you?"

"Who do you think you are? This NAPO award was not vetted through the commissioner's office. It's the prerogative of the police commissioner to give cops' awards. They've gotta be cleared through his office. Now you are going to change this NAPO award." All high-level commanders agreed that the issue of clearance was something that Kelleher might have brought up.

"You know what, Commissioner? I'm not even going to argue with you on the phone. I'm not going to say a word to you on the phone. I am going to have hand-delivered to you in five minutes the rules and regulations of how the Top Cops awards are picked. Obviously you think I had something to do with picking the awardees. I had nothing to do with it, Pat—or do you want me to call you 'Commissioner'? I'm going to send you the rules and regulations and I know you're man enough to call me back and apologize. That's all I have to say. You understand."

"Yeah, OK," Kelleher mumbled, his tone softened somewhat. Scotto stood up and walked into the hall. He couldn't imagine that Kelleher would turn on him and talk to him like that and curse him out unless he'd been ordered to do so by the police commissioner. It was no secret that Scotto and Safir didn't see eye to eye. "It wasn't like Pat to act like that. It had to be Safir. Safir must have told him, 'You get that little bastard,'" Scotto explained.[13]

Immediately, Scotto sat down and drafted a letter stating the rules for the Top Cops award. He printed the letter on the stationery of the National Association of Police Organizations and signed it "With warm regards." The original letter was hand-delivered to Kelleher's office and a copy was put in the police commissioner's mail at One Police Plaza. The letter, dated August 21, made several key points that are abbreviated here: "Any law enforcement officer can nominate another officer or group of officers. This method helps eliminate the political sway that would be inherent in allowing only departments or police chiefs to make nominations. . . . NAPO welcomes and appreciates the nominations of chiefs of departments. . . . The winning submission for Top Cops is based solely on the merits of the individual cases. . . . the judging is independent from the status of the nominating officers. . . . As the president of NAPO, I eliminated myself from the initial selection process. I participate in the final selection process but I am one of many who serve on the final judging board. Final selections are made by representatives from law enforcement groups such as the National Law Enforcement Officers Memorial Fund." The letter concludes with an invitation to Safir and Kelleher to attend. "It would be a great honor . . . if Police Commissioner Safir or you or the both of you could attend and it would be my privilege to make such an arrangement."

Around 2:30 that afternoon, Scotto got a response in the form of phone call from John Santamauro, nicknamed "Johnny Murder" when he was the commanding officer of Brooklyn South Homicide. Johnny Murder was Kelleher's administrative lieutenant and worked at One Police Plaza.

"What's going on with you and the boss?" Santamauro said, according to Scotto, when he answered the phone.

"Johnny, he had a misinterpretation of the Top Cops award."

"Well, he came out this morning all pissed at you and everything."

"What are ya gonna do?" Scotto said, shrugging his shoulders.

"He wants to see you right away, as soon as you can get down here."

"OK. Tell him I'm on my way," Scotto confirmed. Less than twenty minutes later, Scotto arrived at Kelleher's office and was ushered inside.

"Can I call you 'Pat' now?" Scotto asked.

"It's always 'Pat,'" Kelleher responded, "Now stop breaking my balls and sit down. I read this and I just want to get some clarification." Scotto proceeded to give him a history of the Top Cops award and repeated the rules as outlined in the document.

"I had nothing to do with these guys getting the nomination, my secretary, Sam Katz, put their names in, not me, and she has every right to do so." Kelleher might have been skeptical because it was hard to believe a civilian "PAA" (secretarial assistant) working in the Police Department or a police union office would be allowed to initiate such an action without authorization from a boss.

"You're telling me your secretary did that?" Kelleher asked.

"Yes, I am."

"And you didn't know about it?"

"Yes, I did."

"You let a secretary do that?"

"She's ballsy. You'd have to know Sam. She had the right to do it, with Victor Cipullo signing off on the submission." Not that Scotto cared one way or another if a law enforcement officer was involved, but those were the rules.

By the time Scotto said good-bye, relations between them were cordial and Scotto assumed the Top Cops business was settled and that everything would follow the regular process that had taken place in the past. While Kelleher may have misunderstood the NAPO process and wanted his boss to control the award, he had a point in wanting NYPD nominees vetted through the Office of the Police Commissioner. It could prove embarrassing to the department if one of the winning officers turned out to be under investigation by Internal Affairs or another agency.

o o o o o o o

The Top Cop ceremony was scheduled to take place on October 8, 1998. Throughout the month of September and into the first week of October, the officers involved were greeted with one obstacle after another, most of them petty, irritating, and some more threatening. Ray McDermott was the first to alert Scotto of what was going on.

"Tom, I just want you to be aware, the orders have come down. They have to take the time off to go down on their own. The department is not giving them the time to go to Washington for the award, and they can't wear their uniforms or guns."

"What? This is absurd. Guys going down there are uniformed guys! You want to display the pride of the Police Department. You wear a uniform. That's part of the game!"

"I'm just letting you know what it is," McDermott explained. Even before the orders came down, he had been faced with a constantly changing set of instructions. "It became a nightmare for all of us. At first they said we could go, and then they said we couldn't go, and then they said we could go but not wear our uniforms. . . . They took what was supposed to be a beautiful occasion and made it like they were stealing into the middle of the night. These men deserved to be recognized for their actions. They really did. What could have happened that day if they didn't do what they did? I don't want to think about it," McDermott recalled.

Scotto doesn't remember exactly what he did after he hung up the phone, but believes he put in a call to Kelleher and made an appeal. "Pat, this is terrible. I know it got off on a bad leg, whatever the heck it was. But it's crazy. We got the pride of the Police Department at stake. These guys are getting a national award. The president and the vice president will be there. They go to the White House with their families. We sit in the Rose Garden. It's an unbelievable thing. To tell these guys they have to go down there, one, on their own time, and two, they can't wear their uniforms, it takes the joy out of it. You should be praising these guys and giving them medals, instead you're kicking them in the balls!"

The controversy didn't end until the day before they were scheduled to leave. "I got a call from someone in the first dep's office—from the same guy whose job I would have a few years later when Joseph Dunne became first deputy commissioner—the caller said we could go and wear our uniforms, but we had to take our own time, which is what we did," McDermott explained.

o o o o o o o

On October 7, the NYPD Top Cops set off on a four-day trip to Washington, D.C. They would be entertained like royalty, welcomed at tourist destinations, and wined and dined with Hollywood actors, congressmen, the attorney general, and the president of the United States. Before they left, the officers and their wives submitted their social security numbers for preclearance into the White House. Department policy dictated whether they brought their guns to D.C., but their weapons weren't allowed in the president's home.

Ray McDermott and the six officers on the entry team drove down with their families in separate cars. The National Association of Police Organizations arranged private bus transportation inside the capital. Nick Mancini was the only Top Cops winner who didn't go, due to another commitment. He had flown first-class to the Dominican Republic to greet the country's president as part of a delegation from the Federal Office of Emergency Management. Included among the celebrity delegates was Bernie Williams, the New York Yankee baseball player.

When the New York delegation arrived in D.C., they checked into the Omni Shoreham Hotel. The Top Cops from across the country soon began to make each other's acquaintance. Ten men from the Los Angeles Police Department (LAPD) had been involved in the 1997 North Hollywood shootout. Some were members of L.A. Swat, considered one of the premier tactical teams in the nation. Their job involved an attempted bank robbery. The two suspects were armed with assault weapons and body armor. Seven civilians and eleven officers were injured before one perpetrator committed suicide and the other was shot and killed by the police.

Officer Malcolm Thompson of the Kissimee, Florida, Police Department won the award for the Top Cop of the Top Cops. While investigating a felony suspect, Thompson was shot four times, once in the carotid artery. The perpetrator fled in a cab holding the driver at gunpoint. The pursuit ended when Thompson shot the suspect in the head through the window of the taxi. An Arkansas State trooper named Ted Grigson was another Top Cops winner. After rendering first aid to a neighbor who fell off a ladder and broke his neck, Grigson organized a team of volunteers to care for the man's farm. For months, Grigson worked two jobs, one as a cop and the other taking care of the farm. The other seven Top Cops had exhibited equally stellar acts of courage in the face of adversity. They came from big and small departments across the nation, including Indianapolis, New Hampshire, Utah, Washington, D.C., Virginia, West Virginia, and Wisconsin as well as New York City.

Their first night in Washington, the officers and their families attended a cocktail party at the Omni Hotel. Newt Gingrich, the House speaker, gave the welcoming speech. Guests included celebrities Richard Belzer from *Law and Order*, Ed Marinaro from *Homicide: Life on the Street*, and Lynn Russell from *CNN Headline News*, whom the cops viewed as a "hottie." The manager of the Washington Redskins was among the other rich and famous guests.

The Top Cops ate dinner together, exchanging war stories and joking about the size of their "elephant balls." Despite the nature and location of the event, echoes of the ongoing political struggle continued to haunt the cops from New York. Ray McDermott took the heat when he answered his cell phone and nearly choked on a piece of steak. An irate boss from the Office of the First Deputy Commissioner was on the line and ordered McDermott home. McDermott told him that he'd be back in a few days. The boss threatened him with a demotion to captain and the loss of his command.

"Do what you have to do. That kind of runs in the family," McDermott responded, alluding to his father, a cop's cop and legend in the Police Department whose commitment to his cops resulted in his demotion. He was the only assistant chief in the NYPD to have ever been demoted to inspector who was able to rise through the ranks to become assistant chief again.

"What was that about?" John English asked. He'd heard one end of the conversation and suspected there was trouble from New York.

"I got threatened with a demotion. They want me back in New York. We're here now, and we're gonna stay here. I may not be with you when we get back, but I'm here now." The harassment upset the Emergency Service cops, who feared for their boss's career. They, and possibly McDermott as well, believed that the threats that were being transmitted through Kelleher's executive officer were ordered by Kelleher himself. High-ranking officers familiar with events surrounding the trip to Washington deny this was the case. Instead, they believe the executive officer was acting out a personal grudge against Ray McDermott, although he might have falsely thought he also had the blessings of his superior.

Regardless of who initiated the threats, they had to be taken seriously. Still, each hostile call appeared to reinforce McDermott's resolve to stick with his moral principles and support his men. McDermott accounted for his leadership style by noting that he'd been raised by some of the NYPD's greatest leaders, mostly old-school Irish Democrats who came from poverty and believed in the Constitution and civil liberties and tried to apply their principles not only to policing the public but also to respecting the rights of their officers. They all knew that the best way to lead is by example and that loyalty is a two-way street. "I've been very lucky. I worked with Bill Morange, Joe Dunne, they're the same kind of people. I like to think that some of that rubbed off on the way I do things. We know to stick up for our people," McDermott later explained.

On October 9, the officers were driven to the White House to meet the president. They waited with Tom Scotto inside a conference room adjacent to the Oval Office. Janet Reno soon joined them, sat down, and talked candidly for twenty minutes. It didn't take too many words before she'd earned the respect of even the men who did not share her politics. They liked her warmth and sincerity and the way she looked them in the eye. They knew she'd earned her battle scars. An aide soon joined the gathering and began prepping the officers for their meeting with the president.

"If you have any gifts or anything you want to give the president, do not hand it to the president. Hand it to his assistant. You can also give it to the aide who will be standing beside him."

"Ray, I'm gonna hand him a cigar," Dwyer said to McDermott, who likely turned pale. "No, no. It don't have nothing to with that," Dwyer insisted, referring to Monica Lewinsky's testimony during Clinton's impeachment hearings regarding their sexual foreplay.

"OK. You'll each file in one after another, and the president will say a few words and shake your hands," the aide continued.

"I'm still gonna give it to him," Dwyer said. One by one, the Top Cops made their way into the Oval Office and joined the president. He greeted them each by name and thanked them for what they'd done. "Janet Reno was really pleasant, too. She made us feel very comfortable," Ryan said. "It was sad that people two hundred miles away could make us feel uncomfortable when everyone else went out of their way to treat us like family." When it came time for Dwyer to meet Clinton, he reached into his pocket and thrust the cigar in his direction.

"Lieutenant, I'll take that," Clinton graciously said, and gave the cigar to his aide. The aide rolled his eyes. Keith Ryan, Joe Dolan, and Ray McDermott stood there, mortified.[14] "I found that to be extremely distasteful, and I was embarrassed for him, even though I don't think he was embarrassed for himself. He did it to be funny but there are six other guys with him that you're dragging everybody down a little—but he did what he wanted to do and there's no stopping him, so there's nothing you could say," McDermott recalled.

After the president welcomed the officers, they headed to the Rose Garden through a glass-covered passageway surrounded by flowers. Their families were waiting inside. Tom Scotto, Bob Scully, Janet Reno, and four or five congressmen were there. When the president joined the crowd and the press conference began, Tom Scotto walked up to the podium and introduced Clinton as "a dear friend of law enforcement." At 10:57 A.M. Clinton began his speech. He thanked the executives of the National Association of Police Organizations, the attorney general, and members of

Congress in attendance. Then he congratulated the Top Cops, highlighting their accomplishments, courage, and dedication.

"The men and women we honor here today put on their badges every day, prepared to make the same kind of [life-and-death] sacrifice for their own communities. They are true American heroes. They have done astonishing acts of humanity and heroism—from crossing the line of fire to rescue wounded fellow officers, to confronting criminals armed with assault weapons and body armor, to nursing a seriously injured neighbor back to health, to breaking in on a person with a bomb that was partially activated and, thank God, did not go off and blow them all away. And one of these officers, shot four times . . . maintained his consciousness enough to save the life of a cabdriver when the person who shot him had a gun at his head. . . . We owe a great debt of gratitude to our nation's police officers. . . ." Clinton said.

At every Top Cops ceremony during Clinton's administration, new proposals on behalf of law enforcement were announced. The 1998 initiatives included $30 million in new grant money to help hire more police; $40 million to help local police departments computerize the criminal history records that were used for background checks; and a new law providing states with more than $1 billion over the next five years to modernize and upgrade their communication and criminal identification systems. Finally, Clinton concluded his speech by thanking the families in attendance. "Now before I close, . . . I want to thank all of you who are members of their families. In so many ways, you make these achievements possible. You share the sacrifice, and you share the fear, and sometimes you share the loss. We know that. Therefore, you have to provide your own special brand of courage, and for that we are profoundly grateful. . . . Thank you very much, and God bless you."[15]

The top cops and their chiefs joined in the applause. Howard Safir was the only head of a department not represented at any event in Washington D.C. McDermott believed his absence had more to do with politics than a grudge against the cops. "It became one of these things where we had a Republican mayor, Republican governor, and a Democratic president and we were going to be recognized by the president."

For almost two hours, Clinton mingled with the officers and their families, posing for pictures, chatting, and enjoying the crowd. John English stood by his wife, holding his son, John Jr., in his arms. The boy had been born in the wake of the raid at 10:30 the night of October 22, 1997, after twenty-two hours of labor. English had taken the week off to be with his wife for the delivery. Compared to what she'd done, he believed the courage that he'd displayed during the raid on the terrorists was insignificant. "If men had to get pregnant, we'd be extinct. I don't care what you paid me; I would never do that. . . . You know it was unbelievably beautiful but I would never do it, never," English explained.

Keith and Caroline Ryan were standing on the edge of the lawn watching two little boys, sons of a police officer, marching behind the president as he worked the crowd. One boy grabbed the president's coattails and pulled. He pulled a second time and Clinton turned around. The boy looked up and proudly boasted about his father.

"Do you know who my father is? My father's a Top Cop. My daddy's a Top Cop." Clinton laughed.

"Where's your dad?" he asked. The boy turned around and pointed toward his father. Clinton picked up the youngest child and took the other's hand and walked them around the Rose Garden. "He treated them like gold. Everywhere he went, they went with him. It was amazing. It really was a real honor and a privilege to be there," Ryan explained.

o o o o o o o

Under the administration of Bill Clinton, the domestic economy was flush, international relationships were as friendly as they would be for a long time, and the dollar was strong abroad. All of Europe and even Latin America liked President Bill Clinton. Germans were fast replacing Americans as the ugly tourists. The crime rate was falling all across the United States including in New York. But the war in the Middle East continued, and like it or not, the United States was involved.

Not long after the cops returned to New York, hundreds of people were killed in simultaneous car bomb explosions at the U.S. embassies in Tanzania and Kenya. These attacks were linked to local members of the Al Qaeda terrorist network headed by Osama bin Laden. In response to the bombings, President Clinton ordered Operation Infinite Reach, a series of cruise missile strikes on terrorist targets in Sudan and Afghanistan.

Meanwhile, back in Manhattan at Police headquarters, Nick Mancini was promoted to deputy inspector. He was the only officer involved in the Brooklyn case whom the mayor and the police commissioner granted a discretionary promotion.

8 FRIENDLY FIRE

SIX TRUCK WAS FORTUNATE, OR SOME might say unfortunate, in having four sergeants with different and complementary leadership styles. Tommy Murphy was generally popular among the cops because he was fun and acted more like a cop than a boss and had a buddy boy relationship with his favorite subordinates. On the down side, according to some of his peers, he tended to take sides in arguments among cops rather than mediate impartially. Sergeant Jimmy Ortiz was universally recognized as an all-around nice guy and an old-timer. However, he had recently survived a serious illness and was contemplating retirement and may have had less at stake in the inner workings of the squad than when he was younger. The result was that he might have preferred avoiding conflict and allowing others to do the dirty work when an argument arose.

Jack Cambria, the third Six Truck sergeant, was an involved and popular leader among cops, peers, and brass. The 5'9", solidly built boss was known throughout the department as "Gentleman Jack" because of his diplomatic manner of dealing with civilians, including suspects, subordinates, and superiors. A skilled negotiator in every sphere, Jack could "talk the ears off of a statue," Joe Dolan recalled with admiration. He was also known as Gentleman Jack because he dressed meticulously. "He is the only guy I ever saw who could chase a perp underneath a subway and come out with his clothes clean and unwrinkled," one boss explained.

As a result of his gentility, honesty, integrity, and all-around skill as an "E-man" and top-of-the-line mediator, Cambria was often called in to handle the most delicate jobs involving, for example, suicidal members of the service. Liked and trusted by the officers in his command as well as those outside, cops often came to him when they had problems at work or at home or complaints about the job. Ray McDermott believed Cambria was "the epitome of what a supervisor should be. . . . . He was the voice of the truck. . . . You could rely on him to tell you straight up. He always had the interest of his men and women and he put it above his own. He made sure his people were warm when it was cold and they were fed. People would seek him out to talk."

Joe Dolan emphasized that part of what made Cambria such a good boss was consistency of temperament. "I don't think I ever saw him lose any amount of composure, no matter what was going on. He was the calmest, best-dressed ESU cop I could ever meet. He never deviated from that personality. Never had a problem with Jack Cambria; he was the same way every day. He was the constant in a changing universe. Nothing would shake him. It made it easy to work for him."

Tony Rizzo was the fourth Six Truck sergeant. He and Cambria had once partnered together when they were cops and probably made a good team because they valued excellence and complemented each other's working styles, easily assuming in different scenarios the good and bad cop roles, depending on demand. At 5'7", Rizzo had a strong build with the expanding girth of a lot of veteran cops who eat pasta, meat, and "takeout" food from neighborhood restaurants. He had workman's hands, dark eyes, and a receding brown hairline. His eyes glowed and his cheeks puffed up in a wide, warm grin when he talked about his days in Emergency Service. Rizzo was the most controversial of the four sergeants because he enforced the rules as he saw fit, sometimes with a heavy hand. Bosses tend to play different roles in particular units, and Rizzo wasn't ashamed to admit what his was. "See, I was the disciplinarian of the truck, no doubt about that. Jack Cambria used to call me his pit bull. As a boss I won't take money out of your pocket. I won't put you on paper [for doing something you're not supposed to] but I am gonna penalize you."

Rizzo had been a cop as well as a boss in Emergency Service, was trained by some of the most experienced old-timers, and believed he knew how to best handle a job. He was strict in that he wanted jobs done according to his exact instructions unless situational contingencies altered the frame of events in a way that he could justify a change in a plan. An Emergency Service boss from another truck who liked Rizzo a lot and considered him a friend smiled when he told me, "Tony Rizzo is the type of guy who would give you the shirt off his back and then tell you how to wear it." An Emergency Service cop who wasn't in Six Truck and never had a problem with Rizzo did note that he changed when he became a sergeant. "I knew him when he was a cop and he was a pretty good guy. Something happened when he got promoted. I guess he got a little power and something happened after that." Whatever it was, Rizzo tended to be direct, blunt, and sometimes tactless when dealing with subordinates. I suspect the officers who loved him most took orders well, had a low tolerance for ambiguity, and didn't chafe at the bit when confronted with what others might perceive as rudeness or rigidity or over-control. Some cops in Emergency Service were loyal to Rizzo because he was a competent E-man who had the "balls" to stand up for them in the face of difficult and intimidating superiors.

Whatever his flaws, he wasn't an opportunist who "kissed up and kicked down" the ranks to get ahead. He didn't mince many more words when he dealt with bull-headed superiors outside his command than he did with subordinates. More than once Jack Cambria had to bail him out by rephrasing something he said in a less-than-deferential tone in a way that the commander in question could hear without taking offense. One cop recalled a time when an arrogant duty captain tried to take Rizzo to task because he refused to wait the three hours it took for the captain to get to the scene before executing an Emergency Service entry. Rizzo stood his ground, insisting he didn't wait because that would have increased the risk of the mission to his men.

Whether they liked him or not, there wasn't a soul in the unit who didn't respect Rizzo as a cop. Ryan noted with admiration that Rizzo was a competent "E-man" and master electrician. Others remarked on his skill as a tactician and expert in using every piece of Emergency Service equipment, thus living out in his abilities the principle of redundancy the officers in the unit held dear, that every cop is trained in the same way and should be competent at every skill and able to handle any job. Rizzo was also brave. According to several police officers, on one occasion he threw himself on top of what all believed was a live grenade to protect the crowd. Ray McDermott explained, "At that time [Million Man March in Harlem] somebody threw what appeared to be a hand grenade into the crowd; Tony Rizzo actually jumped on it. That's the kind of guy Tony Rizzo is. He's also a first-rate E-man, an outstanding boss, master electrician, and a guy you could rely on to get the job done."

Rizzo did not mention the incident until I asked him precisely what happened. "To set the record straight, I did not jump on the hand grenade. As I was going over to it, I was going to place my ballistic helmet over it to try to contain the explosion and push it into a nearby sewer if possible to eliminate as much shrapnel as possible." I found it striking that, whenever Rizzo spoke of any action involving danger and weapons, he was careful to neutralize the glory implicit in the rumored versions of events and clarify his decision making so I wouldn't see his behavior as crazy, thoughtless, reckless, or excessively gung ho.

o o o o o o o

Rizzo believed that his problems with Ryan began just before he transferred to Six Truck in the pool of blood in which a pit bull was lying, whining and gurgling and moving his head back and forth like it was detached from his neck. Rizzo recalled that the job started out OK. He was leading an Emergency Service team on a warrant-based entry into the basement of a building in Brooklyn where some suspects were hiding out. According to Rizzo, he was walking along the side of the building when he noticed two pit bulls, peering through a glass window, neither of which seemed aggressive. Rizzo thought about reaching his hand inside and petting the dogs. "Just yell if they move," he instructed Ryan, then left the cops alone to check on other team members who were making their way through the back.

At this point, some of the officers threw some flash-bangs into the boiler room, creating a lot of noise and smoke in an effort to disorient the suspects. When the flash-bangs went off or maybe before, the dogs moved away from the window and began cowering behind a sewer pipe that extended from the floor. Then one of the officers ran into the room next to the boiler room and apprehended one of the suspects. Shortly after, Rizzo heard Ryan and his partner open fire. Rizzo knew who was shooting because he recognized the sound and Ryan and Tony, his partner, were the only guys carrying MP-5 submachine guns. What, are you crazy? Rizzo thought. Why were his cops firing weapons?

According to Rizzo, frightened by the blast, the dogs charged in the direction of the officers who then unloaded their weapons in self-defense. "It started from them [Ryan and his partner]. Then it drove the dogs into the rest of the team. Then they had to fire. They had two wounded animals charging at [them]. Five guys fired a total of about forty shots. . . ." I didn't ask Rizzo from which vantage point he was observing events or if his memories were filtered by the accounts he later heard from some of the cops who were at different vantage points in relation to the shooting.

Rizzo ran toward the boiler room, fearing that one of his cops was shot. After he learned that everyone was OK, he gave Ryan a look that could have burned through steel, I imagine, and headed toward the dogs. One dog was lying dead on the floor, riddled with bullet holes. The other dog was making a God awful sound and his head was flopping back and forth like his neck was broken or his spinal cord severed. Rizzo planted his feet firmly in the pile of projectiles, aimed his gun down toward the dog's head and pulled the trigger once. "That was the only time I discharged my fire-arm, and the only reason I did was so it wouldn't run by them again and they wouldn't let another hundred shots go . . . I think Keith fired sixteen shots at those dogs. His partner fired eight. He wasn't even in the room with the dogs. He was outside. . . . If I'd have stayed there and not walked around, the shooting never would have happened. When I saw the dogs, I felt sorry. . . . I had to put him down. I couldn't watch the dog making the noises he was making. To this day that was the only shot I ever fired on the job," Rizzo said.

Tony, Ryan's partner at the time of the incident, is now deceased, hav-ing committed suicide sometime later. His version of the story was there-fore unavailable and neither Rizzo nor Ryan was willing to say much about his role out of respect for a cop who could no longer speak for himself. As is almost always the case in situations involving interpersonal conflict, Ryan's account of the shooting differed from that of his boss. Ryan main-tained that the shooting was partly the fault of an officer who threw in another set of flash-bangs after the first. It was the noise and smoke that frightened the dogs and sent them running in the direction of the officer who was inside. The dogs had thus been running toward one of the cops before Ryan and his partner fired their weapons.

Ryan explained. "We went down into the basement with the devices [i.e., flash-bangs]. They exploded, and then the two guys [i.e., suspects] ran into the back and secreted themselves near the boiler room. As we [continued toward the] back, we threw in more flash-bangs. There were two pit bulls in the basement on the side, but they were contained and there was no reason to fuck with them at this point. So what did [some of the cops] do? They threw in more flash-bangs and scared the shit out of the dogs. . . . It was John who did that. There was no need to throw more flash-bangs at that point—that's what set the dogs off, and Rizzo blamed us.

John went in and the dogs started coming out. I heard Tony [my partner] in front of me yelling, 'The dogs, the dogs!' and he discharged his weapon. I look over and saw the dogs running, and I think they're going after the two guys who are inside. I think I fired eleven rounds, and he fired eight. Me and Tony saw what was happening and started shooting at the dogs because we thought they were going after John. . . . Then Rizzo comes over . . . [He] saw the dog lying on the floor and, to make a point, he had to 'mercifully' put him down so he shot him in the head. 'Because of your ignorance,' he [turned to me and] said. You know what? I've had animals all my life. I would not hurt a dog . . . 'Why would I hurt them?' I asked."

When the duty captain came to make a report, the tension between Ryan and Rizzo escalated considerably. Rizzo was under the impression that Ryan had fired about sixteen rounds because of what he recalled hearing and what made sense to him; it takes only one pull of the trigger to release sixteen rounds when an MP-5 is on full automatic.

"You were on automatic?" Rizzo asked.

"No, Sarg, I wasn't on full automatic," Ryan responded.

"Keith, you were on full automatic," Rizzo said.

"No, I wasn't on full automatic," Ryan said.

"Keith, you want me to go in there and tell the captain that you are a jerk and pulled the trigger sixteen times?" Rizzo asked. At some point during the conversation, he told Ryan in an I don't know what kind of tone of voice, and said that the department didn't care how his weapon was set; they just wanted an explanation that they could swallow without being forced to investigate. Shooting pit bulls and other "dangerous" dogs is not unusual in the NYPD. Nevertheless, procedure demands that every weapon discharge is written up and accounted for, and this one involved a total of forty shots.

"I wasn't on full automatic." Ryan said.

"Shut up and let me finish with the captain," Rizzo said, then disappeared into another room with the captain to discuss the report. Whatever was put on paper that day was never questioned by management. Regardless, Rizzo remained incensed that Ryan and his partner had fired their weapons when Rizzo didn't perceive a threat. He was also annoyed because Ryan was making Rizzo's life difficult by sticking to a story that he didn't think would hold water in the eyes of those above. Ryan was angry that Rizzo didn't believe him and insisted that he wasn't on full automatic. "You never put an MP-5 on automatic, because it's difficult to control and it's very dangerous, but single-shot . . . I could fire single-shot almost like an automatic . . . the gun is easy like that," Ryan explained.

It was after the pit bull incident that Rizzo began to question just about anything Ryan said and assume that he was lying much of the time. He also began to watch him more carefully than the other cops in the squad with whom he'd worked before and trusted to do their jobs. Later, when Ryan and Dolan were partnered, one troublesome incident after another seemed to occur or was remembered, blurring the generally excellent police work the officers did. These incidents didn't involve use of force or a problem in handling serious jobs. Instead, they involved minor sorts of perceived indiscretions that, if discovered, could bring attention from above and embarrass the bosses in the unit. As Rizzo firmly believed a combination of heavy supervision and penalty could whip a cop into shape, each time the officers got involved in something he didn't like, he would call them into his office, ream them out, and punish them with a bad assignment that made them unhappy but didn't enter their personnel file and cause irreparable harm to their careers. It didn't take much time before Rizzo was questioning their "decision making" and calling them names behind their back—and maybe in front of cops and peers. Ryan and Dolan began to view Rizzo as a bully who relentlessly tormented them because he could, ignoring violations by his favorite cops because he didn't count them as egregious, or didn't know about them, or maybe didn't care because he was willing to do what a lot of good bosses do for loyal cops in an organization in which resources are scarce. Meanwhile, Ryan and Dolan suffered because "when he [Rizzo] hated somebody, God help you. There was no stone that he left uncovered to hurt you or try to hurt you." Even officers who loved and respected Tony Rizzo confirmed that Ryan was right; when Rizzo got his teeth into someone, he didn't let up.

Ryan never claimed that he and Dolan were angels, but he didn't think they were any worse than some of the other cops in the squad who sat on their butts and didn't carry their load but managed to stay under the radar nonetheless. There is a logical explanation for this. Officers who avoid work and engage in minor transgressions that mostly effect their peers don't get into trouble because they are able to maintain low visibility as long as they abide by other key cultural rules and don't do anything that will make their colleagues jealous or mad enough to rat on them or lead them to be labeled a risk or high-maintenance from a supervisor's point of view. A cop whose personality gets under a boss's skin, engages in activities that add to his workload, or creates the potential for danger or embarrassment are much more likely to suffer punishment. If top brass get word, for example, that a physical fight has occurred and someone was seriously hurt, then the supervisor's "ass" is on the line. There are times when fistfights do occur between peers, and supervisors look the other way or leave the scene. In such situations, the cops involved have probably not been labeled as trouble, and the bosses believe that the cops will end the conflict before someone is hurt. In contrast to some of their peers who probably violated their share of minor rules, something about Ryan and Dolan's behavior struck a discordant note among Rizzo's cops in particular and thus their actions tended to draw the boss's attention as well.

In some ways the situation in Six Truck was even uglier than Ryan imagined. He didn't believe that peers betrayed him to bosses and aggravated the mess. I think they did; at least some of Rizzo's cops teamed up and went out of their way to leave Dolan and Ryan exposed. A few overtly "ratted" them out. In other ways, the situation wasn't initially as bad as the two officers sometimes believed. Rizzo just wanted to "straighten them out" and believed that the best way to do that was by administering penalties. "Part of my role as a sergeant is protecting men from themselves . . . I thought maybe I should just put [them] on paper and end the problem for me, but I didn't believe in doing it that way. . . . Still, I'm going to make your life miserable. You are going to pay for what you do until you start to do what you're supposed to be doing."

There is thus little doubt that Ryan and Dolan were being singled out and persecuted, which added to the paranoia and unhappiness of their daily lives. It got to the point where they felt that whatever they did, right or wrong, was going to be seen as bad. Ryan recognizes that he probably fed Rizzo's negative opinion of him by sometimes taking the blame and refusing to give up his partner. Ryan's view was that if he was in the truck, he was also responsible for what happened, regardless of which one of the partners did what when. Rizzo couldn't be faulted for what he didn't know or suspect. What strikes me as sad is that this otherwise competent E-man and knowledgeable boss was unable to recognize that his punitive philosophy of management didn't help Ryan or Dolan do what he wanted and probably wouldn't have worked for other officers with similar personalities who were also basically good cops.

∘ ∘ ∘ ∘ ∘ ∘ ∘

After the raid, the first signs of trouble in Emergency Service didn't come from Tony Rizzo. Instead, they involved digs and innuendos from peers and bosses who worked in other trucks. According to rumor, Ryan was going around boasting that he'd saved the lives of his peers by shooting the terrorist suspects. I don't know how this rumor got started. I've interviewed a number of cops and detectives who'd worked with Ryan in other units and described him as a humble and quiet man, not a boastful one.

Regardless of how it arose, I suspect that the rumor was inflated by the collective memory of the article that had appeared in the *New York Post*. Larry Celona's story haunted Ryan like the death of a buddy in combat, infecting his dreams and daily life and peers' and bosses' perception of him. "I think Keith thought he was a hero and he should have been awarded. . . . You got guys jumping off buildings and . . . they expect nothing. It's not what the unit is about. It never was, and hopefully never will be . . . You don't look for recognition. You run into problems when you are trying to get it too much. You want to see heroes, you go to One PP and read the wall, those are the only heroes. There are guys who have done heroic acts here or there, but the real heroes are dead. . . . None of these jobs, the crane job and the raid, none of them are one- or two-man jobs.[1] There is no number one on a team. It's a team. That came from Chief Anemone. . . . We might take a guy with a gun down but the detectives and the police officers all did their work (too) . . . Nobody did it by themselves. It was a team effort, and that is why when some people get recognition, it's like no. . . . The fact of the matter remains [that] Larry Celona was [figuratively] in [Ryan's] living room and [he was] the one that did the talking. . . . There had to have been a lot of resentment when that story came out," Rizzo explained, relying in part on stories he'd heard from other cops to aid his interpretation of events.

In the light of the newspaper article, Rizzo was loath to believe that Ryan concurred with the other members of the team in attempting to limit public exposure by not appearing at the press conference, a stance Rizzo understood and would have likely supported had he been one of the bosses involved. Another Emergency Service sergeant disagreed. He believed that Dolan and Ryan were instrumental in pushing the issue. While this boss did not speculate how the *Post* article came about, except to note how manipulative Celona was with cops, he thought that its untimely appearance added insult to injury in the eyes of the police commissioner and made things worse for the team. John English seemed to take the Larry Celona debacle in stride, as one of those things that happens in real life, like "Shit happens," as a result of some combination of miscommunication, human error, and misplaced trust and/or exploitation by a journalist. In contrast to Rizzo, English believed that Ryan and Dolan did deserve special recognition in the form of the Combat Cross at least, and that all the cops on the raid should have made detective. "Nobody expected anything, but when you see a guy getting promoted to detective specialist, which is what I think Joe, Keith, Mike and Mario would have gotten, for coming up with a great computer program that they are able to use for CompStat and then four guys don't get promoted because of that? On Medal Day, Joe and Keith Ryan should have gotten the Combat Cross, which is, as you know, one step above the Medal of Valor, but we thought we weren't even going to medal day . . . because with all of the other persecution that everybody suffered from this, I thought we would never see anything from the job at all."

Around the same time that people were spreading the rumor that Ryan was saying he saved his teammates' lives, Dolan learned that Tommy Stokes, a lieutenant from another squad, was claiming that Dolan and Ryan were strutting around like peacocks with their feathers spread, boasting about other aspects of their role in the raid. "They didn't do anything special and now they're walking around thinking they're better than anyone else in the Division," Stokes said. Dolan hadn't heard his partner running his mouth and hadn't been boasting himself and couldn't figure out where Stokes was getting his information. One day, when Dolan encountered Stokes in the hall, he decided to ask. "Tommy, I don't know where this stuff is coming from. Have you ever seen us gloating or running our mouths about what we did?" Dolan said. Stokes chatted for a few minutes, said good-bye, and walked away without answering the question.

Later, Ryan ran into Stokes's secretary, who started spouting accusations that sounded like something that came from her boss. "You and that Brooklyn bomb job, you guys are getting all these dinners for free and, you know, you didn't do anything nobody else in this unit hasn't done before!" she said. The veins in Ryan's neck swelled. Maybe he wanted "to crush her cranium into the desktop," to borrow a phrase he once used in reference to a female supervisor loathed by all of the cops. "If I hadn't of walked away, she [the secretary] would have had my palm imprinted on her face. I've never hit a woman. A fuckin' civilian! Where do you get the audacity to talk to me like that?" he asked.

Perhaps I should have been offended by his cursory dismissal of civilians, the way some female researchers today get bothered by even moderate forms of what they see as sexual harassment in the field. In my work with police I've always viewed sexual overtures as valuable clues to culture and dynamics of rapport. So, in a similar vein, I understood where Ryan was coming from even if his opinion hinted at transference—reflecting, perhaps, some unconscious ambivalence toward me.[2] I'd estimate that 99 percent of police officers believe that civilian members of the service are inferior human beings who aren't cops and don't carry guns and are therefore outsiders. Some officers assume that civilians don't have the guts or intelligence to take the test and join the force. Most important, they've never worked the street and therefore can't understand the job and have no right Monday morning quarterbacking the actions of cops, regardless of what they think and hear. "Ah, you're still riding that wave" was another one of the relentless trail of cutting comments coming from cops and, on rare occasion, civilians, that followed Dolan and Ryan around for months to come.

One night, during a week of cold rain and wet snow, when tensions were high in Six Truck and Dolan and Ryan were getting tired of being harassed by peers and bosses for "bullshit," Dolan almost inadvertently ended his career by landing his fist on the base of lieutenant Lonnie Jones's nose. Dolan was sitting in quarters and eating a rotisserie chicken when Jones walked in with a friend who was a retired NYPD boss. Neither Jones nor his friend had ever worked in Six Truck and therefore, in a sense, were coming in as uninvited guests of the squad. Everything was OK until Jones started talking trash, a habit that Ryan could tolerate because it wasn't directed at him and, for reasons he didn't understand, Jones's abrasive remarks usually seemed to roll off his back.

"See this guy over there, he was involved in one of the biggest jobs this job has ever seen, and he fucked it up! We gave him a man's gun and he couldn't do [finish] the job," Jones said, pointing his finger in Dolan's direction, alluding to the fact that the suspects weren't killed. Dolan's eyes got black and beady, his brow came down, his ears turned red, and his face contorted into something that reminded his partner of a bulldog.

"Since you were on that job, why don't you tell me what I did wrong?" he asked.

"I wasn't there."

"Then shut your fuckin' mouth!"

"All you had to do was suck a little dick, and you'd have gotten a gold shield," Jones said. Dolan shoved the chicken out of his way, pushed his chin forward, hunched his shoulders, and leaned into the table with a menacing look that no crumpled-faced dog could imitate. Jones's friend took a step back and froze in his tracks. Seconds ticked by and tensions mounted as if everyone knew an assassin was lurking in the shadows but couldn't see where he was.

"We're not like you," Dolan finally said and then stuck his fork into a piece of breast meat. The lieutenant's friend suggested they leave and accompanied Jones out of the room. Ryan relaxed and put his hand on his forehead in a gesture of relief. "I thought Joey was going to kill him," he explained. "I sat there and it's one of the few times that I ever thought, if Joey went nuts, that I couldn't control him and get to the rational side. . . . We'd been through so much bullshit, and to hear that was like, you're in *my* house, you're not even my truck lieutenant, you're at my table. If you got nothing good to say, say nothing at all . . . It was really bad, and that hit more of a spot with Joey than it did with me because I knew how to ignore Lonnie."

Ryan and Dolan weren't the only men involved in the raid taking heat from cops and maybe bosses. I suspect Keenan and Zorovic were as well. John English recalled that the guys in his squad chided him too but, being who he was, he responded with humor that neutralized tension and jealousy. Once a couple of guys were making comments about his endless attendance at banquets and asking English when and if he was ever going to start working again. English responded by noting that he was also sick of going out and looked forward to a return to his normal life. "I didn't take it personally. . . . it was done in a joking kind of way and it wasn't that often," he explained. However, he noted that the comments directed at Ryan and Dolan were more hostile and the gossip and rumors surrounding their actions ballooned out of control, undermining their reputations and sabotaging their state of mind. "I think there was a lot of jealousy on the part of a very few people. The guys kept going to these dinners and awards. It was just a very few people but in Keith and Joe's case, they began to influence some other people and then it got out of hand."

The result was that Dolan got mad and sometimes confrontational and Ryan's moods turned black and he walked around with a sullen look on his face. When someone pushed him hard enough, he'd push back and the situation would escalate, creating, I suspect, a perverse form of entertainment for the tough-guy type of Emergency Service cop who liked to prey on peers who appear emotional, humorless or otherwise weak and vulnerable in the cultural and/or individual eye. The angrier Ryan and Dolan got, the less pleasant they were to be around, and soon everyone but maybe their closest friends tried to steer clear. Meanwhile, the two officers took the job home with them, allowing the cops and bosses involved to live rent-free in their brains. At work, Ryan walked around wary and vigilant, wondering which one of his actions was going to be questioned next.

He didn't have long to wait. Several incidents took place in close proximity and heightened tensions with Rizzo and other bosses in the squad. Some officers recalled that the incidents happened on one very bad day. Others suggest that they occurred consecutively on different days when the two officers were assigned to the same miserable detail to guard and maintain the light towers in Central Park where there had recently been a rape. I have condensed the incidents here, not because I have a preference for one over another person's remembered chronology but simply to minimize repetition of what were similar and equally trying events for all involved, Ryan and Dolan in particular. "A broken record," Ryan recalled.

At some point during the midnight shift, while Ryan was driving, Dolan discovered he couldn't open the door to the passenger side of the truck and get out. Unknown to him, the cops on the previous tour had discovered the door was out of alignment and fixed it well enough so they didn't have to take it out of service during their shift. Dolan tried and failed to open the door several times and, growing increasingly impatient, started cursing the air. Finally, he crawled across the gears, got out on the driver's side, walked around the truck, stood in front of the offending door, grabbed the handle, and pulled as hard as he could with all his considerable muscle. When he heard the screeching sound of metal caving in, he realized he'd gone too far.

"Oh, shit!"

"Joey, what have you done?" Ryan asked, looking aghast from where he was standing on the pavement still on the driver's side.

"I guess I shouldn't have done that."

"Ahh, Joey. He's gonna fuck with us now!"

The same night or the next, the two officers discovered that the light towers in the park were nearly out of fuel. Apparently, neither officer had anticipated needing a large amount of gas. One officer said that cops from the previous tour assigned to the detail are supposed to ensure the tanks have plenty of fuel before the next shift arrives. This makes sense. The same applies in regard to gas in patrol cars and trucks. Of course, oversights do occur, cops complain, and bosses have to address the problem by developing measures to ensure the rule is enforced. Faced with a near-empty tank, Dolan called quarters and spoke to the desk officer, Tony Ferretti, and asked him to bring them some fuel. Ferretti refused.

"Whaddaya mean? We're on a fixer, we can't leave," Dolan said.

"That's too bad. You handle it."

"Will you get your ass outta that chair and get up here!"

"Fuck you!"

"Fuck me? Fuck you, you lazy son of a bitch, we're up here freezin' our cocks off and you're sitting there behind a desk. Listen, you tough fuck, I'll come down there and wipe the floor with your fat ass!"

"Well, I'm here all night."

"What did you say?"

"You heard me," Ferretti said, with Ryan sitting there listening to Joey's words but not taking action to abort the development of a minor disaster. This is gonna get even worse. Joey is getting crazy. I'm fucked. We're fucked, Ryan thought.

"I'm coming down, you little fuck!" Dolan said, and put his foot on the gas, landing at Floyd Bennett Field in record time. With Ferretti standing there in front of him at the desk, Dolan dared him to say what he'd said on the phone to his face so he could "Kick his ass!" or something to that effect. Ryan recalled that Ferretti backed down first and then acted like he'd been kidding around.

Probably nothing much would have come of the incident had Rizzo not found out from Ferretti what happened. Ryan didn't believe that Ferretti was being malicious when he let it slip that he'd seen the pair at quarters when they were supposed to be in the park. I think Ferretti told Rizzo intentionally because he wanted him to handle the affair as he saw fit. Apparently, Ferretti claimed to his boss that he didn't back down and that Ryan and Dolan threatened him if he sent them to the park again. Who backed down first during the confrontation is anyone's guess. In disputes with male police officers of every rank, testosterone mediates memory, compromises reason, and so no one will ever admit that they did what I, as a civilian, might view as the sensible thing to diffuse the situation.

The next day or maybe another, Rizzo was in the garage helping the cops transfer their load from the truck with the broken door to another truck when he noticed a section of garden hose. Although he knew the hose wasn't Emergency Service equipment, he didn't think much about it until he got a phone call from a lieutenant in Central Park Precinct who explained that he'd gotten a complaint: some NYPD Emergency Service cops had cut one of the Park Department hoses and used it to put fuel into the light tower. "The guy from the park [who complained] is a real nice guy and he doesn't think it's something to worry about but he wants to talk to you before making out the report," the lieutenant said.

Rizzo drove into Manhattan to see the damage and talk to the Parks Department official, get the number of the truck responsible, and assure him that nothing like this would ever happen again. The following morning, Rizzo called Ryan and Dolan into his office and confronted them with what he'd learned. I don't know when the issue of the hose arose and what was said. Ryan insisted they didn't make the hose disappear or try to minimize discovery of what they did because, when they were in the park, they tracked down a Parks Department employee who gave them permission to section the hose and use it as they saw fit. "We were in a marked car. Why would we do something like that? Everybody could see the number on the truck. Joe and I spoke to the guy. Maybe his supervisor got mad, and he didn't tell him what he said to us." Regardless of what actually happened, according to Ryan, Rizzo was disrespectful during the conversation, cursing and calling him a moron and a "no good piece of shit." Rizzo insisted he spoke directly but chose his words carefully because if "you push cops too far, there's no way out": you have no choice but to put the affair in writing and suspend them.

"First thing I wanna know, how is it that you started out in an Emergency Vehicle without gas [for the fuel tank in the park and/or for your truck]? I gotta call from a lieutenant up in Central Park saying you guys [used one of their hoses] to siphon in gas."

"We didn't think we could leave the park." Dolan said.

"I don't get it. Why didn't you call Two Truck, they're just north of the park?"

"We were on a fixer. We didn't think we could leave Central Park," Dolan said. Dolan and Ryan understood they were on a "face-to-face" fixer and weren't supposed to leave until their replacement arrived and the actual exchange took place.

"Well, you had no problem going to Floyd Bennett Field to pick a fight with the desk officer."

"So I should just take shit from somebody over the phone, when we're trying to do the right thing?" Dolan replied. Ryan was standing there listening when the conversation between Dolan and Ferretti flashed through his head.

"That's not the point," Rizzo said. Ryan turned his gaze outward again. It occurred to him that there was nothing he could do or say to come across as reasonable in Rizzo's eyes. Ryan remembered that Dolan and Rizzo were screaming at each other and going back and forth.

The point is whatever you want it to be. It's not the truth. It's Joe Rizzo's truth, Dolan thought or said, no one recalled for sure which.

"There's the door, too," Rizzo continued, looking at Ryan this time, thinking that he, not Dolan, was responsible. "I come in and the door of the truck is bent up. What's wrong with you guys? You ruined that door!"

"The fender got hung up when we tried to open it," Ryan explained.

"Where's the fuckin' accident report, then?"

"We didn't get into an accident."

"We fixed it yesterday, so you must have hit something!" Rizzo said, figuring they they'd probably hit a couple of bumps in the road and the door had shifted position and gotten jammed.

"I pushed the door open. I didn't think it was going to get creased like that," Ryan said. "You know, your guys fucked up the door. You come after us and you didn't tell us your guys damaged it earlier," Ryan added, defending himself but also probably adding fuel the fire.

"That's got nothing to do with it."

"That's got nothing to do with it?" Ryan said. "We get blamed for their screwup! How come your guys didn't put in a report? Your guys don't do anything wrong? Why didn't they put the car out of service and send it to the shop instead of you and your genius mechanic, trying to fix the truck? he said or thought, echoing sentiments I'd heard expressed by some of the sergeant's friends and peers: Rizzo's cops were no less petty and "sinful" than other officers in Emergency Service who acted like children a ridiculous amount of the time.

"That's my car and you damaged it. You don't do that to my car!"

"That truck doesn't belong to you. It belongs to the City of New York!" Ryan responded. Who the hell do you think you are? You're not my fuckin' father! he thought. Enraged and sick of the argument, the tone of Rizzo's voice when he spoke to him, the seemingly relentless number of accusations, the favoritism and harassment, Ryan put his hands on Rizzo's desk and pushed his body forward, getting almost as close as he could to the sergeant in the nanosecond it took before Rizzo stood up.

"Keith, Keith. Calm down. It's not worth it. Come on," Dolan said.

"Everybody in the truck knows who really fucked up that door," Ryan muttered and walked out of the room. "Rizzo doesn't know how close he came to being able to fire Keith and have him arrested for assault. I bent the door. But being the partner that he was, he took the blame for it," Dolan explained.

Ferretti was one of the cops Rizzo liked and respected and, whether or not Ferretti's version of events was partly or wholly true, Rizzo assumed that Ryan and Dolan had, indeed, threatened him. The result was that Rizzo made the decision that from that day on Ryan and Dolan were going to get every park detail that arose. "Ferretti is a great guy. He was at the desk [that day], and when they came and threatened him that they shouldn't be sent to Central Park . . . when I found out that they did that, now you're going more . . . You are going to be the Central Park kings," Rizzo explained.

I asked Ryan why he didn't say anything to keep the situation from escalating out of control. "I don't know how a simple request [for some fuel] got so blown up. I knew it was bad judgment and that anger [was ruling] over common sense. It was like watching my brother doing something idiotic and, even though I don't agree, I can't say anything. I can't fuck up [my relationship with] the one person who loves me more than anything. I have to give him moral support. I had to give Joey support. He did that for me. We each had our [areas that triggered] blind rage but [those that] upset him didn't bother me and those that got to me didn't get to him. I guess the harassment just got to me after a while and I started to second-guess everything everyone did. Maybe it clouded my judgment. I didn't want to second-guess my partner. We didn't want to have to be watching each other like we had to be watching everyone else. It was my error to let myself get caught up in the frenzy."

As time went on and one petty incident followed another, the anger and resentment consuming Dolan and Ryan began to infect their partnership. There was even a brief period in which they got so fed up with the situation that they stopped talking to each other. "I mean, we laugh about this shit, as fucked up as it got and we would just laugh about it, but it got to the point that Joey felt uncomfortable with Rizzo fuckin' with me and he could do nothing about it and I got to the point I didn't want to be around anybody," Ryan explained. Their partnership finally ended when Dolan switched to the 4:00–12:00 shift to spend more time with his family. Alone, Ryan became a more vulnerable target.

○ ○ ○ ○ ○ ○ ○

Tony Abate was well known in Emergency Service for his laziness, a characteristic that bosses and peers acknowledged but that seemed to elicit little more than occasional bitching. "No doubt about it, Abate was lazy," Rizzo said. Years later, at Abate's retirement party, he would receive recognition of his skill from his peers in the form of an award for being the man "who was best at doing nothing at all." It was therefore no surprise that Abate wasn't doing anything significant related to the job on the night he refused to take a call on Ryan's sector when Ryan and his partner were in the midst of a "10-13," assist officer. Ryan had just put his foot on the pavement when the dispatcher requested that an Emergency Service unit meet an off-duty police officer who had locked himself out of his car. Ryan picked up the radio and told the dispatcher that he was at the scene of the 10-13 and asked if she could assign the job to someone else. The dispatcher responded by giving the call to Abate and his partner, who worked the neighboring sector. A few seconds later, Ryan got a call on the cell phone.

"I ain't going on this job. You're Adam car, you go," Abate said, as best as Ryan recalled.

"What? You're ten minutes away. Go to the fuckin' job. We're still out on that 10-13."

"I told you I ain't going!"

"You're outta your mind. There's a cop locked out of his car!" Abate refused, hung up the phone, and then got on the radio.

"Central, reassign that job to Adam Six," he said over the air so every Emergency Service officer could hear. Bobby, Ryan's partner, called Abate back and asked him to take the job with the MOS (Member of the Service), explaining they were out on a huge brawl. An evidence search was involved. It was in the 7-2 Precinct, miles away from the 6-6, where the cop was locked out of his car.

"Ray, what the fuck is your problem? We are at this 13. We are in the 7-2 Precinct. We've got an evidence search. You're not doing nothing. You take this job and we'll take care of the rest of the night," Bobby said.

"Fuck you, Bobby, I ain't going," Abate responded.

Furious, Bobby turned to Ryan and said, "Do you believe this guy? He just told me to go fuck myself. He's not taking the job." This time Ryan called Abate back on his cell and admittedly "went ballistic."

"Tony, go on the fuckin' job, we're still here! We're gonna be here for a while. We got an evidence search. This is cop out there. How long ya gonna keep him waiting?"

"I ain't going nowhere."

"Tony, go on the fuckin job!"

"What are you threatening me?"

"I ain't threatening you. I'm just telling you to do your job. . . . I'm telling you when I come to quarters we're going straighten this right out. You don't go on this job then, you're going to have a problem." After Ryan and his partner finished their role in the 10-13, they headed to the location of the call with the off-duty cop. When they arrived at the scene, they saw that the officer was still standing there, waiting outside. Ryan apologized for the delay and unlocked the door of the officer's car, using a tool they kept in the back of the truck. Ten minutes later Ryan rolled into the parking lot and speed-walked into Emergency Service quarters with Bobby running up the stairs following on his heels. Inside, Ryan discovered that Tony Abate was stretched out on a cushioned bench and his partner was sitting in a chair a few feet away.

"Tony, get up. Get up," Ryan yelled. "Get up! You've got a big fuckin' mouth. Why don't you get up and talk to me now . . . Get the fuck up and talk to me like a man!"

"I ain't getting up," Abate said and grinned.

"Get up!" Abate didn't move and again Ryan tried to get him to stand up and face him like a man. "Why, you son of a bitch! You left a cop standing on the street for an hour and one half. Tony, get up!" he yelled. Helpless and infuriated when Abate still didn't budge, Ryan walked up to the couch, grabbed the table to get it out of the way, accidently flipping it over. He stood above Abate, still screaming at him to get up. Abate lay there and smirked, sending another flash of rage through Ryan's gut. By this time Bobby was in the room and cursing Abate out. Abate's partner then grabbed Ryan, who told him to take his hands off of him. "You should have left that piece of shit in the truck and done the job yourself," he said. Bobby then grabbed Ryan by the shoulders.

"Let's go. It's not worth it," Bobby said. Ryan got ahold of himself, and he and Bobby left the room, walked out of quarters and spent the rest of the night outside. Ryan didn't find out until later that he'd bent the leg of the table.

o o o o o o o

The next morning another cop discovered the broken table and started bitching, "Who broke the table? We just fixed that thing up." Sergeant Tommy Murphy heard the complaint but didn't know what happened until Tony Abate told him his version of events. Abate and he had been friends for a long time, and when Murphy needed a driver to do his rounds or go in on jobs, he often asked Abate to accompany him. It might strike some people as odd that a sergeant would ask a cop who was well known for indolence to be his driver, a position that often involves some degree of compliment or acknowledgment. Ryan explained their partnership by saying, "They both lived on Staten Island. Tony's not a bad guy. He was just burnt out and waiting to retire and didn't want to do anything." He didn't find it a problem that Murphy liked to partner with him.

Certainly the chemistry of police partnership is as difficult to analyze as its sexual counterpart. Seemingly odd combinations of people can survive lengthy periods of time scrunched together in a patrol car without getting on each other's nerves. I've seen deputy commissioners driven by fools who serve no other purpose in their boss's working lives than to transport them here and there and admire, amuse, and make the boss feel good, smart, and powerful. I've also seen chiefs driven by officers who serve more as administrative lieutenants than cops, trusted individuals who are able to keep their bosses' secrets, arrange their schedules, confirm the logistics of meetings, and make sure they have what they need even before they know what that is. Sometimes, the assignment to drive a superior involves a favor or the simple fact that the cop and the boss get along like a well-matched married couple. It was the latter type of relationship that appeared to characterize Murphy and Abate's occasional partnership. In view of the time they spent together and the way they got along, it was, of course, inevitable that Murphy believed Abate's account of the episode, which I suspect minimized his responsibility for the fight and made Ryan out as a violent guy who went berserk, threatened Abate, and broke the table in a fit of unprovoked rage that would have resulted in serious bodily harm if other cops hadn't intervened. "I wished they'd just gotten the tapes out of the queue (from Central Communication) and listened to them," Ryan said.

○ ○ ○ ○ ○ ○ ○

Jack Cambria was aware of the problems in Six Truck before Dolan and Ryan began to confide in him and seek out his advice. After Dolan switched tours and Ryan and Murphy began to have problems, Ryan went to Cambria and asked him to intervene on his behalf. Cambria agreed to mediate—for selfish reasons, he would have claimed, because he couldn't stand going to work when there was tension in the truck. He appealed to Murphy and urged him to talk to Ryan and try to work things out. Murphy agreed, with one caveat. Ryan had to come to him first. After all, Murphy was the sergeant and, as a result, wasn't going to kowtow to a subordinate. Ryan agreed to Murphy's terms but failed to follow through. I'm not sure why. Maybe approaching his sergeant and one-time friend felt too much like groveling on top of the other humiliations he had been suffering. In retrospect, Ryan recognizes that he "should have gone to talk to Tommy. I guess I felt like all my integrity was being questioned. I messed it up by not talking to him. [It felt like] I was walking around in a booby-trapped jungle with everyone second-guessing everything I did, right, wrong, or indifferent." It seemed to me that Ryan couldn't talk to Murphy because he was crippled by hurt and rage, which were exacerbated by all of the partial understandings, confused communications and interpretations, favoritism displayed by some bosses toward particular cops, and the betrayals he'd experienced during the past year. "It killed me that Tommy didn't believe me. He knew me. I had a history with Tommy. I loved working with Tommy when I was a young cop. I just got angry at him for thinking that I would do anything to undermine him. Rizzo poisoned his mind. Rizzo poisoned everybody's mind. . . . The anger just overwhelmed me," Ryan explained.

Not long after the failed mediation attempt, Ryan got so upset he even offended Jack Cambria, whom he respected and considered his only possible ally among the bosses in the truck. "Jack was an archangel in purgatory," Ryan explained in retrospect, thinking about the boss he loved. Cambria was sitting at his desk when Ryan came into the office to check the roll call. When he lifted the roster off the desk and saw that his name was down for yet another detail flying to some place in faraway Queens, he threw the papers back down on the desk and walked out of the room. In a matter of seconds, they slid off the table and hit the floor with a bang. Aghast, Cambria called Ryan back into his office and confronted him with the question, "What have I done to deserve such disrespect?" Ryan apologized profusely and explained that he hadn't meant any disrespect but that he didn't know what to do; every day the same thing kept happening over and over again. He'd come into work and discover he'd been given yet another miserable assignment. Cambria denied knowledge of what was happening and told Ryan that he should discuss the issue with those responsible.

○ ○ ○ ○ ○ ○ ○

The final showdown between Ryan and some of his bosses occurred almost a year after the eight men in Emergency Service received the Top Cops award. According to Ryan, he was working a midnight tour, driving sergeant Jimmy Ortiz, when he discovered a nearly new locker that had been discarded on the street. Ryan asked Ortiz if he could pick up the locker and put it in an unused shower stall that had been housing a broken bench for years. Ortiz agreed. Ryan explained, "That time we [me and Ortiz] were in the truck together and I found a locker, and I said, do you mind if I take the locker? I need another locker. I could change [my clothes] and keep all my money and stuff in there. See, I used to go running after work every day. As soon as I finished my tour I would go and run seven, eight, or ten miles and then come back. He [Ortiz] was like, sure, no problem, go ahead." Ryan loaded the locker in the truck and later, when they got back to quarters, he installed it in the shower stall.

It didn't take long before two cops complained to Rizzo, who quickly discovered that Ryan was involved. Rizzo insisted the shower was functional and that the cops who complained used it sometimes, although I suspect their reasons for complaining were mostly based on petty resentment that Ryan was getting something more than them. Regardless, as a sergeant, it wasn't Rizzo's job to analyze the motives of his officers in this sort of situation. He only had to resolve the conflict in the best way he saw fit. Rizzo didn't think that Ortiz was involved at all and doubted he'd given Ryan permission to assume the space for his private use without consulting him and other truck bosses. Besides, Rizzo didn't think Ryan should put an extra locker in the shower stall because safety issues were involved. "Two guys who used the shower were talking to me about it. I look at it and the bottom line is that, irrespective of that, it's everybody's safety. If some sort of battery acid . . . Guys get caustics on them. I've got the two showers [available]. . . . He [Ryan] wasn't making any friends. Somebody gets pissed at him and they turn the shower on his things. Now I have an internal investigation because somebody damages his stuff. For me it was a win-win situation to get the locker out of there. . . . I don't recall [if Ryan told me that Ortiz said he could put the locker in the shower stall] . . . but even if he did, it wouldn't have mattered. . . . Jimmy Ortiz is a very nice guy. . . . The bottom line is that it didn't belong there. I might have told Keith I don't care what [Jimmy Ortiz] said. Get your locker out of the shower. But before I would do that I would talk to Jimmy about it . . . and maybe we did. It was a long time ago. As sergeants we stuck together and before we would do anything we would discuss it amongst ourselves . . . Like I said, I was the disciplinarian, I would straighten things out that needed straightening out. . . . I definitely would have doubted his story about Ortiz. . . . I would have talked to Ortiz right away. . . . I wouldn't have overruled another sergeant . . . We would have discussed it. Jimmy would have agreed. Maybe I was [the one who was] going to deliver the message. Guys would try to play [us off] one against the other. We all had an agreement. We speak as one."

As soon as Ryan came back from his morning run, Rizzo confronted him and ordered him to take the locker out. Ryan decided to wait and speak to Ortiz instead, who told him that he could keep the locker where it was and that he would talk to Rizzo himself. "Rizzo had a hard-on for me, for what reason I don't know. He told me to move my locker, and I went to Sergeant Ortiz and I said, 'Look you've got to talk to him, tell him that it was OK to put it there. I'll move it but, you know.' Ortiz tells me to wait and he'll talk to Rizzo and straighten it out. To this day I don't know who told the truth and who lied," Ryan said. Assuming that Ortiz was going to talk to Rizzo and everything would be all right, Ryan went home.

The situation turned ugly the next day when Ryan came back from his run after working the midnight to 8:00 A.M. shift and Rizzo came in, discovered the locker was still in the shower and called Ryan into his office. Ryan claimed that Rizzo spoke to him in an abrasive and demeaning manner and that the situation escalated to such a degree that Rizzo stuck his finger into Ryan's chest and threatened to suspend him for insubordination. "Rizzo grabs me in the locker room and starts digging in to me. Look, I said, I'm off duty, I went for a run. I've gotta go home. He stood up and he pokes me in the chest and says, 'You're a piece of shit, you don't belong in my fuckin' truck. . . . If I knew that you were going to be like this I never would have let you into my truck.' I said, 'First of all, the truck belongs to the city of New York, the police commissioner, and the mayor, not you. Now, if you touch me again, I'm going to knock your fuckin' teeth down your throat.' . . . He looks at me and he says, 'Well, I'm going to fuckin' suspend you.' 'Oh yeah,' I said. 'You're gonna suspend me? What the fuck makes you think you're gonna survive the beating I'm gonna give you. Take your shirt off, take those stripes off and let's go downstairs, man to man. You have a big mouth. You're a real tough guy. I am leaving, and if you want to suspend me, you know where I live.'"

Ryan thinks that what stopped Rizzo from escalating the situation was that there was a witness, that a cop was standing in the back listening. I don't know if this was true or not. Rizzo described the conversation so differently that it wouldn't have mattered who was there in terms of his account. He insisted he didn't use demeaning terms or, more importantly, touch Ryan at all, although he might have threatened to suspend him if he was acting insubordinately. "I did not touch him. If it had gotten to that point, I would have suspended him. Never to this day . . . I never laid my hands on him," Rizzo explained.

After the locker incident, Rizzo and Murphy met with Ryan and told him he had to speak to a peer counselor or they'd send him to Psychological Services. "They blackmailed me," Ryan explained. "Rizzo and Murphy did, I don't know if Jack was in on it. I don't know if Jimmy Ortiz was there. I know Rizzo and Murphy grabbed me, called me into their office and told me that I had serious psychological problems, that I had violent tendencies. . . . They beat the shit out of me in that room. It was like a one-two punch, one said and the other agreed . . . They said I was violent and I was walking around like in a manic-depressive state."

Rizzo more or less confirmed Ryan's account of this conversation. "Absolutely, there was a time we met with Keith and told him he had violent tendencies. Me and Tommy definitely did that. He was threatening other cops. We said this can't happen. There were other cops on the late tour . . . I probably did mention [something] about his being violent." At this point in my interview, I asked Rizzo why he didn't call Psychological Services and have Ryan assessed for fitness for duty if he thought he was violent. Rizzo explained, "We didn't feel that was necessary that, if we had a strong presence on him, we could get him in check. You don't want to hurt the guy. You send a cop to Psych Services, he may never come back to full duty . . . I do believe we said, 'You are going to Psych Services if you don't straighten up.' Absolutely, I believe that that is true." I guess, then, that Rizzo wasn't really convinced that Ryan was angry enough to hurt someone. The one boss in Emergency Service who was probably best qualified to make a psychological assessment of his personnel didn't believe Ryan was ever out of control in the sense of prone to physical violence.

By this time, the conflict in Six Truck had reached the upper levels of management and McDermott had gotten involved. Ryan believed that McDermott tried to protect him as best he could and was successful until the situation deteriorated to such a degree that he had no choice but to transfer him out of the squad. McDermott called Ryan into his office or spoke to him on the telephone and suggested that he transfer to Seven Truck. "Yes, it is like a family," McDermott explained. "It's like anything else and, when people get singled out, remember, even in trucks, in a truck, it's like a small miniversion of [a family]—actually, it's an extended family, to be honest—and when certain people get singled out . . . You know [some of these guys], they've been doing jobs like this for years, . . . and all of a sudden they [the officers on the entry team] get all the praise and the accolades, and jealousies come out and people get a little upset and the fact that they're [also] friendly with the commanders and this and that—then jealousies come out and that plays into everybody. . . . I don't remember the whole thing [with Ryan] but I do remember there was a lot of resentment from certain guys [because of the] accolades that these guys got—and there was a lot of ribbing that was going on, some of the trucks, one of them being Six Truck. You know the nature of people. Keith is a wonderful, wonderful guy, and he is sensitive—and I mean that in a good way . . . I love Keith like my own brother. Take this the right way: he can be very sensitive, and unfortunately there are guys that play on that and what they did was the old ball-breaking. You see with Joe [Dolan], they won't [do the same thing], because he has that attitude like I'll see you downstairs, and he would be waiting for you outside. Keith is not like that. Keith tried to resolve everything. He tries to be gentle and calm and just be allowed to do his job. So I believe [that] a group of people were actually starting to mess with him. . . . I think there was a lot of resentment over the [press and other] coverage, the way these guys [involved in the raid] were being portrayed and a lot of guys [in the truck] were resentful of that and I think that's what really came into play. Tony [Deluca] was the truck lieutenant so he would come to see me with the sergeant [Rizzo or Murphy] from the truck and after Joe [Dolan] left, Keith was kind of by himself; that's really what it came down to and I even talked to Keith about it, and I know he went to Seven Truck because he had a better group of people that were real friendly with him. . . . You see, Seven Truck was also John English's truck, and he [Keith] knows John and John was obviously on the job [raid]. . . . Unfortunately, what happens is that when things start bubbling over . . . Keith was really amenable about moving, so that's why he got moved."

Dolan interpreted the squad dynamics that led to his partner's transfer differently; from the perspective of a cop who had been on the receiving end of some of the same bosses' wrath rather than that of a high-level and even-tempered commander who was above the fray and empathized with the conflicting dilemmas of all involved. In Dolan's eyes, Ryan got caught up in a web of personalities, some of whom were good-hearted but ineffective and others of whom were harsh and unfriendly and also able to dominate. "Rizzo wasn't really liked by anybody but his own guys. Then you had Tommy Murphy, who was a paperwork nightmare, and then you had Sergeant Ortiz, who was indifferent to everything, and then you had Jack Cambria, who was running around like a little boy trying to stick his finger along the cracks in the dike to keep it from breaking apart. You had three misfits and a decent boss, and the decent boss has got to be overruled by popular opinion. . . . So Keith was done," Dolan explained.

Dolan went on to elucidate his personal feelings about the pros and cons of Rizzo's leadership. "I don't dislike Rizzo. There are times I didn't like what he did or how he handled people, but there were times I liked the guy—[like when my police officer brother was shot in the face and he told me to go up there to Rhode Island and let him know what I needed and he would take care of it]. I just think his supervisory skills with talking to guys and how he handled things, I think, he was wrong. . . . Otherwise, he wasn't a bad guy to me. If he was convinced that you did something wrong, he wouldn't listen to you no matter what. Like one time he insisted that I'd been involved in a car accident and then left the scene. In fact, I wasn't involved. There was no damage to my truck, not a dent or a scratch, and there was a lot of damage to the car. But that didn't matter. In Rizzo's eyes, I hit this woman's car and left . . . That was his personality, and I believe that's the wrong way to be." For his part, Ryan was mostly disappointed, not just in Rizzo but in the department for not putting a check on the behavior of bosses who got out of hand. "It broke my heart [that] no one stopped this guy [from doing what he did to us] and [just] say enough is enough."

Rizzo looked at the situation in yet another way, interpreting his actions in terms of his role as the squad disciplinarian attempting to meet the needs of everyone in Six Truck and neutralizing any discomfort he felt about the position he took and the decisions he made in terms of his love for and loyalty to the unit as a whole. "I had to look at the whole picture. I had thirty guys working there. I can't have you doing whatever you want to do. . . . The job is pretty clear, what you should do. I was trying to keep it from the job but still you are gonna be penalized. . . . I have loyalty to that unit to this day. I loved that unit. I wouldn't even [have retired]. I would still be there [today] except for my wife, my kids. My wife didn't want me working after 9/11. . . . She was starting to get nervous. We lost fourteen guys in the building. I retired a year after 9/11. I had twenty-two years in."

As much as he disliked Rizzo for how he treated him, Ryan understood where Rizzo might have been coming from in the situation involving the locker, at least. "If Rizzo didn't believe I talked to Ortiz and Ortiz never talked to him, I don't blame him for [reacting] as he did. I mean, if I was a sergeant and I thought a guy was undermining me, I'd have to penalize him. He's got thirty cops in the squad. He can't have one acting insubordinate. It doesn't set a good example and makes him look like he's not in control," Ryan explained. To some extent, Ryan also understood his own role in making a bad situation worse. "It killed me that Jack [Cambria] would be angry at me because, to this day, I have so much respect for him. . . . I created all sorts of problems for me. There were rumors that I lost my mind. Guys were afraid to even talk to me because they thought I was going to snap and kill everybody in the truck. I was like a man without a country. It broke my heart."

Rizzo was less sympathetic to Ryan, claiming on the one hand that neither he nor Dolan meant anything to him in his present life and that he never hated either cop when they did and, at the same time, claiming confusion about why they brought him up to me at all. It was, however, clear that he had little ambivalence about his role as the disciplinarian and few second thoughts about how he had handled things. I could see the element of harshness in this otherwise accomplished and direct man who was committed to his job and whom I enjoyed talking with.

Maybe I also saw a glimpse of his gentler side. Before he left, he told me he wished Ryan and Dolan luck and hoped that they were happy in their current lives. Although he thought he handled the situation as best he could under the circumstances, maybe he understood more of where they were coming from. It's hard to endure injustice and/or abuse by someone in a position of superior power perceived or real, right or wrong, partly self-created but always also interactionally constructed in the dynamic of the two or more personalities involved. This is not to say that Rizzo didn't have his reasons for assessing some of the cops' actions in the way he did. Regardless of his ambivalence toward the cops and how he chose to handle the dilemmas that confronted him, Rizzo did respect Dolan and Ryan in certain ways. "Keith and Joe were active cops. . . . I had to respect them for that. If they could have just toned it down and made some of the decision making better, we would have two excellent cops, no doubt about it. . . . They could have been stars," Rizzo said, almost sounding disappointed that he hadn't been able to whip them into shape and realize the potential he saw in them. Another boss echoed his positive sentiments when he emphasized the strong contribution Ryan and Dolan made to the squad. "They were active and picked up jobs. They worked hard. A lot of [other] guys [ask for] the midnight shift because it's not that busy and they don't have to do much work." Still other bosses, including their top commanders, emphasized without ambivalence that Dolan and Ryan were some of their "very best" cops.

Ryan recalled an incident in which he saw the part of Rizzo I suspect Jack Cambria knew and liked and the glimpses I got during our interview of the kind of man he was with the people he trusted and loved. Rizzo and some of his cops were up at the range one day. Two little sparrows had gotten inside the building and were running about on the floor, squawking and assaulting each other. Ryan bent down and scooped up one of the birds. He held the sparrow, petting its tiny body, smoothing its feathers and calming it down. Rizzo looked at Ryan with genuine interest.

"What are you doing?" he asked in an open and friendly way.

"Well, this one's the bully. I'm going throw him outside where he belongs."

"I didn't know you could do that. I never saw anybody do that before," Rizzo said. "He looked at me differently then," Ryan explained. "It felt good. There was this moment of harmony, the way it should have been [with us]."

o o o o o o o

Ryan transferred to Seven Truck "under a cloud" with John English his only ally among the bosses in the new squad, some of whom didn't know how he worked and believed the gossip they'd heard. On his first day on the job, Ryan's new lieutenant called him into his office and warned him that he wasn't happy he'd been transferred into his truck and that "the first time you screw up here, you're done. You're outta here." During Ryan's first few months in the squad one sergeant trashed his evaluation, a rarity in the NYPD unless a boss is covering his ass, taking revenge, or plotting to get rid of someone.

However, it didn't take too many months before the bosses and cops in the truck began to see that John English was right, Ryan was an asset in the squad, an active cop who made good decisions and could be relied on to handle his jobs and carry his load and more. "Like I said," English explained, "All you had to be was around him and he would prove himself to you . . . A guy like Keith, he'd get in the truck and he was off and running. You could count on him at any job. New Year's Eve on a job on Eastern Parkway, and it was a perp search and I think we were shorthanded . . . And we were going in to search this house, and Keith was right up front with the first bunker guy, never a hesitation. I mean, this was long after the whole bombing incident, and he never missed a step."

A year after Ryan transferred into Seven Truck, his lieutenant pulled him aside and apologized for believing the rumors and assuming the worst when Ryan had first arrived. "It blew me away. I never had a lieutenant talk to me like that before [and apologize]," Ryan explained.

Still, regardless of how much better things were in Seven Truck and how much love and respect he had for John English and his lieutenant as well, scars remained from the year after the raid as deep and apparent to him as the one on his face when he looked in the mirror to shave. I believe they also remained for Joe Dolan. They would be reinforced and reinterpreted in the light of what occurred during 9/11.

o o o o o o o

Ryan left Emergency Service shortly before 9/11 and transferred to the Intelligence Division with the help of Bill Morange and Ray McDermott. Dolan also transferred out and into the Bomb Squad. The shift from Emergency Service to either of these units is considered a good career move from a financial point of view, because it takes a cop into the detective career path while teaching new skills. Cops who go into these units automatically make the rank of detective third grade. Ryan found a solid partner and didn't appear to encounter the sort of trouble with bosses that he'd had in Six Truck, although there were superiors he liked better than others and one whom nobody in the unit liked at all.

One day after I began researching this book, I was talking to Ryan on the phone while he was on his way to a bird sanctuary in Brooklyn. He had just rescued a goose with a broken wing that he'd seen wandering on the highway. He had pulled his car over as soon as he spotted the bird, picked it up, and wrapped it in a blanket. It bothered him that no one had stopped before because the bird could easily have been killed by a passing car. He told me to hold on for a minute while he talked to the park security guard and then let the bird go. Although he couldn't fly, he was otherwise healthy and would survive. When Ryan got back on his cell phone, he described what had happened, how as soon as the bird spotted the other geese, it waddled right over to the lake to join them, "happy as a clam." "All he [the bird] wanted was to be with his own kind," Ryan explained, with a sad tone to his voice that pierced my heart. I was sure he was talking about himself as well as the goose, how injured he felt by all that happened to him in Emergency Service and how much he missed being a cop in that unit before the raid, when things were good.

9/11

WITH THE APPROACH OF THE NEW
millennium, concerns about terrorism
rose to the forefront of police conscious-
ness only to momentarily dissipate under the weight of a bloody fiasco.
On February 4, 1999, a twenty-three-year-old African immigrant, Amadou Diallo, was shot by police forty-one times while he was standing in
the hallway of the apartment building where he lived in the Bronx. It's
typical in organizational accidents to attribute blame to the lowest-rank-
ing participants.[1] In this case, responsibility for the shooting was placed
on the shoulders of four plainclothes officers in the NYPD's Street Crime
Unit. After all, Sean Carroll, Edward McMellon, Kenneth Boss, and
Richard Murphy did pull the trigger that killed an unarmed man.[2] When
Carroll realized that Diallo had been holding a wallet, he dropped to his
knees and started to cry. He opened Diallo's shirt to try to resuscitate
him, then stopped when he saw the two bullet holes piercing his gut.
"Keep breathing. Please don't die, please don't die," Carroll said, and ca-
ressed Diallo's face with his hands.[3]

Twelve hours after the shooting, every one of the almost 40,000 police
officers in the NYPD knew of the incident. Keith Ryan doesn't remember
precisely what he was doing the moment when Diallo died, except that
he was working a midnight shift in Seven Truck. He did recall a conversation he had with lieutenant Rodney Gillis, one of the few black officers
in Emergency Service. "They just assassinated the guy," Gillis said with a
horrified look in his eyes. Then he added the multilayered caveat that every
officer understood: the shooting of Amadou Diallo was a tragic mistake
that almost any cop could have made in the flurry of clarity and confu-

sion that can accompany that split-second decision that may determine the rest of his life.

Most every cop had a theory about why the shooting occurred, some of which became part of the collective memory of the event that persists today. Rich Teemsma suggested that one of the problems was that cops no longer receive the same training in trigger control with semiautomatic handguns that they'd had in the old days when they used Smith & Wesson 38 revolvers that fired one shot at a time. Joe Dolan thought that the use of metal-jacketed ammunition contributed to the situation. "What happens with a copper-jacketed round is that, as it passes straight through [the body] and the hole behind closes back up. People are less likely to be dropped. Hollow points go in and flatten out so they've got a little more stopping power. That was the problem with Diallo; all those rounds were penetrating his body and he wasn't dropping. That's why they changed to hollow points after." A detective who'd been at the crime scene explained that Diallo was standing at the end of the hall and the wall propped him up until his legs finally crumbled.

Chief Lou Anemone confirmed that the metal-jacketed rounds were a factor. Those that missed Diallo bounced off the wall and ricocheted in the direction of the officers. The officers misinterpreted the projectiles as shots being fired at them and returned fire. Anemone also noted that the high-gloss paint on the door reflected the muzzle flash of the officers' weapons. They misread the light as a muzzle flash from something fired at them. One commander who was familiar with crime scene reports said that the location of the projectiles didn't support all of these conclusions. Only one round was found in the street and it had likely been kicked outside from the hallway. Another round was discovered in the superintendent's apartment to the left of the building entrance. A third was on the floor by the stairs. Most of the forty-one bullets were lodged inside Diallo's body, in the wall, the door, and the floor.

Regardless, it's clear that the four Street Crime officers misread cues. They mistook Diallo for a rapist maybe because he resembled the sketch of the suspect. He was also peering in and out of the vestibule in a way that struck them as odd. The officers didn't imagine that Diallo lived in an apartment inside. They didn't think that he might be behaving the way he did because he was curious about why four white men were approaching him from the street. They seemed to assume he was African American rather than African, that he spoke English, that he would recognize them as police officers and not agents from Immigration and Naturalization Services. It didn't occur to the officers that Diallo might have reached for his pocket because he thought they wanted to see his ID. Instead, they mistook his wallet for a gun. After Carroll yelled "Gun!" McMellon stepped backward and tripped down the stairs. Thinking McMellon had been shot, Carroll and the rest of his teammates opened fire.

Howard Safir and Rudy Giuliani have never publically acknowledged their responsibility in the Diallo affair. Some believe that Safir set the organizational preconditions for a tragedy to occur when he placed the goals of high arrest and crime reduction ahead of protecting innocent lives, including those of his cops.[4] In February 1997, Safir ordered the rapid expansion of the Street Crime Unit and divided it into borough satellites in order to "enhance the effective deployment of officers."[5] The expansion of the unit to a total of 438 officers by 1999 took place against the advice of its commanding officer, Dick Savage. Savage argued that growth was possible but required additional time. At the time of the incident, the Street Crime Unit was in the Special Operations Division. "That cost Dick Savage his command," Morange explained. "When they wanted to expand it, they had us come down, and they were telling us everything they wanted to do. Dick came to me and said, 'I can't do it . . . We can do it, but we shouldn't go so fast.' Anyhow, we brought all these issues downtown and he [Safir] said, 'No. It's going to be done.'"

The chief of the department, Lou Anemone, supported the Unit's expansion although he understood the need for extra time in order to get qualified and properly trained candidates. He'd been a lieutenant in Street Crime in its early days and knew the work was delicate and dangerous. "My sense was that we could use a few more cops there. We were doing great things. . . . In the back of my head, 300 cops in a department of 40,000, we should have been able to do that. The only issue that I could argue with Safir about this whole Street Crime thing was that it was placed on the fast track. We went from 100 to 300 [and then to 438] in a fairly short period of time. We had a great captain over there, Dick Savage, who argued against rapid expansion."

Still, when Savage continued to hedge, Anemone began to think twice. He recalled an incident in 1996 when Savage had made a decision that cost him his troops' respect. Police officer Kevin Gillespie, a cop in the Street Crime Unit, was murdered in the Bronx while Savage was skiing in Vermont. Savage was notified, but he didn't come back from vacation. Nor did he attend the wake or the funeral. His cops "never forgave him for that." In regard to the expansion, Anemone was getting pressure from Safir and in turn pressuring Mike Tiffany, who was next in the chain of command. Tiffany told Anemone that Savage was undermining the process and named some specific ways. Trusting Tiffany's judgment, Anemone surmised that Savage was intentionally disrupting the expansion in an attempt, perhaps, to win back his officers' confidence. Anemone then decided it was time for a change. "So we moved Dick out, and I got a guy I'd known for years, Jeff Jones.[6] Now, Jeff is a great guy, [but he's] really a patrol guy. Maybe he wasn't the best fit for Street Crime. Mike Tiffany did a great job of getting the interviews done and selecting the people," Anemone explained.

When Savage was in command, he'd personally interviewed candidates and excluded any officers with a prior history of civilian complaints, departmental charges, or involvement in incidents in which they'd fired their weapons. In order to facilitate the rapid expansion, this screening process had to be compromised. Some new members had less street experience than Savage had required, and others had histories that would have excluded them from membership in the unit as it once had been.

Nevertheless, Safir, Kelleher, and deputy commissioner of Policy and Planning Mike Farrell didn't suggest in their report to the City Council that the new screening process compromised the quality of the officers. Lenny Levitt, in his book *NYPD Confidential*, disagrees. He notes that two out of the four officers involved in the Diallo shooting had histories of weapons use or civilian complaints. Officers who volunteered for the Street Crime Unit after 1997 were required to have three years of street experience. They had to undergo an interview with the Street Crime Review Board, whose members considered such factors as arrest activity, sick record, annual evaluations, and civilian and internal complaints. The Street Crime Review Board then made recommendations to the commanding officer of the unit, who handled the process from there.[7] In terms of the interview process, Anemone believed that he, Savage, and Tiffany were all looking for the same kind of cops. He didn't believe the screening process had changed. "Whenever a new unit is created, generally the officers selected have no experience in that area until they learn by doing," Anemone explained, noting that this was also true when the City-Wide Anti-Crime Unit was first formed in 1971, which would later morph into the Street Crime Unit.

In the wake of the Diallo shooting, Anemone appeared alone among members of the top brass to take responsibility for some of the mistakes that he believed might have contributed to the tragedy. "I didn't follow up on the limitations of the training, on the supervision, and the provisions of the cars, seeing that they were equipped. I thought they had whatever they needed. . . . We had new people assigned to Street Crime who really had no idea how to operate in plainclothes, what it takes and what they should and shouldn't be doing. The idea of four cops riding around in a car is a waste of manpower, and it was a common occurrence . . . I blame supervisors for putting four cops in one auto. Two or maybe three cops you can get away with," Anemone admitted.[8] He went on to explain that tactics were a problem. "None of the four officers got out of the car to conduct surveillance before confronting Diallo. When they did approach, they didn't use speed and surprise. I don't blame the officers for any lack of training or not knowing how to work in plainclothes, but when you look at the cops involved in the event, you realize they may not have had the best training. Their being put in that situation and then their misinterpreting Diallo's actions, misinterpreting the shots, misinterpreting his falling, and the ricochets coming back at them. . . . I feel that it was a series of mistakes that led to this tragedy, but it was never criminal."

Morange echoed Anemone's sentiments but focused on inexperience rather than training. "Jeff Jones worked for me. He was another great commander. Everything that could possibly go wrong went wrong that night. There was a language barrier. Sean was the kid who yelled 'Gun!' He wasn't out of patrol much [time before he was transferred to Street Crime]. He saw this thing come out, and he yelled 'Gun!' McMellon was backing up because of the shots and he falls down, so when he falls, they hear shots and think he's shot, so they start shooting. That was a tragedy and a half. It never should have happened . . . The sad part is the loss of life and a family loses a son. I mean I never could even imagine. I mean, I lost a son. So I know the family end of it but also with them there was . . . It never should have happened. I felt really bad for [Sean Carroll], because I don't think he will ever recover from this thing," Morange explained.

The killing of Amadou Diallo set off a public furor that reverberated around the world and fueled internal fires that had been simmering in the department for years. In the wake of the tragedy, Howard Safir heightened the tension by flying to Los Angeles to attend the Oscars on a corporate-sponsored junket that cost $7,100. Unhappy with the never-ending contract negotiations and the city's stubbornness in resisting pay raises for cops that would put them nearer to departments in New York's Suffolk and Nassau Counties or other big cities like Los Angeles, and looking for a reason to wipe the commissioner's face in the mud, the Patrolmen's Benevolent Association (PBA) cast a vote of no confidence on April 13. In an article appearing in 1999 in the *New York Times*, the PBA president sounded more like a 1960s student radical than a representative of the New York City police. "When zero-tolerance tactics were first introduced by the department, crime was at an all-time high. . . . Now that crime is way down, an adjustment of the strategy is required. If we don't strike a balance between aggressive enforcement and common sense, it becomes a blueprint for a police state and tyranny."[9] The PBA was also quick to point out that Safir's trip constituted a conflict of interest that would have resulted in the suspension of any police officer who had been the recipient of such a gift.

Meanwhile, it was no longer a secret that power in the top ranks was shifting. In the wake of the Louima assault in 1997, Safir and Kelleher had convened a Management Review Task Force that excluded Lou Anemone. When he saw the report after weeks of delay, Anemone could barely contain his rage. He asserted that Kelleher "was dishonest about the way he handled [the report]. He empowered this committee to look at the issues and make recommendations, and then he forced them to change their recommendations. When I found out about it, I confronted him. I was very disappointed because I had some positive recommendations, and I had to forget mine and allow Kelleher and Safir to sit on the report for months."

On January 13, 1998, Anemone sent Kelleher a scathing critique of the report in the form of an official Police Department document, called a "49." By then, relations between the two commanders had deteriorated to such a degree that they could almost be heard arguing in the halls. "I was trying to do police work, right, and I wouldn't back down, and I guess I caused them controversy . . . Kelleher and I had blowouts in front of Safir," Anemone said. A union official put it a different way. "You had the asshole factor with Safir. Then you had the Kelleher factor. Kelleher gradually had more and more power with Safir, to the point where it seemed like the shift was going from Safir to the team of Safir and Kelleher, and Kelleher was not one to negotiate." In 1999, Anemone got fed up and retired. He left behind a legacy of rigorous leadership spotted with brilliance, commitment, dissension, and debate.

On February 25, 2000, the four officers who shot Amadou Diallo were acquitted of murder, a charge that would have been difficult for any district attorney to prove, even without a change of venue to upstate New York. Negligent homicide perhaps, but only a parent blinded by grief or a cop-hating victim of police abuse would believe that the Street Crime officers intentionally killed an unarmed man in cold blood because of his race. Less than a month later, tensions in the city heated up anew when Patrick Dorismond was shot and killed. The twenty-six-year-old black security guard, who was not a dealer, was approached by undercover police who asked if he had drugs to sell. After Dorismond reacted angrily, a fight broke out, and he was shot by a member of the backup team. Under orders from Giuliani, Safir released the victim's criminal record in an effort to justify the officers' actions and diminish the negative image that had plagued the administration for years.

There were also a series of gaffes that Giuliani perpetrated with or without Safir's help that continued to alienate the public as well as a lot of the cops. In 1998, he tried to remake the city in Germany's image by insisting that police officers enforce the laws against jaywalking. Some of the cops who were ordered to enforce the law in midtown ignored the request. Others laughed at the absurdity but did what they had to do when directed by an equally helpless boss. Then, in 1999, Giuliani filed a lawsuit against the Brooklyn Museum regarding an upcoming show that included some controversial pieces he found "sick" and "disgusting." His open affair with his girlfriend and the nasty way he treated his wife in the face of the public added to the demise of what little was left of his reputation, none of which had anything to do with Safir except as guilt by association.

It was within this backdrop of the administration's attempt to enforce petty laws and violate the basic constitutional right of freedom of expression, as well as the racial tension in the black community, the public protest about the Diallo shooting and other events, and conflict with the Patrolman's Benevolent Association and other police unions, that Howard Safir chose to retire in 2000 before his term was up, despite the support of a number of well-regarded, high-ranking bosses who appreciated his leadership. Patrick Kelleher left the department around the same time as his boss, leaving two top-ranking positions vacant.

The major contenders for the job of police commissioner were Joe Dunne and Bernie Kerik. Dunne was the favorite of the rank and file as well as the top brass. He had moved up the ranks from street cop to chief of the department when Anemone left, while gaining the respect of even his very few enemies. Kerik retired from the Police Department while only a detective. Since then, he'd held different jobs, including commissioner of Corrections. Most important in terms of his current status was his service as a member of Giuliani's security detail years before.

On September 5, 2000, Rudy Giuliani swore in Kerik as police commissioner. "Today, it gives me great pleasure to swear in as police commissioner a man of proven ability, talent, and judgment," Giuliani said. He then swore in Dunne as first deputy commissioner a few minutes later, lauding him as "a superb police officer and a superb man, whose talents and experience in the NYPD will serve him, and all New Yorkers, well in his challenging new job."[10] Chief Joe Esposito replaced Joe Dunne as chief of the department, and Kerik tapped Bill Morange for chief of Patrol, a position Morange considered the greatest honor of his career. Meanwhile, the millennium had passed without incident, and every member of the brass who'd spent the six months leading up to this worrying about a terrorist explosion in Times Square were breathing a collective sigh of relief. No one anticipated what would occur almost precisely twelve months after the swearing in.

o o o o o o o

I first met Joe Dunne in his office in the investment banking firm where he'd been working as director of security since he retired from the NYPD after 9/11. I was still in the Training Division of the Police Department and wanted his advice on revisions of the executive curriculum. I'm sure Dunne was assessing my character from the moment I walked into his office, but I couldn't tell. He was warm, welcoming, and direct. He carried himself with an assuredness and command presence that I liked, although I could see it might intimidate some if his temper ran short or he questioned a presentation at CompStat. His voice got loud and animated when he began to talk about some of the issues police bosses face during moments of crisis, and it was obvious that he'd loved being a cop and commander in the NYPD. While his current position might be building his bank account, his heart remained on the job. Later, when I interviewed him about 9/11, he told me he was grateful for the money he'd earned but would give it all up to be back in the NYPD as chief of the department.

Dunne never admitted to me that he was chagrined when Kerik was appointed "PC" or that he felt perturbed at having to report to an inexperienced boss. The over 6'4" solidly built Irish street cop with the tough but tender heart and down-to-earth manner just shrugged his powerful shoulders when I suggested as much. All he would say was that he was disappointed that Giuliani hadn't let him remain as chief of the department. On 9/11, when Dunne felt the debris flying around him, breathed the toxic air, and watched the chaos unfold, he felt the loss of that job more acutely than ever before. He explained, "It pained me that day, not because I didn't think Joe [Esposito] was capable of it, but that's the job that I had just the year before, the job that I loved, but I took this job as the 'first dep' after the mayor put pressure on me to do it. I didn't want the damned job, I was happy being the chief of the department and if I stayed the chief of the department I'd still be there today, but that's another story."

The morning of 9/11, first deputy commissioner Joseph Dunne had gotten up early because he wanted to vote in the primary before going to work. He had a meeting at 9:30 at One Police Plaza with George Grasso, the deputy commissioner, Legal Matters, to discuss the department's DWI policies for cops but nothing pressing before. It was a cool, sunny morning and he hung around his house for a while, "lingering." Around 7:30, his driver, detective Dennis Sheehan, picked him up and they headed around the corner to the polls. Dunne voted, then chatted with the cop who was assigned to the post and also with some of his neighbors.

Dunne and Sheehan headed into Manhattan around 8:00 A.M., monitoring the citywide Special Operations Division radio because that was Emergency Service's frequency, and any event of importance would be announced there. Dunne recalled sitting in the backseat, trying to reach Grasso on his cell phone with the radio humming in the background. "Precinct cops will tell you . . . you hear chatter; the drone of the voices on the radio but you can multitask because your mind is set on your code like Frank or Boy [the name of your sector car] or you just have a sense for an important job [from the] tone [of voice]; the anxiety that you detect." Then Dunne heard a sound that didn't belong, a word that stung or a change in pitch and he knew something was wrong.

"Dennis, what was that?" asked Dunne.

"Boss, I think they said a plane went into the Trade Center."

"You gotta be shittin' me!" Dunne tried to look up at the Manhattan skyline, but they were nearing the entrance to the Midtown Tunnel and all he could see was sun and blue sky behind him.

"George, did we have an accident in the Trade Center?" he recalled asking Grasso when they finally talked on the phone.[11]

"Not that I know of."

"See what you can find out," Dunne said as the car entered the tunnel.

Grasso recorded his experience of 9/11 in a personal diary written shortly after the disaster. What is particularly remarkable about the account is not only the grasp of detail and chronology but also his insight into his moods, fears, strengths, and human flaws. After Grasso and his wife cast their votes in the primary, he got in his car and headed toward headquarters. He was still in Queens when he received a telephone call from a detective in Dunne's office, saying that the "first dep" was trying to reach him. Grasso told the detective that he was heading into the Midtown Tunnel and would call her back when he got to the other side. When he did, she laughed because Dunne was now in the tunnel and couldn't get a connection. Grasso was in the middle of saying he'd try calling again in five minutes when she started shouting.

"Did you just hear that explosion at the World Trade Center Tower? I think a plane might have hit the towers!" Then she hung up. Grasso turned on the radio news and put his foot on the gas. He was around 24th Street, driving south on the FDR Drive and, when he looked up, he could see the gash in the skyline. "With a backdrop of a crystal-clear beautiful blue sky, I saw the north tower . . . , standing with a hole so large, gaping, and monstrous it literally defied belief. Out of that hole poured thick, black smoke, being fueled by an orange fire that was clearly visible inside the fatally damaged building."[12] Upon seeing the extent of the damage, Grasso thought that terrorists had once again attacked the building.

When Dunne got out of the tunnel, he recalled Grasso telling him that a commercial airliner had hit one of the towers. Most likely, the detective in Dunne's office was the person who called and gave him the news, as he and Grasso were still playing phone tag. Dunne then called the operations center to get additional information. "Yes," the officer confirmed. The crash was "big." Dunne explained, "I thought [then] it was the second terrorist attack . . . We were thinking terrorist attack since '99, before the millennium when I was chief of the department. If you remember, Customs grabbed that guy coming in from Canada who was on his way down to LAX [Los Angeles International Airport] with the explosives in his car."

The plan to bomb the airport had been launched by a twenty-three-year-old Algerian man, Ahmed Ressam, who had been trained in explosives in Afghanistan before illegally immigrating to Canada in 1994. After learning that his associates couldn't get into Canada or the United States, Ressam decided to execute the plot alone. On December 14, 1999, he drove a rental car to Victoria, British Columbia, and boarded a ferry to Port Angeles, Washington. From there he planned to go to Los Angeles and, on January 1, 2000, detonate the bombs at the airport. The plot was aborted when U.S. custom agents noticed that Ressam seemed nervous and referred him for further inspection. When an agent started to pat him down, Ressam got scared and tried to run. Inspectors searched his car, found explosives, and put him under arrest. Weeks later, Ressam confessed the names of the principals involved.

"The Mayor of Seattle cancelled the New Year's Eve celebration. . . . In addition to that, what a lot of people didn't know is that one of the terrorists arrested had a cell phone number in his pocket and they traced it back to a house in Brooklyn, so during the millennium preparations we were in fear of an attack," Dunne explained. No wonder, I thought, that Lou Anemone had recommended they cancel the New Year's celebration. It seemed as much a matter of luck as law enforcement intelligence and tactics that nothing occurred, not even the mass computer [Y2K] meltdown that was supposed to cause disruption around the globe. Now we know that the seeds of 9/11 were planted before the millennium and that the terrorists waited to execute their plot until they were prepared and U.S. defenses were down.

Dunne got off the FDR Drive and headed toward Building Seven, located across from the World Trade Center site, where the Office of Emergency Management [OEM] was housed. He arrived to discover the office was gone. "The building caught fire and was evacuated, and so our $40 million-plus facility, which was supposed to be the be-all and end-all of communication, went out in the first round. . . . I think that was a significant issue in our interoperability [in terms of communicating with the Fire Department and other agencies] because every [one] was represented in OEM. We [had] told them that was not the place to put it, but that's another story."

When he approached the World Trade Center, Dunne saw "a little debris on the ground," a "crystal-clear" street, and a building that was on fire. "It was just like a chimney effect with all that smoke rising and none of it filtering down to the ground." Around 8:45 A.M. he struggled to get out of the car. He had a ruptured Achilles tendon and was dependent on crutches to bolster the cast he was wearing from the knee down. He left his sport jacket in the car and put on an NYPD windbreaker "so that someone could identify me from the back as a cop, not as somebody who needed to be evacuated or kicked in the ass and told to get out of there." Dunne had only been standing on the street a short time when he heard "this tremendous roar and an explosion," which he thought was a secondary blast in the north tower.

By this time, Grasso had parked his car in the garage at Police headquarters and got on the elevator and headed up to the fourteenth floor. Inside, he encountered Chief Charles Kammerdener, who was also going upstairs.

"This doesn't look good," Grasso said.

"No," Kammerdener responded. "Charlie was the duty chief in the 1997 raid on the terrorist cell . . . and I thought of that then. I knew we were thinking the same thing; that this is terrorism, although I didn't yet know for sure," Grasso explained. When he entered the area outside Dunne's office, the detective at the desk told him that Dunne had responded directly to the scene. "Of course," Grasso wrote, knowing that a "cop's cop" like Joe Dunne wouldn't be anywhere else but with his commanders and rank-and-file officers on the street. Grasso was still talking to the detective when he looked at the TV screen and saw a plane crash into the south tower. "I felt a chill go down my spine, and any doubt as to whether this was an accident disappeared. I knew the City of New York was experiencing a deliberate terrorist attack," Grasso wrote.[13]

o o o o o o o

Rudy Giuliani was standing outside the Peninsula Hotel on 55th Street in Manhattan when he heard news of the crash. "My first assumption was that it was some nut flying a small plane."[14] He and staff were driving south on Seventh Avenue when he saw flames on the horizon but thought the situation looked manageable. He passed St. Vincent's Hospital in Greenwich Village and noticed the medical staff bustling about outside the emergency room preparing for the flood of injured people who would never show up. It wasn't until he was on Canal Street heading toward the new Command Center on the 23rd floor of 7 World Trade that the second plane hit. It occurred to him then that terrorists were involved.

○ ○ ○ ○ ○ ○ ○

Police commissioner Bernie Kerik was taking a shower on the fourteenth floor of One Police Plaza when he heard people kicking the outer door of his office and someone yelling, "[Boss], they're saying a plane hit the building but you should see the fuckin' hole!"[15] Assuming a small plane had accidently crashed into the World Trade Center, Kerik walked into the conference room and looked through the large picture window. He saw a "huge hole" in the top of the north tower with coal-black smoke billowing out.

"Get the mayor on the phone," Kerik said, then headed into the garage, got into a car with several of his staff members and began driving toward the building.[16] Three minutes later he was on West Broadway and Vesey, near the mobilization center that Chief Joe Esposito had just set up. Kerik got out of the car and looked up at the north tower. "I couldn't believe my eyes. A black cloud poured from the side and the fire—fed by a full tank of jet fuel—was burning up to the higher floors. Debris was raining from the sky [and people were jumping out of the windows] . . . A few held each other as they jumped. It was a vision that I will never forget."[17] Aware that 7 World Trade Center might not be safe, Kerik ordered his staff to locate a command center somewhere else. Shortly after, he saw an "orange and black fireball" but didn't realize it was the back draft from the commercial airliner that was smashing into the south tower. Thinking that terrorists might be bombing the buildings, he ordered the evacuation of City Hall and One Police Plaza, but the phones were tied up so nothing was done.

A few minutes later, Giuliani arrived, picked up Kerik and headed toward the West Side Highway, where the Fire Department and Emergency Service had set up another mobilization point. There they spoke to Pete Ganci and William Feehan, two of FDNY's highest-ranking members. When Giuliani asked if it was possible to send helicopters in for rescue, Ganci told him no because the "smoke" and "swirling matter" wouldn't let the choppers fly in so close. "We can save everybody below the fire. Our guys are in the building, about halfway up the first tower," Ganci said.[18] After telling Ganci to move his command center further north, Giuliani and Kerik headed up to 75 Barclay Street, where they'd established their temporary headquarters. Meanwhile, the mayor's chief of staff had contacted the White House and confirmed it was a terrorist attack. Seven planes were still unaccounted for. The chief of staff ordered the evacuation of City Hall.

○ ○ ○ ○ ○ ○ ○

Moments after the second crash—what most at the scene interpreted as a secondary explosion—Dunne found himself awash in a storm of debris. "All kinds of debris started raining down on us. Some of it hit the car. I think a piece took the [hatch] window out that Dennis had lifted up [to get the windbreaker] and this stuff is coming down. I said, 'Holy shit, we need to take cover.' So we were right next to Building Five [in the World Trade Center complex] which is on the corner of Church and Vesey. . . . Those buildings were built with overhangs, so we were able to get under there and protect ourselves. [Debris] hit the ground and bounced. . . . I think I was lucky we weren't struck. I remember seeing an off-duty cop down there, a Spanish cop, and he came over and said, 'Boss, what the fuck we gonna do?'

"Calm down. Let's see what's going on," I said. Now people are streaming out of the buildings; there are lots of people on the ground. As I walked up to the corner, I saw a young female cop in uniform and she looked stressed but she was doing fine; she was doing her job.

"What are we doing, Boss?" she asked.

"Tell everybody to get out of here. Tell them that they're safe now, they're OK, but to move north or east, tell them to get out of the area and tell them to get off the cell phones!" I said. Everybody had a cell phone in the area, I mean, everybody. I said to a few people, "Hang up the cell phones, and give us a chance to communicate, get out of here, pay attention to what you're doing now, and get yourselves out of here, because there's debris on the ground."

Shock shadowing his face and stealing the light from his eyes, Grasso and his aide, detective John "JT" Totano, headed downtown. As head of legal affairs and an expert in dealing with different city, state, and federal agencies, Grasso thought his best plan of action was to find the commander in charge of southern Manhattan and act as his shield, running interference between him and the different agencies involved. With Grasso's help the police, fire department, state, and federal agencies could coordinate efforts with minimal confusion, conflict, and overlap.

As Grasso and JT were passing City Hall, the air began to fill with smoke. They were walking by St. Paul's Chapel on Vesey Street when Grasso looked down and saw hundreds of shoes on the ground; mostly scattered pairs of women's high heel shoes, lost or discarded by people fleeing the firestorm. At the corner of Vesey and Church Streets, he spotted Chief Esposito, standing there hatless, directing traffic and clearing the way for emergency vehicles. Grasso spoke to Esposito, then continued toward the Twin Towers.

Around the time Dunne met Esposito, he was standing near Bill Morange and several other members of the brass. Dunne recalled him and "Espo" going through "that imaginary list [of] did you [do this] and did you [do that]. Just about everything I spoke to him about, he was doing or in the process of doing." One of the issues discussed was whether to put a helicopter on the roof or rappel officers in for a rescue. Dunne thought it was "too dangerous" and "wouldn't accomplish much" with the smoke and cable and "every other goddamned thing up there." He didn't mention what Lou Anemone had said: that no one could have gotten onto the roof because the doors were locked.

Listening to Dunne tell his story, I was struck by his and other commanders' courage and the enormity of the decisions they made in the spur of the moment with limited vision and knowledge. "The people that are listening to the radio and to the TV probably know more about this unfolding event than I do, and that's not unusual. It's the fog of war, you know, the people sometimes closest to the action have a very parochial view of what's going, while even though we're the leaders of the agency, we're trying to get our arms around the whole thing," Dunne explained.[19] Also intriguing were the thoughts and images that informed what he did. Dunne mentioned his years of training and experience. He told me that he believed in the unity of command, and because Esposito was operational head of the agency, he made the decision not to use his radio. He didn't want to add to confusion by replicating or contradicting directives or creating a question of who was leading the troops.

A book he read as a teenager served to guide his sense of how a leader should act in such a crisis. "I remember I read a book called *Horatio Hornblower*. He had a young ensign officer on the deck who was about to embark on a mission. Hornblower was standing there calm, cool, and collected, and his young officer was running around the deck kind of like a chicken without his head, and Hornblower came over to him and said, 'Mr. Whatever, we must remain calm. The men are watching and if they see you running around like that, you're going to unnerve them.' . . . Something in my mind just said, listen, remain calm, keep it together, don't lose it, there's going to be a lot of things we need to do today. Don't raise your voice or yell at anybody; you just can't do that.

This is serious shit now. This isn't some bullshit, make-believe police operation. We're in trouble."

After he and Esposito finished talking, Dunne assigned members of his security detail to find the police commissioner so he could brief him and get more information, perhaps. As he waited, Dunne watched a group of Emergency Service officers gearing up and putting on their oxygen tanks. "What I remember is that they were calm and professional—no one was running. I remember one of them saying to me, 'Hey boss, we have some extra helmets in here, I think it would be a good idea if you put them on.'" Later, Dunne took off the helmet, gave it to someone else, and ordered other officers to put one on. "I wasn't being a hero giving it away . . . I was on crutches and this thing [the helmet] wasn't fitting me properly and there weren't enough to go around.

"It turns out [Deputy Commissioner] Maureen Casey and [Captain] Teresa Tobin were there and I told them, 'Look, if you people are going to stay here, I want you all to have helmets on.' Most of them put helmets on. Terry put on one." Around this time, one of the cops returned with information about the police commissioner and the mayor. Both men were a block away, in the basement of 75 Barclay Street. Sheehan brought around the car, and Dunne hopped in.

o o o o o o o

Grasso stared at the burning tower. Before Dunne had left, he'd heard him say where he was going but they hadn't had time to talk. Grasso decided to report to him before returning to the towers and looking for the Patrol borough commander of Manhattan South. Grasso was rapidly walking toward Barclay Street when he spotted Terry Tobin, who asked if he was heading up to the mayor's command post. When he confirmed that he was, she jumped in front of a police vehicle.

"Stop for Commissioner Grasso!" she yelled. This bothered Grasso a little. He was focused on getting there and thought walking was faster than taking a car. Still, he stifled the urge to say no and acknowledged her courtesy by getting inside. Glancing at Tobin from inside the vehicle, Grasso thought of how incongruous she looked, as odd in a different way as had four-star Chief Joe Esposito directing traffic without a hat like a rank-and-file cop. Tobin is 5'6" and was wearing an Emergency Service helmet that was twice the size of her head. Grasso rode less than a block and then jumped out of the front seat and started walking ahead. Then he heard JT yelling. He and Marty Gleason, another member of Grasso's staff, were stuck in the backseat, trapped by the locks that had been installed to prevent prisoner escape. Grasso doubled back to let his men out of the car.[20]

Dunne was standing on crutches outside 75 Barclay Street when Grasso arrived. They talked and stood side by side while looking up at the burning towers. At this point, it didn't occur to Grasso that the buildings would come down. He was still thinking it was a terrible disaster, but mostly related to fire. Grasso saw what looked like confetti from a ticker tape parade raining down from the windows. Dunne noticed that the south tower wasn't clearly visible. Then he saw chunks of debris falling out of the windows, did a double take, and realized it wasn't debris. Arms and legs were running in air, or trying to break the fall, like in a dream except that those who were conscious knew that their fate was sealed. "Your mind's eye won't accept it. Your mind's a pretty clever machine, and when it sees something that's so horrible, it tricks you but, as I looked more closely, I said to [George], 'These are people.' 'Jesus Christ Joe, are those people?'

"'Yeah,' I said. There were scores of people falling off that building, it wasn't just one or two, and you know, you look and you're mesmerized, horrified for a few seconds and then you gotta get going. There's shit to do. I think the beauty about having something to do in a crisis is that you don't absorb all the horror. I could say, look, that's happening here [but] I can't do anything about [it], but we can put personnel in [strategic locations] to try to help and rescue people. There's other shit we have to do too. . . . Are we evacuating the city? Are we locking down the city? Where are our people coming from? Where are they going once they are here? Were the streets clean so emergency vehicles could get in? How was our equipment getting in?"

By this time, Grasso had told Dunne what he wanted to do to help the borough commander of Manhattan South. Noting that they would be dealing with this situation for a long time, Dunne directed Grasso not to return to the World Trade Center but to go up to the command center at Police headquarters instead and assist with operations there. Dunne planned to join him as soon as he could. Later, Grasso would think that this brief conversation may have saved his life. Instead of being in or next to the towers when one or both fell, he'd been on his way uptown.

○ ○ ○ ○ ○ ○ ○

A few minutes after Grasso left, Dunne heard the roar of a jet overhead. "So everybody kind of like hunkers down, and then somebody yelled, 'It's all right, it's one of ours!' and I'm thinking, how bizarre is this conversation? This is New York City, I'm a cop, and I'm looking for air support. 'That's one of ours.' This is B-movie dialogue that I'm participating in, and the thought just ran through my mind. I didn't focus on it, but this is just what was going through my mind, how totally bizarre this unfolding episode was. And looking at these buildings, I was thinking, they were going to come down," Dunne explained. Seconds later, he walked into the basement of 75 Barclay Street and briefed Kerik about what he and others had seen. He also spoke to Joe Esposito or another police commander, who told him about the crash in Pennsylvania and the attack on the Pentagon.

"Listen, are we going to get air support here or what?" he asked the mayor, the "PC," and the other commanders in the room.

○ ○ ○ ○ ○ ○ ○

As JT, Marty, and Grasso headed to headquarters, they spotted a street vendor, and Grasso decided to get a cup of coffee and something to eat. He didn't know why he was hungry in view of the devastation he'd seen. He bought a cup of steaming hot coffee and a chocolate donut. While standing in front of the vendor he tuned in to snippets of several bystanders' conversation. "They just crashed into the Pentagon," one man said. "They are going to destroy this country," another man told his friend. Grasso thought that this was preposterous. He wanted to give the guy a lecture and tell him he was getting hysterical, that no one could destroy "our" country. Instead, he handed his cup of steaming hot coffee to JT and ate the donut as fast as he could. He looked up and saw an NYPD Aviation Unit helicopter hovering above him, assumed that meant they had been given an all clear on the airspace, and felt comforted. A few seconds later, while Marty Gleason was talking on his cell phone to his wife, saying "Don't worry, I'm with Commissioner Grasso. Everything is going to be all right," Grasso heard a vibration, rumbling, and then a "loud, crashing roar."[21]

"We just got hit again. One of the bastards just hit us again!" Marty screamed. JT pushed Grasso back in an effort to protect him and Grasso, then shoved him to the side. Grasso rounded the corner and saw "a thick, massive expanding cloud of smoke," like a combination of a nuclear mushroom cloud and a tornado, swallowing the space between the buildings, consuming the street, and heading in their direction at a high rate of speed. If the cloud catches us, we're dead, he thought. The three officers ran.[22] When Grasso reached Church Street, he saw a police car parked on the side with its engine running, ready to take off. Believing escape in the car was their only chance of survival. Grasso sprinted forward, punched the trunk, and yelled for the driver to stop. He, Marty, and JT jumped in.

"Go!" Grasso yelled, but they were already caught in the wave, and everything turned jet black. Knowing they couldn't move in the fog of the dark, he jumped out of the car, heard his men yelling and suddenly remembered the safety locks in the backseat. He paused to open the door so JT and Marty could get outside. Later, upon reflection, he would think back to what Terry Tobin did. He believed that things happen for a reason. If she had not commandeered a car to take him to 75 Barclay Street, he wouldn't have known about the safety locks. In the midst of the chaos he might not have had the presence of mind to realize his men were stuck in the car and open the door. They might have died as a result.[23]

Disoriented, Grasso stood on the street, choking and gasping for air in the almost solid mass of dust and smoke. Convinced he was going to die by drowning in the cloud, he thought of his family. He'd been annoyed at his wife that morning. They'd argued at the polls over an insignificant matter. All that was forgotten under the weight of debris and his belief he would not see his wife or two sons again. In a moment of utter despair, he imagined his family getting a formal notification of his death from the department where he'd worked for most of his life. It couldn't have been more than a second before his despair turned to rage. These bastards are not going to take me down, not in my own city, he thought, and yelled for JT.[24]

"Boss, I can't see you," JT yelled back. Both officers followed the sound of their screaming until they found each other and locked arms. Neither one knew until later that someone had just been killed a few feet away on Church Street. A block and a half behind them, Terry Tobin had been hit in the head by a piece of debris that cracked the helmet that saved her life and put a gash in her back. Still not seeing his face, JT pulled him onto the sidewalk. They saw a deli and took refuge inside. As they entered the premises, a man jumped over the counter and tried to lock the door.

"Don't lock that fuckin' door!" Grasso screamed. At that point, he didn't know if he wanted to stay or leave. He only knew he wanted the option. He and JT took a moment to plan their escape and then went outside. Using the scaffolding as protection, they hugged the building line as they made their way past City Hall. Grasso assumed that most of the officers he'd left behind were dead, Dunne included, but remained focused on the mission ahead. At about 10:00 A.M., they entered One Police Plaza. The cops at the door took one look at the specter of their commander, sculpted in dust with the color bleached out of his face and clothes, and got scared.

"Commissioner, can I get you some water?" "Commissioner, can I get you an elevator?" "Commissioner. . . . ?" Grasso stifled the mild sense of irritation he sometimes got when even well-intentioned people hovered too close in a crisis. It didn't occur to him that his annoyance was also a signal that unpleasant emotions were brewing inside. Back in a familiar environment, the anxiety he'd been holding at bay began to erupt, radiating through his limbs and creating images of death and destruction. He believed that the attack on New York had just begun. He didn't know if One Police Plaza was a target or whether the building could sustain a crash from a jetliner. He thought that the elevator could be a death trap. He didn't know where Marty was and whether he was even alive. He feared that Dunne, Kerik, and Giuliani were dead, buried inside the building on Barclay Street.

"Get me to the eighth floor," Grasso said, and one of the cops led him and JT to an open elevator and turned the key. "I was quiet and intense on the outside but on the inside my thoughts were churning. I half-expected to feel and absorb a catastrophic explosion prior to reaching Command and Control," Grasso wrote.[25] The command center was buzzing with activity when he walked in. Jimmy Lawrence, the chief of Personnel, was there, and Ray McDermott, along with dozens of other officers. Lawrence and McDermott looked at Grasso like they were seeing a ghost. Less than an hour before, McDermott had stood next to Lawrence and watched as the south tower crumbled, knowing that all of their senior commanders were there.

"Jimmy, I think you're police commissioner. They're all dead," McDermott had said in a soft and serious tone. Grasso walked over to Lawrence, who accompanied him to a table in the back where phones and TV monitors were installed. Grasso looked through the large picture window and watched as droves of New Yorkers fled Manhattan over the Brooklyn Bridge. He told Lawrence about "the hell" that lay a few blocks southwest and said that he wasn't sure who could have survived.[26] He asked Lawrence if he had heard from the mayor, the "PC," the "first dep," or the chief of the department. When Lawrence replied in the negative, Grasso quietly directed him to assign a team of officers to try and establish contact with them if possible.

Lawrence gave Grasso a description of what he'd learned so far. The phones were out at One Police Plaza, but officers were still pouring into designated mobilization spots. The Pentagon had been hit, and U.S. airspace was shut down. "I was churning inside with emotions and fears that [I'd] never experienced," Grasso said and, in a similar vein as Dunne, vowed "to remain calm and not show any temper or emotion in order to set the best type of example as I could to all of those who were looking to me for leadership in the midst of such a previously unthinkable crisis."[27] In a matter of just a few hours he'd come full circle, from feeling helpless in the face of death to having critical responsibility for New York City's response to the most terrible manmade disaster that had ever occurred on U.S. soil.

∘ ∘ ∘ ∘ ∘ ∘ ∘

Trying to phone the vice president, the mayor was sitting in a cubicle adjacent to the office where Dunne, Kerik, and the other command staff were waiting inside the basement of 75 Barclay Street. Giuliani had been told that the White House was being evacuated and that the president was not available. He didn't know that George W. Bush had been struck temporarily speechless and paralyzed in a classroom while talking to schoolchildren when he'd heard news of the attack and was now hiding somewhere in Florida, protected by his handlers and the Secret Service. Giuliani was still trying to talk to the vice president when the south tower started to crumble.[28]

Joe Dunne heard a thunderous noise that sounded like a train. Then he heard "things crash and then cracking and then the windows start blowing out and somebody yells, 'Get down!' So we get down, and I'm thinking, they must have hit this building. I think, this fuckin' building's going to come down around us. Some bad shit is happening. Then somebody says that the tower fell. So my mind's eye told me that a portion of the tower may have [fallen off] because of the fire but the building must be still there . . . , [only] the top of the candle broke off." Giuliani's recollections were similar. He heard Joe Esposito yell, "It's coming down—everybody down!" Thinking that only the radio tower had fallen off, Giuliani stayed on the phone until a staff member grabbed his arm and said, "Boss, we've got to get out of here."[29]

At this point, the entrance to 75 Barclay Street was submerged in a lake of debris so Dunne sent some officers to look for an alternative exit. It wasn't long before they located a maintenance worker who told them there was a way out downstairs that led underground to 100 Church Street.

"The whole building came down," Dunne heard someone say as he, Giuliani, Kerik, Joe Esposito, and the rest of the group emerged into the lobby.

"What do you mean, the 'building'?" Dunne asked.

"Boss, the whole fucking building's down."

"Holy shit! Are people getting out of the north tower? Get everybody out of there, are we getting them out?"

"Yeah, they're evacuating now."

"The south tower [is down]?"

"Yeah, the south tower."

"When was that hit? Well, tell them they better hurry. . . . We better get out of the north tower as fast as we can. Get our people the hell out of there. Evacuate that whole building!" Dunne looked in the direction of the World Trade Center but couldn't see anything. "You can't see your hand in front of your face out here, you better get something on," he said, then turned to a building worker who began to distribute some of the paper masks he used on the job. Police officers started randomly walking in the direction they thought might be an exit until Dunne called them back.

"Listen, we ain't going anywhere until we find out how to get out. I'm not going to hop around with these crutches, I'll be dead." After a while, some officers found a path out up some stairs and told Dunne to lead the way. "No, I'll be the last person out of here," he replied. "My motive for that wasn't heroic, hey, if I'm in somebody's way and they get nervous they're going to knock me over, you know what I mean? And by me going slow upstairs it's only going to increase the anxiety level of someone else who wants out, so I was the last one up the stairs and that was the only reason," Dunne explained.

"You better get out of here, look at you! You're on your fuckin' crutches! Get back to headquarters," Kerik said to Dunne, as he and Giuliani headed uptown on their way to the new command center at the Police Academy. No, Dunne thought. "I had to get back down to where I saw my cops the last time. I needed to go back to where the cops were and I just said to myself, I'm not walking away from this scene and leaving my cops back there. This is in no way, shape, or form a judgment on the police commissioner. He belonged with the mayor, but I was kind of like the free agent right then and there. I didn't need to be anywhere."

Like a lot of the officers I interviewed about 9/11, I noticed that Dunne kept switching from past to present tense as he talked. His pattern of speech begged for analysis. Dunne is an educated man with a college degree and postgraduate training who sometimes speaks "colloquial" police but understands correct English grammar and verb tense. In this case, I suspect that anxiety and defense were involved. When he started to talk about something that generated a painful feeling or image, he switched tense to push it away. I noticed his use of the possessive term when he referred to the cops on the scene. I thought I knew what he meant but wanted to make sure.

"When you say 'my cops', you mean, all the cops?" I asked. His quick and adamant response radiated such a poignant combination of outrage and grief that I could sense that a well of tears hovered beneath.

"Of course, they're all my cops, I love them all!" he said, implying, I think, how dare you ask? "So I get back to Church and Vesey and the images that you see really make you proud to be a cop. Cops were left out there on the post and the building came down and they got roughed up. They took cover underneath cars, wherever the hell they could find a place to protect themselves and stay alive. Think about that: you think you're going to die; these guys, they thought they were going to die, I'm sure."

"Did you think you were going to die?" I asked.

"I consciously said to myself early on that day after that first thing when we almost got brained under there, when I was standing back on the corner and giving out the helmets, I did, I consciously said to myself, you know, I may not live through this day, I don't know what's in store for us, and I didn't mean that I was going to do anything heroic, I just meant that we were all in trouble, we were in jeopardy of life and limb and if other things happened, I could easily be a victim of these terrorists, here on the street, and I just thought, let it at least be a good day for me in terms of trying to do the right thing. You're the first one that asked me that, and yeah, it was a thought, but actually you're the first person I shared that with. Only a fool would think that they're going to be perfectly OK, but I didn't obsess over it, I was relatively calm about this."

Dunne looked around the site of the disaster. He saw some of his cops and asked if they were OK. He didn't recall hugging anyone but later some-one showed him a photograph that pictured him with his arms around a police officer or a facilities worker, he wasn't sure which. After he'd been there a while and most of the people had gone, the officers in his detail started to urge him to leave. Dunne turned and spoke to the group of civilians who remained.

"You need to understand, you're not safe. You've got to move as quickly as you possibly can out of here. It's not over," he said. "I knew if the south tower was down, this other goddamned thing's coming down any minute and we're a lot closer to the north tower where we were standing." After officers discovered Dunne's car had been incinerated in the fire, they spotted a Bomb Squad SUV and waved it down.

"Listen, we got to put the boss in here, we're going north, and we're falling back to headquarters." Dunne squeezed into the back of the van next to the Bomb Squad dog. He doesn't remember hearing the sound of knocking just as they were about take off. Joe McGuire, who was driving, put his foot on the brake when he recognized Joe Dolan dressed in jeans and a shirt, covered in blood. Dolan opened the back door and looked at Dunne. "He was standing with his cast on and his crutches and his eyes are, like, this big."

o o o o o o o

Dolan's day had started uneventfully. He'd headed into Manhattan about 7:10 A.M. to give him time enough to handle some issues related to his pension before attending a meeting at One Police Plaza. Usually he and Ryan drove into the meeting together but Ryan had errands to run and was coming in an hour or so later. As Dolan approached the Brooklyn Bridge, he noticed sunlight cascading over the towers, creating a sparkling glow as if someone had climbed up and polished them during the night. "I wish I had that picture now, I really do," he said, tilting his head and looking up at the ceiling fan in the screened-in porch where we were sitting at my brother's house on Kiawah Island, South Carolina. Dolan parked his car near headquarters, walked into the building, and took the elevator upstairs. People were drizzling into the room while he was "bullshitting" with friends when the attack began. "All of a sudden you heard it, the explosion. It shook Saint Andrew's Church." At first, he thought that there'd been an accident or explosion in the subway that runs underneath the Municipal Building.

"You're in the Bomb Squad? You better go take a look at that," the sergeant said.

"I haven't been to school yet so I don't know what I'm looking at," Dolan replied and got up to leave. He headed uptown toward the Federal Court-house but didn't see smoke coming out of the train station. Instead, he saw people running north in the same direction he was walking. Dolan was wearing his shield on his chest so they could see he was a cop.

"The World Trade Center, something happened in the World Trade Center!" a woman ran up and said. When Dolan came around the back of the Municipal Building, he looked up and saw smoke pouring out of the top floors of the north tower. He called the Bomb Squad office.

"I think a bomb went off at the World Trade Center."

"No, it was a plane, a small plane flew into the World Trade Center."

"Well, something happened because there is smoke all over the place and people are running. I'm heading over there."

"We got a car coming down. See what's going on." Dolan tried to flag down a radio car but no one stopped. After a short wait, he caught a ride with a "federal cop." He jumped out near the World Trade Center just as an Emergency Service truck was pulling up. Dolan helped one of the team members distribute equipment, strapped a Scott pack [respirator] on the back of another officer, grabbed a medical bag, and accompanied the team up the escalator. On the way up, he ran into sergeant Rodney Gillis but didn't know that was the last time he'd see him alive. Then the officers turned the corner and walked under Five Financial Building. Nothing Dolan had ever seen in almost twenty years on the job could have prepared him for what was there.

"There were bodies all over the place, so it took me a few seconds to realize what was going on. There weren't only whole bodies. There were body parts all over. There was a loud, constant noise in the air. We're trying to run across and get into the building to start upstairs. The lieutenant says, 'On three, we'll start running'—you're trying to make it across so you don't get hit with debris. He starts counting down and we hear, 'One, two—' and then there's this *grrrboom*! We backed up under the overhang and all this stuff starts falling into the courtyard. You could see the bottom of the south tower but you couldn't see the top."

"We have a secondary explosion from the north tower," the lieutenant said, an assumption that another officer had expressed over police radio [Central Communications].

"Negative, Central! Negative! We have a second plane into the south tower," a different cop shouted over the air. "You knew it wasn't an accident at that point. They're trying to kill us. Then I think I heard someone say, '[Central], notify Washington because New York is under attack,'" Dolan explained.

When the storm of debris subsided, he and the Emergency Service officers prepared to run across the courtyard. "I saw a lot of things were falling but your mind shuts a lot off, by putting it into your head that it was just debris; not paying attention to how many bodies were actually falling." It wasn't until months later, when Ryan and Dolan were in California, that he allowed himself to feel what he saw, Ryan recalled. "He [Dolan] broke down one night, and he just started crying. I mean, he was holding this shit in for a long time and there was nothing we could do. He had to get it out when he was ready. To hear him talk about it, watching the bodies explode. He remembers seeing one of the torsos on fire. So it was tough."

Dolan continued. "Bodies are all over the place. About five or ten yards away, there was a girl laying face down. She was nicely dressed, but only half-dressed. She had on a skirt and black stockings but her shirt had been torn to pieces. I don't know if she came out of the plane or if she was in the office. We made the dash across and I looked down [and] passed a guy lying in the corner and, behind him, there was a perfect male's arm and shoulder. You could see his pin-striped shirt sticking out. It caught my eye."

The officers got to the first landing and were about to begin the climb when the lieutenant looked at Dolan and said, "You can't go. I'm sorry, man. You got no equipment. You can't come with us." Knowing he'd be a hindrance without the proper gear, Dolan handed the medical bag to the officer with the Scott pack, who cursed at the extra weight. Then Dolan turned around and went downstairs to where a crowd of about fifty people were now milling around. Alarmed, he ordered them out of the area.

"What are you here for? You've gotta get the hell out of here!"

"Where do we go? We don't know how to get out," one said. Dolan didn't think it was in their interests to send them back the way he'd come to see what he had seen and weather the storm of debris so he directed them left, in the direction of West Street. He stayed around for a few more minutes to make sure no one else needed help and then he turned right. "I thought I'll go the way I already know. . . . There was a bunch of stuff still coming down and I was standing next to the guy's shoulder, waiting for a break. I ran and made it to the overhang and went downstairs. Joe McGuire and another guy from the Bomb Squad were standing around. I walked up to Joe and said, "No accident."

"No kidding!" McGuire replied, then told Dolan to go up to the Bomb Squad office to pick up equipment and bring it back down. While Dolan was in the office looking for something to wear that would identify him as a cop, he heard on the news that the south tower had collapsed.

"It's down. It's all the way down. Let's go," he said to another detective and got into a truck. Two other officers followed in an SUV with a dog in the back. They parked near the remains of the south tower and left the dog inside the van with the air conditioner on. Dolan led the way into the building in search of the Emergency Service officers he'd left behind. He spotted the escalator, sitting there in a vacuum. "My God, the building is no longer there. You can see straight past, like it's part of the building but there's no tower anymore," he recalled.

"I know that there are guys in that tower because I put them there," Dolan told the detectives.

"What tower?" the detective said, confused.

"I put them there so let's go over and see if they need help." When they ran past the overhang, Dolan didn't see any of the men from the team that he'd left behind. Instead, he saw a few of the guys from Seven and Ten Truck, including Mike Curtin, Joe Vigiano, and John D'Allara. Curtin was smiling as usual and shook Dolan's hand. They stood there talking until Dolan looked up and saw more debris raining down. He watched the lieutenant try to jump out of the way and then grab his arm. When the lieutenant turned in Dolan's direction, Dolan saw that his arm had almost been sliced off and was hanging loosely from his shoulder. His thumb was also cut and partly detached from his hand. Dolan ran up and clamped his hands around the arm to try and cut off the blood supply. He and one of the Emergency Service officers walked the lieutenant down the escalator out onto Vesey and Church Streets. They saw an ambulance, but the emergency medical technicians were busy working on someone else. Dolan asked for supplies and they threw him a roll of gauze. The lieutenant held his arm in place and Dolan put the thumb where it belonged and bandaged him up as best he could. Both men started laughing. All of it seemed so bizarre. "We just kept laughing, trying to soak up and stop the blood." Dolan looked for another ambulance and came up with the Bomb Squad SUV.

He banged on the back until the door opened up and saw Joe Dunne standing on crutches inside with a shell-shocked look on his face.

"Excuse me, sir, I'm sorry," Dolan said, apologizing for his intrusion into the space of someone of such high rank.

"No problem," Dunne replied. Dolan walked up to McGuire, who was driving.

"Joe, where are you going?"

"I'm taking the first dep out of here, and we've got to meet up at the north side of City Hall. That's where the lieutenant is gonna be."

"OK. Look, I got a lieutenant over here. He's got to get to the hospital. His arm is almost hanging off."

"Put him in the back." McGuire replied, directing Dolan to the area in the SUV where the robot was stored. When Dolan opened the door, he saw another Bomb Squad detective who'd managed to squeeze in by wrapping his body around the robot. Just as Dolan was clearing some space, an ambulance pulled up. The EMTs helped the lieutenant crawl in the ambulance, the Bomb Squad van left, and Dolan started walking down Vesey back toward the escalator. When he reached the curb, he heard someone yell.

"It's coming down!" Dolan looked up. "It didn't look like it was coming down at the time. I don't know if maybe they had seen [the building] shift or heard the floors pop. . . . I take a few more steps [back] and now you hear it, the cracking, I hear this *pop, pop, pop* as it started coming down and then it was just a low rumble. It keeps getting louder and louder." Dolan ran. He could feel the street vibrate around him and under his feet as he pounded the pavement. Make it quick. Just don't let me be buried. Don't let me lie here for three days buried, he thought, then grabbed his radio intending to call the Bomb Squad. He didn't bother to press the transmitter when he heard the cacophony of panicked voices swarming Central Communications. He was running up Church against the tide of more than three inches of fast-accumulating powder when the north tower came crashing down. Suddenly the radio went dead. "All those voices one by one dropping off, like they're disappearing as time is going on, so you know these guys are being buried by stuff."

Dolan turned and looked behind him. "The dust cloud was coming and that thing was moving and I thought, I'm not getting out of the way of this fucking thing. I know that for a fact. I saw this ambulance sitting there and, when [the cloud] hit, the shit went under the ambulance. . . .

I turned around and started running [again] and got about six steps and then it was like somebody threw a blanket over my head. How am I going to explain this to my wife? I thought. How's my wife going to explain this to my daughter; that her stupid father didn't get crushed? He smothered to death a block and a half away from the building. I started laughing. It would be just like me to do that. There was nowhere to hide. Every time you took a breath your mouth filled with stuff and you're spitting it out. When I was in the cloud, it got quiet . . . you could hear the wind whipping around but there was no more rumbling. There was no talk on the radio. There was nothing. It was just dead."

Dolan and I had been talking for several hours. It was dark now and still humid but the temperature had gone down. Dolan glanced at his wife and daughter, who were inside in the air-conditioned living room watching TV. I thought of him buried in dust. I recalled seeing the cars in my neighborhood the day after the towers fell. You knew they'd been downtown because they were plastered in white powder that looked nothing like sand or snow. I thought that he must have felt like the last man standing in the wake of a nuclear holocaust.

"What did you think?" I asked.

"I think they're all gone. I didn't know. I felt like I was the last one in the world to make it through and all I kept saying to myself is, keep walking, keep moving. That's all you could do. It wasn't like you could see where you were going. It was walk by feel on the building. You'd feel a doorway and through the haze, you could see flashing lights on the back of something. I felt the edge of a building. I made it up to Broadway and I see two lights flashing in the distance and I stumble up and I realize it's a Chevy. I knew because of the way the lights wrapped around the back. I felt along the side of it until I came to the door handle, opened it up and fell into the car with all this crap coming in after me. I looked up and there was a guy sitting behind the wheel, looking at me with these huge eyes. It turned out he was a fire marshal. I closed the door and the air conditioning was on and I remember that I felt so good because he had fresh air."

"I'm sorry," Dolan said, at which point "all of this crap" fell out of his mouth.

"That's all right. Where the hell did you come from?"

"I was down at the World Trade Center."

"Holy shit!"

"Yeah, I know."

"Where's City Hall?"

"Right now I don't know where it is. The last time I saw it, it was across the street. But don't take my word for it," the fire marshall said. Dolan started to get out of the car but the man grabbed his leg.

"Where are you going?"

"I got my people on the other side of City Hall." Dolan thanked the man, stepped into the street, and started wandering in the slowly dissipating smog. He ended up on the corner of Chambers and Broadway, where he saw a Bomb Squad van and waved it down. It was the same van he had encountered before with McGuire at the wheel.

"You got blood all over you," one of the officers said.

"I'm pretty sure it's not mine. It's the lieutenant from Emergency Service." Rich Teemsma appeared on the street from inside another van. He heard Dolan's explanation but wasn't convinced that he was OK. Teemsma started pouring water over the bloodied shirt until he was sure there wasn't an injury underneath.

"Where's everybody else?" another detective asked.

"I think they're gone," Dolan replied.

"What?"

"I know where I left them and I don't think they're here anymore. I think they're all gone, but I don't know." Dolan climbed into the back of the van with the other detectives. They started moving, and then Dolan asked them to stop. He must have sounded serious, because McGuire didn't ask questions, just put his foot on the brake. Dolan got out and stood alone on the street and tried to clean out his eyes. One of the detectives got some bottles of water from the van and tried to help. "Now that I was out of the cloud, I guess it started to sink in what had happened. My eyes were starting to burn and my throat was burning and I couldn't breathe. I guess it was nerves finally catching up." A couple of hours later, when Dolan was leaving the Bomb Squad office and walking to his car, he thought about who he'd seen in the building before the tower collapsed. As he was telling me this, he started rubbing his eyes. I wondered if he was reliving the pain or fighting back tears.

"You're rubbing your eyes," I said.

"All day my eyes burned but I ended up going back down because I was the only one [who wasn't hurt and at the hospital] who knew who had been down there and where they had gone. We were there for three hours, calling out their names, to no avail. . . . Then they came out with the list of the guys that disappeared. I knew them very well. I worked with them for ten years. I knew I'd never see those faces again. I think, I'm not seeing Mike Curtin anymore and Joe Vigiano. I missed them all."

Around 1:00 A.M., Joe Dolan walked into the front door of his home on Staten Island and was greeted by a call from an officer who worked in Seven Truck in Emergency Service. The officer was in training in Alabama and desperate for news regarding his partner and friends.

"You got names?" he asked.

"I got the names," Dolan replied.

"Who?" the officer inquired. Dolan began to list the names of the men in Emergency Service who he thought were dead but stopped when he got to the guys from Seven Truck.

"I got to go. I can't do this no more," Dolan said.

"OK, I'll call you tomorrow," and he hung up the phone. "I just couldn't do it to him, you know, and I got down to the guys in his squad and he was like, oh my God. He and [one of the missing officers] were partners," Dolan explained. His wife, Nancy, was sitting in the living room listening to her husband on the telephone. She could tell from the look on his face that he was suffering and couldn't talk to her yet. Comforted by his wife's presence and the knowledge his daughter was sleeping upstairs, he summoned the energy to lift his body out of the chair. He climbed the stairs and went into the bathroom. He turned on the water and got in the shower and tried to wash "the brick out of my eyes." He lay down in his bed but couldn't get comfortable, not because his eyes were still burning, which they were, but because he felt vulnerable. He got up, retrieved his gun, and put it under his pillow. "I slept with that fucking thing under my pillow because that night I could not feel safe at all. That thing was not more than two inches from me for the whole night. I couldn't get comfortable and I just didn't feel safe for weeks after that. That was the only time I ever [had a] gun close [to me so] I could get through the night. I never slept with my gun like that before. After 9/11, I felt insecure in my own home. . . . I just lay there in bed that night and, at some point, I cried myself to sleep."

o o o o o o o

The day before the World Trade Center disaster, Rich Teemsma was talking on the phone to his friend and former partner of three years, Danny Richards. They'd worked together until Teemsma had transferred up to the range a few months prior and Richards had stayed in the Chelsea office to do administrative work. Richards had called to warn Teemsma that the "backstabbing" had started again after a detective with a little more time in the squad but less time on the job had gotten wind from their new lieutenant that he was going to put Teemsma in for a promotion.

"I have more to tell you, but I've gotta go. I'll call you tomorrow," Richards had said as he hung up the phone. "The next day was September 11th, and Danny was already dead before we could talk. He was the only one in the Bomb Squad who was killed on 9/11," Teemsma recalled. Teemsma had just started his tour and was using a large machine to clear the parking lot of the mountain of junk that had been there since the space had been used as a dump. He'd been working for ten minutes when another detective came outside and told him that his wife, Kim, had called.

"She says a plane hit the World Trade Center." Teemsma climbed down from the vehicle, walked inside, and turned on the TV. "My first thoughts were a twin engine plane. Who is the moron who bounced this plane off the World Trade Center? I used to love flying. I still do. I had a friend who had a little Cessna he'd invite me up and, years ago, we used to fly above the World Trade Center." As soon as he saw the big hole in the tower on the TV screen, Teemsma realized he was wrong. "I got a sick feeling. . . . It's a beautiful day up here. You can see this thing twenty-five miles away, so how can anyone just come up and hit that thing the way it was?" He thought back to the bombing in 1993 and recalled what he'd seen and said when they'd opened up the sidewalk: "Hijack a 747 and crash it into the building. You will knock it down." He recognized then that the hole was caused by a hijacked plane. After he saw the second plane hit, Teemsma turned to Kenny Silva, another detective and said, "We gotta go."

"Let's go," Kenny responded. Teemsma grabbed his personal bag and headed toward the van. "Can I drop off the dog first?" Kenny asked, wanting to put Buster, one of the Bomb Squad dogs, in the kennel before heading into a bad situation that could last all night.

"Yeah," Teemsma replied. "I'm driving, OK?"

"No, I don't want you driving." Kenny didn't like Teemsma to drive because he drove too fast and rode the sidewalks to get through heavy traffic.

"Yeah, OK," Teemsma said, thinking that maybe it wasn't a bad idea, because "I gotta slow up on this because it's going too fast. It's way over our heads. We're in deep waters. . . . It all worked out because when we pulled up on the other side of Building Number Seven and were coming around the corner, the second tower came down. We were just far enough away so we didn't get hit by anything. When we were leaving, I got out of the van because I had the mask."

Teemsma stopped talking, as if these last fourteen words summed up his whole experience. His face looked sad and drawn. It was clear that this conversation was more intimate than any we'd had in my living room where we'd first met to talk about the raid. Now we were sitting alone in the family room of the house on Long Island he'd practically built himself. I remained silent, increasing the pressure, perhaps, but mostly giving him time to decide if he was comfortable revisiting the past and sharing his recollections with me.

"OK, I'll tell you the whole story," he said, backing up his narrative to when they first arrived at the scene. "When we get down there, I see everyone covered with dust. Everybody had a handkerchief. The thing I always did since the first bombing in 1993 was always keep the particle mask with me. I cleaned it and got new filters and kept it in my bag of tricks. Anyway, we went down this side street on the West Side. Just as we were around Building Seven, Building Two [the north tower] came down. It turned black. We drove a little further, but you couldn't see anything. You could hear it and we just sat there in the van. Looking through the windshield is like watching on TV. It was starting to clear up a little but you could hear it all coming, banging, echoing—very strange. We just sat there and we were thinking, we're done. This is it. We just sat there waiting to die, really. We couldn't see so we couldn't run anyplace. Eventually, it slowly stops and we waited a while. We still couldn't see ahead of us.

"We couldn't breathe, so we had to get out of there. So I said, 'I'm going to get out and walk us out of here. I'll get out and put my hand on the windshield.' He could see my hand but he couldn't see beyond that." Teemsma walked on the side of the van with his arm stretched out and the palm of his hand face down on the window, guiding Kenny past the steel beams and crater-sized holes that restructured the street around them. "He watched my hand and I looked ahead and we headed out of it and went north where there was clean air. We sat there and then two Bomb Squad vans pulled out of this big cloud of dust. I looked at everybody. I saw Joe Dolan first, and he was covered with blood."

"Joe, where are you hurt?" Teemsma asked.

"I'm not hurt. It was a lieutenant that I was taking care of. He lost his arm or something," Dolan said but Teemsma didn't believe him and started pouring bottles of water over the area he thought was cut until he realized that he was OK.

"You're all right," Teemsma said and put Dolan in the back of the van. At this point another detective turned to Teemsma and said, "We lost Danny [Richards]. He's gone."

"How do you know?"

"I saw him and then there was this big hole."

I was quietly listening when I heard Teemsma's voice crack. I think I resisted the urge to touch his hand or arm and just sat there silent and motionless, waiting for him to catch his breath.

"I gotta stop," he said. "I'll be OK in a second." After a few minutes, he collected himself and bravely went on. "So we decided to go back and look for Danny, me and Kenny. We headed back to the World Trade Center and everybody else went to the Bomb Squad office and the [two] guys who were hurt went to hospitals. Before we left, I looked at Fatty [Joe McGuire]—you know how a cop's mind works—like, where were you? I can tell from what he was wearing. They came out of this cloud and he and his partner were spotless. So they were ahead of this thing in the van or something. I'm looking at him like, don't you be telling me stories later. It turns out he was taking pictures of people jumping off and different things. What is he, a fucking photographer, taking pictures [while] everybody else was getting hurt? So we went back to look for Danny. One of the guys told me where he was. I knew the exact spot. We'd been there before. When we got there all I saw was a big hole. The top of the tower came down in this hole and he was there under tons of debris."

"We are not going to get to him. He's buried in here somewhere," Teemsma said.

"Listen, you guys gotta get out of here. Number Seven is coming down," a fire chief came up and told them. Teemsma saw flames shooting out the seventh and eighth floors.

"Yeah, you are right," he said then turned to Kenny. "Well, Danny is dead. There is nothing we can do right now. This thing falls and we're just gonna kill ourselves. We'll wait and go back in." He and Kenny left the area. After Building Seven collapsed, they searched for a while longer and then gave up, knowing that Danny was buried too deeply for them to get to him. Teemsma told me a little more about his partner and then pulled out his wallet and showed me a photo of the Bomb Squad dog. "Buster saved our lives. That's why I have his picture. He just slowed us up enough so that we didn't get there and have the whole thing come down on us. Good old Buster," he said.

When Teemsma got home late the night of 9/11, Kim met him at the door.

"You all right?" she asked.

"Yeah. I gotta take my clothes off here. I don't want to bring this into the house." He undressed in the garage, put his clothes in the washing machine, and went upstairs and took a shower. He and Kim talked for a while and then he went to bed. "I don't know if I slept or not, but I went to bed."

o o o o o o o

John English still has mixed emotions when he thinks about Mike Curtin buried under the rubble when it could have been him. For reasons he doesn't understand, fate or God or something else intervened to save his life. The spring of 2001, Curtin was working as a sergeant in the Emergency Service Apprehension Team whose members were assigned to execute high-risk warrants and make a lot of arrests. English called Curtin and asked if they could switch jobs during the summer as English was thinking of retiring in January and wanted to build up some overtime. Curtin agreed, so English joined the Apprehension Team and Curtin went back to Seven Truck. They were supposed to switch places again in early September but the transfer orders didn't come down so Curtin stayed in the squad for another few weeks. On the morning of 9/11, Curtin was working in Seven Truck while English was home, painting his house on his day off. A little after 8:00 A.M., his wife called him inside.

"Come here. You have to see this on the news!" He went into the living room, looked at the TV and saw a gaping hole in the north tower. He didn't think it was caused by a commercial airline but he decided to call Emergency Service headquarters to find out if everyone was coming in.

"No, we don't know what we have yet," the desk officer said. English abandoned his brushes in the yard and sat inside with his wife, watching the news. When they saw the second plane crash into the south tower, he got up.

"I'm leaving."

"All right. Please be careful," she replied.

"You know I will." English drove to Fort Totten where the members of the Apprehension Team were assigned to mobilize. Shortly after the south tower fell, the officers grabbed their gear and piled into their truck. They were going over the Triborough Bridge when the north tower collapsed. "I remember driving down the FDR Drive. I didn't hear anything after the second building came down. There were no more radio transmissions. There was no traffic going downtown. You couldn't see the tower. I couldn't believe it actually fell, but we were trying to see just where the smoke was. As we were coming down the FDR, we saw thousands of people walking northbound on the roadway of the drive. It looked like a science fiction movie, something from *War of the Worlds*. We go under the underpass at Battery Park and it went from this roll of sun to everything gray and full of smoke. I couldn't orient myself to where I was," English explained. The team pulled over a few blocks south of the World Trade Center and English told his men to "stay together until we find out what's going on."

On instructions from another boss, they mustered at a school, but the situation was chaotic and slow to get organized. Frustrated by the delay, English and the other members of the Apprehension Team "snuck out" and walked to the World Trade Center. "I got there and the whole place was collapsed and it was like the beginning scene of the movie *Terminator*. There's that part where they're fighting these alien robot things. . . . They're laying there and there's fire around them . . . all kinds of fire and smoke and all this bent-up steel and concrete rubble," English said.

The team started to look for survivors until a commander pulled them out of the area before building Seven fell. The officers returned to work when the situation was stable again. "I knew my friends were there because I heard them on the radio before the collapse, and also my cousin Paul [Talty] is in Ten Truck." English had changed to the present tense when he mentioned his cousin, in an effort to deny his death like in a dream when we find ourselves talking to someone we know is gone but wish were alive. "There were guys in my squad I worked with every day— Ronny [Kloepfer], Santos [Valentin], and Mike Curtin—[who] were missing and, I thought, dead. You think, if I was there would I have taken a left instead of a right? I don't know. I'm glad I'm here for my family but I just wish, maybe I could have taken them in a different direction. But there were good leaders there too. It's amazing but Bill Fiori and Mark DeMarco actually survived. They sucked in all the debris in Building One before it fell around them. Somehow they managed to dig their way out. They came back after they got out of the hospital to show us where they'd been. There was nothing there. It was a big pit and you could see Mark's and Billy's handprints on the wall where they felt their way out of the building."

English left ground zero around 1:00 A.M. and got back home about 2:00. His wife met him outside on the grass and they embraced. "I just started crying because I just told her, they're all gone. I knew they were and I never cried like that in my life. I just remember holding her on the front lawn."

"Did she say anything?"

"No, she didn't say anything. She just held me. She said, 'I know.' I was going to stay there all night, but we finally went inside. I took a shower. I don't think I slept that night, and I left at 5:00 A.M. Everything after that is just one day [blurring] into the next. There wasn't much time to think and you just had to get into robotic mode and keep going. Occasionally, you get to think about it but I don't think that I cried [after that], except for at the funerals, because you didn't have time." At one point, while we were talking, English choked up. I'd had to fight to keep the tears from flooding my eyes.

o o o o o o o

Keith Ryan was home when the first plane hit the north tower and he knew right away that it wasn't an accident. When he told his wife that it was a terrorist act, she insisted he was being paranoid. He remembered the bomb job in 1997 and the vacant, soulless look in the terrorist's eyes. It was then that he knew what terrorists were capable of. His recognition was not an abstraction or something he read about in the newspapers but an emotion carved into his gut. If only the police commissioner and the FBI had listened. If they'd understood the raid in the same way that he, Dolan, English, and maybe the other cops had, maybe then someone would have put the pieces together before the towers were struck. Ryan had seen the size of the hole in the tower on TV and knew it wasn't made by a small plane. He'd survived one near disaster and was shocked but not surprised when terrorists launched yet another assault.

Ryan didn't tell his wife, Caroline where he was going when he "snuck out" of the house and jumped in the car. He had a medic bag and triage kit in the back and figured he'd head to the World Trade Center where he was sure he'd find Dolan and they'd start triaging people, maybe with other cops. As he was crossing into Manhattan, he called his lieutenant in the Intelligence Division to notify him what was going on.

"Look, I'm heading down there now, and if you need me you can reach me on the cell. This is where I'm gonna be."

"I need you back here."

"What do you need me there for?"

"Keith, I gotta have you here. You're the only guy who knows about ESU."

"Don't blow smoke up my ass!"

"I'm telling you, Keith."

"I can't hear you. You're breaking up."

"Goddamn it, Keith. Don't fuck around. I'm giving you a direct order!"

"OK." Ryan turned around and headed back into Brooklyn. On the way, he tried contacting Dolan but the cell phone lines were overloaded and he couldn't get through. "I was worried about Joey and pissed that they didn't let me go there because I was already there, but you know what? Somebody was watching over me because I probably would have been dead. I would have gone right into that fucking building like everybody else."

Ryan spent the next few hours working in Brooklyn. He wasn't the only cop who felt helpless because he couldn't go into Manhattan and contribute to the rescue. Hearing about the catastrophe and loss of life, it was hard for a lot of the Brooklyn precinct cops to accept that they were playing an important role by guarding the tunnels and bridges in the event of another attack.

Before he went home that night, Ryan and his sergeant went into Manhattan and walked around the mountains of wreckage on Vesey and Church Street. "I just looked and looked and I thought about Manny [Suarez] and Ronny [Kloepfer] and Tommy Langone and all the guys that were missing. I just dropped to my knees and I started sobbing. I couldn't stop crying. I just couldn't. It's weird, because I remember thinking about when I was a kid—I was a big history buff. I used to watch *The World at War* and all these other documentaries. I could understand what those people felt like who were in London when the Germans were bombing them. I knew what the Poles felt like with the French; I understood those documentaries with the people walking dazed in the streets. I understood the loss; not only the loss of people they knew but of soul and of spirit. It's all gone. It's just empty. You're overwhelmed with this emotion. It overtakes your whole body, even talking about it now. I feel it in my arms and legs. I feel numbness come through my whole body."

A few days after 9/11, Ryan was transferred back to Emergency Service to help in the rescue and recovery operations. Not long after that, he ran into his lieutenant in the Intelligence Unit and thanked him for what he did.

"Lieu, let me tell you something. Someday I want you to go in front of Macy's window and I will kiss your ass in front of everybody because you probably saved my life, by ordering me back. You don't know it, but you probably saved my life."

o o o o o o o

On the morning of 9/11, Paul Yurkiw was off duty working his second job at an attorneys' breakfast for the United Jewish Appeal at the Marriott Hotel. About 8:20, someone asked if he knew anything about the plane that had just hit the World Trade Center. Yurkiw hadn't yet heard the news. He recalled that a small private plane had once hit the Empire State Building and figured that maybe the same thing had happened downtown. When he had a break and could go downstairs, he found an office with a TV and turned it on. When he saw the gash in the north tower, he called the Bomb Squad office.

"Yeah. It's a plane hit the World Trade Center," the detective said.

"I'm in Manhattan on 45th and Broadway at the Marriott."

"OK, we'll call you if we need you to come in." A few minutes later, Yurkiw heard that the south tower had been damaged in a secondary explosion or hit by another plane. When he called the office again, they confirmed that a second jet had crashed into the World Trade Center and told him to come right in. Unable to find a cab or a radio car, Yurkiw jogged south. He stopped to rest at 34th Street. "Everybody was leaving. You know something was wrong. Nobody was picking up the phone at the Bomb Squad. Nobody was picking up the phone at Central [Communications]. The line was busy, busy, busy." He walked two blocks and then jogged down to Fourteenth Street. When he finally got to the Bomb Squad office, he changed into a jumpsuit and boots and was about to head downtown when the lieutenant told him he needed him there. Yurkiw and his boss got into an unmarked car and started answering jobs. "We were absorbing Central's jobs on suspicious packages and vehicles, going from one job to the next, to clear them so Central could deal with the situation downtown. We didn't know what the magnitude was until the south tower collapsed. You can hear it over citywide radio, people screaming. We started clearing more jobs in case there were other attacks. We heard about the Pentagon and the crash in Pennsylvania. So we knew there could be a kamikaze assault on the tunnels and bridges or another jet down in Times Square or Wall Street."

After the north tower fell, Yurkiw and the lieutenant drove south through the cloud of debris. "It was like not being on earth, like being in a movie set. It was so real, it looked fake; like when you see a dead person for the first time, it almost looks like a mannequin. I guess that is a defense mechanism. This is really not happening. But you are in it. Our back window was blown out. I don't remember what happened but just that the whole inside of the car was full of debris. I remember there was a Barnes & Noble near the corner. We were about fifty yards away. The heat was so intense you couldn't get any closer. You could feel it through your jumpsuit. You couldn't stand it. I remember seeing water being put down from a block away. You see streams of water, trying to cool the heat down. I remember hearing that they couldn't find Danny [Richards]."

Around 1:00 P.M., Yurkiw and the lieutenant split up. "I did the drone thing and he did the boss thing. I continued to pick up jobs for the rest of the day. Then I spent the night at the range, and went down in the morning to help look for survivor," Yurkiw said.

∘ ∘ ∘ ∘ ∘ ∘ ∘

Startled by a noise outside the operations room at headquarters, deputy commissioner George Grasso stopped working and tried to assess what was happening. He heard the door open behind him and turned his head. There, leaning on crutches, wearing an NYPD baseball cap, covered in a mantle of white dust, stood Joe Dunne. Grasso felt energized by his presence, and relieved. Weight remained but it was weight he could carry and share.

Dunne walked up to Grasso, planted his large frame in the next chair and demanded a cigarette. Grasso leaned over and whispered, "Joe, we still don't know what the fuck we got in our lungs—are you sure you want a cigarette?" He didn't think of the chocolate donut he'd craved a few hours before. I suspect that Dunne craved a cigarette for the same reason that Grasso sought comfort in junk food in the wake of his brush with death.

"Get me a fuckin' cigarette!" Dunne yelled and tossed his arm in a vehement gesture of no-nonsense command. Grasso stifled a smile. "Joe was back, he was pissed off, and we were going to be all right," he thought.

"The NYPD's toughest and most experienced field commander, my boss, and . . . my friend, [had] emerged from the deadly mushroom cloud."[30]

As soon as Dunne lit his cigarette, he started asking questions. He wanted to know where Bill Morange was and if he or any other street commander needed anything and what the department was doing to meet their requests. He asked about the status of communications. He wanted to know whether all the commercial airlines in the United States had been accounted for. In the midst of this exchange, the chief of the department, Joe Esposito, walked into the room. Grasso voiced his concern that One Police Plaza might be a target and initiated discussion of whether they should evacuate the building and set up a command center somewhere else. Dunne inhaled his cigarette, looked around the room, glanced out the window at the volcano erupting outside, paused for a minute, and quietly said, "We are not getting chased out of One PP—we cannot afford that kind of disruption in command and control operations, so we are staying here." He brushed his hand across his brow. "You people look like shit. We are going to be here for a while—I want you to start taking showers and changing clothes. We will open up the equipment section and provide them."[31]

Grasso looked at the ravished faces around him, locked eyes with JT, and got up. He headed upstairs to his office, walked in and closed the door. He got undressed and stepped into his small private shower. Once again, he felt the same anxiety he'd experienced in the headquarters' elevator when he'd come into the building from downtown. It shot through his abdomen and he could almost feel the walls vibrate as the water streamed down, massaging his skin and rinsing away the residue of compressed metal, paper, plastic, glass, bone, and human flesh. He dried himself off and put on the extra suit he kept in his locker. If he dared to look at himself in the mirror, I doubt he recognized his eyes.

Twenty minutes later, Grasso joined Dunne at the table in the command center, surrounded by other bosses and cops. The television was on and information was piling in. Hundreds of cops and firefighters were still missing. While police radios were still functioning, the telephone service was hardly working at all. Still, offers of help kept coming in from the military, National Guard, State Police, Coast Guard, and the Office of Emergency Management. Verizon workers teamed up with cops and went to the roof of the building to rig up a microwave antenna that allowed for some degree of cell phone capability. After a few hours, a police officer approached Dunne at the table, leaned over and whispered something in his ear. Grasso noticed a shadow of anguish swell in his friend's eyes. When Dunne rose from his chair and walked into the hall, Grasso followed him there.

"Where are my boys? Where are my boys, Joe? I just want my boys back," retired firefighter John Vigiano said when he and Dunne came face to face. One of Vigiano's sons was a firefighter, who, by then, I suspect, was dead. The other was the Emergency Service detective Joe Dolan had seen inside the north tower before it fell. Dunne spoke quietly when he said that they didn't know anything yet but were doing everything they could to find their missing personnel. When Vigiano and Dunne embraced, Grasso could see that his friend's eyes were moist and red.[32] Dunne knew Joe Vigiano. He'd been one of his cops when he'd been the commanding officer of Brooklyn's 7-5 Precinct.

Reading Grasso's moving description of the exchange, I thought of Bill Morange. As soon as I saw the depth in his dark blue eyes and heard the earnest warmth of his voice, I understood why his men loved him so much. He'd had a son who'd died some years before. Now he had lost large numbers of officers he personally knew and loved. I'd done seminars with police commanders who'd lost officers in line-of-duty homicides and suicide and all of them felt partly responsible. They'd had to put aside their personal feelings in order to comfort the officers in their commands. I guess this was one of the reasons Morange wouldn't talk to me about 9/11. The pain was too much.[33] I won't forget how respectful he was of the Muslim community. He was the only officer with whom I talked about the raid who emphasized how brave the Muslim informant had been; a stranger in the country, approaching police he didn't know, and telling them what he knew. Even in the wake of 9/11, Morange didn't succumb to stereotyping any ethnic, religious, or cultural group.

An hour or so after Vigiano left, Dunne received a call from Barry Mawn, the director of the New York office of the FBI, requesting a member of the top brass come to their center of operations and represent the police commissioner and maintain "real time contact" with the Command Center of the NYPD. Dunne turned to Grasso and told him that he was their man. "Get over there and get him whatever he needs from us. Establish a phone line if you can. Call me in this room and give me the number. Keep us in the loop."[34] At about 5:00 P.M., "just like that, in the context of a minute—that's how decisions were being made in the SR [command center] that day—I was thrust into the apex of the federal investigation into the devastating domestic sneak attack that eclipsed even Pearl Harbor," Grasso wrote.[35]

o o o o o o o

Rudy Giuliani and Bernie Kerik had been at the Police Academy since noon. They'd made sure the airports were locked down and the airspace closed and run new phone lines into the Police Academy to facilitate communications. At some point, Giuliani had called Dick Grasso to find out when he could reopen the New York Stock Exchange. Giuliani also met with Charles Hirsch, the city medical examiner. Hirsch had headed toward the towers shortly after the first plane crashed and was still covered in dust and debris when he walked into the building on Twentieth Street. "I saw cuts all over his face and noticed the Frankenstein-looking stitches all over the back of his hand," Giuliani wrote, describing the way the medical examiner had stitched his own hand.[36] Hirsch let the mayor know then what he didn't share with his top police command until several days later: that it was unlikely that anyone would survive the 2,000-degree heat or the collapse of the Twin Towers into piles of molten steel. "Most of the bodies will be vaporized. We're going to end up with biological stains, where the tissue has become shapeless, amorphous masses of matter," Hirsch explained.[37] When Giuliani learned that his friend, Barbara Olson, had been on the plane that crashed into the Pentagon, he ducked into an office and cried. Then he collected himself and went back to work, asking questions and making the hundreds of decisions that had to be made that day: "Was Grand Central Station covered? Were there reports of any more attacks? How would the construction equipment get into the city and where would it come from? How could they find enough lights to illuminate the area so people could work all night on twelve-hour shifts?"[38]

o o o o o o o

When Grasso arrived in the temporary offices of the FBI and started to work with Mawn and his colleagues, he quickly discovered that communications were even worse there than at Police headquarters. The only way that Mawn was going to be able to talk to the police commissioner was if they met in person at the Police Academy. After several failed attempts to establish telephone contact, Grasso personally drove Mawn and Mary Joe

White, the United States attorney for the Southern District of New York, up to 20th Street.

It was a little before 7:00 P.M. when Grasso, Mawn, and White walked into the Police Academy office where the mayor, the governor, the police commissioner, the fire commissioner, and other top city and state officials were meeting. Kerik, Giuliani, and Mawn exchanged a few words, and the FBI director discussed the status of the investigation and what little he knew about the possibility of additional attacks.[39]

George Pataki then began to ask Mawn a series of questions. As the governor of New York, Pataki had to make the decision about whether to close the bridges and tunnels into the cities and needed every bit of information available. Still, during the meeting as a whole, Giuliani was clearly in control, rapidly making decisions and issuing orders. At one point, he asked if anyone had a plan for body recovery. When no one volunteered a solution, he began firing questions at fire commissioner Tom Van Essen. His sun-wrinkled, life-beaten face was riddled with grief and fatigue, and it seemed as though he was barely hanging on, knowing that hundreds of his men were lost and probably dead.[40] Giuliani kept on hammering, forcing Van Essen to either rise above his emotions and focus on the situation or give in and collapse. "Rudy's way was like applying smelling salts," a commander explained, noting that the mayor's method served its purpose and Van Essen got ahold of himself and did what he had to do. Grasso didn't say what he thought when he discovered the number of missing firefighters and how long it took to determine their names. Other police commanders did.

"I don't know how to fight a fire," one top-ranked member of the brass said. "I know it's very dangerous work. I know that the executives at the Fire Department are probably the best-trained and most knowledgeable in the world and their people certainly are up to the task, without question. But I think what happened after 9/11 and what I found to be typical of the Fire Department is that they play a blind game. I am not and I don't claim to be a student of the fire response and the interviews that were conducted of fire chiefs who survived that day, but, at the end of the day, their tactics sucked—and how do I know that? Because they lost 364 people."

Lou Anemone was also critical but focused on the issue surrounding the doors. "It took them [the Fire Department] days to figure how many had died . . . I thought of the roof doors locked and [I felt] rage. I was very angry for a while. I sat through those [9/11] hearings [on TV] and [watched] the executive director of the Port Authority rewriting history, explaining why they couldn't use helicopters; trying to get around the decision [made with the Fire Department] to lock the [rooftop] doors."

o o o o o o o

While Grasso attended to the FBI, Dunne continued to coordinate activity in the command and control center. At different times during the afternoon, he talked to representatives of various agencies. He also made sure they kept tabs on where his officers were assigned and what they needed. At one point, early in the evening he advised civilian and some police staff to go home. "I think we ordered all nonessential personnel out. I remember going up to my office later that night and I saw most of my people were there, including civilians, and I said, 'I thought I gave an order to get you people home.' They said, 'Well, which one of us do you think is not important to you?' I said, 'Never mind . . . Thanks for staying,'" Dunne explained.

By 9:00 P.M. the command staff had concluded that twenty-two police members of the service were unaccounted for. They added another officer the next day. John Perry had put in his retirement papers in the morning and then responded to downtown. "We didn't find that out until the next day when his mom was calling, saying, 'My son, where is he? He didn't come home.' It turned out he was dead. Fourteen of the twenty-three NYPD police officers killed were from Emergency Service and nine from other units [including Patrol, Housing, Transit, one Bomb Squad detective, and an officer in the Police Academy Video Production Unit]. The Port Authority numbers [were] thirty-two and the Fire Department was three hundred sixty-four," Dunne explained.

o o o o o o o

After finishing his work with the FBI around 10:00 P.M., Grasso returned to One Police Plaza. Dunne was sitting at the head of the table, assisted by deputy commissioner Maureen Casey and Charles Campisi, the chief of Internal Affairs, who was fielding calls that didn't need Dunne's attention. Soon after Grasso sat down, Esposito and Bill Allee, the chief of Detectives, walked in. They were covered in powder and their eyes were bloodshot and burning from the grains of compressed glass in the air. Grasso recalled that "the expressions on their faces evoked the thought of the look men have after. . . [they've been] swimming literally in death."[41]

The question of how to deal with the bodies was discussed and initial plans put into place; the National Guard would assist in their handling while the Police Department and other qualified workers managed the rescue and recovery.[42] According to some of the officers I interviewed, something went amok in terms of the National Guard. At some point, they acted on orders that only federal law enforcement personnel were allowed on the site. A confrontation occurred, and Emergency Service officers pushed their way through. On occasion, fights broke out between firefighters and police. However, when bodies emerged, all nascent tensions ceased. The police turned over their grim discoveries of firemen's uniforms to their rivals, and firefighters did the same when they found a cop.

Health issues ran rampant in the first few weeks, in particular. Except for a few officers in Emergency Service, workers had no respirators on-site. Tom Scotto did an interview with FOX News in which he announced this lack. Three or four hours later, an eighteen-wheeler truck, loaded with respirators, pulled up at the Red Cross station at the corner of Church and Chambers Streets. No one realized then that different types of respirators filtered for different things. "So a lot of people were under the impression they had respirators on but they didn't have the proper filtration system for the toxins there," Scotto explained.

Around 11:00 P.M. on the night of 9/11, Dunne requested that they set up a place at headquarters where he could talk to the families of the missing police officers. "Listen, we've got to get our families here because people are calling. Get them all together at headquarters, and I'll talk to them," Dunne said. At the expense of a private foundation, the Police Department also provided a hotel where the parents, spouses and children could stay. About thirty minutes later, the families began to gather in a cordoned-off area in the auditorium where food and coffee were served. When it was time to go downstairs, Dunne got up from the table with a look of "grim determination on his face."[43] He and Grasso got in the elevator, but neither commander said anything.

Father Romano, Monsignor Cassata, and Rabbi Kass were waiting in the auditorium along with relevant police personnel. Grasso and Dunne spoke to the religious leaders first. A spiritual man raised Roman Catholic, Grasso was touched by the presence of three men who represented different faiths. Dunne then walked over and embraced each family member. "There was crying, but it was muffled, and I could see that he [Dunne] also appeared to indicate, as he was embracing each of the people, in some unfathomable way, he was absorbing some of their pain. It is hard to put into words exactly what I felt as I was watching, other than to say it appeared his emotion and embrace was permitting people to deal with the horrible anxiety and grief to transfer some of it to him," Grasso wrote.[44]

Dunne considered his decision to meet the families one of his most important accomplishments. "It was a hard thing to do. . . . At that time [police officers] were still missing and so I had to assure [their families]. I'd listened to the experts who told me there's a chance that, when the building came down, they may have found a void. It's not uncommon. You know [in] mine accidents, it happens all the time. So we really were hopeful that some of the men were able to fall into voids and might still be alive. I told [the families], 'We have a bad situation but don't despair. There are hundreds of police and firefighters on the pile right now. We're convinced that we will be able to rescue some people. We think that there may be voids down there.' But it wasn't meant to be. Giuliani told me much later that, early on, he'd talked to the doctor [who] . . . told him that it would be impossible for anyone to survive that collapse. . . . It's flat as a pancake, a ten-story building squeezed into [a pancake]."

While Dunne was talking to family members, one of his staff members tried to penetrate the area reserved for the meeting and speak to him. Grasso blocked his way and asked what was going on. The staff member explained that the police commissioner was on the phone and needed to speak to Dunne right away.

"Did you tell the PC what Commissioner Dunne is doing?" Grasso asked.

"I tried, but they told me to get Commissioner Dunne," the staff member replied. Grasso took the phone and walked away from the crowd. He identified himself to the "PC," who he assumed was on the line.

"How can I help you?" Grasso said. His question was greeted by silence and he didn't know if Kerik was listening or had shifted his attention to something else. A few seconds later, an aide got on the phone and Grasso explained that Dunne couldn't be disturbed because he was talking to the families of the missing cops. The aide confirmed that Kerik could wait until later to talk to the "first dep."

A few hours after he finished talking to the families, Dunne faced a command center full of exhausted officers and told them it was time to go home and try to get some sleep. Grasso asked if there was anything he needed before he left. Dunne shook his head.

○ ○ ○ ○ ○ ○ ○

Three or four nights after 9/11, Joe Dunne met with Mike Curtin's wife, Helga, in front of headquarters. "Mike Curtin was a Marine gunnery sergeant in the Reserves. He was also a FEMA-certified rescue worker and had been to Oklahoma City after the bombing. They have three beautiful daughters," Dunne explained.

"Listen, I need to talk to you," Helga Curtin said.

"OK," Dunne replied.

"I keep telling my kids that there's a chance we can find Dad, you know, it's getting late. What can I do? What should I tell them?"

"Do you want to be honest with them?"

"Yes, I want to be honest with them."

"He's dead. It's been four or five days. If you and I were locked in a room for four or five days without water or food, we'd be close to death. If he was alive when the building came down, he would have been injured and he would have been pinned someplace. He couldn't possibly be alive. You need to prepare your daughters for the fact that he's dead."

"Well, I needed to hear that from somebody."

"It breaks my heart to tell you that."

"I know."

No formal announcement was made proclaiming when the rescue became a recovery. "It just gravitated to that," Dunne explained.

○ ○ ○ ○ ○ ○ ○

It was well past 1:00 A.M. when Grasso opened the door to his home in Queens. His wife, who had spent most of the day worried and distraught, quickly came down the stairs to greet him as he entered the house. He put down the bag with the tainted clothes he'd worn earlier that day. They hugged.

"It was close, very close, but thank God I made it. A lot of people aren't so lucky," Grasso said. His eldest son joined them in the kitchen and Grasso recounted the events of the day. He didn't omit his brush with death or the numbers listed as lost. At a time like this, he believed that secrecy would only breed anxiety. He assured his son that the country was strong and wouldn't be undermined. Before he went to bed, Grasso checked on his youngest son. The child looked peaceful in his sleep, and Grasso kissed him on the forehead.[45]

o o o o o o o

In the weeks after 9/11, Larry Dwyer and John English worked the midnight shift together on the pile. English recalled one night when they joined some cops working on Liberty Street who needed a relief team to help them dig a hole where they believed people were buried. "It was still burning," English said. They climbed over a mountain of debris to get to the location and then started to work about ten feet below. Each man dug for ten minutes and then was replaced by someone else, because the hole was so small they had to take their air packs off. English doesn't know what time they freed the dead Port Authority cops. Later, when he started digging on top of the chimney of the north tower, he found dishes from the restaurant, Windows on the World. He remembered another night a cop suddenly jumped off a huge pile of debris and alerted his colleagues to the fire beneath.

"Be careful, my shoes are melting," he'd warned. English went on to describe finding the remains of some of his friends. "I wasn't there when they found Mike Curtin, but I was glad they did. I was there when we found John D'Allara. We didn't know it was him until we found his boot and leg and his Spyderco knife. He was a big Spyderco knife guy. We didn't find much else, some fragments and stuff. . . . Mike Curtin was pretty much intact except for a couple of things, but most everybody else we pulled out was just pieces with the hope that maybe somebody would be able to identify them. It's amazing when you think that they're not with their families anymore. That's what bothers me. I'm with mine and I'm so grateful for it now more so than ever but the fact that they're not with theirs just kills me."

Around 2:00 A.M. on the third or fourth night working the pile, Dwyer suggested they take a ride to headquarters and talk to the families of the missing officers. "We walked in there and we got mobbed, rightfully so," English recalled. His cousins, Mr. and Mrs. Vigiano, and Helga Curtin were among the family members who came up to them and asked what was going on.

"Listen, I'm not going to tell you it looks great but what we're trying to do is find the voids. I'm not going to tell you we're optimistic but I'm still hopeful. It's still a possibility. But I'm not going to lie to you," English said, his words vibrating with contradictions he didn't quite recognize. "I tried to put a positive outlook on it, and I still had some hope but later on, my cousin told me that when I talked to them that night, he knew it was over."

"I could tell you were lying," his cousin told him.

"'I was trying not to," English responded.

"It wasn't that you could see you were lying, but you were the first ones that talked to us who'd come from the site."

Even today, years after the World Trade Center attack, English still thinks of his friends. "I drive past certain places in Brooklyn, I'll think about Mike Curtin or Tommy Langone, who also died. I remember one day me and Ray Buckowitz were in Seven Truck on Flatlands Avenue, which is part of our sector, and we see Tommy [Langone] and Jimmy [Leahy] there. I stopped and said, 'You guys poaching over here?'

'You know, you guys have better stuff going on,' Langone said.

'I miss it. I miss the ghetto, you know?' Leahy said. We laughed for an hour, just standing outside on the sidewalk. That's a small, insignificant thing, but every time I drive by there I think about that. I also think about Ronnie [Kloepter] and Santos [Valentin]. They were the most unlikely partners. Ronnie was a family guy and an athlete. He did everything with his family and he worked second jobs as a carpenter or plumber. Santos was single and smoked. He thought exercise was a waste of valuable time. He spent a lot of time on the computer in chat rooms. They were total opposites who worked perfectly together."

○ ○ ○ ○ ○ ○ ○

On the morning of September 12, 2001, Joe Dolan stepped out of his front door and looked across the street at his neighbor's house and saw six firemen's wives sitting on the front steps. "My wife said that she felt a little uncomfortable about that. You know, my husband survived and hers didn't, so I had to say something because I made it out of there," Dolan explained. He walked across the street, knocked on the door, and asked the man who answered if he could speak to his neighbor's wife. When she came outside, Dolan explained that he had been there for "the whole thing" and he hoped that "everything would work out." He nodded his head good-bye, turned around, and walked back into his house. "Every day they had a vigil out there, the six of them, and every day I'd walk out to go to work and see them sitting on the front porch. He was never found. He just disappeared. He was a young fireman, too. He had just gotten the job. I don't think they'll ever find him. People just went to work and disappeared."

For months Dolan could smell the burning rubble in the police vehicles that had been downtown. "I can tell you which ones they are. You could smell it in there. It's a distinct smell. I haven't smelled it since. I can only smell it there [at the site of the disaster] and, to this day, I go near the World Trade Center, I can still smell it. Maybe it's being in the area that makes me smell it, but I decided that there's a distinct smell of wet cement, wet paper, . . . decaying bodies, fire, burning rubber, and everything all mixed into one. . . . At certain times one smell will dominate, like the dank, musty smell of wet cement and blood and bodies that are smashed together, the smell that the human body would give off, whether it was decaying or not. You have that, and you have the smell of burning bodies that were in the rubble, leaking through the different openings. All different types of smells."

○ ○ ○ ○ ○ ○ ○

After the World Trade Center disaster, Keith Ryan was transferred from the Intelligence Unit back to Emergency Service for the duration of the search and recovery operation. His first few days, he was assigned to Bellevue Hospital to support the injured cops brought in. "We thought there would be so many casualties that every hospital would have been overwhelmed, not realizing that everybody was pulverized." When the department recognized that the few officers injured were treated in the first few days, Ryan was transferred to the morgue. "It got worse and worse as they brought more bodies in. There were a lot of firemen. It was painful to see. Most of them were decapitated or shredded. On some, you could see the fibers from their muscle, the way it was torn. It was really fucked up. I can't imagine what they went through in the last few seconds. I can't even imagine. One of the guys told me that he saw a woman with half her torso on the ground and her arms tied behind her back with wire. He figured she had to be one of the stewardesses," Ryan recalled.

Some days Ryan was assigned to the pile with other Emergency Service officers. As he described to me what he did and saw, he began to relive the sensory horror of the memory, as if the air in my living room was saturated with death. "The mind is an incredible animal because now I can smell and taste the morgue. I can taste the smoke. I can smell it like I'm leaning over the dirt and I'm getting that whiff of a corpse and I'm looking for a body but there's nothing there. I guess you can smell their DNA in the dirt and concrete dust. I keep digging but I can't find anything. I remember moving some dirt and putting my glove up to my face and I could smell death on my hand, along with PCBs and every other fucking thing that was there, all simulated into one product. It was hard, going into those voids and not finding anything. Then, every now and then, you would find body parts. We went into one void and found nothing but a torso and shredded clothes. We found a guy on the roof as flat as a pancake, so I imagine he was somebody who jumped out of one of the windows or was blown out.

"I can still see the faces of all the guys and how tired we were and how angry we were because the more we dug the angrier we got. . . . A month later, we kept going down to the pit. Everybody was looking for closure but you really couldn't get it, and it was just the strangest feeling. It was so somber there. I'll be the first one to tell you—I did not want to go down there every day after a while. It depressed the shit out of me. I flew down there with Gary and Eddie three out of five nights a week, sometimes four. A couple of guys just quit going. It got people a little bit bent, the sort of things that went on, but I think that we all just didn't know how to deal with it. It changed our whole way of life forever. I feel sorry for my kids. My kids will never grow up with the freedoms and the liberties that I had—never, not as long as these fucking people walk the face of the earth. They have no value for their own lives, why would they have any value for yours?

"One thing that survived was paper and résumés. We kept finding people's résumés, résumés that were rejected, with little comments on why they rejected them, and I would think, I bet you thought it was bad when you lost your job, but not now. Whoever wrote on these things is probably not here anymore. How many people have the idea that the person that rejected them saved their lives in some bizarre way? God has a funny way of doing things. It was hard going down to the armory. It was hard to support the president while we're still at war in Iraq. We do not associate a face with a death. Like when this happened, we heard all kinds of numbers; I thought there was 20, 30,000 people dead in that building. It's a number and, as great a number as it is, it's just a number. But when you went to the armory and you started seeing people post photos of the numbers, it's not a number now. Now it's a human being. I think if the news did what they used to do when I was a kid, like with Vietnam, where they would actually show the kid's photo, this shit would be over. If they showed these kids coming back blind, paralyzed, amputated. We know about the ones that don't come home, but what about the ones that do come home and have lost their limbs? You don't hear about it. Does anybody really know or see this shit? Does anybody? I think that if people saw and associated the face with the number, this war would be over. Bush would have never got elected."

o o o o o o o

After 9/11, Rich Teemsma spent his regular tour on patrol, picking up calls in the outer boroughs for Patrol as well as the Bomb Squad. "We took Queens and Brooklyn and just drove and picked up the jobs that came in." Sometimes, on his days off, he worked with other bomb technicians, observing detectives sift through debris in the landfill on Staten Island. At other times, he went to the hole and dug. His first day there he hooked up with sergeant Tommy Murphy and other guys from Emergency Service. "Don't go too deep in the pile," because it's dangerous, Murphy told them. It wasn't long before he ignored his own command. He and Teemsma both knew that Danny and other dead cops were buried under layers of beams.

"See you," Murphy said as Teemsma watched him ride the girders deep into the ground. Teemsma told an officer standing by to remember where he was heading, hopped on a girder, and followed in Murphy's wake. By this time the sergeant had disappeared in the earth and Teemsma was alone. "I got down about four floors. When I first got below everything and hit ground I saw this fire. I kept going down and then looked back and the fire was growing, and it got so big that I know the whole south part of this thing was gonna go. I went underneath a slab of concrete. Then there was a collapse and all this debris was coming down. Then I just shot up this mountain of crap and the next thing I know I was in a tree. I look across and there is this fireman just staring at me. My heart's going, 'You're scared.' My mask is clogged and I'm trying to breathe because I'm not going to take my mask off. I must have sat there for five minutes," Teemsma explained.

Then he went on to describe a discovery that still haunts him today. "One day I was down digging with this guy and he looks down and says,

'What is that?' I look, and I see a hand.

'Well, that is a hand,' I said. I picked it up and held it in my hand. It was the left hand of a female from the wrist up, no wedding ring, nothing, so I knew she wasn't married. The hand was beautiful. Sometimes you look at a woman's hands. It was manicured. It was beautiful. I thought of my daughter's hand. I connected with it. What does she look like? I'm thinking. She had to be beautiful. Her hands were beautiful. On 9/11 we had these ceremonies. I can't do them anymore. Walking through the crowd, everyone is holding these pictures of the people who were lost and every girl I looked at, it was like that was her with the beautiful hand. It plays on you really hard. Even today if I see a picture of a girl who died there I always think of that body part that I picked up. . . .

"At one point I was so exhausted. I was so much in shock. I was taking the train back and forth and I was on the train coming back home. I looked around and I couldn't recognize where I was anymore. I couldn't recognize the Bellmore Station stop where I parked my car. I stood up, and I asked the conductor, 'What station are we at?'

'Bellmore,' he said.

'Bellmore?'

'Yes.'

'Thanks a lot.' He looked at me—he knew where I'd been because of my clothes—and I remember him going back out to the door.

'You better take it easy,' he said." Rich Teemsma retired on January 25, 2002. He went down to One Police Plaza, signed out for the day, and handed in his shield. He left headquarters and went down to the World Trade Center to talk to Danny for the last time. "I walked down into the hole where I knew Danny was and I said, 'Sorry I didn't get you.' Then I went home. It was the hardest thing to leave a man. You shouldn't leave him there, but there was nothing I could do and they weren't going to start digging there until a couple of months down the line. They had it planned out where they were going to dig, and he was in the last spot when they found him six-and-a-half months later. He was the most preserved, but he was under the crease of a slab. So I hope he was killed instantly, but now I know he lived. They found him sitting up with his face in his knees. I guess he just went to sleep and died that way. I'm sure he had a lot of injuries. I just hope he didn't suffer. I think he did."

○ ○ ○ ○ ○ ○ ○

Paul Yurkiw worked at the landfill on Staten Island from September until Christmas when the twelve-hour shifts ceased. Detectives were assigned to sift through the debris in search of evidence, personal items, and human remains. Yurkiw and other Bomb Squad technicians observed the process in order to identify explosive parts. The first few days, officers were issued paper masks that provided little protection from the toxic dust. "They didn't work well because the mask got filled up with debris so quick that after a while you had to shake it out and put it back on your face again so the inside got contaminated as well as the outside. It tasted like you were breathing in very fine powder," Yurkiw explained. Detectives were also eating in the same area that they were working with contaminants. At some point Union president Tom Scotto threatened to pull out his officers if the situation didn't immediately improve. Joe Esposito reached out to Tom Scotto, acknowledged the problem, and asked for a little more time to address the issues at hand.

A few days later, a separate dining area was built and decontamination zones established where detectives could take showers. Still, a lot of officers neglected to clean up until they got home, partly because they didn't get overtime pay for using the facilities and bosses weren't ordered to enforce the rules. Machismo also played a role, denial of vulnerability, and also perhaps some dimension of guilt about surviving a catastrophe in which so many friends and colleagues had died.

While the physical situation improved, the operation continued to take an emotional toll. "It was absolutely terrible. I got there at night and left in the morning. We had lights in the area where they would dump the trucks full of new debris and it would be put on a long conveyer belt and sifted through by hand," Yurkiw explained. He and other Bomb Squad technicians answered detectives' questions and looked for explosive materials. "What looks to you like a top to a bottle could be some sort of device that was used in the jet. The spoon from a grenade you might think was a piece of tin. The pin might look like a key ring to you but to me it would look different. . . . I remember seeing a woman's foot with nail polish on it, part of a hand, bone fragments. Most of the flesh was gone so you'd see bone and part of the skin, like part of the foot, part of the toes. After a few weeks you couldn't see anything until someone brought it to your attention. It was like a blank stare. Pretty much everybody got on each others' nerves, from being exhausted, and Danny [Richards] was missing."

While he was working the landfill, Yurkiw sometimes thought of the crash of Flight 800 and also of Pearl Harbor. "We did the same sort of thing with the crash. . . . There were over three thousand people killed in Pearl

Harbor and we weren't at war with anybody, just like with 9/11. Something just happened unexpected. There is not a minute that I see a 747 go by, like when I'm on my boat, that I don't think of it coming down in your backyard. At the time of the Cuban missile crisis, we were the strongest country in the world. Now you look at Korea and all these other countries that have almost as much as we do. We are so thinned out because we have so many people in Iraq and Afghanistan. Over three thousand soldiers have been killed. There were so many signals before the attack on Pearl Harbor that should have been picked up on and it could have been avoided or wouldn't have been as bad as it was. Same thing with the World Trade Center."

o o o o o o o

One of the worst parts of the post-9/11 experience was the endless flow of funerals. "When the funerals began, I recall attending sometimes four or five in a day. When you lose 363 firemen and 60 police officers all in one day, the funerals seem endless.[46] I cried at every one. As a union president, I tried to honor them all but it got to the point where I was numb and I couldn't attend any more," Tom Scotto recalled.

"They were just horrible. It got to the point with everybody where you couldn't bear going to another one; to see the families and the kids. . . . At Vinnie Danz's funeral, I couldn't stop crying, I just couldn't. I liked Vinnie. He was a funny guy, great guy, normal, squared away guy. Rodney Gillis was the worst, to see his brother, his mom. Rodney was like a brother to me. I loved him like a brother. It made you angry, you know. There are so many assholes in the world, and God has to take somebody with so much talent and potential. Rodney could have been a four-star chief on this job. I named my kid after him, Mathew Francis Gillis. And Johnny is named after Chief Morange, John William," Ryan explained.

o o o o o o o

Joseph Dunne knows that there could have been many more police funerals. He is proud of how his cops and commanders performed on 9/11. Commanders made crucial decisions that saved the lives of hundreds of officers who would have been dead had they disobeyed orders and run blindly inside the building. Cops mobilized at their assigned locations and followed their bosses' orders. "Ronnie Wasson was the "CO" of Emergency Service. The Manhattan South Task Force reported to the location with about 50 or 60 cops. Their [commander's] idea was to go into the courtyard of the World Trade Center to direct and assist people out of there. This was before either building fell. Wasson told them, 'No fuckin' way. It's too dangerous in there. There's shit falling from the buildings and I don't want [our cops] out there, exposed.' They could have thrown another 50 or 60 into the pile of the dead if it wasn't for Ronnie's leadership skills and his intelligence and understanding of the event as it was unfolding," Dunne explained.

Lieutenant Larry Dwyer emerged from the wreckage a more thoughtful leader than I'd imagined he was from what I'd heard from some of his peers about his involvement in other incidents. During 9/11, he probably saved the lives of his team by ordering them to pull back and wait in a safe place. Sergeant Tommy Murphy also made a decision that kept his men alive, John English explained. "Tommy Murphy got there and his guys were going to go in but he told them they should go tactical because everybody else was doing rescue work. He felt somebody should take up a tactical mode; stay back and get suited up in case there was another attack of a different type. . . . So they weren't in there [when the buildings collapsed]. It saved their lives."

Some cops did run in the building. Police officers Moira Smith and her partner Bobby Fazio came down from the 13th Precinct, parked their car, and started to help the people who were inside. Moira was seen bringing two injured civilians outside and going back in for more. "We know the fourteen Emergency Service officers who were in there because we sent them in. The other nine were initial responders who ran in to help people. What they did was noble but they weren't directed in there. It's right that they were there. Don't get me wrong, but I think the way we were able to control our response to the event helped save lives. We wanted to have an organized, effective response and the only way to do that is to assess what's going on and then apply your personnel where they're going to be most useful. Our primary responsibility is not to mitigate the fire. That's the duty of the Fire Department. We have a small cadre of our Emergency Service people who are trained in that type of rescue and who had the equipment and were able to go into a smoky building with respirators. The rank and file don't have that. They don't belong in there. Our casualty rate could have been much higher. It was still awful to hear that we lost twenty-three people, murdered, in a few minutes," Dunne said.

Retired chief of the department Lou Anemone had been at the gym when he learned that a plane had hit the World Trade Center. He'd gone into the city to attend to his family, one of whom worked in the towers and was thought to be missing for a while. A day or so after the disaster, Chief Esposito walked him around the area. "It was sobering," Anemone said. "You turn to the guy who is next to you and say, 'Jesus, where would we have been? Would we have been here? Would we have known to pull back? Would we have been able to save somebody?'"

Conclusion

Readers want clean-cut stories with good and bad guys who exist within a black-and-white world. They want their heroes to emerge at the end of a narrative, if not unscathed, then transformed and newly able to love and work with joy, depth, intensity and success. Most everyone knows that such endings are figments of fantasy, sort of like winning the lottery, vaguely possible but highly unlikely developments that don't do justice to the dimpled complexity of human life. "Cops are people too," Rich Teemsma reminded me with a trace of a smile in his eyes. None of the police officers involved in the raid and its aftermath survived without scars, although some weathered conditions with sufficient resilience to temper the disappointments their work bestowed. "It's a job you love that doesn't love you back. That's a known fact," explained Bill Morange, as if those words could account for the roller coaster careers of five good NYPD cops and detectives and hundreds more like them of every rank. "Everyone leaves angry," a just retired NYPD inspector explained, referring to the ambivalence experienced by a multitude of officers of every rank when they finally decide to abandon the job to which they've devoted their lives and still love in their hearts.

RICH TEEMSMA

Rich Teemsma looks almost the same a dozen years after 1997, except his hair is mostly gray and a few extra lines crease the skin around his eyes and bury them deeper into his face. When Teemsma speaks of his decision to turn in his shield, he thinks of the 1997 job and how it made him stop, step back, and think before he dived into the wave of burning debris that flooded the streets after the planes struck in lower Manhattan. "You see, the Brooklyn job saved my life. . . . It was the way we were treated after that job by the job . . . that made me realize it wasn't worth staying and risking my life. I realized the mayor didn't really care. Normally I just go full speed ahead to do what I gotta do, but when I saw the towers hit, I knew they were coming down. I knew the job was over my head and I had to slow myself down. There was nothing we were going to do, and what was the point of getting killed? I'd be a headline for a couple of weeks. You ask anyone the names of the officers who died that day and they don't know. You see, after the Brooklyn job, I realized that they didn't really care what happened to us, and then 9/11 came along and I knew there was going to be another attack at some point. So why should I stay and wait for another attack and get killed?" Teemsma asked.

He went on to discuss the event that finally pushed him out the door. He was up for promotion again, this time by the lieutenant who had replaced Black as head of the Bomb Squad. The mayoral election had just taken place, and a new administration was soon coming in. "My lieutenant turned around and told me he couldn't get me promoted to detective second grade because they had to promote the chief's drivers . . . You see, it's all political," Teemsma explained.

Rich Teemsma enjoys his current job as manager-consultant for Homeland Security. He doesn't feel the loss of the NYPD because he's around cops all the time, giving classes on counterterrorism, bomb technology, and disaster management. He laughs and explains that teaching is like being in psychotherapy, "because what I do is I talk to cops every day. . . . I talk about how they can help others and themselves . . . so they can understand why certain things happen and what they can do. I tell them about 9/11 and about the cops who died. I love this job. I love cops. They're like my brothers and sisters. Now I get to help them to remember what happened and try to think a little bit about what they would do if it happened again. And it will happen again. So it's good therapy."

PAUL YURKIW

Paul Yurkiw has lost fifteen pounds and looks young, healthy, and strong. His hair is red with only a blush of white hiding beneath his ears. Yurkiw retired in April 2002. He does private corporate security and also works as a consultant-instructor with Homeland Security, teaching cops in Brooklyn.

Every now and then he brings in his bulletproof vest with the burn marks on the chest from when he was shot. He shows his students the vest and talks about what happened that day. He doesn't need to say much to get them to understand that they must always wear their ballistic-resistant gear. Sometimes he tells his classes about the 1997 bomb job in terms of the technical issues involved in dismantling IEDs (improvised explosive devices). He doesn't tell them about the other lessons he learned from the Brooklyn job that led him to retire as soon as he had twenty years in. He doesn't talk about the dissension and jealousy that mediates the world of police.

To this day, he believes that the issue of credit for the job was cut-and-dry. He doesn't understand why it had to sink into the childish political game of "who had the juice" to get recognition for what had been done. Yurkiw believes that the credit didn't belong to Mancini, Black, or Bajek or anyone else who acted as though they played a bigger role than they did and were nuzzling up to the top brass and playing power politics. It belonged to the officers who confronted the bombs "up personal," including the six men on the Emergency Service entry team and the two detectives from the Bomb Squad. He doesn't feel bitter now. The job opened his eyes and taught him who his friends were. It dawned on him then that the lives of the officers involved in the job mostly seemed to matter as a stepping stone to enhance some boss's career. Today Yurkiw doesn't talk a lot about the good and bad of the cop he once was. Now he enjoys being on his boat in the summer when the weather is nice. He loves sharing his time with his two grown sons. He pulled the boat out of the water early this year to spend more time with his family.

JOHN ENGLISH

John English still looks youthful but also wizened and weathered from all he has seen. There's little gray in his short brown hair, but he struggles to control his weight and stay healthy and fit. He didn't want to retire from Emergency Service in March 2003, when he did, but after putting his heart into one project after another and never getting promoted to sergeant special assignment, he knew it was time to leave. Now he works for another law enforcement agency with Carlos, his Belgian Shepherd partner whom he trained in narcotics detection. English talks about his decision to retire from the NYPD by describing a conversation he had with a chief whom he ran into while he was working at JFK Airport. The chief knew English had been in Emergency Service and wanted to know when and why he got out.

"I'll be honest with you," English explained. "I loved the job until the day I left, but it was primarily financial. I kind of got sick of seeing the sergeant from Telephone Control get special assignment or the sergeant from the video unit. I'm ten years in ESU, going through doors after people . . . I let it be known to all my bosses that if I got special assignment, I'd probably stay because financially I could justify it, but if not, then I can't stay. They said that 'I really can't tell you you're going to get it.' So I left."

"I'm a three-star chief and I can't even get somebody special assignment," the chief replied, referring perhaps to the current police commissioner—whom another commander called a "bottleneck" boss because he controls everything, including promotions and transfers. "Years ago, you used to go to these things [i.e., retirement affairs] about every seven years, and people had twenty-eight or thirty years on, but not anymore. Now it's just twenty years." The chief went on to explain, somewhat sadly, how the department has changed. I guess he remembered the days when police officers viewed their work as a calling, not just a job.

During the summer of 2009, English gave a talk about the 1997 raid at a conference on special weapons and tactics. He lauded the bravery of Chindluri, the Muslim informant, noted the contribution of the Long Island Railroad cops who helped bring him into the precinct, and discussed the tactical plan and the confrontation with the suspects. He did not mention the political lunacy that followed in the wake of the entry. Still, when he reflects on the raid and its aftermath, he feels a flash of irritation.

"I think Joe, Keith, Mario, and Mike should have been promoted to detective that day, and the fact that they weren't underscores how that whole administration was. Nobody expected anything but when you see people getting promoted to detective specialist for coming up with a great computer program that they're able to use at CompStat, and then these four guys don't' get promoted. Or in my case, it would have been like a sergeant in the Telephone Control Unit who got promoted to sergeant special assignment because he got the chief cell phones every year. Those are the things that annoy you on the job. The fact that these guys didn't get promoted really annoyed me," English confessed.

JOE DOLAN

Joe Dolan still wears the mischievous grin that lends his handsome face a boyish look. He lifts weights and is almost as powerful as he was in his youth. The sleeve tattoos that were only half-formed when we first met are complete now and cover both his arms. Dolan "pulled the pin" in 2003, sold his house on Staten Island, and left New York. I wasn't the only one of his acquaintances and friends who didn't know he'd retired until he and his family were already living down south. Now he works on patrol and as a member of the bomb squad in a local police department and is a drummer in the pipe band. Dolan didn't tell me why he left so abruptly. I imagine he got tired of dealing with bosses and politics and decided it wasn't worth the emotional sacrifice.

He did talk about one of the catalysts that led him to transfer out of Emergency Service shortly before 9/11. He was involved in an incident in which an Emergency Service cop was shot and left behind by his sergeant during a firefight. Instead of helping the wounded officer out, the sergeant ran into the street and took cover behind a car. A few seconds later, a lieutenant and a group of Emergency Service cops went into the hallway and pulled the officer to safety with Dolan helping from the other side of the door. It angers Dolan that the sergeant was never held accountable for his actions and was still in Emergency Service when Dolan retired. What I found striking in his account was how it echoed a central theme of this book: that too many bosses seem to abandon their cops or leave them unprotected in order to save themselves or proffer some gain.

Like the other cops and detectives involved in the raid, Dolan is convinced that Safir could have handled their concerns better than he did. Dolan also thinks they made a mistake by not going along with the press conference as though there was no risk. Still, it irks him to see how Giuliani continues to use the 1997 job to promote himself in the public eye. "Giuliani was in London and they [the reporters] were talking about the terrorist attack on the buses and subway and he turned around and said, 'Not too long ago back in '97, we thwarted a terrorist attack in the subways of New York.' It was on the news. Can you beat that? He's still standing on his fucking soapbox over that thing. Nobody else is walking around talking about it, but there he is in London. He hasn't been mayor since 2002 and he couldn't have given less of a shit about that job when it happened because he didn't get enough political gain out of it and now he's up on his soapbox every time it becomes convenient for him," Dolan explained.

I didn't tell Joe Dolan about Safir's portrayal of the raid in his book, *Security: Policing Your Homeland, Your State, Your City.* Safir stresses the damage that could have incurred had his police officers not intervened. Safir seems to have revised his original portrayal of the terrorists as isolated extremists: "Abu Mezer had been arrested in Israel and was linked to the Hamas movement." At the same time, he suggests that he was aware then that the plot might involve more people and an extended plot. "During [a several-week period after the raid], additional officers were assigned all over the city because we were unsure how far-reaching the scope of their plan was."[1] I don't know whether the transformation in his depiction of the terrorists reflects a post-9/11 reconstruction or an effort to seek political and economic benefit by redefining the threat.

Like many official shooting reports, Safir's account erases the ambiguity that haunted the real event and creates facts where uncertainty exists. He writes that "ESU opened fire when, after officers yelled, 'Police! Don't move!' one of the suspects lunged for a bomb in his backpack. The bomb was built to be detonated by three switches, and the terrorist flipped two of the three switches before they [the cops] shot him and wounded the other suspect."[2] In reality, the officers didn't "open fire" at the same time when one of the suspects lunged for the bag. As far as I know, the bomb was not designed to go off when "three" switches were turned on. The four switches were redundant, and no one was sure why the device didn't go off when one—not two—was put in the on position. It's a stretch to present as absolute truth that one of the terrorists touched the switch when he lunged for the bomb, although the officers assumed this was the case in retrospect.

I also didn't tell Dolan that Safir's account doesn't fully acknowledge the officers who were directly involved in the job. He doesn't name the six officers on the entry team, although none would object at this point in history. He doesn't discuss the role of the detectives who dismantled the bombs. Instead, he stresses that the Emergency Service officers weren't the only heroes and names Chief Charles Kammerdener as the reigning champion. In so doing, Safir might be following informal rules that dictate that the most senior commander gets the credit regardless of who does what. It's also possible that his most recent account of the raid reflects lingering resentment at the cops for giving him a hard time.

The last time I spoke at length with Joe Dolan, I asked him about his tattoos. One depicts the face of Jesus Christ rising over the backdrop of the

Twin Towers. The other, commemorating the 1997 raid, portrays Michael and the Seven Deadly Sins. Dolan explained that he "wanted Michael the Archangel but I didn't want the usual Michael standing on the devil. I felt after the Brooklyn bomb job that someone was there helping us so I thought of the patron saint of police officers. I thought of the one who cast the devil out of heaven and I figured it was him [who helped us survive that job]. There's one head and one torso for each of the seven sins and they all wind around into a circle. I didn't want the usual one devil because, being a cop, you battle so many different things. The devil is found in so many different places and different ways. Cops just have an array of things to constantly put up with, and they get bombarded every day."

KEITH RYAN

Keith Ryan has the same short blond hair and scar punched into the side of his face that he's always had although I hardly see it now. He is heavier than he was in 1997 but has recently lost weight. He still radiates the same intelligence and competence. The vibrant smile that once lit up his face appears but with less frequency than before. Ryan retired in April 2007, more than a year after he was back working full-time in the Intelligence Division. After he left the department, Ryan worked for a few years as head of security at a hotel, then decided to go back on patrol with a specialized law enforcement organization. He also does executive dignitary protection.

The high point in his career as a detective in the NYPD came some years after 9/11, when police commissioner Ray Kelly appointed Charles Kammerdener the chief of the Special Operations Division and Ryan became his driver. As such he acted the role of a loyal subordinate and an administrative lieutenant, organizing the chief's schedule, and dealing with bosses and cops in ways "the K-man" probably didn't know about but appreciated none the less. As demanding as the chief could be, Ryan welcomed the challenge of working for him and grew to love the man as a partner and friend. In turn, Kammerdener loved and respected Ryan and treated him like a son sometimes.

Ryan remains as devoted to Chief Kammerdener today as he was in 1997 when he uttered the words during the briefing that helped convince Ryan that he had support from his boss. "My first encounter with [Kammerdener] was one of the most positive encounters with anybody. . . . The fact that he believed in us that night and gave us that reflection is what saved us, because I wasn't afraid to go in there and do what I had to do, based on his attitude," Ryan said.

Once I spoke to "Chief K" on the phone to inquire about a personal issue unrelated to this book and happened to mention Ryan's name. Kammerdener's voice turned as warm as the tropical sun and I could almost see the smile spreading across his lean, tough, generation-Vietnam, former Marine face. While working for Chief K, Ryan became more like the man he was before the raid; humble but dignified and easy to get along with. His good humor returned, he smiled easily and he seemed to walk more lightly on his feet like the slim, gifted athlete he'd been in his youth. "No wonder," a chief from another bureau explained when we were talking about the positive changes in Keith, "the K-man treats him well." Still, Ryan missed then and misses today being just a cop in Emergency Service, assigned to a truck on patrol, hanging out with guys at quarters, exchanging jokes, stories, complaints, pranks, and landing in the "pickle barrel" once in a while.

Ryan's thoughts about the raid and its aftermath are similar to those of Dolan, Teemsma, and English. He cannot forgive Howard Safir for the "disgraceful" way he treated the cops on the entry team, as if what they did was "insignificant." "They didn't take care of us . . . They didn't protect us like they should have. . . . and we did the right thing." He went on to reflect on how the 1997 job changed him as a man. "I hated everyone then. I didn't trust anyone. Why do you think I wear a gun all the time and carry so many extra rounds of ammunition? That job changed me. I've never been the same. I guess I'm the perfect cop for the department. They can beat me into the ground and I'll come back and work as hard. I'm tired now. They do nothing to keep cops here. It doesn't matter how hard you work. The last time my lieutenant said I'd be getting promoted, I told him, 'Thanks, but I'm fed up with their dangling a carrot in front of my face.' I'm not Bugs Bunny. I'm a lot like Elmer Fudd. I've been passed over too many times. I know it's not him. He's a really good guy, a blessing for all of us . . . At least I can hold my head up. . . . Still, I will never feel right about the way that they punished us and my own feelings of guilt and remorse that I hurt the entire team because I chose not to talk. It hurt them financially. Sometimes I wonder how things would have gone if we would have done everything they wanted. I don't know. Would I have been a first-grade detective now? Would I have sold myself out and lost my soul? I can't ponder what I could have been. I have to go on what is.

If I pondered what could have been, I would lose my mind. I feel terrible that I hurt other people in the process who didn't deserve to be hurt, and I wish to God I could make it up to them."

A supervisor in Emergency Service who knew and respected Ryan and Dolan also attributed the changes he saw in both men to the 1997 Brooklyn job although he emphasized the danger to which the officers were exposed as a result of the tactical plan. "To this day, I believe Joe Dolan and Keith Ryan still carry this heavy weight on their shoulders that there was a good chance they would have died that day. Joe Dolan put a tattoo of the seven deadly sins from the top of his shoulder to the bottom of his elbow. I believe it was because of that [job] that he put it on there as a constant reminder that he saw God that day and these are the seven sins that he must always be cognizant of in order to get his life into perspective. So I think that impacted on Joe. I see Keith's still carrying this weight on his shoulders. He is always very contrite and a little bit reflective. As I remember him [before the raid], he had been more upbeat, more light in his spirit. He loved his job and got along with everybody. He was very harmonious in his approach, in his personality. I don't see that anymore. I think that September 11th just reinforced what he already knew. . . . What did happen on 9/11 could have happened on that night [in 1997], and it profoundly impacted on his life in a negative fashion."

Ryan recently went to a party where he met a distinguished gentleman by the name of Dean Pregerson. Pregerson was nominated by President Bill Clinton in 1996 to the position of United States district court judge, Central District, California, where he remains. When Pregerson learned who Ryan was and what he and the team had done in 1997, he responded with warmth and surprise. "My God! You're what this country is all about. You're a hero. You guys are all heroes," he said. "I'm just a guy who did a job, and by the grace of God I came out alive," Ryan replied.

BILL MORANGE AND RAY MCDERMOTT

Bill Morange retired a few years after the World Trade Center disaster when police commissioner Ray Kelly requested he transfer from chief of Patrol to the Organized Crime Control Bureau [OCCB]. "He [Kelly] told me I really need you over there, that's what I want. And you know with this job you gotta be a team player and I went there, but . . . from that moment on, I knew that I wasn't going to stay. I hit the rank I wanted to hit, never figuring that I would. It's like the poor kid in the neighborhood, sitting in the best seats in Yankee Stadium. I had [more than thirty years] of a great career and never had any problems, and I walked out of there with my head held high, and there aren't too many chiefs who can say that. What more is there? But in reality the job was good to me." Morange is now working as director of security at a public company. One of the first things he did when he got into office was to promote the cops outside the NYPD who had helped bring Chindluri into the 8-8 Precinct station house.

Ray McDermott retired around the same time as Morange. He currently works under Morange as his chief of security. According to rumor, McDermott was forced out of the department because of a personality conflict with first deputy commissioner George Grasso. McDermott denies that he and Grasso were ever at odds and attributes his retirement to an injury he sustained in 2000. "I'd like to say it was heroic, but it wasn't. I fell on the ice and ended up breaking my ankle pretty badly so they put plates and screws in my ankle. The commanding officer of [an outside] division suggested I follow him inside, so I left SOD. Not long after that I worked for Joe Dunne and, after he retired, for George Grasso. Then the medical board told me to put in my papers, and I did."

When McDermott reflects on the raid and its aftermath, he affirms the seriousness of the incident and asserts his belief that the terrorist suspects were connected to a larger terrorist organization. To this day, he regrets that none of the cops on the entry team were promoted. "Looking back, they [the cops] were 100 percent right, you know, you don't compromise your people's security. . . . The problem we had is—and knowing a little more now that I can't get into–but the people that were involved were not just your local friends from around the block, and to think that there were just two of them is kind of having your head in the sand. I think we learned from 9/11, so I mean, you know, you don't—the way I looked at it is that you have an ongoing investigation, you're parading people around and telling them you should'a just—you know. They should have promoted these people. . . . Every one of those men deserved to be promoted, and Bill Morange will say the same thing. . . . They did an unbelievable thing, and they took us to the next level of what we do."

I don't have access to the information McDermott was referring to when he suggested that the terrorists weren't "just your local friends from around the block." I did see intelligence reports written in 2003 confirming that "Mezer and Khalil do not appear to have had ample time, funds or familiarity with the region to have planned and implemented the subway bombing plot without logistical and financial support either from individuals acting independently or from members of an organized group."

THE CULTURE OF POLICING

The story of the raid and its aftermath brings to light a number of features of police organization and culture that have not been fully addressed in the scholarly literature. In her book, based on fieldwork done in the NYPD in the late 1970s, Elizabeth Reuss-Ianni proposed that there are two cultures of policing, which do not share a common vocabulary, work experience, or set of objectives.[3] Management cop culture finds meaning in the theories and practices of scientific management. Police executives minimize the importance of informal personal relationships and information networks and seek to bring rationality and efficiency to the job. Rank-and-file cops derive meaning from the situational exigencies encountered on the street rather than in formal dictates delivered from above. Decisions arise during the flow of interaction, and patterns are evident only when cops pause and reflect in retrospect.[4]

In terms of this study, the differences between cops and management did not revolve around issues of scientific management such as CompStat and other measures of productivity and performance that weren't particularly relevant to the specialized units involved. Instead, differences arose in terms of the strategic management of outside organizations and, most important, the perception of risk. The mayor and the police commissioner appeared to view danger in terms of the public and the media. They saw the raid as a high-profile, newsworthy event that could be used as a vehicle to maximize the image of the department and reap political benefit. In their eyes, the job had the potential to increase public support at a time when the Giuliani administration was under attack for their aggressive "zero-tolerance" policing policies that appeared to target minorities and the poor.[5]

Publically, in interviews with the press, Safir and Giuliani thus emphasized the seriousness of the terrorist plot and the damage the suspects could have wreaked had the police not acted in a timely and courageous fashion. Behind the scenes, a different script was unfolding. Safir minimized the dangerousness of the suspects by presenting them as lone extremists. I don't doubt that he thought he was right. Insulated from physical danger, his sense of truth and notion of right and wrong bolstered by most of his staff, he could only see the officers' actions in terms of a threat to his interests. Safir thus appeared to interpret the cops' hesitation to appear at the press conference as an affront that was linked to the political challenges he had to negotiate every day with minority organizations, advocate groups, the media, and the unions.

In contrast to management, the cops in Emergency Service perceived danger in terms of surveillance by reporters, the public, and superiors in the event the shooting turned out bad, but mostly in terms of the street. For them, the raid was a life-and-death struggle with terrorists that could possibly escalate if they were exposed in a high-profile media event. Their sense of vulnerability was increased by the uncertainty surrounding the identities of the suspects and the ambiguity and unfamiliarity of dealing with Muslim suicide bombers. They could not so easily dismiss the plot as the intention of isolated individuals who weren't connected to a larger organization. By attempting to limit their public appearance, the officers were only doing what they'd learned on the job by minimizing their "threat angles" and ensuring their backs weren't exposed.[6]

In the wake of Safir's angry reaction to their actions surrounding the press conference, the officers became "culturally hypervigilant" and began to interpret every ambiguous communication as harassment or revenge coming directly from the top. This included issues surrounding the selection of medals, Safir's refusal to accompany the officers to Washington to meet President Clinton, the conflicting directives surrounding wearing their uniforms to the Top Cops ceremony, and the threatening phone call to McDermott ordering him back to New York. It was hard for Teemsma and Yurkiw to believe that Black could sabotage their chances for promotion without collusion at the level of the top brass, although Black could have used the self-promotion versus the team rationale to convince Anemone without Safir and Kelleher being aware. I can't fathom why Ryan and Dolan didn't get the Combat Cross unless Safir or Giuliani was involved. Certainly, Safir and Giuliani bore responsibility for the fact that none of the officers on the entry team or detectives in the Bomb Squad got promoted after the raid.

Whoever was responsible for what mixed message, confusion, slight, or attempt to intimidate, the cops resented the way they were treated by the department they served. "I realize that the priorities of the job have to be a certain way, but you cannot have priorities for just the job and forget about the guys; forget about your cops because that's what makes for a lot of animosity and your cops get lost in the shuffle," Joe Dolan explained. I would add that, in situations involving serious physical risk, we cannot expect street cops to suddenly shift their way of understanding the world to suit the needs of high-ranking officials whose sense-making activities revolve around a different set of priorities and notions of danger and risk.

CONFLICT AND CONNECTION: STREET COPS AND MANAGEMENT

While differences between street cops and management were evident in the varied interests and different constructions of danger exhibited by each group, the notion of two distinct and oppositional cultures does not do justice to the power politics involved and the complexity of specialized units and the police organization as a whole. Sociologist Peter Manning notes how the task dependence existing between rank-and-file police and superiors creates a web of solidarity that is reinforced by an informal network of highly personal relations of exchange that link cops, supervisors, and top brass and softens the distinctions in worldview.[7] Vertical as well as horizontal cliques arise situationally, binding cops and superiors. Just these types of horizontal and vertical cliques combined with other factors to hurt Ryan, Dolan, Teemsma, and Yurkiw in various ways.

The division between outside and inside cops and bosses mediates and softens the distinction between the two cultures of policing such that some executives understand and even share street cops' perspectives in certain respects. Outside, cop's cop bosses like Ray McDermott and Bill Morange risked their careers to try and protect the men on the entry team in regards to the turmoil surrounding the press conference. McDermott intervened on Ryan's behalf and ensured his transfer to another squad when he encountered trouble in Six Truck. Morange and McDermott recognized that Ryan and Dolan were some of their best cops and helped them transfer into other specialized units, dismissing the rumors emanating from their former squads as products of jealousy.

In another expression of leadership by a cop's cop, Joe Dunne disobeyed the police commissioner's orders and instead remained with his officers during 9/11, putting his own life at risk so he could protect them as he saw fit. With deputy commissioner George Grasso acting bravely as interference, Dunne also put the interests of the missing officers' families above the demands of commissioner Bernie Kerik, who insisted on speaking with Dunne right away. Had Kerik had real power and been more than Giuliani's sycophant, he might have retaliated for their recalcitrance by putting them in "the penalty box," but that was a risk Dunne and Grasso were willing to take.

Cop's cop bosses bring sanity and balance to police officers' lives, protect them when they are right, and soften the frustrations they meet during the ups and downs of their careers. The problem is not that such men don't exist in the Police Department. As we have seen, they are spattered abundantly throughout the ranks. The problem is that it takes only one or two troublesome bosses to wreak havoc with a good cop's life, infect his personality, and undermine the pleasure and enjoyment he or she finds in the job.

While a division between management and street cops appears in certain situations, this case reveals the multiple ways in which spatial separation of inside and outside soften the hierarchical division between ranks. The dominance of an informal system of exchange also binds members of the rank and file and supervisors to officers at the top of the organization. This study further reveals how different leadership styles among bosses influence the behavior of subordinates, binding them in relationships of loyalty or pushing them away and encouraging them to be passive-aggressive in the way they respond to orders or sometimes politely disobedient if disobedience is necessary to do their jobs with minimal risk. This was evident when Rich Teemsma refused Black's order to dismantle the primary devise first and, again, when both detectives hid the photographs so they could use them to help determine the safest approach. I don't doubt that Teemsma's straightforward approach to dealing with Black's effort to rush the job to show superiors the work of his team and, I assume, claim credit for the success, increased Black's irritation and possibly his desire for revenge.

SUPERVISORS AND COPS

Studies of police deviance and corruption have emphasized the importance of frontline supervision for maintaining the professionalism of the police.[8] What hasn't been fully addressed is how bosses can influence the motivation and commitment of good cops who are positively invested in their roles, feel accountable for their actions, and strive to protect and serve the public as best they can. Bosses are human beings whose particular interactional styles may mesh better with certain cops. Some rank-and-file officers also have more tolerance for the "my-way or the highway," "breathe down your neck," authoritarian style found at every level of the police organization. Other cops experience this kind of management as a strangling disincentive, discouraging motivation and hard work. Only in rare cases do rigidly punitive responses to actions perceived as deviant facilitate reform, improve performance, or increase the allegiance of cops. They mostly do the opposite by creating fear, resentment, and rage when basically good people are involved.

Police bosses don't take lessons in leadership psychology and have to do what they think is best in the way that suits their own personality and management style. Some bosses are naturally empathic and intuitively brilliant at handling people in a way that minimizes conflict and maximizes the productivity of the people they lead. Others prefer to dictate and control rather than understand behavior and negotiate different resolutions, depending on what suits different individuals. Some bosses are also more prone than others to engage in ugly gossip to help neutralize guilt for the aggression that accompanies their punitive acts or simply to let off steam, resulting in further isolation of the target and an increase in his helplessness and rage. Some bosses in the NYPD would argue that fear-and-intimidation, control-freak, authoritarian-style managers are an important complement to other types who don't want to take on the role of the squad pit bull. Cops play games, they would say, and a variety of methods are necessary to keep them under control.

Machismo also rules a lot of interactions, and diffusion techniques for dealing with people, such as stepping back from a confrontational situation and responding with neutrality or kindness, are sometimes viewed as weak. The punitive tactics of bosses may sometimes be more severe than intended because they engage the sadistic impulses of the group to further penalize those involved. Activation of cruelty in otherwise decent men is made easy in Emergency Service, because the unit and those who compose it generally have minimal tolerance for what they perceive as weakness, difference, sensitivity, or fragility among peers. Self-reflection is not a strong point among officers, particularly in high-action units. After all, negotiating a career in Emergency Service involves high-testosterone politics in which self-esteem partly depends on displays of toughness and nerve and in which a minor error in judgment can not only cause embarrassment but also kill.

Exploring the dynamics of the negative attitudes police develop toward the expression of sad and painful emotions, sociologists Pogrebin and Poole note that police "are unable to reveal their feelings to fellow officers, much less discuss them, for fear of being viewed as inadequate."[9] It may be too much to ask action-oriented men who tend to have a black-and-white approach to life to be sensitive to how subordinates feel, feeling being the real "f" word in the NYPD. Yet I have known some very tough men who practiced the "f" word even if they were loath to use it in conversation. One was a former Special Forces soldier who is responsible for managing people assigned to missions in combat zones. Certainly cop's cops like Bill Morange or Ray McDermott were sensitive to the deeper human issues that infused the lives of their officers and practiced the "f" word, too, although *fuck* remains the most frequently used four-letter word beginning with the letter *f* in the vocabularies of even the highest-ranking bosses in the department.

This brings us to a question. Is there a way to train officers to be better leaders of men and women without the training becoming part of the endless stock of exercises that are perceived as a waste of time, touchy-feely psychobabble forced down their throats from above involving principles that few superiors bother to follow themselves? Can a system of checks and balances be implemented in a bureaucracy like the NYPD that would encourage interpersonal reflection and communication without disempowering competent supervisors who must have the support of their senior commanders in order to effectively manage and control the troops?[10] It remains unclear whether top leaders are born or made. If it were possible to implement some such training, it might only enlighten those who would learn through experience anyway.

CONFLICT WITHIN THE RANK AND FILE

By placing emphasis on the strength of the brotherhood that binds rank-and-file officers to each other and distances them from supervisors and higher level management, we overlook several features of police culture that were evident among the elite units studied here. It isn't enough to say there is variation within street cop culture or that cops invoke different normative orders to guide their behavior depending on situational variables and policing styles.[11] There are deep fissures within the world of street cops, animosities and jealousies that fracture the notion of police as a brotherhood. In his study of police corruption, Maurice Punch notes that the organization became "a cauldron of emotions, rumor, infighting, vendettas and guerilla activity" when corruption investigations take place by external agencies.[12] John Van Maanen suggests that, to some degree, distrust, duplicity, and animosity lurk in certain locales under more ordinary circumstances when threats from outside aren't involved.[13]

Cop culture may be more contentious than the "dysfunctional family" metaphor that police typically use to depict the turbulence that sometimes characterizes the relationships in their world. The discord that can arise when individual officers are recognized for special accomplishments may be as troublesome as when the reverse occurs and officers turn their backs on colleagues under investigation for corruption. Within the sometimes jealous world of the police, the rules that structure relations between officers may be violated with impunity in situations in which tensions are raised. Some officers in Emergency Service ratted on others who did not represent a danger on the job, although such allegations were used to justify the officer's isolation and punishment. Peers thus alerted Rizzo that Ryan had had an argument in quarters that resulted in the damaged table. One or more police officers alerted Rizzo when Dolan and Ryan left their post in Central Park. One of the reasons Ryan got into trouble when he put the locker in the shower stall was because unfriendly cops "dropped a dime."

Scarcity aggravates competition and increases jealousy, and cops can be vicious when they think a peer is getting something special or is moving ahead at a faster rate. "If you're working a busy truck and one squad gets a [serious] job, then the other guys are OK because they know, down the line, they'll be next. But when you are in a truck where it's slow then there's a lot of jealousy when a big job comes along," one Emergency Service cop explained. Jealousy surrounding the officers who were involved in the raid was also a factor in creating dissension in the Bomb Squad. "For some reason, Paul [Yurkiw] and I were always getting the big jobs and, after a while, they [the guys in the unit] were asking why. I didn't know. What could I say? I guess it was my bad luck. Like with Fatty McGuire, me and Paul, we already had medals, and McGuire never got a medal. So he was jealous of Paul and me getting invited to all of these affairs after the Brooklyn job, and he started a lot of rumors, and the other guys joined in. McGuire was angry because he let 'the big one' slip out of his hands," Teemsma explained.

Jealousy spawned rumors and exacerbated tensions in the squads, resulting in the negative labeling of particular cops. Joe Dolan addressed the damage that rumors can wreak, noting that "rumor can be as damaging as fact because, if it catches on, pretty soon you're under the weight of it and, if everyone starts saying the same thing, it becomes fact even if it's not. . . . They used to say that, if you do something stupid and you get yourself in trouble, for a little while you're in the barrel, but it's not going to last too long because right behind you there's somebody else who is going to do something stupid and get themselves in trouble, too. It always seemed to me that the guy behind Keith who got in trouble, his trouble would end quicker and then it would spring back to Keith again. I don't know why."

One of the rumors that bore a heavy weight revolved around the issue of boasting or self-promotion. Mancini may have contributed to the problem by talking about the raid in terms of the publicity and profit it could attract. A book written by his friend presents a distorted account of the raid that confirms Mancini's reputation for opportunistic self-aggrandizement and possibly Dwyer's as well. Author Samuel M. Katz thus presents Dwyer and Mancini as playing starring roles that they didn't play during the real event as if they are preparing for parts in a movie. Katz describes Dwyer as "dragging [suspect] Lafi Khalil by the arm, hoisting his motionless body across the courtyard, and then dropping him by Mancini's legs. 'Hey dude,' [Dwyer] smiled and said, as if greeting [Mancini] on a bright sunny day at the annual ESU barbecue. 'Can you keep an eye on him?'"[14] In Katz's account, Mancini and Kammerdener hoisted the suspects onto a stretcher and brought them out to EMS.[15] Everyone I interviewed confirmed that Ryan, English, and McDermott carried the suspects from the apartment to the ambulance with no stops in between. Other distortions appear similar in that they present Kammerdener, Mancini, and Dwyer, the three former Housing police officers, in the most central light, exacting revenge, I suspect, for the problems they experienced years before when the Housing Police Department was merged into the NYPD.[16]

While several sources told me that Mancini continued to talk about the raid long after the fact, no one could confirm that they'd heard Ryan and Dolan boast out loud. According to Dolan, such rumors were false. "I always contested, Mike Keenan always contested, Keith [Ryan] always contested, John English always contested, Mario always contested; this was nothing more than a warrant execution, nothing more than a hit. That's all it was. It was a room entry, no more or less. You open the door, you're going in and you take care of the problem. . . . We never said we did anything special. I don't know if that aggravated people more than if we had walked around and said that we were great. I don't know what about that job [changed things]. It wasn't a problem with a lot of the cops but a lot of the bosses had comments."

The rumors that got linked to Ryan and Dolan likely intensified in the light of the simmering tension between them and Rizzo, who seemed disposed to find them wanting while sometimes turning a blind eye when his own cops did something wrong. Ryan and Dolan were not the only officers who bore responsibility for bad decisions surrounding the broken car door. It wasn't as if Ryan's anger at the lazy cop who refused to take the job with the off-duty officer was totally unprovoked. Rizzo would probably disagree and offer an alternative account. This is one of those instances in which there is point of view but no absolute right or wrong. After all, in many ways Rizzo was an example of a boss who held cops accountable in a manner the public and the department would approve of, although Jack Cambria did the same thing but with a different interactional style. Rizzo justified his actions in several ways that superiors in the department probably wouldn't fault. He appealed to higher loyalties when he said that he didn't want Ryan to keep a locker in the shower stall in case the water was needed to decontaminate personnel in the event of a biochemical hazard. He also claimed he was protecting the unit against an embarrassing scandal if Ryan's locker was vandalized and an inquiry was launched from above. He denied injury by claiming he punished cops with bad assignments but rarely wrote them up in a way that would hurt their career.[17] He was clearly a strong boss who took pride in his role as being the truck disciplinarian and experienced little cognitive dissonance or internal conflict.

Regardless of accusations of self-promotion and the officers' denials that they publically boasted about what they did, it defies imagination that so many officers in the unit insisted the raid was routine. Every cop and boss knew the job was unusual and very dangerous. The tactics had been practiced before. Had Ryan and Dolan been off that night, the other officers assigned to their sector would probably have handled the job. Ryan and Dolan also couldn't have done what they did without the contribution of all the police involved. Nevertheless, the two officers played a highly significant role. All six officers on the entry team risked their lives when they volunteered to go into a situation knowing that bombs were involved.

Only Ryan and Dolan risked their careers knowing that they would likely have to fire their weapons at suspects who weren't traditionally armed. This meant that the two officers had to be willing to use lethal force if the suspects moved in any way that could be interpreted as a threat.

"The cops are going in there prepared to shoot anything that moves. The room is dark. Once they're inside that room, they don't have time to assess if there are really bombs in the room. They can't wait to be sure that the bag the informant claims is inside is there at all. No, whether or not they saw a bag, I can't tell you. I wasn't there but maybe not. If they hadn't done what they did, the job could have literally blown up in their face and some of them would have been killed. If there wasn't a bag or bombs, they would have had to live with the fact that they'd shot innocent men and there's a real question whether the department would have backed them up," one commander explained.

Joe Dolan alluded to the ambiguity of the situation in several accounts. "When you open the door and it's two people with no weapons who start moving around. . . . You have got to remember in the back of your head that the guy doesn't have a gun or knife in his hand and I am shooting an unarmed man at this point. My career is going right down the toilet if these guys are reaching for their socks. . . . [After the shooting] I thought they were dead because they were turning gray. . . . I'm like, all right, we've got two dead guys in handcuffs. Not only is my career dangling but my whole life is dangling in front of me saying, all right, these guys didn't have a gun in their hand. You know that they were moving to something but what were they moving for?"[18]

Not that the utilization of routine tactics in more ordinary situations involving suspects in possession of knives or guns is a guarantee of success. To some degree, every suspect encounter is unpredictable and may demand a flexibility that isn't decreed in formal procedure and prearranged tactical plans. Karl Weick's 1993 analysis of why firefighters died in the 1949 Mann Gulch disaster provides an example. Only the firefighters who violated procedures and dropped their heavy tools and ran survived. Those who died conformed to the stipulation that they always carry their tools. In terms of the police, tactical plans are also assessed in retrospect. If they work and no innocent persons are hurt, the plan is viewed as good and no investigation takes place. Only in the event of a mishap or disaster do tactical decisions come into question. It's ironic that some plans that could be labeled good in terms of risk assessment and chances of success probably end up badly while others that are dangerous and poorly conceptualized turn out well.

LETHAL FORCE

It is within the context of the uniqueness of the raid, its dangerousness, the possibility of mass casualties, and the ambiguity of the shooting that the officers constructed accounts in retrospect to process the event and minimize internal conflict. Most scholarly explorations of police use of force examine the accounts officers used to justify and excuse acts that are viewed as deviant by the public but accepted as normal within the culture of police.[19] However, studies by John Van Maanen and Dave Klinger suggest that even shootings that are justified and celebrated by the police and the public may demand a lengthy period of adjustment that involves the retrospective construction of accounts.[20]

Dealing with the fallout of shooting thus involves a process of working through what happened and transforming the memory of the incident into a narrative that minimizes internal ambivalence and allows the officer to live comfortably with what was a difficult and complex event. In the case of the terrorist raid, the approval of peers and bosses in the immediate aftermath, the congratulations from the police commissioner, the ease of the investigation, and external confirmation that the shooting was justified helped minimize internal conflict and affirm the officers' sense of identity as good cops and moral human beings. However, the retribution that was experienced later in relation to the press conference and other matters internal to the squad could have unconsciously become linked to the shooting, with the result that a satisfactory narrative became more difficult to solidify. The fact that the raid was an important part of police history that kept repeating itself in accounts in the press, in public speeches, and in books, made it harder to put to rest.

During the initial encounter with the suspect, the officers recalled experiencing a sense of disbelief that former LAPD officer and sociologist Dave Klinger calls the "oh shit factor."[21] Disbelief that the suspects refused to follow orders was followed by a sense of recognition that the officers remained at risk and there had to be something inhuman about the suspects that led them to behave so irrationally. The particulars of the vilification of the suspect, or "denial of the victim," were transformed progressively in subsequent accounts. Initially, Ryan talked about the internal conversation he had during the confrontation and stressed the unusual look in the suspect's eyes. "I'm thinking, what the fuck is wrong with you. . . . At one point I could have shot him point-blank in his head but I didn't want to kill him. . . . I'm having this conversation with myself. . . . I wanted him to stop. *He gave me a look like I've never seen. It was wild and at the same time focused and controlled. There was no fear.* I fired a third time and hit him in the torso." Later, Ryan added another dimension to his description that put a label to the look he saw in the suspect's eyes: "I saw it. I'll never fucking forget it. I'm looking at them right now as I talk to you. *I can see them standing right there, looking at me with that stare, that look. It's like looking at the devil.*"

Dolan also vilifies the suspects in different accounts. One of the most striking arose after we'd been talking about the events of 9/11 and then returned to discuss the 1997 raid. "Now what starts coming home is the fact that you had people in the apartment building bombs over little kids, you know. I think that I don't really like these people because they had no ethic, no nothing about anybody. You got something against this country, fine, but don't come over here and start blowing up innocent people . . . I would never find fault in the military for whatever they do. They can do whatever they want over there."

More interesting than the negative labels the officers applied to the suspects were the distortions in memory. Ryan remained convinced that the first man he shot when he entered the bedroom was Abu Mezer, the mastermind of the plot. Crime scene photos and court testimony indicated that this was not the case. Lafi Khalil was the suspect whom Ryan shot first when he lunged in his direction and then grabbed for his gun hand. Ryan shot Abu Mezer next when he reached toward something on the floor. I don't know when Ryan began to develop his recollection of events. As suggested in the chapter on the trial, court testimony indicates that neither officer knew the identity of the terrorists when they entered the bedroom. Perhaps the memory of the shooting began to emerge when Ryan testified in court about the first suspect [Lafi Khalil] and Abu Mezer kept nodding his head as if Ryan was talking about him. Regardless, I suspect that one of the reasons it was important for him to recall events in the way he did was because he wanted to have first opened fire at the more heinous suspect. After all, Ryan initiated the firefight and Dolan followed suit in the context of what he observed.[22] Overcoming resistance to killing is difficult. This is noted by sociologist Randall Collins and military psychiatrist Dave

Grossman when they suggest that only 45 percent of soldiers consistently fire their weapons in combat.[23]

Reassignment of responsibility was a second means by which Ryan and Dolan dealt with the ambiguity of the shooting and developed a positive narrative that minimized ambiguity and internal conflict. In such accounts, the officers suggested that they didn't really choose to fire their weapons. Instead, the suspects made the decision for them. Dolan explained, "What people do determines whether they get shot. The interaction forges the path. . . . What they do . . . that is what helps you make your decision. So it's up to them whether they live or die." Ryan said, "The crazy motherfucker didn't give me a choice. It couldn't have lasted more than ten seconds and I never heard the gunshot. All I remember is seeing the muzzle flash. It's so weird. I screamed but don't know what I said. When he moved, I had to act. It was up to him whether he lived or died."

The officers also developed an effective narrative through a process of role affirmation in which they confirmed their identity as competent police whose mission was to protect, serve, and rescue rather than kill. Ryan said, "We're not paid assassins. Police officers are trained to serve and protect, not kill. . . . As a cop you play God out there, deciding who can live and die. You have to be able to handle that." In another account, he explained, "It seemed like an eternity, [that] ten seconds. Never heard the gunshot. All I remember is seeing the muzzle flash. I'm yelling, 'Police, don't move!' but in my head I'm saying *what the fuck are you doing? Stop, stop, you fuckin' idiot, I'm saying in my mind. I don't wanta fucking kill you. I don't want to kill you. I'm not here for that so it was a very enlightening experience.*" Later, when he thought about the incident, he emphasized his role as rescuer. "I think of it now and I see what they really could have done to us. It's nothing to brag about to take a life but to save lives [that's something to feel good about]. There's no glory in shooting someone. It's about saving lives."

Regardless of the narratives the officers developed in the aftermath of the shooting, it appeared that the formal parameters surrounding the use of lethal force were temporarily lifted in the raid, then justified in retrospect to accommodate the unusual circumstances in which the officers found themselves. In reference to dealing with terrorist suspects in possession of IEDs, the use of deadly force in the 1997 raid can be seen as a precursor to strategies that were not seriously considered in New York until after the World Trade Center disaster. In the event of encounters with individuals who are believed to be suicide bombers by virtue of intelligence or the way they look and behave and how they respond to orders, soldiers and police in combat zones are given permission to kill. Shooting teams in Britain also have explicit commands that free them "to shoot to kill" when dealing with terrorist suspects.

Such "commands" were neither formally or informally in operation during the 1997 raid in New York. Shooting parameters remained stable in that respect, and both officers shot to stop the suspects rather than shoot them in the head. While the rules of engagement in the NYPD have not been formally changed in terms of the recruit student guidelines regarding the use of deadly force, I suspect that confrontations with suicide bombers are now included in simulations training of Emergency Service officers who are considered the first responders in the event of a terrorist threat. I also suspect that "shoot to kill" policies are now under discussion for specialized units like Emergency Service, who are likely to respond to jobs involving suicide bombers.

EMERGENCY SERVICE TODAY

While the Bomb Squad is similar in terms of its numbers and organization to what it was in 1997, Emergency Service has changed significantly since 9/11. The unit has undergone an expansion in numbers that could affect its culture in negative and positive ways. A lot of knowledge and experience was lost with the deaths of so many Emergency Service officers in 9/11 combined with the retirements that have more recently taken place. The unit has also increased the number of captains, many of whom have no prior experience in the unit, leading one veteran supervisor to say that "now we have lots of little Mancini's running around," eager to run into jobs and play the "E-man" role. New training has been added related to hazmat [hazardous materials] and the management of terrorist threats. In 2009, Charles Kammerdener was promoted to three-star chief, and the Special Operations Division was made into an independent command with him still at the helm.[24] Some of these changes may relate to the NYPD's ongoing effort to fight terrorism, and Emergency Service is viewed as the special weapons and tactical arm of the Intelligence and Counterterrorism Divisions and the unit of the last resort. The implications of these changes remain unclear.[25]

ORGANIZATIONS AND HARMFUL OUTCOMES

This study highlights the dynamics of a high-profile police event and the frustrations that greet the efforts of rank-and-file officers to move forward in their careers. It reveals the demoralization that creeps into the daily lives of good cops when they work hard and take great risks to do their jobs and yet fail to get ahead. It shows how the interests of low-ranking cops and detectives get lost in the midst of the shifting priorities and changing politics that empower different individuals linked to particular horizontal and vertical cliques. The result of these organizational dynamics is that some of the city's best, most highly trained, and most committed officers eventually get frustrated and disillusioned and leave the job while still in their prime. While this book focused on only a small sample of officers, their situation is hardly unique. Significant numbers of police of every rank experience similar disappointments resulting in the development of cynicism and demoralization that pushes them out of their jobs. Issues of morale have long plagued cops in uniformed patrol and to a lesser degree those in special units and the Detective Division. CompStat is an institution that has changed the job and influenced how police experience their work in units where it is relevant, including the Detective Division where it was most recently applied in 2009. Regardless, the world has changed. Police work contains far more risks now than before 1993 when the World Trade Center bombing occurred and after 9/11 when the United States began to fight overt wars in the Muslim world. As a result, it is more important than ever for departments to address issues of morale and retention of good cops, supervisors, and commanders.

There is no single theoretical model that allows us to fully understand the paradoxical events that occurred in the wake of the 1997 raid and resulted in the varying degrees of frustration experienced by the cops. In her study, *The Dark Side of Organizations*, sociologist Diane Vaughan explores the social origin of "routine nonconformity," mistakes, misconduct, and disaster.[26] Challenging Weberian notions of rationality in organizational behavior, Vaughan argues that these types of behavior are systematic products of complex structures and processes. When put in social context, choices that appear rational in the abstract can produce unanticipated consequences that may deviate from the organization's formal goals and normative standards and expectations. Any system of action generates secondary consequences that may be considered "suboptimal" in the sense of harmful to individuals, groups, masses, and/or the organization as a whole.

Vaughan's definition of the processes that generate suboptimal outcomes is sufficiently broad to subsume a variety of behaviors that would not be considered abnormal in the sense of illegal, bad, or even outside "normative standards." Within this framework, it's possible to consider organizational collusion in leadership styles that wreak havoc with officer motivation as a form of organizational deviance. We could also consider political dynamics that cater to powerful members of the brass and undermine the careers of good, active cops and detectives as a form of routine nonconformity that results in suboptimal outcomes in terms of loss of productivity, alienation and suffering, and early retirement from the job. The problem is that this model does not take account of the dominance of the informal system of power and the shifting interests involved. While officer demoralization may sometimes constitute an unintended "side effect," the processes involved constitute informal but normative behaviors that allow other individuals and groups to assert their power and get ahead. In terms of the public and the long-term interests of the organization, the loss of such highly trained, hardworking officers deprives the public of experience, education, training, and knowledge while costing thousands of dollars in preparing new recruits and specialists and dealing with the accidents that sometimes occur in the process.[27]

In relation to the short-term interests of rising power elites (cliques and those to whom their members are connected), the loss of these officers is beneficial because it allows them to put their own people in particular positions and strengthen the informal web of exchange that increases their organizational worth and cements their place and those of their followers in the organizational hierarchy. In the afterword of his book *Normal Accidents*, Charles Perrow points to a related issue in explaining the social logic of disaster: "An economic system that runs risks for the sake of private profits, or a government system that runs them for the sake of national prestige, patronage or personal power, is the more important focus and culprit."[28] It's hard for police officers who've risked their lives and careers to represent the department and protect and serve the public to realize that, at the end of the game, they don't seem to count for much except in terms of their families and close friends. But as members of the Police Department, in many ways they are pawns in a game of high-stakes politics that echo up and down the ranks.

While it is unpopular in sociological examinations of organizations to bring in psychology, I believe that personalities also play a role in the production of organizational behaviors that result in suboptimal outcomes. Maurice Punch notes that "as an emergency organization with considerable powers one might expect the leadership would be forcefully present in policing. In practice the top layers of police organizations are, like other organizations, arenas for egos and power-plays, and interpersonal factionalism fosters divisiveness, infighting and paralysis at the top echelon."[29] In his book *Organizations in Depth*, Yiannis Gabriel explores the problem of "egos" with a psychodynamic model in mind. He notes that individuals who reach top positions in particular types of organizations tend to manifest high levels of narcissism, which in moderate degrees constitutes a healthy aspect of personality. Modified by some openness to criticism and other points of view, a modicum of empathy, and other balancing characteristics, narcissistically inclined leaders can institute creative and even heroic endeavors that maximize organizational effectiveness and minimize harmful outcomes. Other leaders who demonstrate malignant degrees of narcissism run the risk of becoming trapped in delusions of grandeur and omnipotence. Seduced by their charm, power, and image, their followers become sycophants. They reinforce their leaders' fantasies of self-perfection and protect them from knowledge that might compromise their vision and reveal flaws in their patterns of thought and behavior.

Narcissism among top-level leaders within the Police Department is particularly problematic in view of its paramilitary organization and the notion many officers share that loyalty is related not only to obedience of legal—and sometimes not so legal—orders but also to agreement. When one police commander told me that Howard Safir's greatest flaw was his unwavering loyalty to Rudy Giuliani, I believe he was indirectly talking about the way a "good" subordinate gets swallowed up in the reality of a narcissistic boss to the point where he can't disagree or disappoint. These sorts of relationships between subordinates and bosses reinforce the likelihood that mistakes are made and tragedies will occur that cannot be attributed to officer error or a few bad apples that bring trouble to all.

It's important to recognize that the forces that resulted in the early retirement of the officers featured in this book are not the product of one mayor or commissioner but continue in other administrations, depending on the kind of leadership style that is encouraged down the line and whether or not processes are put in place that check people's desire for petty revenge and keep top brass appraised of officers who have contributed to the public and the organization in major ways. There were good decisions made during the years of the Safir and Giuliani administration. Many of the same top commanders who officers viewed as cop's cops remain devoted to Safir because they feel he empowered them to do their jobs. A lot of these commanders are not advocates of the administration that followed 9/11 because of its leader's micromanaging style and their belief that the department is going downhill. One explained, "I just feel that if you don't get your chiefs and your top-line managers engaged, they're going to disengage and the job will slip back to the time where higher-ranking officers would just say, 'Listen, the best thing to do is nothing so you don't get yourself in trouble, and if they want me, they'll call.' What happens then is that the agency eventually slips. It's a process that occurs over time. It's like twilight, the sun is going down and before you know it's dark."

Regardless of the particulars of each administration, the highly personal and convoluted organizational politics of the department tends to be reproduced in one way or another with each generation such that there are places in which fine leaders take care of good cops at the same time that they hold them accountable for serving the public and protecting their rights. There are also places in which authoritarian, spineless, or Jekyll-and-Hyde bosses dominate and demand officers bite their tongues and hone their skill at managing up the ranks. Prolonged exposure to certain types of bosses is likely to push good cops away, increase dissension among the ranks, and, in the absence of rewards, including promotion, press officers to retire while they are still in their prime.

This leads us to an important question. If we, the department and the public, abandon good cops when they risk their lives doing their jobs in good faith, will they abandon us when we need them most? All of the officers involved in the raid that averted America's first suicide bombing headed toward the World Trade Center when the planes struck. In contrast, during hurricane Katrina, significant numbers of officers left New Orleans at a critical time. We don't know why, and no serious in-depth interview study has been done to find out. Although the departments are different, it's possible that what happened in New Orleans contains lessons for New York City. It's inevitable that down the road, the city will suffer another terrorist attack, or a high-risk organizational accident, or an unexpected natural disaster. There may then come a time in which we will pay for the omissions the organization perpetuates when it inadvertently or otherwise encourages some of its most skilled and experienced officers to give up and retire.

I will end this book with a memory of a conversation I had with chief Bill Morange. "Yeah, you know you can't figure out the NYPD. You'll never figure out the NYPD," he told me in an earnest, warm, and honest voice that inspired my complete trust. It didn't take more than ten minutes of talk before I understood why his officers viewed him with such love and respect. I thought then that if we could just spawn hundreds of little Moranges and other cop's cops and put them into offices in strategic locations throughout the NYPD, the world of police would be a much better place. What Morange told me was correct. After more than twenty-five years of researching police, I cannot understand what goes on inside the organization. I don't know why some good cops end up in bad places while others who are not better and sometimes worse land on their feet, sometimes on the top of their world.

Epilogue

On May 1st, 2010, a young Pakistani American named Faisal Shahzad planted a vehicle-borne explosive device in an SUV he'd purchased in cash a few days before. He drove the car into Manhattan, parked it in Times Square, and soon headed for the airport where he boarded a flight to Dubai. The car bomb malfunctioned and caused smoke and a small fire but no external damage or injuries to people in the area. One or two local street vendors saw the smoke emanating from the parked vehicle and alerted police. Police and firefighters then arrived at the scene, including officers from Emergency Service and the Bomb Squad. Times Square was evacuated and a massive investigation begun to identify and locate the suspect. The Joint Terrorist Task Force and the FBI as well as Customs and Immigration participated in the investigation and/or the arrest of the suspect on the plane more than fifty hours after the bomb was found. The suspect cooperated with authorities and provided a history of his involvement in terrorism and decision to plant the bomb. The investigation continues today as this book goes to press.

A comparison of the 1997 terrorist plot to detonate an explosive device in the New York subway and the May 1, 2010, incident reveals similarities and differences that relate in part to the fact that this most recent event occurred after 9/11, when the threat of international terrorism is being taken more seriously than ever before. Both incidents appear to have been launched by one or more Muslim terrorist who did not have the ordnance expertise or resources to plan and execute a major bombing attack. Regardless, even primitively constructed bombs can be lethal. A bombing in an enclosed space like a subway is likely to cause more injuries and deaths than a detonation in an open space, depending on the sophistication and potency of the explosive materials involved, the number and location of people exposed, and the kind of fragmentation objects that get caught up in the blast.

It remains unclear whether the terrorists involved in the plots were or are linked to a larger terrorist organization such as Hamas in 1997 and the Pakistani Taliban in 2010, although neither Hamas nor the Pakistani Taliban claimed responsibility. Regardless, in both cases, suspects appeared sympathetic to the ideology and practice of Muslim terrorist groups, may have had some connection to them, possibly by exposure to activities such as training. In Shahzad's case, he also appears to have been inspired by the Jihadist preaching of a well-known radical Muslim cleric. Although the educational levels are different for the Pakistani American who attempted the 2010 bombing and the two illegal Palestinian immigrants apprehended in 1997, none of the three suspects appear to have possessed sufficient funds to finance the plots on their own. In both cases, financial aid appears to have come from relatives, friends, or acquaintances in the Middle East. In the 1997 and 2010 incidents, the terrorist suspects were apprehended because of the timely actions of American citizens or legal immigrants who came forward and informed authorities of their concerns. In 1997, Chindluri, the roommate of terrorist suspects Abu Mezer and Lafi Khalil, left the apartment specifically to look for police and warn them of the plot. In 2010, one or more street venders noticed smoke coming out of the SUV and told nearby precinct and/or mounted police officers what they saw.

This book explores what occurred behind the scenes in the 1997 incident, after the police were alerted, and how they aborted a bombing in the New York City subway that could have cost hundreds or even thousands of lives. It also examines how top-ranking city and police officials attempted to enhance their image and rally public support at a time in which policies linked to zero-tolerance policing were increasingly being questioned. We do not know what is happening behind the scenes in the case of the 2010 bombing in Times Square. What is apparent, however, is that mayor Michael Bloomberg, police commissioner Raymond Kelly, and other top NYPD brass are using the latest terrorist attempt to maximize their political advantage and possibly divert attention away from issues of crime and accusations that pressure down the chain of command is pushing rank-and-file officers to manipulate the numbers for purposes of CompStat (computerized statistical mapping of crime). The mayor and the police commissioner continue to publicize their success although they had minimal responsibility for what did and didn't occur in 2010.

Police in the NYPD did not know about the recent plot in time to arrest the suspect before he parked the SUV in Times Square. Instead, the vehicle-borne explosive device failed to detonate and the street vendor(s) alerted authorities at which point the NYPD, the Fire Department, and external law enforcement agencies got involved. The police did play a role in the ensuing investigation that resulted in the apprehension of the suspect before his plane took off for Dubai. Top NYPD brass, including police commissioner Kelly and deputy commissioner of intelligence David Cohen, also managed to more or less resist the competitive jousting with the FBI and Joint Terrorist Task Force that had undermined the investigation of a serious terrorist plot the year before. This time, with perhaps only minor exceptions, federal and local law enforcement agencies appeared to have worked largely in tandem to ensure that the suspect was caught. In contrast, in the 1997 incident, the NYPD did play the major role in aborting a bombing in the subway with no input by the FBI except during later phases of the investigation when, for example, "the feds" designed and tested a mock bomb. In both the 1997 and 2010 incidents, luck also played a part.

In contrast to 1997, when the suspects were initially dismissed as "lone wolfs" with only vague contact with terrorist organizations in the Middle East, today law enforcement organizations appear to be pushing the envelope to find a link between Faisal Shahzad and the Pakistani Taliban and possibly al Qaeda or other international terrorist organizations. Whether they are exploiting the potential of these connections because it makes for better "spin" by the deputy commissioner, public information, the Police Department's media machine, or law enforcement authorities really believe the connections are real is a question that can only be answered by those privy to the inner workings of the NYPD.

Still, speaking for a number of his active-duty colleagues, one retired member of NYPD's Intelligence Division, with expertise in counterterrorism and explosive construction and forensics, raised a number of questions when I asked him his thoughts about the 2010 incident. Noting that Shahzad was on a federal watch list prior to his becoming a U.S. citizen, he wondered what sort of follow-up the FBI had initiated after their first contact. "Did the FBI ever share what they knew about Shahzad with the NYPD?" With its abundant resources, the NYPD might have been able to keep tabs on someone who had a "questionable background." "Did the FBI ever question Shahzad's neighbors or conduct surveillance?" The retired officer believes that the answer is probably a resounding *no*. "My guess is that Shahzad lived a clean life, married for naturalization, which should always be suspect and again, no one verified even a simple tax record to establish how he sustained himself. That requires getting out from behind the desk and knocking on the door; too risky for the FBI and not much media play for such 'podium posers,'" he explained, sarcastically. The officer noted that the federal agents conducting surveillance on Shahzad temporarily lost him as they made their way to the airport. The officer wonders why the FBI didn't prepare for this possibility by immediately putting Shahzad on the no-fly list so he couldn't have boarded the plane and escaped. The officer went on to explain that the same problems exist now as were in place before 9/11, when the United States had the intelligence to "connect the dots" and two federal agents warned of the possibility of the plot, yet no one took action to stop the worst manmade disaster in U.S. history. "It's gonna happen again. We all know there's gonna be another terrorist attack. It's just a matter of when," an officer involved in the 1997 raid explained. Keith Ryan made additional points. "There are around 300 cops in the area at any particular time. The Task Force, Transit, K-9, Operation Neon Task Force, Atlas, and Hercules cover Times Square at one point or another during the day. Yet Shahzad was able to make a trial run the day before with no problem. Then, on May 1st, he goes in and parks the Suburban and no one sees anything until a vendor spots the smoke. I think this guy was the sacrificial lamb, an amateur put there [by a terrorist organization] to see how prepared we are. Now they [the terrorists] know that the area is penetrable. Next time—and rest assured, there will be a next time—they'll send somebody in who wants to be a martyr and he'll enter the Marriott or other location where a lot of people gather and detonate the bomb and thousands will die. Put me on the lecture tour, and I'll be candid with you."

Appendix
METHODOLOGY

This study is based on hundreds of hours of interviews with twenty-nine police officers and two civilians who were involved in the incident or had special knowledge of events surrounding the 1997 Brooklyn raid. I interviewed officers of every rank from cop and detective to three- and four-star chief and deputy commissioner. Interviews lasted from ninety minutes to four hours and were conducted in person with the exception of three short telephone interviews. In-person interviews were taped with the permission of police subjects. The tape recorder was placed on a table and the officers instructed how to turn it on and off when and if they wished. I did not take notes when they invoked the off-the-record option, and telephone interviews were not recorded.

I developed some of the contacts for this study while working in the Training Division of the Police Department during 2003–4. With three exceptions, I used the names of officers with whom I'd worked when contacting other police. Additional sources of data included internal police reports, the suicide bombers' note, and photographs of the officers in different contexts. I also reviewed newspaper accounts, transcripts of court testimony, and evidence introduced during the suspects' trial. A short piece on the raid based on handwritten notes taken in a limited number of interviews was included in a chapter of the new recruit student guide.

Police scholar Paul Chevigny notes that problems often arise in the wake of police shootings because officers lie about what happened even in situations in which the truth would not undermine their case.[1] Lying is also common in fieldwork and interview contexts that have nothing to do with violence and occupational survival in a punitive world bound by law and procedure.[2] Contradictions in police accounts of critical incidents are not always intentional. Time and stress affect memory in different ways. There is little correlation between accuracy and confidence of recollection, and significant perceptual distortions are experienced during combat situations.[3]

In view of the expectation that police should provide accurate statements in the wake of involvement in critical incidents, it's not surprising that stories don't always converge or that officers sometimes get together to construct logical accounts in an effort to protect themselves. Regardless, even when retelling their stories multiple times, I discovered only a few discrepancies in officers' narratives, some of which could be explained with reference to the lengthy passage of time. Considering the complexity of sorting lies from narrative truth, subjective from objective "reality," police renditions of events are viewed from both symbolic interactionist and psychoanalytic perspectives; as accounts that combine memory with attempts to explain, excuse, justify, deny, and repress thought and action that create moral ambiguity, emotional discomfort, or ego-dystonic images of the self.[4]

Ethnographers typically encounter more than one reality when they interview different sources regarding their experience of the same event, regardless of whether research subjects intentionally lie. Sometimes, these realities represent alternative perspectives that fit into a coherent picture when age, gender, rank, status, and position are taken into account. There are also times when realities conflict, compete or collide, and form a collage of discordant elements that cannot be reconciled. This sometimes occurs when interview subjects leave out aspects of a story that compromise how they want us to know and depict them. It can also result from the fact that remembered interactions are infused with and selected according to the emotions and motives of the teller, providing a truth that eschews the positivist inclinations of videotaped observations. As anthropologist Carolyn Nordstrom points out in her study of war, "Narrative is experience. But it is not the experience of that which it narrates."[5] Whatever problems they hold for writers trying to reconstruct events, conflicting accounts are often instructive. In the case of this research, they alerted me to officers' sense of vulnerability and the defenses they needed to survive. Such accounts also confirmed my sense that police put enormous weight on appearances and will stick to their stories in order to minimize guilt and embarrassment even when faced with discrepancies. It is also possible that officers come to believe that theirs is the only version of truth and that alternative interpretations don't exist.

Conflicting accounts repeated in the context of the research relationship may represent a part of the transference.[6] Interviewees repeat the same patterns of behavior with the researcher that they use with other people in their past and present lives. Some of the officers I interviewed thus revealed in their interactions with me similar modes of behavior that they used with peers and bosses and, I suspect, significant others in their past. In certain encounters I found myself feeling as though I imagined some of their bosses might have felt in similar situations. The transference/countertransference dynamic thus helped me understand some of the problems particular officers faced on the job.

The most challenging chapter to write was "Friendly Fire," which explores the contentious relationships that developed within a particular squad. The dynamics of who did what to whom, when, and why were difficult to determine. It was hard to make sense of some interviews because they felt too close to home. My positive feelings about some of the cops' bosses who were trying their best, however limited, to deal with difficult situations made writing additionally difficult. At times, my fingers felt catatonic as if they were glued to the keyboard and couldn't move for fear I'd hurt someone or unfairly depict the gray versus black-and-white reality of being a cop and boss in an organization like the NYPD.

At the request of officers I interviewed, I have omitted information, changed names, places, and other details of their lives. I have also used my discretion in making additional changes that I thought would help display them in the most positive possible light. In situations in which accounts conflicted and I could not include one version of truth without feeling dishonest or making someone else "look bad," I "diluted" the story and/or included more than one account. This sort of account dilemma is probably common among authors attempting to write chronological narratives based on multiple interviews. After all, individuals want their stories told in the way they think preserves their most cherished image of themselves and the people they love.[7]

I have indicated in the text or endnotes instances when my interviews were too limited to verify realities. I have also made note of instances in which realities collided in ways I could not coherently reconstruct. In situations in which I could not verify accounts with more than two people, I changed the names of the officers involved if exposure could put them in an unfair light. I also changed the names of officers I didn't interview, except for those whose roles were insignificant or who were high-ranking public figures. I have left out certain facts to spare individuals unnecessary embarrassment while including those that are necessary to maintain the integrity of the story and what it reveals about the world of police.

I have never pretended to be someone I wasn't in fieldwork. Nor have I burdened research subjects with details of my personal life and political, social, and religious opinions that might limit what they might say to me or make them feel as though they were being judged when they weren't. Nevertheless, a lot of the cops and detectives I interviewed were aware that I am a "typical" "Upper West Side [Manhattan] liberal" who didn't share their often conservative views. Sometimes I told them this in jest. I knew they could learn a lot about me from a few phone calls to the Police Academy, where I had worked and enjoyed relationships with a number of conservative-thinking officers who didn't share my point of view.

I do not believe the officers' knowledge of and assumptions about my political and religious affiliations undermined the quality of our relationship. I have always found that honesty and a genuine effort to listen and understand, coupled with interview skills, are what are most important in building rapport and gaining access to hidden dimensions of reality once the cultural gate is breached. Deception, too much confession of real or imagined philosophies or experiences, and other attempts to falsely manipulate the interview/fieldwork situation to gain trust may belong in the realm of military and police interrogation but not in that of ethnographic research.[8]

Ethnographers sometimes use the tools of narrative nonfiction to produce accounts that allow the reader to more fully know and experience the world of their subjects. Jonathan Rubinstein's *City Police* provides an example of a classic ethnography that utilizes the techniques of investigative journalism to shed light on the world of policing as experienced by officers in the Philadelphia Police Department at a particular time in history. A more recent work that combines the techniques of ethnography and narrative nonfiction is Robert Jackall's *Wild Cowboys*, a book about New York City detectives. *Cop in the Hood*, sociologist Peter Moskos's lovely account of his one-year experience as a police officer in Baltimore learning about police culture and politics and the fallacies of CompStat from the ground up, provides another innovative approach.[9]

Seven Shots also utilizes writing styles that are not typical of traditional ethnography. I drew on the techniques of narrative nonfiction to appeal to readers' emotions and sense of identification and show them what police officers experienced during the raid and its aftermath. In the introduction and conclusion, I try to tell the reader what happened and make sense of events intellectually, using parts of the story to bring into relief the social dynamics of policing in the NYPD. Police officers' accounts of events typically include conversations stated in terms of what "he said" or "she said." Only on rare occasions did I have to ask officers to try and remember conversations so I could effectively create scenes and reconstruct dialogue. The dialogue quoted in this book thus mostly came directly from interview transcripts. I also used trial testimony, official press releases, and quotations in newspapers accounts. In chapter 2, "10-1," I transcribed a CD of the 911 tape that took place when Yurkiw was shot and quoted it with the minor changes cited in endnotes. There are also a few occasions in which I used creative license to build a scene and create dialogue to provide the reader with a richer understanding of the police world. These instances are documented in endnotes.

Sometimes ethnographers who study similar cultures disagree about what they see and how their data should be interpreted. To some degree, this is the case for me and ethnographer Peter Kraska, who studied what he calls "police paramilitary units" (PPUs) in the United States. The differences in our perspectives are partly rooted in the particulars of the environments we researched as well as issues of age, gender, and temperament. Kraska was troubled by the masculine ethos and "warrior culture" he discovered during his stint of participant-observation among SWAT officers in training.[10] He felt guilty about the ease with which he reverted to traditional masculine interactional styles and his participation in some of the combat games the men enjoyed, as if he'd betrayed his "profeminist" principles and belief that the militarization of police was dangerous to democracy.[11] Kraska suggests that his fieldwork triggered uncomfortable images of wild escapades that had been an ambivalent part of his youth.

I experienced researching Emergence Service cops differently. Perhaps because I am an older woman and did not interact with the cops as a man, I saw different aspects of their world and had an alternative interpretation of some of the things they said. Where Kraska saw masculine power and violence in officer's attire, talk, and behavior, I saw defense, pain, vulnerability, and internal conflict regarding issues of power and lethal force. I also saw variation among officers in terms of their identification with values of the masculine, warrior subculture Kraska describes. A few of the officers I interviewed fit to some degree the stereotypical SWAT cop encountered by Kraska during his fieldwork among officers in training. Most of them didn't fit as far as I could tell.

My interview subjects were probably older and had more life experience than Kraska's. All had spouses and children. Those who'd been through rocky marriages presented a complex picture of their relationships that did not conform to masculine sexist stereotypes and sometimes struck me as sad. Several officers appeared ashamed, conflicted, guilty, or otherwise distressed when they talked of their difficult times. Other officers had close relationships with their wives with whom they shared their work as well as their personal lives. These were family men who enjoyed the masculine camaraderie of the job but preferred to spend their off-duty time with their wives.

All but one of the officers seemed to feel comfortable revealing sometimes strong emotions that didn't necessarily conform to the macho image Kraska describes. One officer wasn't embarrassed to tell me how, during a rough period at work, he'd come home and cried. Almost all of the officers choked up or shed tears when we talked about 9/11. One could barely keep from weeping when he talked of a terrible time in his and his family's life. Anger, expressed directly or displayed in visceral changes in affect and tone of voice, clenched fists, and red faces and necks, were other signs of feeling that more strongly linked to traditional notions of masculinity although I interpreted them differently. I thus found myself immersed in a curious world of fluctuating thought and emotions. No amount of humor, bravado, armor, or weaponry could disguise the tension, anxiety, fear, and moral confusion faced by every officer I interviewed at various moments in time.

Some features of policing that Kraska found dangerous or offensive seemed normal to me, such as their camaraderie and the fun they had working together. I have also enjoyed the times I have been a member of a valued community among friends. I have taken pleasure in those times in my research when police felt sufficiently trustful to include me in their world as friend, confidant, ally or sometimes almost one of them. In contrast to Kraska, I didn't feel conflicted about the pleasure [or other sentiment] I experienced while engaging in or hearing about activities culturally linked to masculinity and combat.

Not that I always had an empathic connection with every cop I interviewed. Sometimes I got annoyed, when, for example, an officer acted in a way I found "difficult," like repeatedly cancelling meetings at the last minute or expecting more than I could realistically give.[12] Once or twice, I felt a mixture of bafflement, guilt, and helpless irritation when I discovered that officers hadn't been forthright with me as far as I could tell yet still seemed to expect me to fix the problem somehow and protect them even though by censoring important information they'd taken away my tools. More often I found I wanted to rescue the cops or make them feel better about some difficult life event.[13] I viewed such responses as a part of my countertransference that, once understood, could help me gain insight into the officers and their world.[14]

When I reflect on this latest research encounter, I think of the words of an NYPD veteran commander who frequently handled situations involving officer death. He told me that cops have three selves. First, there is the public self they show to each other—the tough, fearless, funny, and sometimes angry guy who lives in a world composed mostly of men. The second self he shows to his wife and a few close friends—the tender, loving father and husband, sometimes warm and helpful, on occasion, disgruntled, who does his best to overcome life's obstacles and take care of the family. The third is the private self no one really knows. Parts of it are sometimes hidden in his locker, stored away from his friends and family, unless he unexpectedly dies. Then an assigned officer, who understands the unspoken rules, will open his locker and bury the remnants of his private self as he would have wished; the picture of the lover his wife doesn't know about; the diary filled with frightened ruminations he hasn't dared share; the poems depicting sad and violent death, sometimes his own, all of which reveal his inner life.

I don't know what parts of themselves cops revealed to other police researchers and how these revelations affected their feelings about their subjects, the distance they perceived between them, and their reflections about their countertransference if that was something they acknowledged and understood. Much of the time, I think the cops showed me an aspect of their public selves, what they wanted me to see and what they'd agreed to share in consultation with their partners. At other times, they spoke openly and even revealed bits of their private selves. On occasion, I was also greeted with selective recollections that made the officers look like they needed to see themselves: Hollywood police, heroic, fearless, flawless men fighting the forces of evil. I suspect that Kraska was greeted with similar part-person-cops with the important difference that they related to him as a male. His and my understanding thus represent different aspects of a dynamic cultural representation rather than right or wrong constructions of external reality. The divergent themes we recognized are there in both SWAT and Emergency Service but vary in dominance, depending on the type of team and the larger organization of which it is part.

While writing this book I was often reminded of an incident that occurred in the late 1970s. I was a graduate student doing my second stint of fieldwork among big city police, working a four-to-midnight shift. My cop partner was outside doing a routine check of a factory door to make sure it was locked. I was inside the car. A uniformed cop pulled up alongside, shocked to see a woman in the front seat of a marked car. At the time there were only one hundred female rookies in the Police Department and I was in plainclothes, wearing a pair of jeans.

"*Who* are you?" the officer asked.

"I'm a person, a human being. Who are you?" I responded.

"I'm just a cop," he answered, then drove away. I never saw him again. I believe this interaction epitomized the deeper truth that informed and sustained my relationship with police and that of most other ethnographers and their research subjects. We choose to study particular people because they resonate something powerful and often silent in ourselves. How we feel about and deal with these often unconscious echoes into our past impact on our ability to empathize, see, and hear and on how we interpret the relevant culture. When we are doing our jobs right, we recognize that we are in many more ways than not the same as the people we study.

As best I can as author and interpreter, I have tried to tell the story of the 1997 Brooklyn raid through the eyes of the cops involved, including Keith Ryan, Joe Dolan, John English, Rich Teemsma, and Paul Yurkiw and officers of every status and rank who played key roles or were familiar with the events. I alone am responsible for the mistakes, omissions, and distortions of fact that accompany this narrative.

Notes

PREFACE

   1. Sacks (1972).

   2. Hunt (1984).

   3. Hunt (1984), (1990).

   4. Skolnik (1967); Manning (1977); Kappeler, Sluder, and Alpert (1998); Kraska and Paulsen (1997).

   5. Watson (1999).

   6. Sacks (1972).

   7. Rubinstein (1973).

   8. Van Maanen (1978); Skolnik (1967).

   9. Watson (1999).

   10. During the 1970s, there were a number of sexual discrimination suits filed against big city police departments, including the Los Angeles Police Department and the Philadelphia Police Department, alleging discrimination in the hiring of female officers to the ranks of uniformed patrol and their promotion to supervisory and managerial ranks. Typically these lawsuits argued that women didn't have the physical strength to handle the job and were emotionally ill suited as well.

   11. Hunt (1990).

   12. Van Maanen (1978).

   13. Jeffrey T. Mitchell (Everly and Mitchell 1997) developed a method of critical incident stress management (CISM), which has been subject to much critical scrutiny by experts in the field of traumatic and posttraumatic stress. CISM, also referred to as the "Mitchell model," includes a phase of group discussion that takes place shortly after the critical incident that is designed to mitigate acute symptoms and provide a sense of psychological closure and relief. While ideally the method entails seven phase-specific exposures, in practice "group therapy" sessions may be substantially reduced and occur long after the critical incident occurred. Psychiatrists critical of the method note that, among other serious problems, group "catharsis" in the absence of individual follow-up and psychotherapy may aggravate rather than alleviate symptoms linked to traumatic and/or posttraumatic stress.

   14. This was something an NYPD anticrime officer actually did in the 1970s in

Crown Heights, Brooklyn, where he worked. His actions were viewed as normal among his plainclothes peers.

15. See Hunt (1984).

16. See Slansky and Marks (2008); Levitt (2009c).

17. Herbert (1997).

INTRODUCTION

1. I cannot provide precise figures to support this assertion, but it was confirmed by two persons working at high levels with the U.S. military in Iraq.

2. See Rashbaum, William and Baker (2009) and Levitt (2009b).

3. Herbert (1997); and Marks (2005).

4. Terrill et al. (2003); see also Marks (2005), 20.

5. Marks (2005); Chan (1997).

6. Kraska (1996); Kraska and Kappeler (1997).

7. David Klinger (2004) also supports the view that SWAT officers use lethal force as a last resort and do not "want" to kill anyone. He shows that different officers handle the experience in a variety of ways. None experience the use of lethal force casually. One officer left the unit and went back to patrol after several lethal force encounters left him feeling unhappy (see also Rojek 2005). In statistical studies of SWAT use of lethal force, the findings of Klinger (2004) and Rojek (2005) confirm that SWAT officers do not fire their weapons indiscriminately, resulting in numerous accidents and increasing the rate of death when alternative solutions are possible.

8. Chevigny (1995).

9. Although an emphasis on winning the hearts and minds of the civilian population is popular among a small minority of military commanders who have learned from the mistakes of Vietnam and, more recently, Iraq and Afghanistan, the Army's dominant cultural philosophy remains focused on killing the enemy as the means and solution in war. Neutralizing insurgency through nonkinetic methods by developing cultural intelligence, communicating with and serving local populations, and helping control certain types of crime is viewed by the majority of combat troops and some commanders as low-status activities that have been forced on them from above.

10. Collins (2008), 88–93.

11. Waldren (2007), (2008); IPCC (2006).

12. Jackall (1997), 364.

13. Lenny Levitt (2009d) describes recent incidents in the NYPD in which officers were caught on tape in compromising situations that would have never been captured in past generations. Instances caught on security cameras included the beating of a handcuffed man in a West Side housing project in 2008. Video footage in 2003 revealed that the police claim that they arrested anti-Iraq war demonstrators because they were being unruly and refused to disperse was false. The protesters couldn't disperse because police barricades pinned them down as the mounted units advanced. Video cameras showed that many of the people arrested at the Republican National Convention in 2004 had not broken any law, leading the district attorney to drop every case. These are among just a few of the examples mentioned that caught police committing lies to frame suspects or justify troublesome actions, some of which led to charges of perjury.

14. Van Maanen uses the term "assholes" to describe persons who don't recognize police officers' superior authority in interactions with them. "Know-nothings" include the average civilian who has had little experience with police and knows nothing about their world (Van Maanen 1978a).

15. I was working in the NYPD before the convention and attended numerous meetings in which the deputy commissioner, Training, reminded his staff that the whole world was watching and that they had to be very careful they didn't repeat the events that occurred at the Democratic Convention in Chicago years before.

16. Reuss-Ianni (1983), 63.

17. The detective mentioned an occasion in which he and his colleagues were working inside on midnight shift. They had a party with wine. "We were having such a good time," he said to explain why they hadn't made sure at least one officer remained sober to handle emergencies or inquiries from above. When the lieutenant came in to work in the morning and discovered that all of his officers were drunk, he angrily ordered them home. 'Sir, I can't do that. I'm too drunk to drive,' the detective said. Irate, the lieutenant went to the captain and told him what his men had done. The captain inquired, "Are you going to do anything about it?" The lieutenant paused and said, 'No.' The Captain replied, 'Then why are you telling me? There are some things I don't have to know.'" From the perspective of the detective telling the story, the lieutenant was a bad and spineless boss because he didn't have the courage to handle the situation himself. Instead, he attempted to escalate the situation by dumping it into the captain's lap. The detective considered the captain a good boss because he declined to make an issue of the party and suggested in the way he responded that it should be resolved at low levels in-house.

18. Abbott (1981).

19. I am indebted to friend and colleague Terry Wonder, who used this phrase in reference to a petty, fear-and-intimidation, micromanaging control-freak team "leader" who was causing problems for her during and after a mock military exercise.

CHAPTER TWO

1. The tape said Eight rather than Nine Truck. In fact, Yurkiw was a fly-man from Eight Truck "flying," or going, to Nine Truck to work for the night. The transcription has been changed to reflect that.

2. I don't know for sure whether he pulled the blanket over his face, but the actions match the words he spoke so I took the creative liberty of including them in the sequence.

3. People gave different accounts of how Chindluri came to the attention of the police. I was unable to substantiate the version included here, because the two NYPD cops involved are still on the job and one was apparently ordered by his chief in Counterterrorism not to talk to me when I went through the Office of the Deputy Commissioner, Public Information, requesting an interview. Court testimony indicates that the Long Island Railroad cops called headquarters, and a car was dispatched from the 8-8 Precinct. Other sources claim that Huber and Kowalchuck initially dismissed Chindluri's concerns and sent him on his way. Not long after that, they changed their minds and went to search for him. By this time, Chindluri had run into Christie and Caruso, who took his story seriously and brought him into the station house along with the two Long Island railroad cops who appeared a few minutes later.

4. This material is taken from Kammerdener's testimony in the trial: *United States vs. Lafi Khalil and Gazi Ibrahim Abu Mezer*, July 7, 1998:785–800.

5. I have been unable to learn the identity of the female inspector to verify her position and exactly what she said. However I have no reason to doubt the officers' account of what happened during the meeting.

6. Precinct or unit commanding officers are under pressure from Police Headquarters to meet certain productivity goals, including arrests and summonses which

bring revenue to the city. Since the introduction of CompStat in the 1990s, the "numbers game" has become more pronounced and refined. Borough and precinct commanders are under increased pressure to find ways to reduce crime, sometimes by manipulating the numbers (reducing the severity of the arrest or making sure the rate stays on a steady downward slope and avoiding sudden dips which could be hard to further reduce).

7. Ryan (and other police officers) recalled Mancini bringing in these types of photographs and passing them around. However, I have taken this memory out of the context in which it arose (Emergency Service quarters) and put it here as one of Ryan's thoughts.

8. In most tactical entries, the first and second men in the stack usually carry handguns. The next three officers carry MP-5s. The last man responsible for rear guard security carries the Mini-14. This arrangement helps to minimize the possibility of critical injury by "friendly fire" in the event of a gun battle. The officers' vests will typically stop 9 mm rounds but might not stop high-velocity .223 rounds, depending on the location of the bullet's entry.

9. Emergency Service officers are taught to go for the "fastest reload." In this type of scenario it would likely be his backup gun.

10. *New York Post,* Friday, August 1, 1997, 5.

CHAPTER THREE

1. I am grateful to author "Jolting Ass Pain" for the phrase "two-faced man-hating muncher," which appeared in the NYPD RANT October, 25, 2006. His rant concerned a female chief who was then commanding officer of the Police Academy.

2. Some material in this chapter is borrowed from the author's account of the incident prepared for the New York Police Department Recruit Student Guide, 2003. The account appears in the chapter on domestic preparedness.

3. In order to better describe the illumination in the room at the time of the raid, I borrowed the same type of flashlight that was mounted on Ryan's gun and experimented with the lighting and shadow contrast in two small dark rooms.

4. *New York Times,* August 2, 1997, B4.

5. *New York Times,* August 1, 1997, B4. The first name of Ms. Ortiz is fictitious.

6. *New York Times,* August 1, 1997, B4.

CHAPTER FOUR

1. I visited Methodist Hospital in order to understand the layout and atmosphere in the waiting room at the same time of day that Ryan and Dolan were there. The man eating roti and the way the room smelled were derived from my visit rather than the memory of the officers.

2. This sentence is fiction. I made it up with the help of a police officer-consultant.

3. Procedure has changed since 1997. As soon as cops arrive in the hospital, they are whisked away and segregated from patients. Half of the hospital staff, including the administrator, greets the officers, a duty captain shows up and an entourage follows, including the mayor and the police commissioner. The Police Department takes control of the relevant wing of the hospital and orchestrates the process.

4. The conversation about the blood, Bratton, and walking pathogens is fictionalized dialogue created with the help of a police officer-consultant.

5. The ribbing-related dialogue about Piazza and his partner did occur but probably

a day or so later at quarters rather than at the hospital. The officers don't recall exactly when it happened.

6. While English and Ryan reported having separate conversations with different friends, it's possible that only one officer received a warning and later, as fear spread and actions needed to be explained, the warning became part of both officers' memories and incorporated into retrospective accounts.

7. I toured the 8-8 Precinct around the same time of day as the debriefing occurred in order to reconstruct relevant scenes. A number of details, specifically the description of the bathroom, the detectives' quarters upstairs, the conversation among the detectives about Attica, the suspect with his face pressed against the precinct cell, and the interaction between the prisoner and the officers near the front desk were derived from my visit.

8. McDermott suggested that Bill Morange was instrumental in arranging that the incident be treated like an undercover operation.

9. "FDRB 150 (97) July 31. 1997. *Report Under* I.O 139 s95. From: Duty Inspector, Patrol Borough Brooklyn South. To: Chief of the Department. Subject no. 1—Ongoing Investigation of Suspected Terrorist(s) with Middle Eastern Origins, in Possession of Explosive Devices, within the Confines of the 78 Precinct. No. 2. Firearm Discharge within the Confines of the 78 Precinct by two (2) Uniformed on Duty Members of the Service. Three (3) of the Perpetrators Injured by the Firearm Discharge. Firearm Discharge Tracking no. 150." (Two not three of the suspects were injured during the firefight).

10. Records indicate that the majority of arrests in the Crown Heights riots were made in Brooklyn North by other commanders at the scene.

11. The source for this quote from Safir is a high-ranking member of the Giuliani-Safir administration.

12. The sequence of memories from Anemone is reconstructed from our interviews in addition to photographs of the World Trade Center bombing.

13. Bill Morange was not the commanding officer of the Special Operations Division in 1993.

14. Although all accounts confirm the gist of Dwyer's and Mancini's comments during this meeting, there is some confusion regarding each officer's role in the decision not to talk to the press. Ryan recalls that he initiated the move. English does not know how the conversation started but only that he did not want to appear at the press conference and made known his point of view. A supervisor in Emergency Service who was not present during the meeting insisted the initiative came from all the cops involved as well as John English.

CHAPTER FIVE

1. This is not an exact quote. No one could remember exactly what different officers said in support of the shooters. I asked one officer to think of the sort of remark that might have been made, and he came up with this.

2. This quote is taken from newspaper accounts that appeared the day after the incident and were reproduced in Congressional reports.

3. The quotes from Black are according to Teemsma's and/or other officers' memories.

4. While a similar scene occurred between Ryan and his mother, I made up what she was reading and her quote from Nietzsche, based on my interview with her, my sense of her as a person, and our discussion of her love of philosophy and the books she likes to read.

5. See *New York Post*, Sunday, August 3, 1997, 2–3.

CHAPTER SIX

1. While the scene with Celona is fictionalized here, I based my conclusion about his commitment to writing the story on a telephone call we shared. He was adamant then that, if there was a story hidden in my questions, whatever I said would not be confidential. I'm not sure why I felt this way but Celona seemed sleazy to me. I didn't like or trust him in contrast to several reporters to whom I've referred nonpolice friends who had stories to tell and requested the names of reliable journalists. I also think Celona was truthful when he related what he recalled of his conversation with Ryan, although Ryan remembered it differently.

2. *New York Post*, August 2, 1997, 1, 2, 12. The article that mentioned Dolan and Ryan was written by Larry Celona, Murray Weiss, and Tracy Conner. The quotations suggest that the telephone conversation between Ryan and Celona could have taken place Thursday night, August 1, rather than the night of July 31. Ryan is quoted as saying, "I felt sick when I woke up today. I started to realize I almost wasn't here today" (12).

3. *New York Post*, August 2, 1997, 12.

4. *New York Post*, August 2, 1997, 12.

5. In the 1980s police believed that the mob never hit cops. This myth was exposed when members of the NYPD shot two detectives, Kathy Burke and Anthony Venditti. Burke was hit in the chest but managed to empty her revolver. She had multiple surgeries but survived. Venditti couldn't get to his gun, which he kept in an ankle holster, and died on the street. Accounts of the incident are conflicting, and some police believe Burke didn't back up her partner and was responsible for his death.

6. This account is reconstructed from interviews with friends of Collins, individuals who worked in DCPI, and officers who witnessed events.

7. *New York Post*, Sunday, August 3, 1997, 2–3.

8. Initially, the suspect's family claimed that Kamal was despondent because he had recently lost his life savings. Years later, the family confessed they'd been told to make up the story by a terrorist organization and Kamal had intended on making a political statement in the incident.

9. Although Charles Campisi remained convinced that Schwartz was guilty, a civilian jury found him innocent of holding the door but guilty of perjury in the cover up.

10. O'Reilly is a pseudonym.

CHAPTER SEVEN

1. Anemone felt that the politicking for promotion "detracted from (the two detectives') otherwise terrific performance."

2. Quotations are from "Transcript of Hearing," *United States of America vs. Gazi Ibrahim Abu Mezer and Lafi Khalil,* case no. 97-CR-804, United States District Court, Eastern District of New York, 101–920.

3. In the 1983 Supreme Court decision of the Fourth Amendment case of *Illinois v. Gates*, 462 U.S. 213 (1983), *Gates* overruled and replaced previous decisions, thus allowing for the "totality of circumstances" to be used in support of "probable cause" for police to take certain types of action that might have been ruled as unconstitutional in the past.

4. Crime scene photographs identify Lafi Khalil as the suspect who was shot in the hand.

5. *United States v. Gazi Ibrahim Abu Mezer and Lafi Khalil*, 819.

6. Ibid., 851.

7. I did not interview Michael Corr. The two short scenes that include him are

based on interviews with other officers and documented by materials provided by key personnel from the Detectives' Endowment Association.

8. Tom Scotto's assistant, Sam Katz, included the following names in her Top Cops' submission: Charles Kammerdener, Jim Black, Joe McGuire, Jeffrey Campbell, Richard Teemsma, Paul Yurkiw, Joseph Palermo (8-8 Squad), Harry Antoine (8-8 Squad), Michael Girardin (8-8 Squad), Kent Arthur (8-8 Squad), Laura Pender (8-8 Squad), Thomas Sinclair (8-8 Squad), Robert Moore (7-7 Squad), Lt. Robert Boyce (8-8 Precinct), Lt. Ronald Jacobs (8-8 Precinct), Sgt. Michael Lavin (8-8 Precinct), Sgt. Douglas Lantine (8-8 Precinct), Eric Huber, and John Kowalchuck.

9. Departmental Recognition Request, PD 439-162 (REV, 5-92)-h2. Ref PG 120–134: Pct. Serial no. ESU 11-98. No. of Personnel Submitted for Recognition, 16 of 16.

10. Press release no. 428-98, September 15, 1998. Archives of the Mayor. http://www.nyc.gov/html/om/html/98b/pr428-98.html.

11. Press release no. 428-98, September 15, 1998. Archives of the Mayor. http://www.nyc.gov/html/om/html/98b/pr428-98.html

12. The name of the inspector has been changed. Many bosses would be hesitant about providing this kind of information directly to the rank-and-file officers involved, although leaks are common from both cops and brass.

13. Safir had scheduled an executive meeting at the same time as the union had arranged a memorial service in Staten Island to dedicate a monument to detectives slain in the line of duty. The event was widely advertised and invitations had gone out months before to Safir, his deputy commissioners, and chiefs. Giuliani wasn't invited, which might have influenced Safir's decision to avoid the event and make it difficult for his senior staff to attend. Archbishop John Cardinal O'Connor was at the affair, along with politicians, the families of the deceased, and a crowd of police, totaling about eight hundred attendees. No chief or commissioner was able to attend the service, although the borough commander of Staten Island showed up later. Guy Molinari, the Staten Island borough president, insisted on being seated on the dais with the cardinal. The cardinal waited an hour and still Molinari didn't show up. Scotto finally called his office and a staff member told him that he was in a meeting and would not be attending. The fact that Molinari was a friend of the mayor might have accounted for his last-minute absence and decision not to notify Scotto directly. Safir's actions violated protocol and embarrassed and angered Scotto, who responded by making disparaging comments to the press that were quoted in its coverage of the event.

14. John English remembers the incident differently from McDermott and the other cops. In the conference room outside the Oval Office, McCaffrey said to the president's aide, "Listen, I have a cigar . . . It's not about the Monica Lewinsky cigar. It's a good cigar. I know he smokes cigars." The aide then took the cigar to give to the president. "I'm glad the cigar thing never came to fruition," English explained, embarrassed by even the thought of greeting the president of the United States with such a tasteless practical joke.

15. The White House, Office of the Press Secretary, "Remarks by the President at NAPO Top Cops Award Ceremony," October 9, 1998.

CHAPTER EIGHT

1. The "crane job" refers to an incident in which Emergency Service officers rescued a woman who was caught under a crane. The officer who'd talked to the woman and calmed her down while the rescue was taking place was interviewed for articles that appeared with his name in the New York press, alienating him from peers.

2. Transference refers to the unconscious imposition of archaic and ongoing images belonging to other people and situations onto the person of the researcher. Countertransference refers to the researcher's unconscious and conscious reaction to aspects of the subject's person, talk, and transference (see Hunt 1989).

CHAPTER NINE

1. Perrow (1999), 360.

2. Murphy fired four shots, none of which apparently hit Diallo.

3. See Levitt (2009c), 174.

4. See Levitt (2009c).

5. Safir, Kelleher, and Farrell (1999), 2.

6. *Jeff Jones* is a pseudonym.

7. See Safir, Kelleher, and Farrell (1999), 6.

8. Familiar with academic studies of police, Anemone told me that one of the factors determining use of force was number of officers at the scene.

9. Michael Cooper, "Vote by P.B.A. Rebukes Safir and His Policy," *New York Times*, April 14, 1999.

10. Giuliani (2000).

11. Dunne's and Grasso's recollections are complementary but somewhat different. As Grasso recorded his experience of the day shortly after 9/11, his account may more accurately reflect certain details, such as when he and Dunne talked and what was said. Nevertheless, I have included Dunne's as well as Grasso's accounts in order to do justice to narrative recollection as well as that which may be closer to "fact." In the case of these quotes, Grasso does not recall telling Dunne that a commercial airplane hit one of the towers. Dunne most likely learned about the event in a conversation with the detective in his office who was trying to connect him and Grasso when one or the other was entering the Midtown Tunnel.

12. Grasso (2001), 3.

13. Grasso (2001), 3.

14. Giuliani (2002), 5.

15. Kerik (2001), 330.

16. Kerik (2001), 330.

17. Kerik (2001), 330.

18. Giuliani (2002), 8.

19. The "fog of war" is a term developed by military historian Carl von Clausewitz. "War is a realm of uncertainty; three quarters of the factors on which action in war is based are warped in a fog of greater or lesser uncertainty. A sensitive and discriminating judgment is called for; a skilled intelligence to scent out the truth." See Mullaney (2009), 65.

20. See Grasso (2001), 5.

21. Grasso (2001), 5.

22. Grasso (2001), 5–6.

23. Grasso (2001), 4–5.

24. Grasso (2001), 6.

25. Grasso (2001), 7.

26. Grasso (2001), 8.

27. Grasso (2001), 9.

28. See Giuliani (2002), 11.

29. Giuliani (2002), 11–12.

30. Grasso (2001), 9.

31. Grasso (2001), 10.

32. Grasso (2001), 11.

33. Morange is a modest man. I believe that he might also have been concerned that a depiction of him in a book as a hero on 9/11 would have violated cultural rules prohibiting glory-seeking behavior. Perhaps he feared his friends and colleagues might be jealous or otherwise disturbed if he was depicted in a book as the great leader he was when they had also suffered during the disaster and done great things in their careers. One thing that Morange said to me struck me as key to his personality and leadership style. "I left my job with my head held high," he said. "Not a lot of chiefs can say that." In other words, he left the job without ever having sacrificed his men or his ethics in order to promote his own self-interest and move up in his career. In 2009, while I was completing the chapter on 9/11, I received permission from the police commissioner to interview one of his top commanders about his role in 9/11. His name kept appearing in various interviews and I thought his presence would add much to the chapter. Although the commander was willing to be interviewed about other matters, he declined to talk about 9/11. As his highest-ranking associate assured me it wasn't an issue of trust, I suspect his hesitancy revolved around two issues. First, he didn't want to talk of memories that brought pain. Second, he might have been hesitant to be presented as a "hero-commander," lest it create jealousy among peers and subordinates who played equally heroic roles. It's also possible that tensions between him and the police commissioner influenced his decision to talk.

34. See Grasso (2001), 12.

35. Grasso (2001), 12.

36. Giuliani (2002), 22.

37. Giuliani (2002), 22.

38. Giuliani (2002), 24.

39. See Grasso (2001), 14.

40. See Grasso (2001), 14.

41. Grasso (2001), 16.

42. See Grasso (2001), 17.

43. Grasso (2001), 18.

44. Grasso (2001), 18.

45. Grasso (2001), 20.

46. The sixty officers include those from the Port Authority and other police agencies from outside the NYPD.

CONCLUSION

1. Safir (2003), 143–144.

2. Safir (2003), 142.

3. Reuss-Ianni (1983), 68.

4. See Weick (1995); Reuss-Ianni (1983); Manning (1978); Hunt (1985); Scott and Lyman (1968); and Waegel (1984a).

5. See McArdle and Erzen (2001).

6. See Rojak (2007), 149–151 for a description of how SWAT officers are trained to reduce their vulnerability to threat.

7. Manning (1978).

8. Van Mannen (1983) and Punch (2009) both note the importance of supervision.

9. Pogrebin and Poole (1991), 398.

10. Punch (2009, 240) points out that good supervision that controls deviant action among cops must have the support of superiors in order to be effective. Supervisors who feel isolated and abandoned from above are more likely to develop a pattern of "indulgency" in regards to deviation among their cops.

11. See Terrill et al. (2003); Marks (2005), 20; and Herbert (1997).

12. Punch (2009), 96.

13. Van Mannen (1978b), 322.

14. Katz (2005), 217.

15. Katz (2005), 219.

16. The most offensive distortions in Katz's (2005) discussion of the raid involve his depiction of Chindluri, the Muslim informant. He claims that Chindluri was so frightened during the ride in the counter assault team car to the suspects' apartment that he soiled his pants. All the officers I interviewed who were in the CAT car along with Dwyer told me this wasn't true.

17. I have used Sykes and Matza's (1957) techniques of neutralization combined with Scott and Lyman's (1968) notion of retrospect accounts to analyze the vocabularies of motive Rizzo used to explain his actions.

18. In some ways, Dolan and Ryan suffered a similar dilemma as members of the shooting team involved in the shooting of terrorist suspect Jean Charles de Menezes in the Stockwell subway station in London in 2005 (see McLaughlin 2007, 203–212). The Stockwell incident was complex. Surveillance officers misidentified Jean Charles de Menezes as a terrorist suspect. No joint team briefing took place prior to the incident to help coordinate action. The shooting team arrived at the Stockwell station late. Some members of the surveillance team did not think de Menezes matched the description of the terrorist they were looking for. This information was not effectively relayed from the rank and file to the upper ranks and back down to the members of the shooting team. The commanding officer of the incident was not on the scene and communicated orders on the radio to members of the shooting team that they interpreted as a direct order to invoke the shoot-to-kill policy and neutralize the suspect's central nervous system. Her words were ambiguous and, in view of the circumstances, easy to interpret as an order to shoot to kill that inadvertently or intentionally would allow her to deny responsibility in the event the shooting was bad. De Menezes was shot point-blank in the head multiple times while he was sitting in the subway car next to a surveillance officer. Later, police attempted to cover up the incident, describing his ordinary dress and behavior as suspicious and inappropriate. The details of the investigation are available in two reports (IPCC 2006, 2007).

19. See Hunt (1985) and Waegel (1984a).

20. See Van Maanen (1980) and Klinger (2004).

21. The conversation with Klinger took place during a breakfast meeting at the annual meeting of the American Society of Criminology in November 2009.

22. English also assumed that Abu Mezer was shot first. English further vilified the suspects by recalling the part of the briefing that suggested they were cop killers as well as terrorists. "He [the informant] said they're going to get on a train and blow themselves up and kill as many people as they can, and actually they were targeting Jews specifically. So we asked him . . . 'Well, what do you think will happen if we go in there and try to stop them?' He says, 'Well, if they can't kill other people, they'll kill you. . . . if they can't kill [Jews], they're going to die killing somebody.'" Based on a youthful photo of the suspect, I said to Ryan that Khalil had a small build with

shoulders the width of a girl's. Ryan responded, "That little girl would have killed me in a heartbeat."

23. See Grossman (1995) and Collins (2008).

24. There is some confusion regarding SOD's new status in relation to the chief of Patrol or chief of the department. Apparently SOD is still under the chief of Patrol, except for in matters of daily operations and tactics. In other words, SOD would still operate under the chief of Patrol in large citywide operations, such as parades, New Year's Eve events, and so forth.

25. In recent months in 2009, there have been several internally controversial lethal force incidents against nonterrorist suspects. Although the shootings were legally justified, some members of the Police Department think they could have been avoided if the normal checks and balances had been properly working and the input of officers from other key units respected. I do not know if recent changes have resulted in an increase in such incidents and whether they are a result of a change in Emergency Service culture supported by a transformation in the orientation of the Police Department as a whole.

26. Vaughan (1999).

27. One such accident was the Diallo shooting, as discussed in chapter 9.

28. See Perrow (1999), 359–360.

29. See Punch (2009), 35.

APPENDIX

1. See Chevigny (1995), 78.

2. See Nachman (1984); Hunt and Manning (1991); Punch (2008).

3. See Beehr et al. (2004); Artwhohl and Christensen (1997); Klinger (2004).

4. Symbolic interactionist studies in sociology explore how meaning is constructed in interaction and influences subsequent action and the interpretation of new significance. Some symbolic interactionist studies examine meaning in terms of the construction of prospective and retrospective accounts that explain behavior that is considered deviant by members of the larger culture but not necessarily within the studied subculture itself. In contrast, psychoanalytic approaches analyze the unconscious dynamics of behavior and the conflictual relationship that may develop between desire (id), reality (managed by the ego), and the conscience (superego). The ego is the part of the mind that mediates between desire and the demands of the outside world and the demands of the superego. Ego-dystonic behaviors refer to those that create internal conflict between id, ego, and superego and are experienced as anxiety or other type of emotional discomfort.

5. See Nordstrom (1997), 20.

6. See Hunt (1989). In this case, transference refers to the unconscious thoughts and fantasies that research subjects impose on the researcher, influencing how they see her, and what they say and expect during interviews and other interactions. Countertransference refers to the researcher's unconscious reaction to the subjects' transference, combined with the unconscious images and thoughts that she brings to the table and that influence what she hears and how she interprets the subject's words, behavior, and ultimately, how she depicts their world.

7. See Malcolm (1990).

8. In a paper researching police detectives involved in interrogation, Leo pretended to share their conservative views and justified his methods by claiming they were necessary to gain rapport (Leo 1995).

9. See Moskos (2008); Jackall (2005); and Rubinstein (1973).

10. Kraska (2001), 141–156.
11. Kraska and Paulsen (1997); Kraska and Kappeler (1997); and Kraska (2001).
12. See Punch (2008), 187–189.
13. See Vanderstaay (2005).
14. See Hunt (1989); Levine (1981).

Bibliography

Abbott, Jack Henry. 1981. *In the Belly of the Beast*. New York: Random House.

Alpert Geoffrey P., and Lorie A. Fridell. 1992. *Police Vehicles and Firearms: Instruments of Deadly Force*. Prospect Heights, IL: Waveland Press.

Alpert, Geoffrey, and Roger Dunham. 2004. *Understanding Police Use of Force: Officers, Suspects, and Reciprocity*. Cambridge: Cambridge University Press.

Anemone, Louis. 2009. Personal e-mail communication, October 20.

Artwhohl, Alexis, and Loren W. Christensen. 1997. *Deadly Force Encounters: What Cops Need to Know to Mentally and Physically Prepare for and Survive a Gunfight*. Boulder: Paladin Press.

Beehr, Terry A., Lana Ivanitskaya, Katherine Glaser, Dmitry Erofeev, and Kris Canali. 2004. "Working in a Violent Environment: The Accuracy of Police Officers' Reports about Shooting Incidents." *Journal of Occupational and Organizational Psychology* 77:217–238.

Blumberg, Mark. 1986. "Issues and Controversies with Respect to the Use of Deadly Force by Police." In *Police Deviance*, ed. Thomas Barker and David L. Carter. Cincinnati: Pilgrimage.

Bonifacio, Philip. 1991. *The Psychological Effects of Police Work: A Psychodynamic Approach*. New York: Plenum Press.

Chan, Janet B. 1997. *Changing Police Culture: Policing in Multicultural Society*. Cambridge: Cambridge University Press.

Chevigny, Paul. 1995. *Edge of the Knife: Police Violence in the Americas*. New York: New Press.

Collins, Randall. 2008. *Violence: A Micro-Sociological Theory*. Princeton: Princeton University Press.

Cooper, Michael. 1999. "Vote by P.B.A. Rebukes Safir and His Policy." *New York Times*, April 14.

Correll, Joshua, Bernard Wittenbrink, Beradette Park, Charles Judd, and Melody Sadler. 2007. "Across the Thin Blue Line: Police Officers and Racial Bias in the Decision to Shoot." *Journal of Personality and Social Psychology* 92:1006–1023.

Ericson, Richard V., and Kevin D. Haggerty. 1997. *Policing the Risk Society*. Toronto: University of Toronto Press; and Oxford: Oxford University Press.

Everly, G. S., and J. T. Mitchell. 1997. Critical Incident Stress Management (CISM): A New Era and Standard of Care in *Crisis Intervention*. Ellicott City, MD: Chevron.

Friedrich, Robert. J. 1980. "Police Use of Force: Individuals, Situations, and Organizations." *Annals of the American Academy of Political and Social Science* 452:82–97.

Gabriel, Yiannis. 1999. *Organizations in Depth*. London: Sage Publications.

Geertz, Clifford. 1977. *The Interpretation of Cultures*. New York: Basic Books.

Giuliani, Rudy. 2000. Release 332-00. "Mayor Giuliani Swears in Bernard Kerik as 40th Commissioner, Joseph Dunne as First Deputy Commissioner, of the New York City Police Department." *Archives of the Mayor's Press Office*, Tuesday, September 5.

————. 2002. *Leadership*. New York: Hyperion Press.

Goffman, Irving. 1982. *Interaction Ritual: Essays on Face-to-Face Behavior*. New York: Pantheon.

————. 1986. *Frame Analysis*. Boston: Northeastern University Press.

Grasso, George. A. 2001. "My 9/11 Experience." Unpublished manuscript.

Grossman, Dave. 1996. *On Killing: The Psychological Cost of Learning to Kill in War and Society*. Boston and New York: Brown and Company.

Haggerty, Kevin D., and A. Gazo. 2005. "Seeing Beyond the Ruins: Surveillance as a Response to Terrorist Threats." *Canadian Journal of Sociology* 30:169–187.

Herbert, Steve. 1997. *Policing Space: Territoriality and the Los Angeles Police Department*. Minneapolis: University of Minnesota Press.

Hunt, Jennifer. 1985. "Police Accounts of Normal Force." *Urban Life* 13, no. 4:315–341.

————. 1989. *Psychoanalytic Aspects of Fieldwork*. Beverly Hills: Sage.

————. 1984. "The Development of Rapport through the Negotiation of Gender in Fieldwork among Police." *Human Organization* 43: no. 4:283–296.

————. 1990. "The Logic of Sexism among Police." *Women and Criminal Justice* 1:3-30.

Hunt, Jennifer, and Peter K. Manning. 1991. "The Social Context of Police Lying." *Symbolic Interaction* 14:51–70.

IPCC. 2006. *Stockwell One: Independent Police Complaints Commission Investigation into the Shooting of Jean Charles de Menezes at Stockwell Underground Station on 22 July 2005*. Report submitted to the Crown Prosecution Service for consideration, 19 January.

————. 2007. *Stockwell Two: Independent Police Complaints Commission. An Investigation into complaints about the Metropolitan Police Service's handling of public statements following the shooting of Jean Charles de Menezes on 22 July 2005*.

Jackall, Robert. 2005. *Wild Cowboys: Urban Marauders and the Forces of Order*. Cambridge: Harvard University Press.

Kappeler, Victor, Richard Sluder and Geoffrey Alpert. 1998. *Forces of Deviance: Understanding the Dark Side of Policing*. Long Grove, Ill: Waveland Press.

Katz, Samuel M. 2005. *Jihad in Brooklyn: The NYPD Raid That Stopped America's First Suicide Bombers*. New York: New American Library; Penguin.

Kerik, Bernard. B. 2001. *The Lost Son: A Life in Pursuit of Justice*. New York: HarperTorch.

Klinger, David. 2004. *Into the Kill Zone: A Cop's Eye View of Deadly Force*. San Francisco: Jossey-Bass.

Klinger, David, and Jeff Rojack. 2005. "A Multi-Method Study of Police Special Weapons and Tactics Team." *Final Report to National Institute of Justice*. Grant 2000-IJ-CX-0003.

Kracke, W. 1987. "Encounter with Other Cultures: Psychological and Epistemological Aspects." *Ethos* 15:58–82.

Kop, Nicolien, and Martin Eewema. 2001. "Occupational Stress and the Use of Force by Dutch Police Officers." *Criminal Justice and Behavior* 28:631–652.

Kraska, Peter B. 1996. "Enjoying Militarism: Political/Personal Dilemmas in Studying U.S. Police Paramilitary Units." *Justice Quarterly* 13:405–429.

———. 2001. "Playing War: Masculinity, Militarism, and Their Real-World Consequences." In *Militarizing the American Criminal Justice System: The Changing Roles of the Armed Forces and the Police*, ed. Peter B. Kraska. Boston: Northeastern Press.

———. 2007. "Militarization and Policing—Its Relevance to 21st-Century Police." *Policing Advance Access*. Dec. 13: 1–13.

———. 2008. Personal communication, April 24.

Kraska, Peter B., ed. 2001. *Militarizing the American Criminal Justice System: The Changing Roles of the Armed Forces and the Police*. Boston: Northeastern Press.

Kraska, Peter B., and Derek J. Paulsen. 1997. "Grounded Research into U.S. Paramilitary Policing: Forging the Iron Fist inside the Velvet Glove." *Policing and Society* 7:253–270.

Kraska, Peter B., and Victor E. Kappeler. 1997. "Militarizing American Police: The Rise and Normalization of Paramilitary Units." *Social Problems* 44:486–499.

Leo, Richard. 1995. "Trial and Tribulations: Courts, Ethnography and the Need for an Evidentiary Privilege for Academic Researchers." *American Sociologist* 26, no. 1:113–134.

Levine, Sarah. 1981. "Dreams of the Informant about the Research: Some Difficulties Inherent in the Research Relationship." *Ethos* 9:276–293.

Levitt, Leonard. 2009a. "The Police Exposed, Yet Again." NYPD Confidential website, Feb. 6. http://nypdconfidential.com/rpint/2009p/090216p.html.

———. 2009b. "Intelligence Division: Botching Its Biggest Terrorist Plot?" NYPD Confidential website, Sept. 21. http://nypdconfidential.com/rprint/2009.

———. 2009c. *NYPD Confidential: Power and Corruption in the Country's Greatest Police Force*. New York: St. Martin's Press.

———. 2009d. "Cops, Cameras, and Lies." NYPD Confidential website, Feb. 23.

Malcolm. Janet. 1990. *The Journalist and the Murderer*. New York: Vintage Press.

Manning, Peter K. 1977. *Police Work*. Cambridge, Mass: MIT Press.

———. 1978. "Rules, Colleagues, and Situationally Justified Actions." In *Policing a View from the Street*, ed. Peter K. Manning and Van Mannen. Santa Monica, CA: Goodyear.

Marks, Monique. 2005. *Transforming the Robocops: Changing Police in South Africa*. South Africa: University of KwaZulu-Natal Press.

McAardle, Andrea, and Tanya Erzen. 2001. *Zero Tolerance: Quality of Life and the New Police Brutality in New York City*. New York: New York University Press.

McLaughlin, Eugene. 2007. *The New Policing*. London: Sage Publications.

Meyer, Marshall. 1980. "Police Shootings at Minorities: The Case of Los Angeles." *Annals of the American Academy of Political and Social Science* 452:98–110.

Moskos, Peter. 2008. *Cop in the Hood: My Year Policing Baltimore's Eastern District*. Princeton: Princeton University Press.

Mullaney, Craig M. 2009. *The Unforgiving Minute: A Soldier's Education*. New York: Penguin Press.

Nachman, Steven R. 1984. "Lies My Informants Told Me." *Journal of Anthropological Research* 40:536–555.

National Institute of Mental Health. 2002. "Gene May Bias Amygdala Response to Frightful Faces." Press release, July 18.

New York City Police Department. 1990s–. *Patrol Guide Manual*. Serial. Charlottesville: LexisNexis Gould Publications.

Nordstrom, Carolyn. 1997. *A Different Kind of War Story.* Philadelphia: University of Pennsylvania Press.

Paoline, Eugene. 2004. "Shedding Light on Police Culture: An Examination of Officers' Occupational Attitudes." *Police Quarterly* 7:205–236.

Perrow, Charles. 1999. *Normal Accidents: Living with High-Risk Technologies.* Princeton: Princeton University Press.

Pogrebin, Mark K., and Eric D. Poole. 1991. "Police and Tragic Events: The Management of Emotions." *Journal of Criminal Justice* 19:395–403.

Punch, Maurice. 2008. "Researching Police Deviance: A Personal Encounter with the Limitations and Liabilities of Field-Work. *British Journal of Sociology* 40:177–204.

———. 2009. *Police Corruption: Deviance, Accountability and Reform in Policing.* [Devon]: Willan.

Purnick, Joyce. 2008. "Last Week Profiling Was Wrong." In *Racial Profiling: Current Perspectives.* Ed Rodney Brunson. Belmont, CA: Wadsworth.

Rabinow, Paul. 1977. *Reflections on Fieldwork in Morocco.* Berkeley: University of California Press.

Rashbaum, William K., and Al Baker. 2009. "New York Police Official in Terror Unit Removed." *New York Times,* Sept. 24.

Reuss-Ianni, Elizabeth. 1983. *Two Cultures of Policing: Street Cops and Management Cops.* New Brunswick: Transaction.

Rojek, Jeff. 2005. *Organizing to Manage Risk: The Operations of a Police Tactical Unit.* Ph.D. diss., University of Missouri–St. Louis.

Rubinstein, J. 1973. *City Police.* New York: Farrar, Strauss and Giroux.

Sacks, Harvey. 1972. "Notes on the Police Assessment of Moral Character." In *Policing: A View from the Streets,* ed. P. K. Manning and J. Van Maanen. Santa Monica: Goodyear.

Safir, Howard. 2003. *Security: Policing Your Homeland, Your State, Your City.* New York: St. Martin's Press.

Safir, Howard, Patrick E. Kelleher, and Michael J. Farrell. 1999. *New York City Council Public Safety Committee Hearing: Street Crime Unit.* April 19. New York: New York Police Department Internal Publication, Office of Management and Planning.

Schein, E. 1997. *Organizational Culture and Leadership.* San Francisco: Jossey-Bass.

Scott, M. B., and S. M. Lyman. 1968. "Accounts." *American Sociological Review* 33:46–62.

Shengold, Leonard. 1991. *Soul Murder: The Effects of Childhood Abuse and Deprivation.* New York: Ballantine Books.

Skogan, Wesley G. 2008. "Why Reforms Fail." *Policing and Society* 18:23–59.

Skolnick, J. 1969. *Justice without Trial.* New York: John Wiley & Sons.

Slansky, David A., and Monique Marks. 2008. "The Role of the Rank and File in Police Reform." *Policing and Society* 18:1–6.

Sykes, G. M., and D. Matza. 1957. "Techniques of Neutralization: A Theory of Delinquency." *American Sociological Review* 22:664–70.

Teal, Thomas. 1998. "The Human Side of Management." *Harvard Business Review on Leadership.* Boston: Harvard Business School Press.

Terrill, William, Eugene A. Paoline III, and Peter K. Manning. 2003. "Police Culture and Coercion." *Criminology* 41:1003–1034.

Toch, Hans. 1975. *Agents of Change: A Study of Police Reform.* New York: John Wiley.

Van Maanen, John. 1978a. "The Asshole." In *Policing: A View From the Street,* ed. Peter K. Manning and John Van Maanen. Santa Monica: Goodyear.

———. 1978b. "Watching the Watchers." In *Policing: A View from the Street*. Ed. Peter. K. Manning and John Van Maanen. Santa Monica: Goodyear.

———. 1983. "The Boss: First Line Supervision in an American Police Agency." In *Control in the Police Organization*, ed. M. Punch. Cambridge, MA: MIT Press.

Vanderstaay, Steven. 2005. "One Hundred Dollars and a Dead Man: Ethical Decision Making in Ethnographic Fieldwork." *Journal of Contemporary Ethnography* 34:371–409.

Vaughan, Diane. 1999. "The Dark Side of Organizations: Mistake, Misconduct and Disaster." *Annual Review of Sociology* 25:271–305.

———. 2004. "Organizational Rituals of Risk and Error." In *Organizational Encounters with Risk*. Ed. Bridget Hutter and Michael Powers. Cambridge: Cambridge University Press.

Waddington, P. A. J. 1999. "Police (Canteen) Sub-Culture: An Appreciation." *British Journal of Criminology* 39:287–309.

Waegel, William B. 1984a. "How Police Justify the Use of Deadly Force." *Social Problems* 32:144–155.

———. 1984b. "The Use of Deadly Force by Police: The Effect of Statutory Change." *Crime and Delinquency* 30:121–140.

Waldren, Mike. 2007. Personal communication, Dec. 16.

———. 2008. Personal communication, April 8.

Watson, Sean. 1999. "Policing the Affective Society: Beyond Governmentality in the Theory of Social Control." *Social and Legal Studies* 8:227–251.

Weick, Karl E. 1995. *Sensemaking in Organizations*. Thousand Oaks, CA: Sage Publications.

———. 1993. "The Collapse of Sensemaking in Organizations: The Mann Gulch Disaster." *Administrative Science Quarterly* 38:628–652.

Worden, Robert E. 2004. "'The Causes of Police Brutality' Theory and Evidence on Police Use of Force." In *The Police in American: Contemporary Readings*, ed. Steven G. Brandl and David S. Barker. Belmont, CA: Wadsworth Publishing.

Index